T0189462

International Series on Computer Entertainment and Media Technology

Series Editor

Newton Lee,
Tujunga, California, USA

The International Series on Computer Entertainment and Media Technology presents forward-looking ideas, cutting-edge research, and in-depth case studies across a wide spectrum of entertainment and media technology. The series covers a range of content from professional to academic. Entertainment Technology includes computer games, electronic toys, scenery fabrication, theatrical property, costume, lighting, sound, video, music, show control, animation, animatronics, interactive environments, computer simulation, visual effects, augmented reality, and virtual reality. Media Technology includes art media, print media, digital media, electronic media, big data, asset management, signal processing, data recording, data storage, data transmission, media psychology, wearable devices, robotics, and physical computing.

More information about this series at http://www.springer.com/series/13820

Artur Lugmayr · Emilija Stojmenova
Katarina Stanoevska · Robert Wellington
Editors

Information Systems and Management in Media and Entertainment Industries

Springer

Editors
Artur Lugmayr
Visualisation and Interactive Media
Curtin University
Perth, WA
Australia

Emilija Stojmenova
University of Ljubljana
Ljubljana
Slovenia

Katarina Stanoevska
University of St. Gallen
St. Gallen
Switzerland

Robert Wellington
School of Computer and Mathematical
  Sciences
Auckland University of Technology
Auckland
New Zealand

ISSN 2364-947X   ISSN 2364-9488   (electronic)
International Series on Computer Entertainment and Media Technology
ISBN 978-3-319-84156-4   ISBN 978-3-319-49407-4   (eBook)
DOI 10.1007/978-3-319-49407-4

© Springer International Publishing AG 2016
Softcover reprint of the hardcover 1st edition 2017
This work is subject to copyright. All rights are reserved by the Publisher, whether the whole or part
of the material is concerned, specifically the rights of translation, reprinting, reuse of illustrations,
recitation, broadcasting, reproduction on microfilms or in any other physical way, and transmission
or information storage and retrieval, electronic adaptation, computer software, or by similar or dissimilar
methodology now known or hereafter developed.
The use of general descriptive names, registered names, trademarks, service marks, etc. in this
publication does not imply, even in the absence of a specific statement, that such names are exempt from
the relevant protective laws and regulations and therefore free for general use.
The publisher, the authors and the editors are safe to assume that the advice and information in this
book are believed to be true and accurate at the date of publication. Neither the publisher nor the
authors or the editors give a warranty, express or implied, with respect to the material contained herein or
for any errors or omissions that may have been made.

Printed on acid-free paper

This Springer imprint is published by Springer Nature
The registered company is Springer International Publishing AG
The registered company address is: Gewerbestrasse 11, 6330 Cham, Switzerland

Preface

This book was motivated by the current transformation towards digital media houses, which disrupts current media industry business models. In particular, we wanted to advance the research field of information systems in media industry. This resulting book is based on several activities which we have been conducting in the past, and are still undertaking:

- Association for Information Systems (AIS) Special Interest Group (SIG) eMedia https://aisnet.org/group/SIG-eMedia
- European Conference on Information Systems (ECIS) Track: IT in Media Industry
- Pacific Australasian Conference on Information Systems (PACIS) Track: IT in Media Industries

The editors wish to thank all the authors contributing time and efforts to the development of this edited book and contribute to the epistemology of information systems research in media industry. We especially like to pinpoint to the following resources, if you wish to advance your knowledge in this domain:

- Book webpage and eMail list: www.artur-lugmayr.com
- Email list: http://mail.ambientmediaassociation.org/mailman/listinfo/ais-sig-emedia_ambientmediaassociation.org
- Introduction publications: we advise the following publications as starting point for readers in this domain: [1], [2], and [3]

Authors submitted their initial chapters in form of abstracts. The editors of this book invited the most promising chapters for a full chapter submission. These chapters underwent a double-blind review process. We therefore would like to thank all the reviewers for their valuable work and input and fruitful suggestions. From the 30 submitted chapters, 16 chapters made it into the book. It is to state that two chapters have been invited from the ECIS Track 'IT in Media Industry', organized by Cinzia Dal Zotto and Artur Lugmayr in 2015, which leads to an acceptance rate of roughly 50%.

We also would like to thank Springer-Verlag for the very fruitful and easy cooperation, especially for their patience for waiting for the final volume.

As editors, we hope you will be enjoying the fascinating contributions to the book.

[1] Lugmayr, A. (2013). Brief introduction into information systems and management research in media industries. In *2013 IEEE International Conference on Multimedia and Expo Workshops (ICMEW)* (2013) (pp. 1–6).

[2] Lugmayr, A., & Zotto, C. D. (2015). Convergence is not King—The tripe convergence, coexistence, and divergence is King. In A. Lugmayr, & C. D. Zotto (Eds.), *Media convergence handbook (Vol. 1): Journalism, Broadcasting, And Social Media Aspects Of Convergence And Media Convergence Handbook (Vol. 2): Firm and user perspective*. Springer.

[3] Lugmayr, A. et al. (2016). A comprehensive survey on big data research and it's implications—What is really 'new' in big data? It's cognitive big data. In *Proceedings of the 20th Pacific-Asian Conference on Information Systems (PACIS 2016)* (2016).

Perth, Australia   Artur Lugmayr
Ljubljana, Slovenia   Emilija Stojmenova
St. Gallen, Switzerland   Katarina Stanoevska
Auckland, New Zealand   Robert Wellington

Contents

Part I
Content, Service, Application, and Artistic Viewpoint on IS&M in Media and Creativity Industries

An ARTISAN Perspective for Software Development, Commercialisation and Artistic Co-creation: A Case Study

John R. Taylor

Abstract Making music is a very personal endeavour, where artistic bias can impact artistic collaboration, software development and the commercialisation of software generated through the creative process. This investigation provides an understanding of the behavioural characteristics, artistic and technical knowledge and application, and industry contexts, of two groups of electronic musicians using a shared software platform. Under investigation are the commercialisation and collaborative opportunities within in the Max/MSP and Ableton Live! artistic and economic communities (ecosystems), of which, Max for Live! is a shared sub-ecosystem. This investigation presents two frameworks: "The Five Cs" framework and the "ARTISAN" framework, designed to reflectively reduce the effects of artistic, technical, and psychological biases, that can serve as a barrier to driving innovation, commercialisation opportunities and collaboration.

1 Introduction

In 2010 the global music industry's estimated value was US$160 billion [8], of which the audio equipment industry is valued at approximately US$15 billion, equivalent to 24 % (we are mainly interested in the software component of this industry herein). The Audio Engineering Society (AES) began standardisation in 1977 [21], which globalised products in the audio equipment industry. Artistically, these standardised, global products (think of your favourite pre-bought digital audio workstation (DAW) or software synthesiser) inhibit artistic exploration by limiting the user's ability to customise the tool for new, creative purposes, beyond combinatorial effects processing and parametric manipulation. As such, a need arose for a software program that facilitated the creation of custom software instruments for composition.

J.R. Taylor (✉)
Sydney Conservatorium of Music, University of Sydney, Sydney, Australia
e-mail: john.taylor@sydney.edu.au

© Springer International Publishing AG 2016
A. Lugmayr et al. (eds.), *Information Systems and Management in Media and Entertainment Industries*, International Series on Computer Entertainment and Media Technology, DOI 10.1007/978-3-319-49407-4_1

In 1988 at IRCAM, Miller Puckette wrote Max, a program that addressed this need and allowed composers to create their own instruments [1, 11, 14, 22, 23].

One of the main pre-requisites for creating new software using Max/MSP is an understanding of digital sound synthesis and programming, which for a long time was restricted to scientists and researchers in institutions and companies (old world). Nowadays, Max/MSP is available commercially, and has been integrated with other DAWs, driving its popularity amongst creative enthusiasts and consumers (new world).

These enthusiasts have also adopted knowledge of programming and synthesis and, combined with artistic expression, demonstrate 'lead user' behaviour by experiencing and identifying early needs for a novel product [18–20, 28], and by being 'ahead of the market-place' [2–4, 20, p. 227], driven by both artistic vision and practical need. Another component that defines lead users is the high amount of expected benefits from an innovation [3], with a comparable example presented in which hobbyist animator may expect higher benefits from a solution than an established company such as Pixar [3, p. 303] suggesting that user-centric innovation paradigms are not uncommon in multimedia industries.

Despite an increased possibility for co-creation, innovation, and greater commercialisation opportunities due to a larger number of users, there are still vast differences in the two distinctly different user groups that prevent creative collaboration and the co-creation of custom software for artistic purposes. These can be broadly categorised into three areas: end-user/innovator characteristics, functional and conceptual implementation, and industry context, as shown in Fig. 1.

A distinguishing feature between the old world and new world users of Max/MSP is their respective sub-ecosystem use of the internet and technology [9, 13]. Despite this, and their different needs and implementations, they can both still operate within a common environment [10]. For the purposes of this investigation the key sub-ecosystem difference between the two is that, in the old world, Max/MSP is pre-dominantly used as a standalone application whereas, in the new world, Max/MSP is fundamentally linked to a commercially available DAW called Ableton Live! This is shown in Fig. 2.

Despite these differences, the technical and artistic application of software created in Max/MSP can be both interchangeable as a component of a common environment, and simultaneously prohibitive in use between the two users as a result of restrictions imposed by the Ableton Live! (Ableton). A secondary effect of the greater numbers of Max/MSP users developing custom artistic software is the

Fig. 1 The user characteristics, functional and conceptual implementation of software, and industry context to be analyzed in this case study

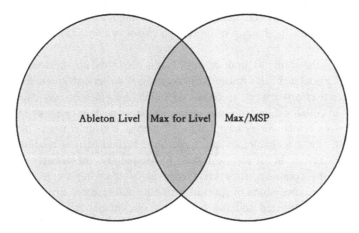

Fig. 2 Common ecosystem in the Max/MSP and Ableton Live! environments

increased artistic competition, whereby innovation in an artistic sense, operates in an increasingly smaller conceptual space. Furthermore, the scope for creating disruptively innovative artistic software becomes narrower due to increased competition and the decentralisation of artistic functions to single software applications (in contrast to DAWs, that are extremely multi-functional in a single software application).

This investigation takes an holistic informations systems and management approach, by examining the people, technology and information perspectives of this common ecosystem [16, 17]. More specifically, this investigations seeks to uncover the core similarities and differences in old world and new world Max/MSP users' artistic and technical ecosystems, which includes the analysis of technical knowledge and artistic experience, creative and technical application, and industry context within the Max/MSP platform ecosystem in order to present generic frameworks for encouraging co-creation and driving innovation, by maximising the artistic and technical similarities between the two groups, in order to make the best use of any potential commercialisation opportunities for both parties.

1.1 The Creative Knowledge Environment

The three barriers to co-creation described in the previous section (user characteristics, implementation, and industry context) can be considered different aspects of what is known as a creative knowledge environment, which is the influence of the environment upon the production of creative products [7]. On the premise that there are many external factors (including uncontrollable factors such as government regulation) of an environment that can affect the production of creative products, and that an environment can be influenced by the creator of the products to achieve similar results (i.e. design of a studio layout for enhancing a creative workflow), this must be thought of more as a two-way interaction than a one-way external influence.

Creativity is the ability to produce work that is novel and appropriate [12], and is a term often associated with musicians, composers, writers, painters, and videographers, where creative work is produced either individually (i.e. Stockhausen, Pollock) or in collaboration with others (i.e. The Beatles, Van Gogh and Gauguin). While advances in technology have led to widespread consumer use of high quality creative tools, these technologies and tools have facilitated new mediums of collaborative endeavour in all artistic forms. Consequently, the creative knowledge environment, the complementary knowledge ac-companying the technology [7], that was once the cornerstone of specialist training and research institutions, can be more rapidly disseminated and has become as important, and as popular as the technology and tools themselves. With creativity forming the basis for new products or services [26], the commodification of creative knowledge is likely to supplement the economic impact of creativity, through increased innovation. In addition, such commodification in the research environment is both the result of, and has the effect of, reducing artistic and technical knowledge to a 'routinized and codified product' [27, p. 938].

Exactly how the creative knowledge environment affects the economic impact of creativity varies, depending on the business environment. The term 'economic impact' implies the commercialisation of a creative idea, although from a commercial standpoint, creativity may not always be innovative from the outset. A common view is that creativity and innovation is not the same thing; creativity is the generation of ideas, the production of something of value [5, 6, 24], while innovation commercialises; generates business value from the idea [6, 25]. Therefore, the creative knowledge environment in this context relates primarily to product development, and technical and artistic application, rather than commercialisation. In the context of creative technology, the commodification of creative knowledge from traditional specialist training and research institutions will increase the numbers of higher quality creative products in the marketplace, thus making the market more competitive and making new product innovations increasingly more difficult.

From the perspective of an artist making and using creative technology, this commodification presents both new opportunities and new challenges within the global Max/MSP environment: (1) there is a larger consumer base, with the capability of producing new creative products as competitors; (2) there are enormous differences in creative knowledge environments between artists as a result of a wider artistic experience, appropriation, and creation; (3) the disparity in creative knowledge environments can differ to the extent that it has a polarising effect on co-creation despite similar artistic visions, together with different implementations of software; and (4) there are an almost infinite number of technical configurations available, a result of (1), which directly affects (2) and (3).

So far a broad spectrum of user segments have been identified, ranging from professional and academic researchers, to creative hobbyists and everything in between, all of whom exist in different sub-ecosystems, differentiated predominantly by technical knowledge, and artistic knowledge/experience, and all sharing a common ecosystem. The next sections will describe the motivations and methodology and describe the key research questions under investigation.

2 Motivation

The motivation behind this investigation stem from the author's five years of experience in both target groups, having used both Ableton Live! and Max/MSP extensively. During that time, a significant amount of knowledge of both software platforms and user groups has been gathered. This ethnographic data collection forms the foundation of the current research strategy, facilitating 'cultural reconstruction' of both user groups, and the 'acquisition of first-hand, sensory accounts of phenomena as they occur in real world settings' [15, pp. 387–389]. A second motivation behind this investigation is the author's development of a software tool with musical application, developed using Max/MSP that, as part of a three-year research project, may or may not be suitable for commercialisation. The development of reflective and advisory commercialisation frameworks would have been of significant benefit during the software conception phase of this research project, to increase the suitability and commercialisation potential of the software program for both sets of users.

3 Methodology

As described previously, this investigation seeks to determine the core similarities and differences in old world and new world Max/MSP users' artistic and technical ecosystems, which includes the analysis of technical knowledge and artistic experience, creative and technical application, and industry context within the Max/MSP platform ecosystem, in order to present two generic frameworks for encouraging and enabling co-creation, and driving innovation, by maximising the artistic and technical similarities between the two groups in order to make the best use of any potential commercialisation opportunities for both parties.

The frameworks presented in this investigation will be drawn from a qualitative approach that seeks to understand the in-depth knowledge, experience, and user habits of the two key target segments. This approach has been chosen for this investigation in order to generate a greater understanding of the area of artistic experience and technical knowledge of the ecosystems in question, which to date has seen little research. A qualitative approach was chosen over a quantitative method as this investigation seeks to identify and explore the stories behind the participant's experiences, perceptions, artistic attributes, knowledge levels, and behaviour relating to three user groups, for which a quantitative method would be less suitable. Limitations of the qualitative approach taken in this investigation relate to sample size; the respondents interviewed may not be representative of the wider user group to which they are attributed.

This qualitative investigation will aim to understand the three key issues—user characteristics (needs, knowledge), artistic and technical implementation, and industry context of each of the interviewees, who will be drawn from different user segments (new world and old world). This will be done using semi-structured individual and group interviews, and seeks to further provide an in-depth understanding of the key issues that relate to the user segments, including:

1. The main behavioural, technical, and artistic characteristics of each user group.
2. How each user group implements and develops software from a technical and artistic perspective.
3. The key industry attributes that influence the users' software choice and development.

The first interviewee (Participant A) is an old world user who, as an internationally recognised and commissioned composer, is currently active in academic research and has developed numerous creative software programs for composition and multimedia using Max/MSP. Participant A has been using Max/MSP for fourteen years. The second interviewee (Participant B) is a professional technical support manager/music studio engineer, with experience of supporting academic research/artistic development with specialist technical requirements, and working in recording studios with more consumer-focussed products and artistic goals. Participant B is 'platform neutral' in this investigation as they do not use Ableton, Max for Live or Max/MSP as their main software platform. They do, however, have experience of both platforms in professional and creative capacities, and can provide an objective perspective of the issues under investigation. The third interview comprised of three participants (Participants C1, C2, and C3) who are a collaborating musical group of new world users, who currently operate internationally, and have a history of playing large international music festivals and venues, and are credited with four albums and six EPs. This group currently provides tuition on Ableton, and has experience using Max/MSP.

The analysis of these interviews will enable the formation of two creative software design frameworks, applicable to all users, to encourage co-creation, innovation, and commercialization opportunities, irrespective of artistic endeavour, genre or multimedia discipline.

4 Findings

4.1 Views of the Platforms

In expressing their views on both platforms, each of the respondents describes how the platforms fit within their creative context. Participant A describes Ableton as being more suited to composers 'creating soundtracks in more commercial-based applications, electronic, techno, dance music' and cites the layout of the software and user interface as being the main reason for this. From a creative standpoint, Participant A describes how the layout of Ableton creates a 'predefined framework' producing an implied 'creative system'; one that can be applied to 'several styles'. As a result, Participant A describes how Ableton is 'by itself a bit limiting' but the integration of Max/MSP 'opens possibilities'. This predefined framework is supported by Participant B, who describes Ableton as a 'more glorified playback, backing track', although describes how Ableton is creative with particular functionality, in that 'you can loop sections, you can take in and out parts'. The creative functionality of Ableton is a fundamental aspect of creative choice for Participant C3, whereby, if Max was integrated into 'any other [DAW] I wouldn't get it for the Max integration'.

Regarding Max/MSP, Participant A describes how the lack of predefined framework makes it 'possible to explore the dimensions, or explore the compositional boundaries', and describes this aspect as 'the major artistic difference between Max/MSP and Ableton'. In contrast, Participant C3 describes how in trying to learn Max/MSP initially they 'got a bit frustrated with it and didn't end up building anything useful with it'. Nowadays, Participant C3 uses Max 'for doing stuff that's very simple and specific and that's why it doesn't exist as a VST—because only 1 in 10 people would want to make such a stupid sound are going to want that tool'. Describing Ableton with Max for Live (M4L), Participant A asserts that the existing predefined framework on it's own is 'limiting' but offers an advantage to Max users in that there is 'an existing interface and you can add all of the plugins and it's a multi-channel environment', where the 'interconnection between Max and Live is probably a very strong feature, a very useful feature'. The usefulness of having Max functionality within Ableton is also shared by Participant C3, who states that 'the only reason I would want to use Max is if there wasn't a tool already that did it [a function]' to create something that is 'not achievable in anything apart from Max'.

Participant B describes how Ableton 'is really tailored towards commercial music because it allows you to get all your parts and be very interactive and loop it, loop sections. In some respects you can actually jam with your music'. In addition, Participant B continues to describe how the ability to 'jam' with your music 'gives you greater control' compared to alternative sequencers and software because they are 'not as interactive that way because they are more geared around more kind of traditional composition or more traditional recording and mixing', with the biggest benefit of Ableton being for 'live performances' where users can 'take the patches that they have created in Max/MSP' and use it interactively during a live performance. However, noting that there is significant overlap in functionality between Ableton and Max/MSP, Participant C3 describes how generating MIDI Control Change (CC) data for control external devices was done differently in Max compared to Ableton and, although they achieved similar results, 'the Max version of it was slightly more generative than the Ableton one, but the Ableton one was more precise', which may be important during a live performance and may affect software choice.

Aside from the artistic advantage highlighted by Participant A (above), Participant B describes one of the key benefits of using Max/MSP whereby:

> You can actually program and create what you want. Just say you want to create a filter plugin then you can basically create that or if you want to create a certain synthesiser, you can create that. You are not reliant upon some company to create that, you can go out and do that yourself.

This further highlights the differences in the use of Max with Participant C3, who only uses it for small, specific tasks. Participant C1 highlights one key strength in Max/MSP by stating that 'with cross-platform media, Max is the way to go over Ableton or something else'. This view was further supported by Participant C2 who asserts that:

> Another good thing about Max is that it's a good bridge. You can bridge any program to any other program using it. Or you can bridge it to your phone or your iPad or something like that. You can use Max and input and output it as anything. You can basically take any out from any device to any other device you have. So it's heaps good as like a bridging function as well.

In addition, Participant C2 describes how integrating Max into their existing artistic workflow can be more difficult but more functional: 'it's a little bit more technical with Max, like integrating it into a session is easier with some other software but more functional with Max if you know how to use it'.

4.2 Views of Users

So far, the findings suggest that the views on the different software platforms are polarized, with one participant's creativity flourishing (i.e. Participant A in Max) in a software platform that inhibits an opposing party (Participant C3 in Max). In addition, each respondent acknowledges the benefits of the other software despite differences in creative approach and artistic experience. Despite these differences, a common held view is that the integration of Max within Ableton is useful, and the polarising effect on creative workflow may not necessarily be a barrier for co-creation and commercialisation.

Describing the typical users of each of the software platforms, Participant A states that 'Ableton users need to have a basic knowledge of audio... knowledge of music technology is required'. This is supported by Participant B who argues that 'users of Ableton fall into two types. Either someone like me who has an audio-engineering background... or someone doing very much experimental out-there electronic music', where users with an audio-engineering background focus on being creative within the Ableton framework, and experimental musicians focus on being creative by using the Max integration. This division of creativity based upon Max integration is further supported by Participant B who describes Max as 'very experimental'. Participant B goes on to say that:

> People who use Max are very much in the experimental field. I haven't met too many casual dance music producers who write 'four-on-the-floor' type beats who also use Max as well, so it's very much more experimental.

Participant B suggests that this division is 'because it's basically a programming environment it really is going to appeal to a rather niche audience'. Interestingly, this implies that Max users require a higher level of technical (programming) knowledge compared to users of Ableton (without Max) who, as described by Participant A, need only a basic level of music knowledge of audio and music technology to operate the software. This suggests that general technical knowledge is a key differentiator between the two user groups, which can be developed through experience or formal training.

Describing the technical users of Ableton, Participant B argues that 'you are going to get the full broad technical scope of users' where people just want to create 'four-on-the-floor dance music with loops and just bang it out there... the vast majority of users are into more commercial dance music regardless of whatever style you want to call it'.

From a platform adoption perspective, this raises an interesting point regarding the transitioning of a user from one platform to another, as a primary platform, and the associated levels of learning involved in such a migration. Participant B highlights this in more detail:

> For a hard-core Max user they'd find it easier to go to Ableton just because their technical skills are at a higher level. So I'm going to assume that because they can program really interesting synthesisers to use Ableton is not going to be much of a stretch. Where if you reverse it the other way around, someone who is just more of a typical musician, dabbles around with some electronic sounds, it doesn't really go too deeply beyond that there, except just using the tools that they are given, I think it would actually be much harder for them to get into Max because Max is a programming environment. If you do one thing wrong, it isn't going to work. It's not going to create the desired outcome.

Interestingly, Participant A argues that the interaction of Max with other programming environments, such as 'Java, Python, OpenGL, Graphics, Communications Networking, etc.', allows the user to 'think in a more multimedia fashion and integrate other phenomena or other perceptual phenomena into a musical realm'. This enables the user to create 'a multi-parametric and multi-dimensional environment' where full exploitation of the software requires significantly more technical knowledge than Ableton with its single environment and its predefined framework where 'the learning curve is relatively low'.

Similarly, Participant B states that, compared to Ableton users, Max users 'definitely have different technical skillsets' and that:

> It does require a lot of knowledge in the first place. It's like anything, it's a programming environment, you've actually got to sit down and learn the program. That's basically the deal-breaker of Max that 99 % of people don't want to do that, they want to just go 'I want to start doing what I need to do'. So it really does appeal to a very small niche.

This supports the statement made by Participant C3 who described how their initial use of Max/MSP caused frustration that in turn prevented full adoption of the platform. Participant B also describes how 'there are two kinds of Max users. Those who take it to learn about it and they still may have no real technical skills' and 'people who are very technical, who either have a very strong computer programming background or are of a very audio-geeky nerdy background'. Participant B continues and describes how sometimes:

> People with a stronger computer programming background...at times they still don't actually understand the fundamentals of the audio... but they actually are using Max in a very kind of powerful way though still.

This is supported by Participant C3 who describes how, in the first encounter with Max the 'learning curve was too steep', and that they weren't 'capable of building anything useful at the time'. In addition, 'it just didn't make much sense to spend the time on it'. This suggests that the time required to learn the technical knowledge for platform proficiency is a significant barrier to a new Max user.

4.3   Technical Knowledge

It is clear that technical knowledge may, in part, be a contributing factor affecting the adoption of certain platforms. Given the differences in the platforms in each sub-ecosystem, the acquisition of knowledge, and need, is different between the users. The extent to which gaining technical knowledge is a barrier is described by Participant C2:

> You could create your own [EQ] in Max, but again the amount of mathematics that goes into an EQ is probably huge. Although it's not so much knowledge, but time. Time is the biggest factor for me. You can learn all that stuff from research, but it's the time it takes. To make an EQ, it obviously takes a bit of knowledge, but to get that knowledge takes like, to make an EQ even would probably take me a month or so to learn. And I don't have month to spend on making an EQ when I can just go and buy an EQ that has that feature.

When asked about methods of knowledge acquisition required to help overcome any barriers faced when first using Max, Participant C2 states that:

> The inbuilt tutorials in Max, are the best out of any software. I've used the inbuilt tutorials for a load of software, and most of them suck, but the ones in Max are sweet, they explain everything down to a tee.

Despite describing the tutorials as being the 'best of any software', Participant C2 goes on to say:

> I don't think the tutorials are that easy to use, it's just that they are more comprehensive than a lot of other software' cutting out the internet searching time for 3rd party tutorials and 'stuff that users have created on YouTube or articles that people have written on blogs and stuff.

Summarising the effect of the tutorials on access to technical knowledge, Participant C2 asserts that:

For people who want to do that sort of thing [build their own instruments in Max], it's easier than it was before', although from a personal perspective, this was not a factor in Max usage. 'I didn't start using it more to build stuff because it became easier, I started using it because I could build stuff that I couldn't find a VST [virtual studio instrument] for.

This suggests that for typical Ableton users, there are at least three key factors when deciding whether to use Max: the need for the developed tool; access to the knowledge; and time considerations. These three factors could be generalised and applied to any user's decision to use Max to build software, irrespective of their primary platform.

However, upon evaluating these factors, more fundamental biases, manifested through artistic experience, may influence the decision on Max usage.

4.4 Artistic Experience

Artistic experience can be described as a bias for tool and software choice.[1] This is summarised by Participant C1 who states that:

Every producer going to have a very specific set of needs, I mean everyone's got their own style like this is a specific thing I might want, and some other producer might say I don't have any need for that in my music.

However, in the context of Max and Ableton users, the artistic experience between them appears more divisive. Participant A states that, in order to translate a creative vision into software, 'you have to have some sort of analytical basis to begin with', and that programming in Max is part of the creative process:

The results may be unpredictable and that element of unpredictability is also interesting because if you make various connections in Max/MSP you might discover things or lead to unexpected musical results that might sound very interesting. From a structural point of view, from a formalistic point of view, rather than just a sonic perspective.

Interestingly, an unexpected result, or not producing the desired outcome, is considered an important aspect of the compositional process by Participant A. This is also described earlier by Participant B as a barrier to Max adoption. Where Participant A considers programming as part of musical creation (which includes development not necessarily directly generating musical sound), Participant C2 describes their approach to non-musically generating activities by stating that 'if I can do it in two seconds then I'll buy a tool to do that because in the long run it'll save me hours and hours of work'. The emphasis on workflow is reiterated by Participant C3, who states that 'most of the stuff that I bought in the last couple of

---

[1]The term 'artistic bias' can also be described as 'creative preference'. However, in the context of this case study, the term artistic bias will be used in the context of artistic experience being a barrier to creative innovation. It is also acknowledge that in some cases artistic experience can have a positive effect on the management process.

years hasn't been stuff for making new sounds a lot of it has been workflow stuff'. It is clear that workflow is important to each participant. However, it is interesting to also note that the perception of workflow is very different, with Participant A potentially increasing the workflow by using Max, whereas Participants C2 and C3 preferring to streamline the workflow as much as possible.

This active streamlining of workflow by Participants C2 and C3 could be attributed to respective frameworks of the platform, a point alluded to earlier by Participant A. Participant B, who describes Ableton as being 'popular for certain functions', supports this by describing how Ableton's main strengths as a software platform reside in it's use for live performances rather than composition:

> Where it really shines… with electronic producers who very much want to use it either for two things. They might only use it just to perform live with… or there will be people who do both, use Ableton Live! to create their compositions and also perform it live.

This supports the notion that the software framework used mandates specific technical knowledge for its use, which in turn affects artistic experience. This is described by Participant A who, in discussing the link between technical knowledge and artistic experience, asserts that 'the technical aspects are the underlying, sort of, grid or schematics of the composition. It's an integral part. It's an intrinsic and integral part of the actual composition's structure'. Participant A continues:

> Well, say a person does not have the knowledge of Max or the possibilities then there would be no interference because there would not be any knowledge of what's possible. Basically, you try to maximise Ableton [creatively] as much as possible not knowing what is possible with Max.

By extension, not knowing what is possible with Max could also include other multimedia environments thus reducing creative possibilities. However, Participant B argues that technical knowledge isn't necessarily needed if the tools are already freely available; that creativity is not dependant on technical knowledge:

> There's so many freeware plugins or software that you can already buy in the market that would pretty much cover 99 per cent of things that you want to do. So it [Max] really is going to only appeal to people who just want to be completely in control of everything they are doing with music.

Participant B quantifies this position by explaining that:

> With a very creative, talented songwriter, given the right tools they'll just use it and create amazing works. They may not have the technical ability to program the patches but they can use it to actually create some good music.

Participant B also supports Participant A in the view that a lack of technical knowledge inhibits artistic experience regarding use of a software platform. 'If you haven't got a programming background you're not going to get the full benefit of the software [Max]'.

While Participant A focuses more on the depth of the technical knowledge as being part of the creative process, Participant C2 describes how a broader technical knowledge, mostly related to the current users' creative setup, is required in order to make informed artistic decisions about creative software:

> Providing it was something that hasn't been done by another plugin, and providing it was something that wasn't CPU intensive and providing it was something that was not that expensive... depending how crazy it was and the different stuff it did, and providing that all of these things would be the judge as to whether I would pay for it.

It was noted earlier that Ableton is a good platform for 'jamming', which implies that it is also a platform that enables artistic co-creation. This fact was echoed by the collaborative nature of the relationship between Participants C1, C2, and C3. Participant B supports this position 'because of the nature of how the software works. It's very loop-audio based'. In short, Ableton is a very collaborative piece of software in itself.

4.5   Collaboration and Co-creation

However, despite the Max integration with Ableton, Participant A has never collaborated with an Ableton user, citing aesthetic differences between the two environments as a reason for this:

> I think maybe aesthetically, when one uses Max/MSP the type of music that comes out of that particular software environment, perhaps in my case, does not match the aesthetics of the music that would come out of Ableton.

In addition, Participant A argues that, although it would be a personal barrier to collaborate with some with 'limited knowledge of Max', they 'didn't see it as a barrier in general' due to elements of the Ableton environment that can be used (i.e. plugins) and experience with other similar platforms (i.e. Logic).

5   Considerations for Product Development

Throughout the discussion of these findings, there have emerged some indications of the important considerations for both product development and commercialisation, particularly from a consumer perspective. For example, when discussing considerations for commercialisation using Max, Participant A felt that the most important consideration was the 'type of music they [end-users] would like to create'.

> If there's a dimension of experimental music or any form of exploration then the parameters would change, it would not be as much a grid-type music or measure-based, bar-based music but the sort of freedom in time to generate the material that is not based on a traditional rhythmic foundation.

Essentially, Participant A is describing the extremes of the two broad user groups, Max users and Ableton users, which ascertained within the findings are not truly representative of all Max/Ableton users.

In contrast, Participant C3 does not describe important end-user aspects of software in terms of music genre but rather in terms of use and development cost. In their view it should not be:

> Something complex... What's the point? I can just buy something complex [and] something less intense that wouldn't take me six months to build [but should be] something that I could build in a day, and something that doesn't take a huge amount of learning and time out of my life to build.

This indicates that, in the words of Participant C3, there is a trade-off for 'building software over buying it'.

6   Industry Context

The proliferation of these two platforms, and increased number of users building their own software, has led to increased competition in the music software industry. This increased competition is highlighted by Participant A:

> There's a lot of software around and there's a growing trend, I think, that people are trying to recreate the same concepts but through their own, sort of, filter, their own interpretation of what it is they are trying to create.

In addition, 'collectively I think a lot of people are trying to accomplish similar things. So there's a lot of repetition of ideas'. Participant C2 echoes this sentiment stating, 'there's a billion EQs out there already. The same with synthesizers. I would never build a synthesizer in Max as there are a billion synths out there already'. Such competition, and repetition of ideas, means that innovation in software design and development is becoming increasingly more difficult. Moreover, artistic musical software must not only meet the traits of good generic software (i.e. efficiency) but should also have good functionality, and lend itself to artistic innovation, as a tool towards creating a new product, music. In appraising the use of Software developed using Max, Participant A describes how during development, they are able to 'focus on the elements which are important for me in installation and performance' which gives greater control, despite the drawback such as 'lack of user-interface or lack of access to visual representation of sound and music'. Despite these drawbacks, Participant A concedes that 'your own system might be more efficient in conveying your artistic idea' compared to commercially available software that 'becomes a filter to your own idea. It colours it'. This was also a view expressed earlier by Participant A in relation to Ableton.

7 User-Consumer Demands for Purchasing Software

Another important aspect of commercialisation is identifying what the consumer demands are prior to purchasing software. Participant A clearly states his position on this when he says that 'without question I would only use a tool from a good source. As long as it works for me is not a principle'. Furthermore, software 'has to be of high value, high impact, high quality'. This is 'to avoid situations where the lack of knowledge can be an impediment to artistic creativity', whereby knowledge in this context refers to the developers' skills. Additionally, 'it's very important that the software works with my existing set-up', adding that if a hardware upgrade was necessary to run software then:

> I would try to then create my own system in Max/MSP…I'm of the opinion that there's always often a software solution, an efficient software solution, to avoid these hardware upgrades.

Importantly, this view is dependent on possessing the technical knowledge to be able to recreate such a system, which in some instances may not be an option. For Participant B to purchase software, 'it would have to be something that is different or unique to what's already on the market'. Had the software been created in Max, it has to be 'something that's better than what is already on the market'. Although, ultimately, 'it doesn't really bother me if it is done in Max or whatever programming environment because, in the end, I'm still going to assess it on the merits of what it actually does, not what it was programmed with'. Functionally, Participant B applies similar values on software irrespective of platform, such as 'its CPU efficiency [which] is always a consideration with any piece of software. Is it stable? That's with any piece of software'.

In their descriptions of their expectations of software from both a functional and artistic perspective, Participant A and Participant B imply certain minimum levels of quality and performance. This is a view not entirely shared by Participants C1, C2, and C3. Artistically, there are similarities between them. This is highlighted by Participant C3, who states that software must be 'something that does something that nothing else does', or 'because it does something that one of my other plugins doesn't quite do as well'. In addition, Participant C2 identified that software should be something 'that saves me a considerable amount of time, or something that helps me achieve something that isn't possible without it', and 'fulfilled some [creative] need'.

Agreeing with Participant A, Participant C3 asserts that the user interface of the software is not a significant factor in purchase. 'I wont buy a plugin just because it looks good either. That's good as well, if it looks good its awesome. And if its nice to look that's good'. However, Participant C2 disagrees with Participant A regarding the theoretical underpinnings of software. As described earlier, using Max enables the exploration of (theoretical) compositional systems. For Participant C2, theoretical underpinnings of software are not important because 'if they have all this theory behind it, I don't care about how complex it is, if it's just another large synthesiser I'm not going to buy it'.

For Participant C2 'price is definitely important' when considering a software purchase. For example, for any software costing $200–$300, 'I can conceivably see that if I spent a week and did a bit of research I could maybe build that. It's the sort of price where I would just go and build it'. However, this attitude does not necessarily apply to complex software with higher values involving significantly longer development times. For example, Participant C2 asserts that 'you might be able to build something like that with Max, but it would take you like, ten years... I could spend $400 bucks on this plugin or I could, you know, lose income for ten years'. Equally, Participant C3 argues that 'you are paying for ten years worth of somebody else's trial and error'.

This implies that both Participants C2 and C3 appreciate the development costs of such an item and consider the cost benefit over development time, as highlighted previously. Other functional views by Participant C1 are in agreement with Participants A and B, where computational efficiency is a concern, particularly 'if it's something you are going to use on every channel, like an EQ or compressor'. In terms of upgrading hardware to run software, unlike Participant A, Participant C2 indicates that they would be willing to upgrade but only under certain circumstances: 'If it was useful enough to the point where I was like, it is so insane that I have to buy the technology just to use this thing, then no it wouldn't be a barrier, I would just buy the technology'. This approach could be accounted for by technical knowledge and artistic experience.

Another consideration for Participant C2 in purchasing software was the perception of quality inferred by the developers:

> It depends how they presented it I think... dodgy about the presentation... they didn't care and their website crashed everyday, their Ableton session was messy, if it was something like that... I probably wouldn't trust their software. But I mean if they were like pretty professional like, their websites really good and their support is really good and they answer their emails within 24 h... they probably build good plugins too.

When asked about the correlation between price and quality, Participant C1 questioned whether price equalled quality? 'The same goes for patches, there's amazing stuff that's free and paid for it's just a matter of finding it'. More significantly, Participant C3, who had previously described recent purchases as items relating to workflow, describes how:

> I have had a lot of problems with Max patches that I have gotten off the user community for free you know. They aren't very well written and a bit buggy, the CPU just maxes out as soon as you load them, and you know, like session crash and stuff like that. But you know, if you are not paying for them it's not, it's a hassle, but it's not that bad.

This demonstrates a clear contradiction. A user invests in software to help improve workflow efficiency, whereas, free software can in some cases decrease workflow efficiency.. In essence, therefore, the value of the software tool from an artistic perspective supersedes the workflow requirements at the time.

It has been noted that there are a number of different distribution methods available to developers of software using Max, most notably, the possibility of selling the software through the Apple Mac App Store. Participant A considers this method 'a good way to distribute your own projects... to distribute your ideas and knowledge and maybe influence other people's music'. Moreover, Participant A 'would be willing' to use this distribution method for future developments. Participant C2 considered this distribution method as 'pretty cool' but identified the Max Runtime format of the software as the most beneficial aspect: 'you just get a runtime application on your mac that you can just click and you can just open and run'.

Surprisingly, Participants C1, C2, and C3 indicate that they would most likely make the software open-source. 'I think we'd probably give it away... we'd give it away because it's better exposure [for ourselves as artists]... we would consider making a max patch/software open source, for sure'. However, this position is due to two factors. Firstly, they 'design the whole [musical] projects to be around the whole free thing, and just contributing like that and it would give us more exposure, and that's pretty much the ethos of our music', particularly with regards to remix packs, 'its heaps rewarding to see what people do with that stuff [our remix packs] ... especially if they do really, really, innovative things with it'. Finally, and more importantly from a co-creation perspective:

> If you are giving your stuff away for open source and then you see people doing really innovative things with it, it's like they have to do less work, and they are more inclined to do these innovative things than you, and you get it back and think its awesome. Better exposure for you, better exposure for them. A better tool becomes available for everyone.

The preference by Participants C1, C2 and C3 to adopt an open-source approach to software distribution could be explained by their artistic development approach, whereby the development of software for commercialisation purposes is secondary to the music.

8 Conclusion

The findings presented, drawn from a qualitative analysis of the interviews, show that there are clear divides of software choice, usage, and need. These are based upon several biasing factors pertaining to the respondents as creative individuals and include artistic development experience, trajectory, strategy and innovation, and technical knowledge and learning. These factors should be taken into consideration above the typical types of consumer demands of general non-artistic software, such as reliability, efficiency, security etc. It is important that business decisions are made as free from bias as possible, irrespective of industry. This applies particularly to those with an artistic (musical) persuasion. This research demonstrates that creative people can be very passionate about their craft and works, and bias can become a significant barrier to their objectivity, not just in

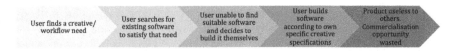

Fig. 3 The path to wasted opportunity

commercialisation strategies but also in initial decisions regarding the purchase of software vs. the building of software. In addition, creative work and creative workflows are highly individual and personal. Except in some cases where there is synergy across several users. For example, in the case of the group collaboration between Participants C1, C2, and C3. This bias is also compounded when the end user-innovator paradigm is taken into account, where the end-users of a product are also the creators of products themselves, as demonstrated by the participants within this investigation. The effect of these biases is shown in Fig. 3.

8.1 Check Your Biases

The resultant effect of bias in this instance will have a significantly greater impact on commercialisation opportunities because the primary focus for software development may be less to do with strategic planning but creative need. In addition, these biases may also impact personal use and commercialisation decisions accordingly.

Table 1 presents a 'Five C framework' that aims to prompt reflective thinking in a creative user, thereby enabling them to make less biased decisions regarding software building and buying for personal use, as well as considerations for commercialisation.

Table 1 The five C's framework

	Buying and building (personal use)	Commercialisation
Creative	Will the software fulfil a personal creative need or is it to be used to improve workflow?	Will this software satisfy the creative and/or workflow needs of other users?
Context	Is there an identified need for this software in popular platforms and, if so, can they integrated?	Will this software appeal to a broad range of users using different software platforms?
Collaborative	Will this software be used individually, in a small group of users, or in a large group of users?	Is this software intended for use by individuals, small groups, or large groups of users?
Continuation	Are you expecting to use this software on an on-going basis or for a 'one-off' project?	Will this software be used on an on-going basis or is it likely to be used only once (i.e. disposable and novel)?
Career	Is this software an integral part of your creative work or career plan?	Is this software intended to form part of a larger business strategy around music products?

8.2 Check Your Parameters

Once a creative user has reached a decision to build software for a specific artistic/workflow need, the next stage is to determine whether the intended functionality is suitable only for personal use or for commercialisation. This may depend on a variety of factors not limited to the scope of the user intention of the software, or the usual software quality considerations. This may also include various other factors relating to artistic lifestyle, which may differ between enthusiasts with 'day jobs' and academics with lecturing and research commitments. Such effects may include time constraints and constraints for on-going support, right through to differences between commercial and university commercialisation policies.

Moreover, the potential software use by a third-party end-user must be taken into account when determining the functional specifications of the software. This may include additional hardware usage and other software integration, which may be significant given the highly individualised nature studio configurations and software environments. The successful commercialisation of such a product may cause significant strain on the support capabilities, particularly where volumes of users require support with appropriate response times.

Having adequate business support functions to maximise the commercialisation opportunity is essential for longer-term success. Such infrastructure can assist in intellectual property leveraging and distribution, particularly where the software is the primary business offering. This investigation has shown that, from an artist perspective, the business aspect of software commercialisation operates in reverse. In other words, the software is not a complementary product that supports existing business functions—the function of making music. In addition, Participants C1, C2 and C3 all indicated a preference for open source distribution over commercial for-profit distribution channels. This is because software distribution was seen very much as a mechanism for generating advancement in their primary activity—making music.

In each of these examples there are clear possibilities, given the individual nature of the creative musical industry, for failure with regards to the capitalisation of commercialisation opportunities. Table 2 presents the ARTISAN framework and has been developed from the analysis within this investigation. The ARTISAN framework has been developed to raise awareness of the wider contexts of the creative individuals that are developing software, by asking critical questions in order to minimise wasted opportunities. In relation to Fig. 3, both the five C's and ARTISAN frameworks are intend to be used at stage three of the process. Figure 4 shows the potential use of the frameworks and the impact that these frameworks can have the path to creating and exploiting opportunity.

By using these frameworks, it is hoped that creative users of all music genres, technical ability, and environmental configuration, may be able collaborate, co-create, and cross-pollenate ideas through innovative music software.

Further research could include a quantitative study to determine the extent to which the biases described affect decision-making in wider user groups and communities. Additionally, a longitudinal study could identify whether these biases change over time and whether technological advancement affects user behaviour.

Table 2 The ARTISAN framework

Parameter	Buying or building (personal use)	Building and commercialisation
Availability	Is the software available elsewhere? Either for free, as a trial, or paid for? Is it readily available?	What is the current competition? Is the core functionality of the software already available?
Relevance	Do you have the relevant technical knowledge? Can you acquire the relevant technical knowledge? Do you have good access to resources? Are the resources easy to use? Are the resources comprehensive? Are the resources relevant?	Do you have technical knowledge that's difficult to learn? Is the software that you require relevant to others? Have you isolated a need within in an existing platform? Does it have/combine multiple desirable functions?
Time	Do you have the time to invest, in order to research and build the software?	Will the development time become a factor in commercialisation? Initial time cost Documentation time Quality Assurance processing time On-going support time
Integration	Will you be integrating this software into many environments or device configurations? Individual Use Group (collaborative use)	Will this software be used on multiple operating systems? Can the software be used in many different software and hardware environments? Does the software adhere to industry standards and communications protocols? Are the parameters of the software changeable by the user?
Support	Does the developer support this product? Has the product undergone rigorous quality assurance processes?	Do you intend to provide support for this software on an on-going basis? General queries Bug fixes Revisions
Additions	How interdependent is the software? Do you need to buy additional software or hardware? Do you need to buy additional software and/or hardware?	How interdependent is the software? Do users need additional software or hardware? Will it meet typical consumer minimum requirements?
Network	Do you have sufficient support networks in place? Is there help via popular user forums and online communities? Can you build it collaboratively?	Do you have sufficient commercialisation networks in place? Do you have correct business support mechanisms? Do you have an existing network for IP Leverage? Do you have a mechanism for distribution/commercialisation? Does commercialisation support the internal business network?

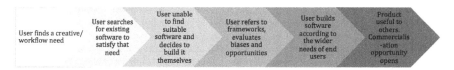

Fig. 4 The path to creating and exploiting opportunity

Acknowledgements The author wishes to thank Adam Wilson, James Vuong, Jarrad Salmon, Jacqui Mees, Maria Rumyantseva, and Leon Gross.

References

1. Bilbao, S. (2012). Time domain simulation and sound synthesis for the snare drum. *Journal of the Acoustical Society of America, 131*(1), 914–925.
2. Bilgram, V., Brem, A., & Voigt, K. I. (2008). User-centric innovations in new product development—Systematic identification of lead users harnessing interactive and collaborative online-tools. *International Journal of Innovation Management, 12*(03), 419–458.
3. Franke, N., von Hippel, E., & Schreier, M. (2006). Finding commercially attractive user innovations: A test of lead-user theory. *Journal of Product Innovation Management, 23*(4), 301–315.
4. Friberg, A., & Sundstrom, A. (2002). Swing ratios and ensemble timing in jazz performance: Evidence for a common rhythmic pattern. *Music Perception, 19*(3), 333–349.
5. Govindarajan, V. (2010). Innovation is not creativity. *blogs.hbr.org.* Available at: http://blogs.hbr.org/govindarajan/2010/08/innovation-is-not-creativity.html. Accessed September 23, 2012.
6. Gurteen, D. (1998). Knowledge, creativity and innovation. *Journal of Knowledge Management, 2*(1), 5–13.
7. Hemlin, S., Martin, C., & Martin, B. R. (2004). *Creative knowledge environments: The influences on creativity in research and innovation.* Cheltenham, UK: Edward Elgar Publishing.
8. IFPI. (2010). *Investing in music: How music companies discover, develop and promote talent, March 2010.* London: IFPI.
9. Kandiah, G., & Gossain, S. (1998). Reinventing value: The new business ecosystem. *Strategy & Leadership, 26*(5), 28–33.
10. Kannan, R., Balasundaram, S. R., & Andres, F. (2010). The role of mulsemedia in digital content ecosystem design. In *Proceedings of the international conference on management of emergent digital ecosystems*, pp. 264–266.
11. Katayose, H., et al. (2012). On evaluating systems for generating expressive music performance: the Rencon experience. *Journal of New Music Research, 41*(4), 299–310.
12. Kaufman, J. C., & Sternberg, R. J. (2010). *The Cambridge Handbook of Creativity (Cambridge Handbooks in Psychology).* Cambridge: Cambridge University Press.
13. Kirikova, M., et al. (2010). Quality of study programs: An ecosystems perspective. In J. Grundspenkis, M. Kirikova, Y. Manolopoulos & L. Novickis (Eds.), *Advances in Databases and Information Systems, Associated Workshops and Doctoral Consortium of the 13th East European Conference (ADBIS 2009)*, (pp. 39–46). Riga, Latvia: Springer-Verlag Berlin Heidelberg.
14. Kirke, A., & Miranda, E. R. (2009). A survey of computer systems for expressive music performance. *ACM Computing Surveys, 42*(1), 1–41.
15. LeCompte, M. D., & Goetz, J. P. (1982). Ethnographic data collection in evaluation research. *Educational Evaluation and Policy Analysis*, pp. 387–400.

16. Lugmayr, A. (2013). Issues and approach in defining a european research agenda on information systems and management in creative eMedia Industries. In E. Stojmenova & A. Lugmayr (Eds.), *Proceedings of the 1st workshop on defining a european research agenda on information systems and management in eMedia industries (in conjuction with eBled, Bled, Slovenia)*. Bled, Slovenia: lugymedia Inc., International Ambient Media Organization (AMEA), 2013, pp. 17–25.
17. Lugmayr, A. (2013). Brief introduction into information systems and management research in media industries. In *2013 IEEE International Conference on Multimedia and Expo Workshops (ICMEW)*. San Jose, California, pp. 1–6.
18. Manning, P. (2004). *Electronic and computer music revised*. USA: Oxford University Press.
19. Mazzola, G. B. (1995). Inverse performance theory. In *Proceedings of the 1995 international computer music conference*. San Francisco: International Computer Music Association, pp. 533–540.
20. Mazzola, G. B. (2011). *Musical performance*. New York: Springer-Verlag.
21. McKnight, J. (2005). History of AES digital audio engineering standardization. *aes.org*. Available at: http://www.aes.org/aeshc/docs/aeshist/standards.hist/digital.standards/history-of-aes-digital-audio-eng-standardization.html. Accessed September 23, 2012.
22. Puckette, M. (2007). *The theory and technique of electronic music*. Singapore: World Scientific.
23. Rath, M., & Waltermann, M. (2008). Exploring the perceptual relevance of inherent variability of drum sounds. *Computer Music Modeling and Retrieval. Sense of Sounds*, pp. 303–312.
24. Runco, M. A., & Pritzker, S. R. (1999). *Encyclopedia of creativity. Vol. 1. A–H*. San Diego: Academic Press.
25. Schoen, J., et al. (2005). The innovation cycle- A new model and case study for the invention to innovation process. *Engineering Management Journal, 17*(3), 3.
26. Sternberg, R. J., & Lubart, T. (2010). The concept of creativity: Prospects and paradigms. In J. C. Kaufman & R. J. Sternberg (Eds.), *The Cambridge Handbook of Creativity (Cambridge Handbooks in Psychology)*. Cambridge: Cambridge University Press.
27. Suddaby, R., & Greenwood, R. (2001). Colonizing knowledge: Commodification as a dynamic of jurisdictional expansion in professional service firms. *Human Relations, 54*(7), 933–953.
28. von Hippel, E. (1986). Lead users: A source of novel product concepts. *Management Science, 32*(7), 791–805.

Author Biography

John R. Taylor is a composer, musician, programmer, and interactive media designer with over ten years experience in the music industry, including several international single releases, and internationally peer reviewed publications. John has a PhD in Composition (Sydney Conservatorium of Music), an MA in Sonic Arts (Middlesex, UK), a Graduate Certificate in Innovation & Enterprise (Sydney), and a BA (Hons) in Music Industry Management (BNU, UK). John is currently a lecturer at the Sydney Conservatorium of Music.

Multi-Screen Viewing and Contents: Understanding Connected TV

Patricia Diego, Cristina Etayo and Enrique Guerrero

Abstract In recent years, the number and range of screens used to watch audio-visual contents has risen, from the traditional television set to interactive Internet-enabled devices. This fact has profoundly changed audiovisual consumption habits in Spain. Firstly, viewing-times have increased across every platform. For example, in the case of conventional television, the average Spanish person watches four hours per day. Secondly, at the same time, younger audiences in particular are increasingly likely to use connected screens. The aim of this article is to analyze which screens are preferred by Spanish Internet users, as well as their reasons for doing so when watching different types of TV contents online, such as fiction series, entertainment shows, films, news and sports. In order to carry out this research, the following screens have been taken into account: smart TV, mobile phones, tablets, computers and video consoles. Of the main findings, two in particular may be highlighted in advance: almost half of Internet users watch TV online, and the most frequently used device to do so is the computer—including laptops and netbooks. A further clear conclusion is that users choose different program genres depending on the screen. The results of this study, based on an original survey carried out online, may prove especially significant in order to discover new audiovisual consumption habits of the Spanish population on the Internet.

P. Diego · C. Etayo · E. Guerrero (✉)
Universidad de Navarra (España), Pamplona, Spain
e-mail: eguerrero@unav.es

P. Diego
e-mail: pdiegon@unav.es

C. Etayo
e-mail: cetayo@unav.es

© Springer International Publishing AG 2016
A. Lugmayr et al. (eds.), *Information Systems and Management in Media and Entertainment Industries*, International Series on Computer Entertainment and Media Technology, DOI 10.1007/978-3-319-49407-4_2

1 Introduction

1.1 Literature Review

Approximately ten years ago, only one option was available to a Spanish viewer interested in watching television contents: the conventional television set. In recent years, however, audiovisual consumption habits in Spain have been radically transformed by the emergence of a multiplatform environment. Audiences can now avail of a wide variety of devices to access television contents, including computers, tablets and mobile telephones, among others. This transformation has been driven by the youngest segment of the Spanish population, which has pioneered the adoption of new technologies [20: 45–46].

There is a great deal of research literature concerning the impact of digitalization on audiences and consumption habits. In broad terms, a number of experts have studied the emergence of the new digital culture and its consequences for media and entertainment consumption [27, 28, 36, 39]. Several researchers have also directly explored the relationship between television, new media and the Internet [1, 13, 14, 24, 35, 44], and its interactive capabilities [3, 5, 11]. In this sense, it should be highlighted the role played by Information Technology (IT) infrastructures in several ways such as the management of digital content and digital rights, or the customer relationship management (CRM) [30]. Besides, studies about media consumption are especially pertinent to the purposes of this paper [6, 34, 38].

In the particular case of Spain, most of the research around this topic—carried out in recent years—has covered issues regarding media convergence and technological migration [16, 37], or the specific relationship between television and new technologies [22, 32]. In addition, some scholars have addressed the consumption of television contents (shows and programmes) via new technologies [9, 29, 33]. Finally, there are a number of studies—mostly based on surveys—that explore the behavior of young population in regard to new technologies [8, 18, 20, 31].

Not only has this new multi-screen environment had an impact on the audience's viewing habits; the television industry has also felt the foundations of its traditional business model begin to crumble, while new opportunities and their associated risks have also arisen at the same time. Thus, the sector faces a changing situation in a state of constant development. Following an initial period of uncertainty, television production companies and channels acknowledged the need to address these new challenges. Many researchers in the field have focused on analyzing the relationship between television business models and new digital media, especially the Internet. See, for instance, Forrester [17], Griffiths [21], Vizjak and Ringlstetter [41], Hoskins et al. [25], Vukanovic [43], Ulin [40], Gershon [19], Álvarez Monzoncillo and Menor [2], Artero [4], Evens [15], Vogel [42] and Izquierdo-Castillo [26].

Doyle [13: 433] argues that a television operator may avail of the following options in designing a multiplatform strategy:

(a) Distribute the contents produced for conventional television broadcasting on other platforms.
(b) Alter and adapt existing contents to the defining features of other platforms, adding new 'layers' that update and enrich them.
(c) Create original contents for online platforms to complement the programming range on offer via linear television channels.

These options are not mutually exclusive: they may be combined in a multi-platform strategy. Nevertheless, given that one of the defining features of digital content is its versatility and ability to cross the boundaries between different media, the debate about content-format should not be limited to the nature of the distribution platform. Content-format and distribution channel are rendered separate by digitalization [41: 5].

1.2 Historical Background

At this point, however, it may be worthwhile to offer a brief overview of the historical context so as to enable a clearer understanding of the present situation. The emergence of a private television sector in Spain in the 1990s also led to the development of a new production model for audiovisual contents [10, 23]. For the most part, television channels opted to outsource to independent production companies rather than to favour an in-house production system; that is, to entrust the production of a significant proportion of their programming schedules to companies specializing in television contents [7: 108]. Thus, the television network funded the project, and the production company provided the creative input. This situation gave rise to an industrial nexus of production companies expert in the creation of entertainment (quiz shows, reality TV shows, comedy programs, talk shows, etc.) and fiction products (sitcoms, drama series, soap operas and TV movies).

The commercial life of most of these productions was relatively 'short-lived' [10: 35]. In short, contents were produced exclusively for broadcast—and possible, future repeat broadcasts—on conventional television. The success of television as a medium shaped its commercial development: the sale of formats and contents. Within this framework, the production company and the television network exercised total control over the distribution of the product. Nevertheless, the spread of the Internet undermined the dominance of both agents insofar as they acted as guardians or gatekeepers to television contents [35: 80–81]. Production companies and television networks were shocked to discover that their products were being distributed illegally over the Internet, and that they would receive absolutely no remuneration or compensation in return. This evolving situation prompted them to set up their own online content players and *apps*, whereby users could access their back-catalogues of series and programs for free or on a pay-per-view basis (pre-mieres, without commercial breaks or in HD format) [22: 370]. To date, free access to television contents following their broadcast on conventional television is the preferred model. However, that audience rating figures remain the key measure of a given product's commercial success should not be overlooked.

As a result, the linear television strategy is shifting towards an à-la-carte approach, where the user becomes the programmer—choosing what to watch, as well as when, where and how to watch it—and even the producer of his/her own contents [12: 334]. Hence, the need to map the new audiovisual consumption habits and their impact on the content production industry and its business models is acute. Television is evolving to a collaborative model according to the next three cate-gories related to interactivity levels [5: 76]:

(a) iTV: Interaction with the media.
(b) Social TV: A step furher, it includes iTV plus social interactions (e.g. instant messengers, social networks, etcetera).
(c) Collaborative TV: It combines iTV and social TV with collaborative services in all stages of the TV production process.

The purpose of this paper is to explore whether Internet users in Spain use different screens or platforms when they view different types of content online (fiction series, entertainment programs, films, news, sports, etc.), as well as their reasons for doing so. A related objective is to establish whether the use of different media devices—Smart TV, mobile telephones, tablets, computers and video con-soles (Wii, Playstation, Xbox, etc.)—is complementary or competitive. The results of this study are of interest to both production companies and television networks in terms of content creation and product scheduling across a variety of platforms.

The paper is structured as follows: first, the technological context in Spain is described; then, the methodology used for the purposes of this study is outlined, based on data from an unpublished survey carried out among Internet users. This background information frames the analysis of results that follows. Finally, the main conclusions as regards the television contents most frequently viewed on each screen, as well as the reasons why, are discussed.

1.3 Technological Framework

So as to offer a comprehensive description of the technological context shaping the television industry and the patterns of audiovisual consumption in Spain, data from the three main sources of statistical information for the country have been taken into consideration: Eurostat, the *Instituto Nacional de Estadística* (INE: Spanish Statistical Office) and the *Centro de Investigaciones Sociológicas* (CIS: Center for Sociological Research).

It should be noted that no general consensus has yet been reached as regards the definition of Internet user as such. Eurostat, for instance, defines an Internet user as any individual, aged between 16 and 74, who has accessed the web at least once a week during the previous three months. Although it refers to the same population and timeframe, the INE does not take frequency of access into account (an Internet user as such is required only to have accessed the web at some point in the previous three months). Finally, like the INE, the CIS does not take frequency of access within the same three-month timeframe into account; however, it also changes the population age-group to individuals aged 18 or older.

The number of Internet users has grown steadily year on year in the main European markets. The figure has doubled over the last ten years in almost all of the countries (Table 1). The UK has registered the highest rate of Internet users in relation to the population as a whole: 84 % in 2012. At the same time, the rate of increase has been highest in Spain in recent years. According to Eurostat, the figure grew from 31 to 65 % in less than ten years. The figures supplied by the CIS are more or less the same, which registered a percentage of 63.6 % Internet users. The INE figure is higher, however, because it does not take frequency of access into account, but does encompass a wider range of young people (Table 2).

In absolute numbers, there were 13.5 m Internet users in Spain in 2004; the INE figure for 2012 reached over 24 m (Table 2). In terms of frequency of access, 72.6 % of Internet users go online every day, and 20.5 % at least once a week. To sum up, 93.1 % of Internet users access the web at least once a week (22,413,941) —that is to say, 65 % of the total population aged between 16 and 74 –. There is a more marked trend in the younger population segment (aged between 16 and 24) to go online every day: 85.3 % of Internet users in this age-group access the web every day, as compared with 72.6 % of the total population.

The desktop computer is still the device that is most frequently used to access the Internet; 63 % of users do so, although the number of laptop/netbook users is not much lower: 57 %. The CIS data also discloses a strikingly low uptake in smart TV use among Internet users in Spain (Table 3).

If the analysis of the data is limited to mobile devices used outside the home or normal workplace, the mobile telephone is the screen that is most frequently used to access the Internet (44.1 %), followed by the portable computer (laptop/netbook)

Table 1 Evolution of Internet users in the main European markets

	2004	2005	2006	2007	2008	2009	2010	2011	2012
Germany	50	54	59	64	68	71	75	77	78
Spain	31	35	39	44	49	54	58	62	65
France	..	..	39	55	63	67	72	74	78
Italy	26	28	31	34	37	42	48	51	53
United Kingdom	49	54	57	65	70	76	80	81	84

Source Eurostat. Figures in percentages

Table 2 Evolution of Internet users in Spain

	2004	2005	2006	2007	2008	2009	2010	2011	2012
Internet users	13,534,664	15,1314,20	15,970,998	17,580,587	19,572,899	20,741,237	22,207,773	23,196,058	24,075,125
%	40.4	44.4	47.9	52	56.7	59.8	64.2	67.1	69.8

Source INE

Table 3 Connected screens and Internet users (everywhere)

Screens	%
Computer	63.0
Laptop/Netbook	56.9
Tablet	3.5
Smart TV	1.1
Smartphone	36.5
Video console	1.5

Source CIS, June 2012

Table 4 Mobile screens and Internet users (excluding home and workplace)

	Laptops/Netbooks	Tablets	Mobile phones (including smartphones)	Other	Mobile devices (total)
% of Internet users	32.8	10.2	44.1	6.5	56

Source: INE 2012
Note The total figure for mobile devices is not the same as the sum of the numbers for each type of device because each user may use more than one screen to access the Internet

Table 5 Places and Internet users

Places	%
Home	90.5
Workplace	34.2
Anywhere: tablet/smartphone	31.8

Source CIS, June 2012

(32.8 %) and the tablet (10.2 %). 56 % of the total number of Internet users access the web using some kind of mobile device (Table 4).

The INE data (Table 4) do not take an account of mobile device use outside the home or normal workplace, although these are the preferred locations for Internet access according to the CIS (Table 5).

As regards technological equipment at home, amounting to a total number of 15,529,687 households in 2012 according to the INE, the most common devices in Spanish homes are the television set and the mobile telephone (Table 6). According to ComScore [48: 14] 66 % of the mobile telephones in use in Spain are smartphones. Spain is the European country with the highest market penetration in this regard. 89 % of smartphone owners use it to access the Internet on a daily basis [50: 5].

Before turning to our analysis of the results of the survey carried out among Internet users, the methodology of the study is set out in greater detail, and the research questions addressed by this paper are articulated in clearer terms.

Table 6 Technological equipment in Spanish homes

	Television	Computer	Laptop/Netbook/Tablet	Mobile phone (including smartphones)
Households %	99.4	47.8	54.6	95.9

Source INE 2012

Note Tablets are included in the same category as portable computers because the INE regards them as portable computers without a physical keyboard

2 Methodology and Research Questions

The main source of data for this empirical study is an original survey administered in May 2012, which was designed by a research team that included the authors of this paper. The survey was carried out online by a company that specializes in such research.

The target population for the survey was Spanish Internet users, in contrast to other studies conducted in relation to biased samples. The definition of Internet user matched that outlined by other organizations such as the *Asociación para la Investigación de Medios de Comunicación* (AIMC: the Communications Media Research Association, Spain), which is responsible for producing the *Estudio General de Medios* (EGM: Annual Media Report), one of the main reports on media audiences in Spain. Hence, the definition of Internet user is as follows: an individual between the ages of 14 and 64 who has accessed the Internet at least once in the previous month. This description is only slightly different to the other definitions cited above (INE, Eurostat and CIS).

The initial objective was to compile a sample of 1200 observations, which involved making contact with 2665 Internet users, yielding a response rate of 45.02 %. Proportional quotas were established for the categories of sex, age and region. The final sample mirrors the structure of the theoretical sample. The proportional quotas were fixed on the basis of the composition of the Internet-user population aged over 14 as indicated by the data supplied in the most recent edition of the EGM. The sample comprises 55 % men and 45 % women. As regards age-groups, 25 % of the sample is between 14 and 24 years old; 29 % between 25 and 34; 24 % between 45 and 54; and 7.5 % between 55 and 64. The regional distribution is as follows: 12 % from the northeast (Catalonia and the Balearic Islands); 15 % from the east; 19 % from Andalusia; 10.5 % from the centre; 9 % from the northwest; 9 % from the north-central area; 5 % from the Canary Islands; 8.5 % from urban Barcelona; and 12 % from Madrid.

Our main purpose in this article is to discover Internet user consumption habits in Spain in relation to different types of contents—fiction series, entertainment shows, films, news and sports—and screens—smart TV, mobile phones, tablets, computers and video consoles. To this end, the research questions addressed by this study are as follows: what percentage of Spanish Internet users watches television online; what screens are most commonly used for this purpose; what types of television contents are most frequently viewed via the Internet; whether there is a relationship between the media device used and the type of content viewed; and finally, the reasons that may have prompted the latter relationship. Another question also arises in this regard: whether different platforms are in direct competition with one another, or whether they are in fact complementary.

Our starting point is a double hypothesis to be confirmed. Firstly, there is a correlation between contents and screens, which means that the audience uses different devices when watching each type of content. In this regard, several factors are decisive: the screen size and its viewing conditions—for instance, some media devices are more appropriate when watching contents on the go. And secondly, the use of different platforms is not exclusive; that is to say, screens are complementary. They do not compete directly for audience time. According to this, using one type of screen does not exclude watching contents on another.

3   Results: Screens and Contents

Prior to offering a detailed analysis of the survey results, it should be noted that conventional television consumption has not been negatively affected by easy access to viewing via other screens. According to the CIS (June 2012 edition), 46.4 % of Internet users said that their Internet use had not disrupted the time they spend on other activities. Although 26.5 % acknowledged that they watch less conventional television, this has not had a significant impact on the average figures for conventional TV consumption: rather than decrease, this has undergone a steady growth-rate in recent years, peaking at 246 min per day in 2012 (Table 7).

Such information suggests that conventional television consumption is compatible with the use of other Internet-enabled devices. This view has been confirmed by a number of studies, including Televidente 2.0, in which 51 % of those surveyed, who have mobile devices (computers, smartphones or tablets), said that they usually use them while watching television (The Cocktail Analysis, November 2012). Moreover, studies such as the AIMC [46] have shown that online television viewing has not led to a reduction in the time spent watching conventional television. In fact, when the two modes are combined, the total amount of time spent on television consumption as a whole is higher.

In addition, another common viewing habit discloses the existence of the multitasking viewer [3, 39] or *double dipper* [24]; that is, users who watch television and surf the internet, commenting on or sharing contents via social networking sites

Table 7 Evolution of conventional TV consumption in Spain

	2004	2005	2006	2007	2008	2009	2010	2011	2012
Minutes	218	217	217	223	227	226	234	239	246

Source Kantar Media. Average minutes per day

at the same time. It reveals a symbiotic relationship between TV and the internet through which the role of each medium is mutually reinforced, especially when young audiences are involved [22: 352].

In relation to the issue of whether or not digital media are siphoning viewers away from television, Gunter [24: XIII] holds that the Internet plays a twofold role: on the one hand, it competes with television in terms of available user time; on the other, however, it also functions as an alternative platform for the distribution of television contents. Gunter argues that the question of whether or not the Internet and television are in direct competition is preceded by other considerations: Do both media meet the same needs? And that being the case, how successfully do they do so? [24: 67]. Rather than coming to a firm conclusion in this regard, Gunter reflects on the issue, reasoning that the Internet cannot be regarded merely as a competitor; rather, it enriches other media, offering a new platform by means of which the audience may be engaged [24: 31–33].

In fact, a reading of the user ratings suggests that TV and the Internet are complementary as platforms. However, this comparison may be rendered obsolete when convergence between the two media is complete. Until that time comes, the notion of multiplatform television involves nothing other than the distribution of contents via a variety of devices. However, the simplicity of this statement occludes the complexity of what it implies for both the television industry and the audience. Rather than replacing the experience of watching television in one's living-room, the possibility of watching such contents on other devices enriches the experience [1: 3].

As things now stand, television as a medium cannot be seen as synonymous with the television set. Television contents are now viewed via a variety of screens. According to the CIS, only 14.4 % of Internet users access the web to watch television. This data is very different to the figures afforded by INE. Table 8 shows that 50.6 % of Internet users—that is, 35 % of the total population aged between 16 and 74—watches television or listens to the radio via the Internet. Such viewing and listening habits are more common among the younger age-groups of users: 64 % of Internet users between the ages of 16 and 24 watch television or listen to the radio online. The marked disparity between the date supplied by the CIS and the INE may be accounted—in part, at least—by the difference in the samples and media analysed: the former takes neither users under the age of 18 nor radio-listening into

Table 8 Internet TV and Radio consumption

Ages	Watching TV/Listening to the radio
16–24	64.1
25–34	60.3
35–44	49.6
45–54	4.4
55–64	31.7
65–74	28.0
Internet users (total)	50.6

Source INE 2012

Table 9 Use of different screens to watch television on the Internet

	Never or almost never (%)	Once a month (%)	At least once a week (%)	At least three times a week (%)	Every day (%)	Total (%)	No.
Computer	3.1	41.1	33.9	11.4	10.4	100	508
Mobile	81.9	8.7	5.7	2.2	1.6	100	508
Tablet	85	6.5	4.5	2.2	1.8	100	508
Smart TV	67.9	11.6	7.7	3.5	9.3	100	508
Video console	90.6	6.1	2.2	0.8	0.4	100	508

Source by the authors

consideration. In Spain, too, the most common form of online television consumption is via streaming, rather than by download [46: 2].

The results of our survey show that 42.3 % of Internet users (508 out of 1,200 individuals) watch television online (Table 9). This figure reflects more closely the data provided by the INE. Table 9 lists the devices used for such television viewing. The computer is, by far, the most frequently used device: 10.4 % of Internet users view television contents online via computer every day, 45.3 % at least once a week, 41.1 % at least once a month, and only 3.1 % never or almost never use their computer to watch television.

The rate of use of other screens or platforms is considerably lower. The second most commonly used device is the Internet-enabled or smart TV, although only 9.3 % of online television viewers said that they use it every day, and 67.9 % of respondents said that they never or almost never use it. The percentages for those using a smart TV to watch television at least once a month or once a week are 11.6 and 11.2 %, respectively.

The use of the other three types of screen is practically negligible. It is worth recalling in this regard that the population surveyed comprises only those who view television online, so the sample is very well-defined. 1.6 % of such TV viewers use a mobile telephone to watch television contents online; 1.8 % a tablet; and only 0.4 % use a video console. Those who watch television at least once a week via these devices might also be described as frequent users: 7.9 % in the case of the mobile telephone; 6.7 %, the tablet; and 3 %, the video console. However, the most striking figures in this regard are that 81.9 % of online television viewers never use their mobile telephone to do so, 85 % never use a tablet, and 90.6 %, a video console.

The next table details information relating to a key issue addressed in this paper and referred to in the title. The research questions covered here include the following: what types of television contents are most frequently viewed online; what screens are most commonly used for this purpose; and whether there is a relationship between the media device used and the type of content viewed.

The data presented in Table 10 shows that foreign fiction series and films (in that order) are by far the most frequently viewed contents among users who watch

Table 10 Contents viewed on different screens used to watch television on the Internet

	Spanish fiction series (%)	Foreign fiction series (%)	Entertainment (%)	Films (%)	News (%)	Sports (%)	Other (%)	No.	%
Computer	37	54.1	36.6	47	31.7	36.8	3	492	96.9
Mobile	20.7	23.9	30.4	23.9	42.4	40.2	7.6	92	18.1
Tablet	36.8	47.4	40.8	39.5	44.7	27.6	11.8	76	15
Smart TV	42.9	52.1	35.6	63.2	34.4	41.1	3.1	163	32.1
Video console	29.2	37.5	22.9	52.1	16.7	27.1	4.2	48	9.4
Any platform	42.5	56.9	43.9	52	40.7	41.9	9.8	508	100

Source by the authors

television via the Internet (508): the results are 56.9 and 52 %, respectively. As regards the screens used, and as noted above, the computer and smart TV are the most commonly used devices in online television viewing at 96.9 and 32.1 %, respectively.

The percentages cited below were calculated in relation to the total number of online television viewers depending on the screen or platform used. The figures show that there are clear differences as regards the types of contents viewed using different devices. The computer is used, above all, to watch foreign fiction series (54.1 %) and films (47 %) and, to a somewhat lesser extent, Spanish fiction (37 %), sports (36.8 %), entertainment (36.6 %) and the news (31.7 %). A similar pattern may be traced for the smart TV, which 63.4 % of online viewers use to watch films; 52.1 %, foreign fiction series; 42.9 %, Spanish series; 41.1 %, sports; 35.6 %, entertainment programs; and 34.4 %, the news.

The video console is predominantly used to watch films (52.1 %) and, much less frequently, for entertainment programs (22.9 %), news programs (16.7 %) and sports (27.1 %). In contrast, the mobile telephone is most commonly used to access the news (42.4 %) and sports (40.2 %), rather than fiction contents. Finally, the tablet is generally used for watching foreign fiction series (47.4 %), news programs (44.7 %) and entertainment shows (40.8 %), and less frequently for sports (27.6 %), although no major differences arise in this regard. As compared with the other screens, the tablet is used to view a higher proportion (11.8 %) of 'other' audiovisual content-types not specified here.

Table 11 traces the relationship(s) between the use of different screen to watch television via the Internet. The information here takes into account only whether or not a given device is used. The frequency or intensity of use is addressed in Table 12. The data presented in Table 11 discloses a number of significant correlations. With the exception of the computer, in general terms, anyone who uses one screen to watch television online is more likely to use the other screens for the same purpose: this pattern is reflected in the findings for the mobile telephone, the tablet, the smart TV and the video console. The correlation is particularly strong in relation to the mobile telephone and the tablet, which suggests that a viewer who uses one of these devices is also likely to use the other. The data for the computer is different to that for the other devices. In fact, the correlation between the computer and both

Table 11 The relationship between the use of different screens used to watch television on the Internet (Pearson's correlation)

	Computer	Mobile	Tablet	Smart TV
Mobile	−0.091**			
Tablet	−0.082*	0.261***		
Smart TV	−0.021	0.137***	0.043	
Video console	0.020	0.093**	0.091**	0.138***

***$p < 0.01$, **$p < 0.05$, *$p < 0.10$
Source by the authors

Table 12 The relationship between intensity of use for different screens used to watch television on the Internet (Spearman's correlation)

	Computer	Mobile	Tablet	Smart TV
Mobile	0.033			
Tablet	0.077*	0.257***		
Smart TV	0.094**	0.142***	0.055	
Video console	0.011	0.095**	0.097**	0.129***

$***p < 0.01$, $**p < 0.05$, $*p < 0.10$
Source by the authors

the mobile telephone and the tablet is negative—in other words, the latter devices are used instead of the computer for the purposes of online television viewing.

In addition to finding out whether or not the various screens are used, the frequency of such use is also significant. Table 12 presents the data concerning frequency of use for each of the different screens. The results for all the devices, except for the computer, parallel the findings detailed in chart 11. Indeed, the correlation figures are very similar, which means that greater frequency of use for any one of these screens (mobile telephone, tablet, smart TV or video console) correlates positively with greater frequency of use for all the other screens. In contrast, there is a marked change in the relationship between frequency of use for the computer and the other platforms. Unlike the conclusion drawn from Table 11, no negative correlations emerge in this case, which suggests that the relationship here is one of complementarity rather than competition. Online television viewers who tend to use the computer more frequently are also more likely to use the tablet and smart TV more frequently. This conclusion confirms the complementarity hypothesis referred to earlier in this paper.

Finally, in light of the data relating to the device(s) used to watch television online, the frequency of use in each case, and the types of content accessed via the different screens, the reasons for doing so are explored. Tables 13, 14, 15, 16, 17 and 18 analyse whether or not there is a correlation between the reason given for watching television online and the type of media device used to do so. Based on the Chi-squared scores for 'I wasn't able to watch them when they were broadcast' and 'I like to watch them again' (Tables 13 and 14) it is clear that there is no link to a greater or lesser use of one screen rather than another.

This is not the case for the reason, 'I missed a part' (Table 15) where viewers are more likely to use a smart TV to complete their viewing experience.

When the reason is 'I like to watch them with little or no advertising' (Table 16), the video console is the most commonly used device.

The video console, along with the tablet, is used most frequently when the reason given is 'I like to decide how to watch them' (Table 17).

Finally, when the reason is 'Because they are not broadcast on television' (Table 18), Internet users tend to access the audiovisual contents via mobile telephone and video console.

Table 13 The relationship between the use of different screens to watch television contents via the Internet and the reasons (I wasn't able to watch them when they were broadcast)

I wasn't able to watch them when they were broadcast				
		No (%)	Yes (%)	Chi-2
Total		9.4	90.6	
Computer	No	18.8	81.3	1.670
	Yes	9.1	90.9	
Mobile	No	8.9	91.1	0.826
	Yes	12	88	
Tablet	No	10.2	89.8	1.830
	Yes	5.3	94.7	
Smart TV	No	10.7	89.3	2.046
	Yes	6.7	93.3	
Video console	No	10	90	1.729
	Yes	4.2	95.8	

$***p < 0.01$, $**p < 0.05$, $*p < 0.10$
Source by the authors

Table 14 The relationship between the use of different screens to watch television contents via the Internet and the reasons (I like to watch them again)

I like to watch them again				
		No (%)	Yes (%)	Chi-2
Total		61	39	
Computer	No	68.8	31.3	0.415
	Yes	60.8	68.5	
Mobile	No	62	38	0.957
	Yes	56.5	43.5	
Tablet	No	61.1	38.9	0.009
	Yes	60.5	39.5	
Smart TV	No	62.9	37.1	1.589
	Yes	57.1	42.9	
Video console	No	61.7	38.3	1.048
	Yes	54.2	45.8	

$***p < 0.01$, $**p < 0.05$, $*p < 0.10$
Source by the authors

These connected devices allow the audience not only to watch contents but also interactive capabilities. With regard to his fact, media industries stand out as a very clear example for introducing organization wide information technology infrastructure [30]. According to our research [11: 185–186], the audience is willing to interact mainly to participate in tele-voting and to criticise via social networks. Increasingly such participation occurs through a connected second screen during the viewing time, given that more than half of the audience are multitask viewers.

Table 15 The relationship between the use of different screens to watch television contents via the Internet and the reason "I missed a part"

I missed a part		No (%)	Yes (%)	Chi-2
Total		31.9	68.1	
Computer	No	43.8	56.3	1.070
	Yes	31.5	68.5	
Mobile	No	32.7	67.3	0.681
	Yes	28.3	71.7	
Tablet	No	32.9	67.1	1.278
	Yes	26.3	73.7	
Smart TV	No	36.8	63.2	11.992***
	Yes	21.5	78.5	
Video console	No	32.6	67.4	1.158
	Yes	25	75	

***$p < 0.01$, **$p < 0.05$, *$p < 0.10$
Source by the authors

Table 16 The relationship between the use of different screens to watch television contents via the Internet and the reason "I like to watch them with little or no advertising"

I like to watch them with little or no advertising		No (%)	Yes (%)	Chi-2
Total		33.9	66.1	
Computer	No	25	75	0.579
	Yes	34.1	65.9	
Mobile	No	33.7	66.3	0.043
	Yes	34.8	65.2	
Tablet	No	34.3	65.7	0.207
	Yes	31.6	68.4	
Smart TV	No	33.3	66.7	0.132
	Yes	35	65	
Video console	No	35	65	2.834*
	Yes	22.9	77.1	

***$p < 0.01$, **$p < 0.05$, *$p < 0.10$
Source by the authors

Connected television in Spain is evolving from a social TV model to a collaborative one [5]. Some fiction, entertainment and news shows are using collaborative tools. For instance, the quiz show *Atrapa un millón*—the Spanish adaptation of the international format *One million drop* broadcast by Antena 3—invites the viewer to play online the same game than the contestant in the studio of the TV show via its website and its mobile application.

Table 17 The relationship between the use of different screens to watch television contents via the Internet and the reason "I like to decide how to watch them"

I like to decide how to watch them		No (%)	Yes (%)	Chi-2
Total		37.6	62.4	
Computer	No	43.8	56.3	0.266
	Yes	37.4	62.6	
Mobile	No	38.5	61.5	0.729
	Yes	33.7	66.3	
Tablet	No	39.1	60.9	2.851*
	Yes	28.9	71.1	
Smart TV	No	37.7	62.3	0.003
	Yes	37.4	62.6	
Video console	No	38.9	61.1	3.586**
	Yes	25	75	

***$p < 0.01$, **$p < 0.05$, *$p < 0.10$
Source by the authors

Table 18 The relationship between the use of different screens to watch television contents via the Internet and the reason "Because they are not broadcast on television"

Because they are not broadcast on television		No (%)	Yes (%)	Chi-2
Total		37.2	62.8	
Computer	No	43.8	56.3	0.303
	Yes	37	63	
Mobile	No	43.8	56.3	2.968*
	Yes	37	63	
Tablet	No	36.6	63.4	0.492
	Yes	40.8	59.2	
Smart TV	No	39.1	60.9	1.707
	Yes	33.1	66.9	
Video console	No	39.1	60.9	7.727***

***$p < 0.01$, **$p < 0.05$, *$p < 0.10$
Source by the authors

4 Conclusions

Technological developments and the spread of the Internet have changed the audiovisual consumption habits of Spanish audiences over the last ten years. Of the main European markets, it is striking that Spain is the country where the number of Internet users has grown most dramatically: the number of Internet users in Spain doubled in the last decade. According to Eurostat, the proportion of the Spanish population who were Internet users in 2012 was 65 %.

In this context, the viewing figures show that conventional television continues to dominate the sector. On average, Spanish viewers spend four hours per day watching television. Nevertheless, this fact has not had a bearing on the consumption of online television contents. Our results show that almost half of the Internet user population watches television on the Internet. Among such Internet viewers, the computer is the most commonly used device (96.9 %). A substantially lower proportion of Internet TV viewers (32.1 %) use a smart TV set. In spite of its increasing penetration in Spanish homes, it is not yet the main screen for connected television. Smart TV devices are still being used in the same way as conventional television sets. Regarding smaller screens, the proportions of people using mobile telephones and tablets to watch TV on the internet are low: 18.1 % of Internet TV viewers use mobile phones for that purpose, whereas the percentage for tablets is 15 %. Finally, video consoles are used by only 9.4 % of Internet users to watch TV online, and thus are the least common platform.

In relation to the viewing of different TV genres on the Internet, our results point to significant variety and diversity among users. The most viewed genres among TV Internet users are foreign fiction series and films, followed by entertainment programs, Spanish fiction series, sports and news programs.

The results also show that users choose different program genres depending on the screen, which confirms our initial hypothesis. As regards computers, smart TVs and consoles, the programs viewed most often mirror those mentioned above in relation to the Internet in general: foreign fiction series and films. In the case of tablets, all the genres considered here are viewed to a similar extent. Mobile telephones are the devices that evince a different pattern: those that use them to view television contents via the Internet are more likely to watch news programs and sports.

Moreover, the results of this study also confirm our second hypothesis, that the various screens are complementary. The data relating to the viewing habits of seasoned online TV consumers are especially significant in this regard. With the exception of computers, viewers using another platform to watch television via the Internet are more likely to use the other devices for the same purpose. In any case, the greater the frequency of viewing via any of the platforms—including the computer, albeit to a slightly lesser extent—is also linked to a higher frequency of use for all the other screens.

Furthermore there is a correlation between the reason for viewing television online and the platform used to do so (excluding the reasons that given contents could not be watched at the time of broadcast or viewers are interested in watching the contents again). When users were unable to watch the complete contents, they use a smart TV to finish their online viewing. However, so as to avoid having to see commercials, they use the video console, a screen that they also use—along with the tablet—when they want to decide for themselves how to watch audiovisual contents. Users interested in watching programs that are not broadcast on conventional television tend to access them via the video console and mobile telephone.

Finally, while television is becoming a collaborative media, at the same time the audience is becoming more active, using online interactive tools. In this sense, further research should continue to assess changing viewing habits with regard to connected TV and its impact on the audiovisual industry and the creative production process of contents.

Acknowledgments This article forms part of two subsidized research projects: *New Consumption Habits in Audiovisual Contents: Impact of Digitalization on the European Media Diet*, financed by the Spanish Ministry of Economy and competitiveness for the period 2011–13 (CSO2010-20122); and *The Impact of Digitalization on the Spanish Audiovisual Industry* (2011–13), financed by the University of Navarra (PIUNA).

References

1. Adams, M. (2009). Bullpen: Implementing multiplatform TV. *Communications Technology, 26*(12), 3.
2. Álvarez, Monzoncillo J. M., & Menor, J. (2010). Previsiones sobre los recursos del audiovisual. La televisión, entre la gratuidad y el pago. *Telos, 85*, 36–44.
3. Arrojo, M. J. (2010). Nuevas estrategias para rentabilizar los contenidos. Distribución y financiación de formatos audiovisuales en Internet. *Telos, 85*, 117–128.
4. Artero, M. J. P. (2010). Online video business models: YouTube versus Hulu. *Palabra Clave, 13*(1), 11–123.
5. Bachmayer, S., Lugmayr, A., & Kotsis, G. (2010). Convergence of collaborative web approaches and interactive TV program formats. *International Journal of Web Information Systems, 6*(1), 74–94. Doi:10.1108/17440081011034493
6. Bondad-Brown, B. A., Rice, R. E., & Pearce, K. E. (2012). Influences on TV viewing and online user-shared video use: Demographics, generations, contextual age, media use, motivations, and audience activity. *Journal of Broadcasting & Electronic Media, 56*(4), 471–493. Doi:10.1080/08838151.2012.732139
7. Bustamante, E. (1999). *La televisión económica. Financiación, estrategias y mercados.* Barcelona: Gedisa.
8. Cáceres, M. D., San Román, J. A., & Brändle, G. (2011). El uso de la televisión en un contexto multipantallas: Viejas prácticas en nuevos medios. *Anàlisi, 43*, 21–44.
9. Castillo-Hinojosa, A. M. (2012). Ficción audiovisual en redes sociales en línea: Prácticas para la construcción de identidad y relaciones en Facebook. *Comunicación, 1*(10), 907–916.
10. Diego, P. (2010). *La ficción en la pequeña pantalla. Cincuenta años de series en España.* Pamplona: Eunsa.
11. Diego, P., Guerrero, E., & Etayo, C. (2014). Connected TV in Spain: Contents, screens and viewing habits. *Revista Mediterránea de Comunicación, 5*(1), p. 179–199. Doi:10.14198/MEDCOM2014.5.1.10
12. Diego, P., & Herrero, M. (2010). Desarrollo de series online producidas por el usuario final: El caso del videoblog de ficción. *Palabra Clave, 13*(2), 325–336.
13. Doyle, G. (2010). From television to multi-platform: Less from more or more for less? *Convergence, 16*(4), 431–449.
14. Evans, E. (2011). *Transmedia television: Audiences, new media and daily life.* New York: Routledge.
15. Evens, T. (2010). Value Networks and changing business models for the digital television industry. *Journal of Media Business Studies, 7*(4), 41–58.
16. Feijóo, C. (2013). Soportes digitales y transformación de la industria de contenidos. *El Profesional de la Información, 22*(1), 5–9. Doi:10.3145/epi.2013.ene.01.
17. Forrester, C. (2000). *The business of digital television.* Boston: Focal Press.
18. Galán, E., & Del Pino, C. (2010). Jóvenes, ficción televisiva y nuevas tecnologías. *Área Abierta, 25*, 1–17.
19. Gershon, R. A. (2009). *Telecommunications and business strategy.* New York: Routledge.
20. González, Aldea P., & López, Vidales N. (2011). La generación digital ante un nuevo modelo de television: Contenidos y soportes preferidos. *Anàlisi, 44*, 31–48.

21. Griffiths, A. (2003). *Digital television strategies: Business challenges and opportunities.* Houndmills, Basingstoke, Hampshire: Palgrave Macmillan.
22. Guerrero, E., Diego, P., & Pardo, A. (2013). Distributing audiovisual contents in the new digital scenario: Multiplatform strategies of the main Spanish television networks. In M. Friedrichsen & W. Mühl-Benninghaus (Eds.), *Handbook of social media management. Value chain and business in changing media markets* (pp. 349–374). Berlin: Springer.
23. Guerrero, E. (2010). *El entretenimiento en la televisión en España. Historia, industria y mercado.* Barcelona: Deusto.
24. Gunter, B. (2010). *Television versus the Internet: Will TV prosper or perish as the world movies online?* Oxford: Chandos Publishing.
25. Hoskins, C., McFadyen, S., & Finn, A. (2004). *Media economics: Applying economics to new and traditional media.* Thousand Oaks (California): Sage.
26. Izquierdo-Castillo, J. (2012). Distribución online de contenidos audiovisuales: Análisis de 3 modelos de negocio. *El Profesional De La Información, 21*(4), 385–390. Doi:10.3145/epi.2012.jul.09.
27. Jenkins, H. (2006). *Convergence culture: Where old and new media collide.* New York: New York University Press.
28. Jenkins, H., Ford, S., & Green, J. (2013). *Spreadable media: Creating value and meaning in a networked culture.* New York: New York University Press.
29. Lacalle, C. (2011). La ficción interactiva: Televisión y web 2.0. *Ámbitos, 20,* 87–107.
30. Lugmayr, A. (2013). Issues and approach in defining a european research agenda on information systems and management in creative eMedia industries. In E. Stojmenova & A. Lugmayr (Eds.), *Proceedings of the 1st workshop on defining a european research agenda on information systems and management in eMedia industries (in conjuction with eBled, Bled, Slovenia)* (pp. 17–25). Bled, Slovenia: lugymedia Inc., International Ambient Media Organization (AMEA).
31. Méndiz, A., de Aguilera, M., & Borges, E. (2011). Actitudes y valoraciones de los jóvenes ante la TV móvil. *Comunicar, 13*(36), 69–76. Doi:10.3916/C36-2011-02-08.
32. Micó, J. L. (2010). Entretenimiento transversal. Convergencia de contenidos entre la televisión, internet y los dispositivos móviles. *Trípodos, 27,* 107–115.
33. Morales, L. F. (2011). La producción de ficción para telefonía móvil: Evolución tecnológica, estado actual y perspectivas. *Telos, 87,* 1–7.
34. Napoli, P. (2011). *Audience evolution: New technologies and the transformation of media audiences.* New York: Columbia University Press.
35. Palmer, S. (2006). *Television disrupted: The transition from network to networked TV.* Amsterdam, Boston: Focal Press.
36. Pavlik, J. V., & McIntosh, S. (2011). *Converging media: A new introduction to mass communication.* New York: Oxford University Press.
37. Ruano, S. (2008). Internet y la telefonía móvil: Nuevos soportes para distribuir contenidos audiovisuales. *Razón y Palabra,* (68). Available in http://www.razonypalabra.org.mx/N/n68/varia/ruano.html. September 26, 2013.
38. Taneja, H., et al. (2012). Media consumption across platforms: Identifying user-defined repertoires. *New Media and Society, 14*(6), 951–968. Doi:10.1177/1461444811436146.
39. Tapscott, D. (2009). *Grown up digital: How the net generation is changing your world.* New York: MacGraw-Hill Professional.
40. Ulin, J. C. (2009). *The business of media distribution: Monetizing film, TV and video content in an online world.* Burlington: Focal Press.
41. Vizjak, A., & Ringlstetter, M. J. (2003). *Media management: Leveraging content for profitable growth.* Berlin, New York: Springer.
42. Vogel, H. (2011). *Entertainment industry economics: A guide for financial analysis* (8th ed.). New York: Cambridge University Press.
43. Vukanovic, Z. (2009). *Television and digital media in the 21st century: New business, economic and technological paradigm.* Novi Sad: Media Art Service International.

44. Ytreberg, E. (2009). Extended liveness and eventfulness in multiplatform reality formats. *New Media and Society, 11*(4), 467–485.

Other Resources

45. Asociación para la Investigación de Medios de Comunicación (AIMC). (2013, February/March). *Estudio general de medios: Audiencia de internet* (first series).
46. Asociación para la Investigación de Medios de Comunicación (AIMC). (2012). *Televisión: tradicional versus online*.
47. Centro de Investigaciones Sociológicas. (2012, June).
48. ComScore. (2013). *Spain digital future in focus*.
49. Eurostat. (2012). *Internet use in households and by individuals*.
50. Google. (2012). *Our mobile planet: Global smartphone users*.
51. Instituto Nacional de Estadística (Spanish Statistical Office). (2012). *Encuesta sobre Equipamiento y Uso de Tecnologías de la Información y Comunicación en los hogares* (Survey on ICT Devices and their Use in Spanish homes).
52. Kantar Media. (2004–2012). Audience ratings data.
53. The Cocktail Analysis. (2012, November) *Televidente 2.0* (sixth series).

Authors Biography

Patricia Diego is associate professor of TV Drama Production at the School of Communication, University of Navarra (Spain). She got a Ph.D. in 2004 with a thesis entitled Production of TV fiction in Spain (1990–2002). History, industry and market, which received the outstanding doctoral thesis award. She has been a visiting researcher at the University of Westminster (2006) and at the Univesity of Cork (2014). She has published several articles, books and chapters about TV production and the history of TV Fiction in Spain. Her current lines of research are production standards in TV drama and the impact of digitalization on the TV industry. Besides she is member of the Spanish Academy of Television Arts & Sciences.

Cristina Etayo is associate professor of Marketing Research at the School of Communication in the University of Navarra (Spain). She develops her research mainly in the area of mass media communication, especially in television advertising. She is currently working in a project on new audiovisual consumption patterns in Europe, where she analyzes the impact of digitalization on media consumption by people and on the media industry. She has been a visiting researcher at the University of Kent (2009 and 2014). She has published several articles, books and chapters about TV consumption habits.

Enrique Guerrero received his Ph.D. degree in Audiovisual Communication (2009) from the University of Navarra and got a certificate in Entertainment and Media Management (2007) from the University of California Los Angeles (UCLA). His doctoral research consisted on a study about production standards of entertainment TV shows. Currently, he is associate professor of Entertainment TV Shows Production and Multimedia Content Management at the University of Navarra. His research is focused on the impact of digitalization on the audiovisual industriy, specially on the production of entertainment formats. In addition, he has been a visiting scholar at Bournemouth University (2011) and The University of Texas at Austin (2013), and has published several books, chapters and articles about entertainment contents for television. Besides he is member of the Spanish Academy of Television Arts & Sciences.

Information and Communication Technology for Government by Design: The New Digital Media, Actors, Creative Influences, and Fields of Play

Shefali Virkar

Abstract Much has been written about the application of the new digital media to government within a growing stream of literature on ICT for development, generating countervailing perspectives where optimistic, technocratic approaches are countered by far more sceptical standpoints on technological innovation. This chapter seeks to, through the use of a case study, unravel the social dynamics shaping e-government projects used to reform public sector institutions. In particular, the research analyses actor behaviour, motivations, and interactions surrounding the conception and maintenance of software platforms facilitating these transformations. The value of such an approach is based on a review of existing ICT and software development literature which tends to be overly systems-rational in its approach and, as a consequence, often fails to recognise the degree to which project failure (viz. the general inability of the project design to meet stated goals and resolve both predicted and emerging problems) is symptomatic of a broader, much more complex set of interrelated inequalities, unresolved problems, and lopsided power-relationships both within the adopting organisation and in the surrounding environmental context.

1 Introduction

Over the course of the last two decades, globalisation and Information Technology have been rapidly dismantling traditional barriers to trade, travel and communication, fuelling great promise for progress towards greater global equity and prosperity. Attracted by the 'hype and hope' of Information and Communication Technologies (ICTs), development actors across the world have adopted computer-based systems and related ICTs for use in government as a means reforming the inefficiencies in public service provision. Whilst a number of these electronic government or 'e-government' projects have achieved significant results,

S. Virkar (✉)
Department of Politics and International Relations, University of Oxford, Oxford, UK
e-mail: shefali.virkar@politics.ox.ac.uk

© Springer International Publishing AG 2016
A. Lugmayr et al. (eds.), *Information Systems and Management in Media and Entertainment Industries*, International Series on Computer Entertainment and Media Technology, DOI 10.1007/978-3-319-49407-4_3

evidence from the field indicates that despite the reported success stories, the rate of project failure remains particularly high.

Much has been written about e-government within a growing stream of literature on ICT hardware and software platform development, generating countervailing perspectives where optimistic, technocratic approaches are countered by far more sceptical standpoints on technological innovation. However, in trying to analyse both their potential and real value, there has been a tendency for scholars to see e-government applications as isolated technical artefacts, analysed solely as a collection of hardware and software. Far less work is based on empirical field research, and models put forward by scholars and practitioners alike often neglect the actual attitudes, choices, and behaviour of the wide array of actors involved in the implementation and use of new technology in real organisations, as well as the way in which the application shapes and is shaped by existing social, organisational, and strategic geospatial circumstances.

This research chapter seeks to, through the use of a case study, unravel the social dynamics shaping e-government projects used to reform public sector institutions. In particular, the chapter analyses the strategic actor behaviour, motivations, and interactions surrounding the conception, development, and maintenance of e-government software platforms facilitating these transformations. The value of such an approach is based on a review of existing ICT and development literature; most of which tends to be overly systems-rational in its approach and, as a consequence, often fails to recognise the degree to which project failure (viz. the general inability of the project design to meet stated goals and to resolve both predicted and emerging problems) is symptomatic of a broader, much more complex set of interrelated inequalities, unresolved circumstances, and lopsided power-relationships, both within the adopting organisation and in the surrounding environmental context.

2   The Medium and the Message: Management Information Systems from eMedia to eGovernance

Information systems play an important role in the management of the contemporary enterprise: be it small-, medium-, or large-scale; a profit-making or a social-service set-up; a public or private undertaking; a creative, manufacturing, or service-oriented venture; a local or a global organisation; or, a start-up or an established business house [27]. More precisely, **Management Information Systems (or MIS)** contend especially with the "...process of managing information as a strategic resource for improving organizational performance [and] involves developing strategies and introducing systems and controls to improve information quality over time" [4]. Worded differently, management information systems deal with processing of information on several management levels within a given organization; both, in actively perusing the goals of a particular organizational level, affording operative staff recourse to the solutions required to cope with their daily tasks, and allowing senior management to gain greater insight into attracting new customers and developing new products with a view to increasing business performance base-lines [20].

Within the Creative Media Industries, Big-Data variants of *information* are obtained in the express form of *content*, and require a particular and industry-specific approach to their production, processing, distribution, and management [32]. On an operational level, therefore, the core of the media industry comprises essentially of any information architecture which deals with the handling of content, together with those other management information systems introduced as the basis of industry in general [19]. Likewise, the work of the public sector has also traditionally been highly information-intensive [31]: government has been, and still remains, the single largest collector, user, holder, and producer of information; and data is considered to be a central resource 'in pursuing democratic/political processes, in managing resources, executing functions, measuring performance, and in service delivery'.

Consequently, and similar to Lugmayr's [20, 19] research on Creative eMedia organisations, a primary consideration taken whilst introducing business information management practices and systems into government relates to the particular adopting sectoral or industry segmentation; wherein each segment requires the particular use of a particular information system at a particular operational- and knowledge-base level. The most significant media segments adept at handling both types of informational content, identified also in Virkar [31, 32], encompass broadcasting, newspapers and magazines, production industries, advertising and advertising agencies, publishing houses, Internet and new media platforms and applications, and computer-moderated gaming. Each of these creative media and e-media components requires a different workflow for information processing [19]; one that also extends towards differences in the conceptualisation of work culture, modes of working, and the manner in which an audience creates and perceives media content.

The main goal of the research presented within this chapter is, therefore, to examine the issues arising from the organisational and institutional transformations that occur in public administration through the innovation and application of creative ICT platforms; from a multidisciplinary perspective, and through the use of a single central case study. The case study from which the chapter's central observations and results are advanced focused on a project aimed at digitising property tax records and administrative processes within the Revenue Department of the Greater Bangalore City Municipal Corporation (*Bruhat Bengaluru Mahanagara Palike* or *BBMP*). In recognising the need to turn property tax into a viable revenue instrument that delivered high tax yields without compromising on citizen acceptance, the Bangalore City Corporation sought to improve its property tax administration system through the introduction of a computerised database supported by back-end digital mapping techniques used to track compliance and to check taxpayer evasion.

3 Research Methodology

The ultimate aim of this chapter is thus to contribute to the development of a conceptual framework that is relevant to policy discussions of e-government software platform design and maintenance within not only an Indian, but also a broader global context. In order to augment theoretical discussions of administrative reform in a digitised world, this chapter uses a case study to explore its central research issues, within which a mixed methods approach using a combination of qualitative and quantitative data was selected in order to inform and strengthen the understanding of the relationships between the actors, inputs, and project outputs. The aim of the study was, therefore, to evolve ideas that could be generalised across similar situations and the research was consequently developed in the following steps:

- In-depth review of existing theoretical perspectives and literature surrounding corruption and tax evasion, ICTs and public administration, and property tax reform
- Qualitative analysis of official documents
- Collection and analysis of quantitative data relevant to the case
- Developing case studies through in-depth personal interviews
- Data analysis and interpretation
- Preparation of conclusions and their validation
- Recommendations for the future.

The use of mixed-method case study research is becoming increasingly popular in the social sciences, and is fast being recognised as a successful approach for investigating contemporary phenomena in a real-life context when the boundaries between phenomenon and context are not evident and where multiple sources of evidence present themselves [35]. The research approach has become a particularly significant technique by which Creative eMedia interfaces are explored and evaluated [25]. The application of data obtained via the use of mixed-methods was, consequently, for this study, considered to be an especially apt way of examining the nature and impact of participant actor actions, motivations, and strategic behaviours on e-government software platform conception, design, and innovation; from whence the aim is not simply to judge whether the project at hand represents a success or failure, but is also to understand the qualities inherent in the systems architecture that have made it so.

More precisely, case study research consists of a detailed investigation of phenomena within a given context, often with data being collected over a period of time. The aim of this approach is thus to provide the researcher with an all-round analysis of the surrounding environment and processes, in order that they might throw light on the theoretical issues being investigated [10]. The phenomenon under examination is thus not isolated from its context, rather it is of interest precisely because the aim is to observe and understand actor behaviour and/or organisational processes and their interplay with the surrounding environment.

The use of a case study itself is therefore not as much a method as it is a *research strategy*, where the context is deliberately included as part of the overall design. Today, case studies are widely used in organisational research across the social sciences, indicating growing confidence in the approach as a rigorous research strategy in its own right [12].

As research conducted by adopting this strategy is typically done in the field, the presence of too many observations and uncontrollable 'variables' makes the application of standard experimental or survey approaches infeasible. Further, information tends to be scattered and generally cannot be picked up using one single method. Case studies thus typically combine a number of data collection methods such as participant observation, direct observation, interviews, focus groups, ethnography, document analysis, questionnaires etc., where evidence may be quantitative or qualitative depending on the research issues at hand. The approach is consequently flexible, allowing for new methods to be incorporated as new sources of data and new actors present themselves. The case study approach may thus be and has been used for various purposes—to provide a descriptive narrative, to generate new theory, or to test existing theory through the triangulation of data [31].

The theoretical framework adopted by this research will emphasise three issues: first, the politics involved in the conception, innovation, and governance of software platforms for public administration, which is related to the set of institutions and rules that set the limits on, and the incentives that result in, the constitution and working of interdependent networks of actors within the industry and within government; second, the concept of electronic government itself as circumscribed by socio-political and economic development; and finally, the relationship and interrelationships between technology, organisation, and institutional change. To do this, the chapter will ground its case study in three major complementary strands of literature:

1. A conceptual discussion of the role and interactions of a multiplicity of actors with diverse motivations and strategies conceptualized as an 'ecology of games', within the umbrella of New Institutionalism, and their role in shaping political organisations and institutions, with special reference to the success or failure of e-government projects.
2. The literature which deals with public administration reform and the role of Information and Communication Technologies in improving the functioning of public administration and reducing corruption in a developing country context.
3. A discussion of the importance of the ICT hardware and software industry, with special reference to software platform design for e-government and politico-economic development in India.

Conclusions will be reached through the concurrent use of three dimensions—theoretically on the basis of existing literature, descriptively on the basis of a case study, and analytically using the concept of the Ecology of Games.

4 Interviews as a Primary Source of Evidence

For the larger study from which this chapter is drawn, 40 personal interviews were conducted over a 24-month period. The interviewees can be roughly divided into four groups based on their relationship to the case: **Senior Civil Servants** involved with the planning and implementation of the project, including current and former BBMP Commissioners, Deputy Commissioners for Revenue, and Revenue Officers, **Revenue and Tax Officials**, primarily Assistant Revenue Officers (AROs) responsible for the in-the-field collection and administration of property tax in the city, **Software Developers** involved in the conception, design, and implementation of the project, and **Miscellaneous Actors** including journalists and external consultants.

Twenty-seven subjects agreed to full-length interviews and to have their comments recorded. This included all six members of the project planning committee, one senior official involved with the implementation of the GIS, and twenty senior revenue officers involved with the system's application in the field. Additional informal interviews conducted face-to-face or over the email were also used to close gaps in knowledge or to follow up new information and anchor the interpretation of events and motives in the perceptions of participants. In addition to the recorded interviews, this chapter uses information and quotes obtained informally from people related to the project who did not wish to be interviewed formally or have their comments recorded, in order to obtain a cross-hierarchical view of the impact of process re-engineering on the organisational culture and practical issues on the ground. Out of the 13 people in this category, 10 were junior revenue officials (Station Managers, Tax Inspectors and Accountants) working under the AROs interviewed, 2 were Revenue Officers supervising the overall administration of the Revenue Offices and one person was a local correspondent from a leading national daily.

From the above discussion, it follows that the use of a case study for this chapter is particularly apt for two reasons. Firstly, the approach is particularly useful for examining research issues that require a detailed understanding of socio-political, economic, or organisational processes through the collection and analysis of rich data. Secondly, as discussed above, case study research design is also more flexible than other frameworks such as laboratory-based or survey-based approaches, in that it is able to reconcile different research methods and harness the evidence gathered to generate novel theory from any creative insights that might ensue from the juxtaposition of data at various points in the analysis. This, despite the truism which states that a single case study cannot always provide an answer to these questions globally; for even the examination of a single case can suggest significant ways of addressing issues that could, through application, be relevant to a wider variety of cases across disciplines.

5   Communication by Design: e-Government, Its Definition and Scope Within the Global eMedia Ecosystem

Simultaneous with the shift towards a more inclusive process of participation in political decision-making and public sector reform has been an increased interest in the new digital Information and Communication Technologies (ICTs) and the ways in which they may be used to effectively complement and creatively reform existing political processes. Developments in communication technologies have historically resulted in changes in the way in which governments function, often challenging them to find new ways in which to communicate and interact with their citizens, and ICTs today are seen to possess the potential to change institutions as well as the mechanisms of service delivery, bringing about a fundamental change in the way government operates and a transformation in the dynamic between government and its citizens [47]. The work of the public sector has traditionally been highly information-intensive; government has been, and still remains, the single largest collector, user, holder and producer of information [43], and is considered to be a central resource 'in pursuing democratic/political processes, in managing resources, executing functions, measuring performance, and in service delivery' [45].

e-Government has today become an influential concept for scholars concerned with public administration reform and better overall governance. In developed countries, large-scale projects at the local level have typically concentrated on the creation of virtual or digital town-halls through the automation and distribution of well-structured administrative services [42]. However, while online e-government service initiatives have become common in many countries, and in a variety of contexts, such applications are characteristically built with a primary focus on administration-citizen interaction, rather than on explicitly supporting plans for strategic organisational development.

Further, although considerable attention has been paid to how e-government can help public bodies improve their services, there are relatively few studies that focus on the long term sustainability of such initiatives, particularly in the developing world. In contrast to most literature in the canon, therefore, this project focused on in this study seeks to illustrate that the potential for improved government-citizen interactions and private-public collaborations for the development of e-government platforms and public sector reform programmes may be realised through not only the development of a 'virtual front office' but also through the enhancement of their positive influence on back-office organisation and culture. In defining e-Government as the use of Information and Communication Technologies (such as Wide Area Networks, the Internet, and mobile computing) by government agencies to transform relations with citizens, businesses, and other arms of government, almost all conceptions of e-government indicate three critical transformational areas in which ICTs have an impact [23]:

The Internal Arena: where Information and Communication Technologies are used to enhance the efficiency and effectiveness of internal government functions and processes by intermediating between employees, public managers, departments, and agencies.

The External Arena: where ICTs open up new possibilities for governments to be more transparent to citizens and businesses by providing multiple channels that allow them improved access to a greater range of government information.

The Relational Sphere: where ICT adoption has the potential to bring about fundamental changes in the relationships between government employees and their managers, citizens and the state, and between nation states; with implications for the democratic process and the structures of government.

Thus, although the term e-government is primarily used to refer to the usage of ICTs to improve administrative efficiency, it arguably produces other effects that would give rise to increased transparency and accountability, reflect on the relationship between government and citizens, and help build new spaces for citizens to participate in their overall development [12].

6 Innovatively, Yours: Digital Storytelling and Electronic Service Delivery Models in Government

e-Government applications tend to develop in two stages [31]. Initially, a back-office system is set up within the adopting agency to handle online processes and information about services provided by the agency is published on a website. The second step involves the setting up of the 'front-office': the use of ICTs in the actual delivery of a service, where citizens can interact with the site to download application forms and information sheets for a variety of services such as filing a tax return or renewing a license, with more sophisticated applications being able to process online payments.

A key three-stage strategy used by actors in games related to the design and development of e-government systems and technology policy, particularly those in developing countries who wish to radically transform public administration by moving government services from manual processes to online systems, is to adopt different models of service delivery at different stages of the development process. The first move generally involves the automation of basic work processes and the online provision of information and services by government departments from computers based within the departmental premises [38].

Citizens interact with a designated government employee or private computer operator who accesses data and processes transactions on their behalf. Locating online terminals within agency premises tends to result in greater ownership of the system by government staff, reducing resistance to technology and facilitating easier acceptance of change. However, the downside of this mode of delivery is that citizens are still required to visit different government departments to avail of different public services, all within their fixed hours of work. In addition, the dependence of an entire agency office on a single person (or small group of people) to operate the system may cause friction.

The second stage in the evolution of service delivery is the use of conveniently located citizen kiosks or service centres in public places, again manned by public or privately hired operators [36]. This mode of delivery scores over the previous one as multiple services—municipal, state or federal—may be offered at each location. Kiosks also generally stay open longer than government offices, both before and after regular office hours, maximising system coverage by allowing working individuals to access services at times more convenient to them. In recent years, citizen service centres have become popular, particularly in countries where Internet penetration is low.

The final platform of e-government service delivery, popular in countries where Internet penetration and skills are high, is the one-stop shop online portal from where citizens with a computer and an Internet connection may, at any time of day, access a whole range of public information and services themselves without having to visit a kiosk or depend on a computer operator [33]. However, for such a mode of delivery to become ubiquitous, a number of conditions need to be in place—citizens must have the technological hardware and skills to access the system, the back-end of the government agency must be fully computerised, government staff must be trained on the new technology, security and privacy loopholes must be closed, and trust in online transactions must be built up.

The step-by-step strategy outlined above is generally adopted by key political and administrative actors involved with the implementation of e-government projects, and if followed may reduce political tensions and controversies that might arise as the result of change by not only ensuring maximum citizen access to services, but also an increased acceptance of the technology by agency staff [38].

7 Design by Information: Understanding Actor Behaviour

The central issue that needs to be understood whilst studying the development of ICT platforms and their implementation in public sector organisations through an analysis of actor interactions is thus: *Why do people do what they do?* One approach to understanding behaviour is to look at the rationality of individual actors, rather than the system as a whole. This is largely because political actors are driven by a combination of organisational and institutional roles and duties and calculated self-interest, with political interaction being organised around the construction and interpretation of meaning as well as the making of choices.

Political actors, in general, have a complex set of goals including power, income, prestige, security, convenience, loyalty (to an idea, an institution or the nation), pride in work well done, and a desire to serve the public interest (as the individual actor conceives it). According to Downs [7] actors range from being purely self-interested ('climbers' or 'conservers' motivated entirely by goals which benefit themselves and their status quo rather than their organizations or the society at large) to having mixed motives ('zealots', 'advocates' and 'statesmen' motivated by goals which combine self interest and altruistic loyalty with larger values). An in-depth analysis of the ICT for development literature by this researcher identified five actor groups involved in games relating to the implementation of e-government projects:

(i) **Politicians**: The first group identified comprises of elected representatives of various hues, guided and influenced chiefly by electoral imperatives and a need to maintain their public image, and are therefore concerned with directing both key economic policy issues as well as issues of public service delivery.

(ii) **Administrators/civil servants**: This group of actors is guided by their perceptions of existing institutional 'culture' and practices and their positive (or negative) attitudes towards internal bureaucratic reforms such as concerns about the down-sizing of administrative services to promote 'efficiency' and a sense of being policed by elected government through the introduction of ICTs.

(iii) **Organisations dealing with technical designing of IT systems for tax collection**: The approach private IT suppliers take to e-government might be considerably different to what the adopting government agency actually needs or wants from a system.

(iv) **Citizens**: This is another particularly interesting group of actors as one is never quite sure what their reaction to the implementation of e-government will be. Whilst in theory citizens should welcome the introduction of a system that simplifies administrative processes, in practice it is equally possible that some citizens might not be very happy if a more efficient system was put into place.

(v) **International donors**: This final actor group controls the purse-strings and oftentimes comes to the table with 'higher' ideals coloured by ideas prevalent in international politics (such as the desire to see a particular brand of 'good governance' in the developing world).

Introducing e-government initiatives into public bodies is a tricky game to play, as computerisation alters the work-load, work profile and content of the average public sector employee; impacting accountability, reducing the opportunities for exercising discretion, making performance more visible and flattening the hierarchy [2], and often forcing the need for retraining and retooling and sometimes creating redundancy. Many projects tend to face internal resistance from staff—particularly from the middle to lower levels of the civil service—with moves made to reengineer processes and effect back-end computerisation having a profound effect on the way civil servants perform their duties and perceive their jobs. Very often in developing countries, it is the fear of the unknown that drives this resistance, especially if the introduction of new technology results in a change of procedures and the need for new skills. Further, in corrupt service delivery departments, there may be pressure to slow down or delay the introduction of technology-led reforms due to the impending loss of additional income.

8 From Human Factors to Human Actors: The Psychology Behind Human-Computer System Design and Innovation

The design and implementation of complex computer systems requires a better understanding in practitioner circles of the users of such networks and the settings in which they work. Part of the problem resides in the implicit treatment of ordinary people as unskilled, non-specialist users of technology and their networks comprising of elementary processes or *factors* that can be studied in isolation in a field laboratory setting [1]. Although psychology has a long tradition of contributing to computer systems design and implementation, it has been a neglected discipline in scholarly circles and key issues such as those relating to the underlying values of the people involved in large-scale system design and their motivation in the work setting have been missed out in recent computer science-based scholarly analysis [28].

Conceptualising and understanding people as *actors* in situations, on the other hand, with a set of skills and shared practices based on work experiences with others, requires a reorientation in the way in which the relationship between key elements of computer system design, namely people, technology, work requirements, and organisational constraints in work settings, is negotiated [16]. The terms 'human factors' and 'human actors' give a clue as to how people in system design clusters are approached [31]. More particularly, the terms highlight difference in how people and their contributions are perceived, the former connoting a passive, fragmented, depersonalised, somewhat automatic human contribution; the latter an active, controlling, involved one [3].

More precisely, within the Human Factor approach, the human element is more often than not reduced to being another system component with certain characteristics that need to be factored into the design equation for the overall human-machine system [6]. In doing so, the approach de-emphasises certain important elements of work design: the goals, values, and beliefs which technologists and system-users hold about life and work [15]. By using the term *human actors*, emphasis is placed on users and developers as autonomous agents possessing the capacity to control, regulate, and coordinate their behaviour, rather than them being on par and analysed as mere information processing automatons [26].

9 The Games People Play: The Ecology of Games as an Analytical Framework

From the turn of the century to the present, there has been a progressive movement away from the view that governance is the outcome of rational calculation to achieve specific goals by a unitary governmental actor, and in that context metaphors based on games have been extremely useful in developing new ways to think about the policy process. No behavioural concept in the scholarly canon has proved more ill-defined, elusive, controversial, and even unfashionable than that of *play*. A look through the literature reveals that although political games have been described by scholars within a range of differing contexts, from electoral politics to administrative functioning, no comprehensive description of the public organization as a system of these various interactions actually exists.

The use of Game Theory and most other game metaphors (although differing widely in their orientation) have had, according to scholars, one major limitation for clarifying policy processes: they focus squarely on a single arena or field of action; be it a school, a county, a legislature, etc. Yet, by their very nature, policy making and implementation cut across these separate arenas, in both their development and impact [11]. In e-government projects for instance, systems built by both public and private enterprises for use by government employees and citizens across different political constituencies must be enforced by legislative acts created and interpreted by national branches of government. In addition, actors at different levels of the policy system encounter divergent problems posed by the system in question and their actions are influenced by varied motives. What is needed, therefore, is a framework that goes beyond single games in order to focus on how games 'mesh or miss' each other to influence governance and policy decisions. One of the few efforts to look at this interaction and interdependence was Norton Long's [18] discussion of "The Local Community as an Ecology of Games."

The Ecology of Games framework, as first laid out by Long in the late 1950s offers a New Institutionalist perspective on organisational and institutional analysis. As with most theories of new institutionalism, it recognises that political institutions are not simple echoes of social forces, and that routines, rules and forms within organisations and institutions evolve through historically interdependent processes that do not reliably and quickly reach equilibrium [21]. Long developed the idea of the ecology of games as a way of reconciling existing debates about who governed local communities as he believed they had significant flaws. The crucial insight in Long's theory however, was not the idea of games per se which, as has been discussed earlier, was already well developed, but his linking of that notion to the metaphor of an ecology [11].

Ecology as a concept relates to the interrelationships of species in their environment, allowing for numerous relationships amongst entities, and has been used to understand the relationships among individuals and more complex social systems. Most obviously, co-existence within a common space results in competition for resources and power between different actors, and can result in unique modes of operation as means of achieving ones aims. This in turn may lead to either mutual non-involvement in the same space, or active co-operation between different actors and the development of symbiotic relationships. All this speaks of a singular interdependence between different actors within a given territory. Although there may be other relationships as well, what is significantly missing is a single, rational, coordinating presence.

Games themselves are social constructs that vary over time and across social contexts [5]. Similar types of games might recur within similar social settings, but all games tend to be uniquely situated in place and time, and any typology of games that might emerge across a cumulative body of studies is likely to remain quite abstract. Despite this, Dutton [8] has identified several key attributes that all games may share. First, every game has a set of goals, purposes, or objectives, with some actors within certain games having multiple aims. For example, a civil servant within the software development game might need to meet efficiency targets set by his department through the taking of decisions regarding the procurement of technology and choice of supplier that conform to stringent budgetary requirements. Similarly, software developers may choose to advertise the quality of their products and maintain their stranglehold over niche markets by quoting top-end prices at the outset of negotiations.

Second, a game has a set of prizes, which may vary widely from profit to authority to recognition, and are distinct from the objectives of the players. For instance, the same civil servant seeking to increase the efficiency of his department and conform to its budget might expect to get a promotion, an honour, or earn a better public reputation outside of the workplace. Software sales personnel may likewise expect to earn bonuses or larger commissions. Third, games have rules that govern the strategies or moves open to players depending on the organisational or institutional settings within which they are played. Any large-scale regulatory game incorporates bureaucrats, legislators, regulated firms, and oft-times entire industries; but also may include the public, the media, the courts, and other actors willing and able to become involved. Rules need not be public or fair (depending on whether public or private interests are involved), may change over time, and may or may not need consensus to be accepted. Finally, a game has a set of players, defined by the fact that they interact—compete or cooperate—with another in pursuing the game's objectives.

For Long, territories (or fields of play) were defined quite literally by being local communities. The notion of an 'ecology' of games underlines not only the degree to which not all players in any given territory are involved in the same game, but also the fact that different players within that territory are likely to be involved in a variety of games [9, 22]). Games can thus be interrelated in several ways. Some actors ('players') might be simultaneously participating in different games, and some players might transfer from one game to another.[1] Plays (i.e. moves or actions) made in one game can affect the play of others. Also, the outcome of one game might affect the rules or play of another. However, although individuals may play a number of games, their major preoccupation for the most part is with one, central game [18]. A researcher might be able to anticipate a range of strategies open to individuals or organizations if we know what role they play in the game(s) most central to them. Conversely, when the actions of players appear irrational to an observer, it is likely that the observer does not know the games in which players are most centrally involved; the players' moves in one game might be constrained by their moves within other games.

---

[1]Long, 'The Local Community as an Ecology of Games', p. 253.

Moved from the community context to the world of e-government platform design, adoption, and implementation, territories may be diverse—from the inner circle of the project design team, through to the adopting organisation, the nation and finally the international policy arena—but the idea of each stage being a political community or a collection of actors whose actions have political implications is still very much applicable. The ecology of games metaphor thus provides us with a useful way to think about how the various players interact in making and carrying out administration and developing policy.

10   Assessing Project Outcome: The Design-Actuality Gap Model

Like all political interactions, the behaviour of actors related to the design and uptake of e-government projects is circumscribed by the organisations and institutions within which they are played out, and by the range of actors taken from the individuals and groups directly and indirectly involved with the process of governance. The outcome of an e-government project therefore does not depend on a single project entity alone, and instead depends on the interaction between different actors in the process and the nature of the relationships between them. Gaps in project design and implementation can in reality be seen as expressions of differences arising from the interaction between different (often conflicting) actor moves and strategies, determined to a large extent by actor perceptions, and played out within the context of set circumstances.

Heeks [14] concluded that the major factor determining project outcome was the degree of mismatch between the current realities of a situation (the 'where are we now') and the models, conceptions, and assumptions built into a project's design (the 'where the e-government project wants to get us'). From this perspective, e-government success and failure depends largely on the size of this *'design-actuality gap'*: the larger gap, the greater the risk of e-government failure, the smaller the gap, the greater the chance of project success. By examining numerous case studies related to ICTs and e-government failure in developing countries, Heeks [13] identified three dominant categories of reported outcome: *total failure*, *partial failure*, and *success*.

- The first possible outcome is *total failure*, where a project is either never implemented or in which a new system is implemented but is almost immediately abandoned.
- A second possible outcome is the *partial failure* of an initiative, in which major goals are unattained or where there are significant undesirable outcomes. Cases range from straightforward underachievement to more complex "sustainability failures" of an initiative.
- Finally, one may see the *success* of an initiative, in which most actor groups attain their major goals and do not experience significant undesirable outcomes.

Heeks also identified three so-called 'archetypes of failure', situations when a large design-actuality gap, and consequently project failure, is likely to emerge: *Hard-Soft Gaps* (the difference between the actual, rational design of the technology and the actuality of the social context within which it operates), *Public-Private Gaps* (the mismatch that results when technology meant for private organisations is used in the public sector without being adequately adapted to the adopting organisation) and *Country Context Gaps* (the gap that arises when a system designed for one country is transferred unaltered into the reality of another).

The above discussion reveals that although the strength of the Ecology of Games lies in its ability to identify and analyse the interrelationships between the different actors involved in the process of e-government system design and adoption, when taken alone it provides no insight into the consequences of this behaviour and its impact on project outcome. Similarly, the Design-Actuality Gap model is able to analyse structural weaknesses in a project's design but doesn't on its own provide an adequate explanation of the decision-making processes that led to such structural deficiencies in the first place. The results and analysis of this chapter will, therefore, rely on the two frameworks being used in combination to arrive at prescribed solutions and examples of best practice within the case study at hand. The advantage of using such an approach is that it allows the researcher to not only identify and analyse patterns of behaviour within the case under study, but also link decisions and actions to specific project outcomes.

11 Digitising Property Tax Records in Bangalore, India: Examining Actor Attitudes Towards, and Perceptions of, Big Data

Against the background of technological innovation in Karnataka state, project planners from the Greater Bangalore City Corporation (BBMP) felt that the manual system of property tax administration was archaic, opaque, and inefficient. All the members of the core project group believed that property tax collections under the manual system had suffered from poor record keeping and bad information management practices, slow processing times, and overcomplicated assessment and payment procedures. These had, in turn, created frustration amongst taxpayers and resulted in low levels of compliance. The computerised property tax system was thus borne out of a need to reform the manual system of property tax administration in Bangalore and improve tax revenues and compliance through the improvement of back-office efficiency, the simplification of tax collection, and the reduction of money lost through malpractice through the effective detection and deterrence of tax evasion—spurred on by the need to enhance power, authority and reputations.

Having identified senior state revenue officials, municipal tax administrators, and local tax collectors as the target users of the system, the ultimate aim of the project designers was to create an Internet-based 'back-office' database which could be used to monitor all aspects of property taxation: in essence property identification, tax dues assessment, revenue collection, and tax compliance monitoring. The application was put together using an Oracle database on an open-source software platform, with the architects using J2E and Java technology to construct the back-end application servers. Personal Digital Assistant (PDA) devices were integrated into the system so that revenue officers could go out in the field to collect taxes, and then use them to upload data back in real time. It was envisaged that citizens would in time also become users of the system, and would be able to have unrestricted access to their property records (and those of the entire city) online. The system's single-most unique feature was to be its eventual use of Geographic Information Systems (GIS) or online virtual mapping tools, to visually aid the revamping of the addressing system and to improve tax coverage through more comprehensive property identification and stricter monitoring [31].

Interviews with tax officials revealed that most felt that there had been serious problems with the manual system of tax administration. They claimed that the biggest hurdles to the efficient administration of tax that they encountered prior to the introduction of the computerised database were poor and haphazard record-keeping and large amounts of paperwork that needed to be done manually. Information was scattered and the process of calculating tax due, administering collections and checking up on defaulters was extremely unsystematic. While, as expected, none of the revenue officials interviewed mentioned government employee corruption as being serious problem, many interviewees spoke of the difficulties they faced in identifying and catching tax evaders.

Most officials interviewed felt that the introduction of technology had greatly impacted old work processes and had helped alleviate the difficulties they faced under the manual system. They believed that the centralisation of data, the ease with which citizens could access their tax information, and the setting up of tax collection points across the city had all helped in bringing more properties into the tax net and contributed significantly towards improving tax payer compliance. All the officials interviewed felt that their interactions with the public had significantly decreased since the introduction of the computerised system, and a little over half them believed their overall relationship with citizens had improved as a result.

However, while acknowledging that the use of digitised records, computer printouts and online databases had had a positive impact on their work, some interviewees were quick to point out that technology had been used simply to automate existing processes, and that old infrastructural problems (such as poor electricity supply and old computers) and problems related to a lack of skills and training on the computerised system had not been resolved. Only a small percentage of revenue officials reported that they had been consulted during the design stage of the project. Further, there appeared to be no mechanism in place to solicit user feedback once the initial system had been developed.

Almost all the officials interviewed said they felt disconnected from system. Most professed a high degree of unfamiliarity with the system, and were completely unaware of its key features. For instance, only one tax official mentioned the introduction of GIS mapping techniques as being useful to his work and that of his staff, a worrying fact given that the core project team had placed much store by the GIS maps as a tool to track property tax payments and identify defaulters. These are not good signs, as effective system implementation requires employees to fully accept and adopt the technology in the belief that it will do them some well-defined good.

Further, none of the officials interviewed knew how to operate even its most basic features. With no scheme in place to give them any formal training on the system, all the interviewees reported to be completely dependent on a private computer operator to feed in, change and retrieve electronic property tax data. This, the researcher feels, created a new problem within revenue offices and limited the effectiveness of the system, as it resulted in a shift in the balance of power within the workplace to the disadvantage of revenue officials and consequently hardened their attitude towards computerisation. Senior officers, once enthusiastic about the system, spoke about the frustration they felt at being unable to fulfil their supervisory role and at being put at the mercy of a junior employee. Junior tax officials, already slightly sceptical of the system, feared that their skill levels would put them at a disadvantage within the office and could eventually result in redundancy.

Opinions were divided about whether or not computerisation of the system that had led to improved tax yields. Most tax officials felt that while the introduction of the computerised system had positively impacted tax collections to some extent, there were many other reasons as to why tax yields had improved. For others, the introduction of the Self Assessment Scheme as a means of shifting the responsibility of tax payments onto the shoulders of the citizens and reducing the workload of revenue staff was almost as (if not more) important as the introduction of technology into the workplace. It may be concluded from the interviews that general citizen apathy towards property tax is to a large extent a consequence of poor public awareness about the benefits of paying property tax, a lack of enforcement measures and a general dislike of cumbersome processes—problems which cannot be solved through the introduction of technology alone.

12 Identifying Games That Impact the Uptake and Management Of ICT-Based Systems Architecture: Human-Technology Interactions Within Bureaucracies

An examination of the interviews and other data collected during field research reveals that the eventual outcome of the revenue department project can be interpreted as the consequence of a number of players making moves within a number of separate but interrelated games related to the project's design, implementation and adoption. At least six kinds of games appear to have influenced the impact the system has had on tax administration in Bangalore city. They include expertise games, power and influence games, policy games, turf struggles, games of persuasion and business games. Within each game, the following elements may be identified from the case at hand to help the researcher arrive at an in-depth analysis of the impact that various interactions have on the outcome of the project under study. They are:

1. **Key Actors**: the individuals, groups or other entities whose interactions shape the particular game being considered.
2. **Game Rules**: the written or unwritten codes of conduct that shape actor moves and choices during a game.
3. **Actor Goals and Motivations**: the aims that key actors seek to attain and maintain from interacting with other players, both broader long-term achievements as well as more short- to medium-term rewards.
4. **Key Strategies**: tactics, ruses, and ploys adopted by key actors during the course of a game to keep the balance of the engagement in their favour.
5. **Key Moves**: decisions and other plays made by key actors to arrive at key goals, usually if not always based on their strategy of choice.

From the games identified during the course of this author's research, a four-fold taxonomy has been developed which classifies and analyses behaviour depending on the level of actor interactions along four different axes: the field of play, the key actors involved, the main objective(s) of the game under study and the nature and/or spirit in which the game has been played. The four categories are elaborated on below:

1. **Arena or Field of Play**: Actor interactions may be classified according to the arena within which they are played out. In other words, this classification—which has its roots in initial work done by Vedel [29] and Dutton [8]—focuses on the reach and influence of actors within a given context, and the impact of their actions (both direct and indirect) on project outcomes.

   (a) **Project-Specific Games**: are generally played by individuals and groups of actors directly involved with the case under study. Such interactions usually occur during the planning and execution of a project and impact.
   (b) **Organisation-Specific Games**: are played out within the department or organisation within which the case study is based, involving not only actors directly concerned with the case study but also others within the institution whose moves come to bear influence on the project at hand.
   (c) **City or Regional Level Games**: include those interactions between actors whose power or reach extends to the level of the city or region within which the project is based, and who are playing power games for relatively high stakes. The goals, moves and strategies chosen by actors at this level may or may not have a direct link to the case study, however they come to bear either a direct or indirect influence on its eventual outcome.

(d) **National Level Games**: involve players who have their eye on attaining some sort of national prestige or who are influenced by other actors or discourses operating at the national level. Here again, actors may or may not be directly attached to the project or organisation under study.

(e) **International Level Games**: are played chiefly by actors or groups of actors possessing international clout and/or aspirations. Games played at this level usually do not have a direct bearing on the project under study, however, actors might indirectly influence outcomes by attempting to gain power/prestige through adhering to popular trends, binding project planners to third-party conditionalities or merely by subscribing to certain schools of thought.

2. **Key Actors Involved**: Games may also be classified according to the key actors involved in each interaction studied. This axis thus aims to study interactions within the context of the key players—who they are and who they interact with.

(a) **Interactions Internal to the Project Planning/Core Group**: includes any games being played exclusively between constituent elements of the project planning committee or the core group responsible for the design and execution of the project under study.

(b) **Core Project Group versus Other Members of Implementing Department**: cover games played between members of the core project committee and other individuals and/or groups within the implementing department who are otherwise not directly involved on the project at hand.

(c) **Games within the Implementing Organisation**: are played out between groups and individual actors who are members of the implementing organisation. Such interactions may or may not be directly related to the ICT4D project, but their outcome would have an impact on its eventual success or failure.

(d) **Department/Organisation versus External Players**: cover interactions between the implementing department/organisation acting in a unified, institutional capacity and other external players such as the media, citizens and civil society organisations.

(e) **Games Played by External Actors**: which have little or no direct connection to the current project, but which nonetheless have a significant impact on its eventual success or failure.

3. **Actor Goals**: A third way of classifying actor interactions is based on the goals that different actor groups seek to attain by engaging with other players. Actors within each game are bound to have multiple goals that motivate them to act in certain ways, and thus it is important when applying this classification to identify the primary motivating factor behind each move.

(a) **Games of Power and Prestige**: involve moves to enable actors to gain or shore up their individual power and prestige or those of their group.

(b) **Games to Maintain Status Quo**: are those interactions whereby players seek to maintain the status quo. These games are generally played when actors perceive a threat to their current position or status, and thus act to preserve their current standing in the hierarchy.

(c) **Games to Achieve Change**: are those interactions that attempt to change a current situation or process within a department or organisation, primarily through the attainment of project goals and objectives.

(d) **Games to Achieve Political and Policy Aims**: are those moves and strategies played by actors to achieve certain political or policy aims which may or may not have a direct relationship or bearing on the project under study.

(e) **Games to Further Ideology and/or Discourse**: comprise chiefly those games played by actors who are generally driven by a particular ideology or discourse and wish to use their political influence to impose their ideas on either the implementing organisation or on the project planners themselves.

4. **Nature of Game Play**: The final axis against which games may be classified analyses the nature of the political dynamic between the key actors within which the project was conceived and implemented. In other words, this axis differentiates between positive and negative actors and the impact of their actions on their sphere of influence.

(a) **Constructive Game Play**: includes altruistic and other positive moves, where competition is seen to be constructive and controlled/restrained rivalry brings about positive results. Such games are therefore win-win situations, and include all those moves that have a positive impact on the adoption of new technologies within a development context

(b) **Destructive Game Play**: involves fierce rivalries and negative competition, resulting in zero-sum games where actors act purposefully to win at the cost of their so-called 'opponents', thereby creating a negative project environment and often resulting in a large wastage of time and resources.

13   Playful Interaction, Serious Games: Collaborative Production, Process Re-engineering, and Public Sector Reform

Information and communication technologies bring about rapid changes in management patterns, such as the breakdown of traditional administration hierarchies and the streamlining of decision-making within and across agencies. Steps to adopt and use ICTs in government are thus generally taken as part of a broader reform or change-management agenda driven by actors from different levels, where new technology is introduced to solve existing administrative problems. The re-engineering of administrative processes is possibly the most important step in implementing an application, as it requires that an agency undertakes substantial reform of its organisational structure [2]. This is particularly true as using ICTs with out-dated or inappropriate processes can increase corruption and other forms of poor governance by providing opportunities for officials to perform dishonest activities faster and still avoid detection [24].

Re-engineering processes often involves playing games to change the mind-sets and culture of an organisation's workforce, including using strategies that recognise the need to train employees, improve skill sets, and deploy appropriate supporting infrastructure to enable online processes that are useful to both the user and the implementing organisation. A common strategy in a successful implementation game is to map existing methods and procedures, usually followed by the simplification of these procedures in such a way that the overall task can be completed in as few steps as possible [47].

The looked-for outcome of such an exercise is that of mutual cooperation; where all the players in the game accept the modification of processes that result in fewer steps, any eventual reduction in the number of people needed to perform tasks, and the automation of certain operations that result in eventual back-end computerisation. However, this is not always the case, and re-engineering games may get stymied in conflicting moves made by different key players. This thesis argues, therefore, that the use of ICTs alone will not guarantee the success of a project in achieving its objectives and reaching its full potential. Successful e-government systems and re-engineered processes standardise rules and procedures, but it is the well thought-out games played by project designers and implementers which ultimately bring down resistance and fear, reduce opportunities for exercising discretion, and create an environment conducive to the adoption of the new technology.

Related to this, project managers whilst implementing a project have to decide whether they will adopt a top-down approach to decision-making, or whether they will select a more participatory style. Whilst a top-down approach to project management does yield a number of benefits—including the speeding up of decisions that might otherwise be difficult to make (particularly true for cases like the one under study, where employees might attempt to resist the introduction of technology when faced with dramatic changes)—such an approach means that during the planning of a system, priority goes to those features and aspects which are seen as important by a select, centralised group of planners. There is a danger that some of the priorities of the main users, the staff on the ground, may be overlooked and any mismatch between design and user needs may result in employees rejecting the system. To add to this, most of the literature on organisational change in the private sector stresses the importance of employee participation in the planning of change-inducing projects [17], particularly to enhance staff morale, an idea that is fast catching on in public sector management and e-government circles [44].

14 The Case of the Greater Bangalore City Municipal Corporation (*BBMP*): Digital Content, Material Gains

The State of Karnataka is particularly interesting when studying the various games and interactions related to the use of Information Technology for public service reform within Indian government departments, as ongoing processes of change within different government agencies in the state have had the use of ICTs deeply implicated in them, and many government and quasi-government bodies have entered into partnerships with private and non-profit organisations. In recent years, there has been growing pressure placed by citizen groups, international agencies, and the local media on both city corporations and the state government to rationalise existing revenue collection structures and improve the collection of property tax in the field, both within cities and across the State at large.

In view of the need to turn property tax into a productive tax instrument, the Greater Bangalore Municipal Corporation (BBMP) teamed up with a series of private and not-for-profit technology firms in partnerships which aimed to improve property tax collections across Bangalore city using computerised revenue records and Geographical Information Systems (GIS)-based property mapping. Against the background of technological innovation in the State, project planners decided to do away with the manual, paper-based system of property tax administration considering it to be increasingly archaic, opaque, and inefficient. In particular, members of the core project group felt that property tax collections under the manual system had over the years suffered consistently from poor recordkeeping and bad information management practices, slow processing times, and overcomplicated assessment and payment procedures.

This had, in turn, created frustration amongst taxpayers and resulted in increasingly low levels of tax compliance. The computerised property tax system was thus borne out of an ever-growing need to reform the old system of property tax administration in Bangalore city and to improve tax revenues and compliance through the improvement of back-office efficiency, the simplification of tax collection, and the reduction of money lost as a result of malpractice through the effective detection and deterrence of tax evasion. Concurrently planners were also spurred on by the need to enhance their own power, authority, and reputations with their respective spheres of influence and beyond.

Interviews with key people involved with the design and implementation of the project, conducted between 2005 and 2009, brought to light a number of games or interactions operating at different levels or 'arenas', all of which had an impact—direct or indirect—on the effectiveness of the system and its eventual performance. These are outlined in Tables 1, 2, 3 and 4.

Table 1 Project Planning Committee games

Games	Key players	Key objectives	Nature of moves
e-Government movement	Various current senior BBMP officials, software providers	Encourage BBMP departmental reform through the use of technology	Positive game play
System conception and design (a) Formation of the Core Project Planning Group	Various current senior BBMP officials, software providers	Take credit for the initial design idea and design process	Negative game play
(b) Initial design and conception of the system	BBMP officials on the project planning committee, eGovernments Foundation representatives	Design and launch a successful system	Altruistic game play
Digital democracy	Senior BBMP officials and eGovernments Foundation members	Seek to influence the design of the PTIS to support their conception of democracy	Negative game play

Source Author Analysis, 2010

Table 2 BBMP Revenue Department games

Games	Key players	Key objectives	Nature of moves
System acceptance games	Project planning group (Senior BBMP officials, software providers, external consultants), senior and junior revenue officials	Get officials on the ground to accept and adopt the system	Positive game play
Efficiency games	Senior BBMP officials, Assistant Revenue Officers, and junior revenue staff	Hold down costs and increase tax revenues by improving efficiency	Positive game play
Management control	Senior BBMP officials, Revenue officials	Expand power and decisional control	Negative game play
Game to control petty corruption	Senior BBMP officials, Revenue officials	Reduce revenue losses from petty corruption	Negative game play
Revenue office politics	Revenue Officials, Assistant Revenue Officers, Station Managers, junior revenue staff	Assert 'superior' status, retain power and authority within the field office	Negative game play

Source Author Analysis, 2010

Table 3 Bangalore City Games

Games	Key players	Key objectives	Nature of moves
Image building game	BBMP officials, the media, citizens	Improve image of the BBMP as an accountable, modern and responsive government agency	Positive game play
Tax compliance game	BBMP officials, the media, citizens	Encourage citizens to pay taxes through a mixture of carrot and stick initiatives	Largely positive game play

Source Author Analysis, 2010

Table 4 National-level games

Games	Key players	Key objectives	Nature of moves
The innovation game	BBMP officials, non-profit software providers	Introduce and be associated with a new idea, policy, or technology to improve the national image of the city and agency	Positive game play
The game for business competition	Software developers	Be associated with a successful project to gain national recognition	Positive game play

Source Author Analysis, 2010

15   What's in a Game? Discussing and Analysing e-Government Success and Failure Within the Context of Management Information Systems Research

This chapter sought to unravel the social dynamics shaping e-government projects used to reform public sector institutions. In particular, its chief aim was to analyse actor behaviour, motivations, and interactions surrounding the conception, development and maintenance of e-government software platforms facilitating these transformations. The principal approach of this research to the issues thrown up by these cross-sectoral interactions was the use of an empirical case study dealing with the design, implementation, and subsequent use of an electronic property tax system based in the Revenue Department of the Greater Bangalore Municipal Corporation (BBMP).

The overarching aim of the computerised system was to improve tax revenues and tax compliance through the streamlining of tax administration processes by increasing back-office efficiency, simplifying methods of tax payment, reducing the amount of money lost through petty corruption, and improving tax yields and citizen compliance through the speedy detection of tax evasion. Designers of the project sought to use automation and digitisation to improve data management in the revenue offices, reduce the use of discretion by government officials in revenue-related decisions, and make property tax collection processes more transparent. In particular, the system sought to increase revenues from property tax through better quality data, quicker evaluations, greater computational accuracy, and positive psychological reinforcement; whilst at the same time reducing losses in revenue occurred as a result of back-office inefficiencies and fraudulent practices through the use of digital databases and GIS maps. However, as illustrated by the case study, the underlying motivations for the individual partners and actors within each of the participating organisations turned out in some instances to be widely divergent, resulting in several highly divisive and negative outcomes within the context of the project under study.

As the analysis in previous sections has shown, certain key games with local impacts get played out in different arenas between actors influenced by not only local but also national and international factors. An examination of interview data and other documents brought to light a number of games in different arenas, each involving key actors related to the project, whose interplay had a bearing on the project's eventual outcome. No single game can account for the ultimate outcome of the Revenue Department project at the time of writing, and instead the impact that the system has had on property tax administration can be best understood as an 'interacting set' or 'ecology' of games—as discussed in previous sections. Games that shaped the development and adoption of the system appear to have be layered or 'nested', with some contained within others.

Key games found to have significantly shaped the outcome of the system appear to have been played during the initial stages of the process, either during the time of its conception (in the form of positive and negative interactions between members of the project planning committee) or at the stage of internal implementation and adoption (in the form of friction between the core project team and the intended end-users such as the field officers), corroborating the findings of the quantitative data analysis set out in the previous section of this chapter. The only city-level game that had any significant impact on the project appeared to be the Tax Compliance game, played between the BBMP and the taxpayers of Bangalore. Other games at the city and national levels were primarily found to be ideological games and games centred around the interplay of market forces, thus having little direct bearing on the tax administration system and its eventual fate.

Questions remained, however, as to whether conflicting motivations and interests could be aligned to ensure win-win situations for all actors concerned and to promote the long-term sustainability of the project at hand. The discussion of the case study in previous sections also reveals that at the heart of each game lay a design-actuality gap, usually brought about from a power struggle stemming from a deep-seated mistrust between different actor groups. In particular, the case study demonstrates that gaps arise because those with the power and authority to take design or implementation decisions at different key stages of the process are usually unwilling to allow any initiative to go ahead that would give the other actor group (s) in the game more autonomy over the system or more control over their actions. Design-actuality gaps also arise when key actors refuse to acknowledge the impact that external, tangential factors and circumstances have on the shaping of decisions and government policy.

In recognising that design-actuality gaps open up and give way to unfavourable project outcomes if designers and top managers assume that localised outcomes result only from direct local influences, discounting the impact of other factors external to the project at hand, preliminary findings suggest that the project may at the time of writing be classed as a *partial failure* under Heeks' three-fold categorisation. However, as evidenced by the discussion, this so-called 'failure' is neither a straightforward case of the outright inability of project managers to achieve stated objectives nor is it a so-called 'sustainability failure'. Causes of failure to meet stated aims appear to be two-fold: manifested through Hard-Soft gaps, stemming from competitive and divisive moves made by actors in key games relating to the system's design and implementation that generated conflict and disharmony in later attempts by users to adopt the system, and Private-Public gaps, rooted in fierce competition and oftentimes rivalry between key executive members on both sides of the profit- non-profit divide that stemmed from their differing values, work cultures, and agendas.

16   Government and the eMedia Industry: The Consequences of Innovative Change Management for the Strategic Political Environment

Rapidly evolving economic and social contexts mean that political institutions and the people who constitute them cannot afford to get bogged down in traditional work practices or be impervious or resistant to change themselves. Whilst this does not necessarily mean a wholesale rejection of what has gone before, it does mean that there needs to be a constant assessment and reassessment of workplace values and current practices, eliminating those which result in behaviours that are detrimental to the functioning of the organisation and encouraging those that promote positive interactions.

Organisations and institutions, particularly those which form the political core of a society, cannot afford to be seen to have been left behind, as the people within those institutions are generally looked to as political trendsetters and role models in addition to being responsible for societal welfare. Software platform development for e-government thus needs to be able to respond to swiftly and appropriately to these changes, and the growing demand for cost-effective high-quality programming has resulted in several collaborative cross-sectoral partnerships between software developers and government organisations globally. However, as illustrated by the case study, the underlying motivations for the individual partners and actors within these partnerships can be widely divergent, and may result in highly divisive and negative outcomes.

The discussion put forward in this chapter reveals that at the heart of a political game usually lies a power struggle, brought about through a deep-seated mistrust between different actor groups. This holds particularly true for the process of software conception and design wherein, as the case study put forward demonstrates, gaps in quality and overall technical applicability arise because those with the power and authority to take design or implementation decisions are usually unwilling to allow any initiative to go ahead that would give the other actor group (s) in the game more autonomy over the process or system. Further, certain key games with local impacts get played out in different arenas between actors influenced by not only local but also national and international factors. Problems arise if designers and top managers assume that localised outcomes result only from direct local influences, discounting the impact of other factors external to the project at hand.

Added to this, there is a tendency for power élites to lose touch with ground realities when devising projects for their organisations as well as for their citizens, especially when planners comprise the higher echelons of government and operate within a top-down command-and-control system of management. There is also a danger that high-level project planners will, in looking at macro-outcomes, ignore outliers and how these may precipitate unexpected turns of events. This holds particularly true when existing patterns of communication and information exchange either fail to be flexible or prove unable to adapt to changing situations.

17 Conclusion

In modern times, people and their governments have struggled to find easy, cheap, creative, and effective ways to run countries. ICT-based applications have the potential to revolutionise patterns of communication between authority and citizenry, radically restructuring politics and governance at all levels by making systems more integrated, transparent, and efficient. However critics of e-government, and more particularly of its introduction into developing country contexts, contend that administrative reform is not an important enough issue to justify exposing cash-strapped governments to the risks and opportunity costs associated with ICT projects.

Whilst it is widely recognised that ICTs are strategically important to a country, and the need for investment in e-government is generally well-accepted, questions related to the balancing of investment in ICTs with the need to give priority to other basic infrastructural requirements still need to be answered, and there is apprehension in some quarters that money used for e-government will absorb scarce developmental resources whilst not delivering on potential benefits. Further, it is still unclear whether administrative reforms stimulated by e-government will in the long run feed into a country's other economic, societal, and development goals, or simply divert resources away from areas where they are needed into already cash-rich sectors and industries such as those related to software design and development. Only time and further research will be able to tell.

Key Terms and Definitions

Actor(s): the individuals, groups or other entities whose interactions shape the direction and nature of a particular game being considered.

Actor Goals and Motivations: the aims that key actors seek to attain and maintain from interacting with other players, encompassing both broader long-term achievements as well as more short- to medium-term rewards.

Actor Perceptions: include the preferences and opinions of key institutional players that help determine the disjoint between project design and current ground realities, together with the nature and direction of organisational reform and institutional change.

Country Context Gap: refers to the gap that arises when a system designed in theory for one country is transferred into the reality of another.

Design-Actuality Gap Model or Framework: is a framework for project evaluation which contends that the major factor determining project outcome is the degree of mismatch between the current ground realities of a situation ('where are we now'), and the models, conceptions, and assumptions built into a project's design (the 'where the project wants to get us').

e-Democracy: may be defined by the express intent to increase the participation of citizens in decision-making through the use of digital media and the application of Information and Communication Technologies to political processes. e-Democracy may be subdivided into **e-Engagement** (or **e-Participation**), **e-Voting**, **e-Consultation**.

(1) **e-Engagement** (or **e-Participation**): refers to the overall enhancement of opportunities for greater consultation and dialogue between government and its citizens through the encouragement of online citizen action and citizen participation in political processes electronically.

(2) **e-Voting**: may be defined broadly as the expression and exercise of fundamental democratic rights and duties online through specially developed digital platforms.

(3) **e-Consultation**: refers to the process whereby citizens are given the opportunity to provide feedback to government online on matters of public importance and participate in the shaping of issues relevant to them via the new digital media.

e-Governance: refers to the use of ICTs by government, civil society, and political institutions to engage citizens in political processes and to the promote greater participation of citizens in the public sphere.

e-Government: refers to the use of Information and Communication Technologies by government departments and agencies to improve internal functioning and public service provision. Broadly speaking, e-government may be divided into 2 distinct areas: **e-Administration** and **e-Services**.

(1) **e-Administration**, which refers to the improvement of government processes and to the streamlining of the internal workings of the public sector often using ICT-based information systems,
(2) **e-Services**, which refers to the improved delivery of public services to citizens through multiple electronic platforms

Game(s): arena(s) of competition and cooperation structured by a set of rules and assumptions about how to act in order for actors to achieve a particular set of objectives.

Hard-Soft Gap: refers to the difference between the *actual, rational design* of a technology (hard) adopted within a project and the *actuality of the social context*, namely people, culture, politics, etc., within which the system operates (soft).

Managerial Variables: are those institutional variables relating to project management and other *soft* variables of project design and implementation, which include the efficiency and effectiveness of a supply chain, the characteristics of an agency's culture, and the capacity of an adopting agency to adapt to and to manage change.

Moves: may be defined as actions, decisions and other plays made by key actors taken to arrive at key goals, usually if not always based on their strategy of choice.

Partial Failure: of an initiative is a situation in which major goals are unattained or where there are significant undesirable outcomes.

Political Variables: are those *soft* institutional variables relating to the perceptions and impressions that public servants have regarding potential labour cuts, administrative turnover, and changes in executive direction generated by the development of e-government.

Private-Public Gap: refers to the mismatch that results when technology meant for private organisations is used in the public sector without being adapted to suit the role and aims of the adopting public organisation.

Project Outcome: or the sum total of the interaction between organisational and institutional realities and the project design carried out within the constraints of the current organisational and institutional set-up.

Rules: the written or unwritten codes of conduct that shape actor moves and choices during a game.

Strategies: include tactics, ruses, and ploys adopted by key actors during the course of a game to keep the balance of the engagement in their favour.

Success: of an initiative is a situation in which most actor groups attain their major goals and do not experience significant undesirable outcomes.

Technological Variables: are those institutional variables relating to technology and other *hard* elements of project design and implementation, which include the ability of a user-population to access ICTs, the quality of the user population's Internet use, the availability of an internal technological infrastructure, and the provision of technical skills to the government workforce.

Total Failure: of an initiative is a situation where a project is either never implemented or in which a new system is implemented but is almost immediately abandoned.

References

1. Bannon, L. J. (1991). From human factors to human actors: The role of psychology and human computer interaction studies in system design. In J. Greenbaum & M. Kyng (Eds.), *Design at work: Cooperative design of computer systems* (pp. 25–44). New Jersey, N.J.: Lawerence Erlbaum Associates, Inc., Publishers.
2. Bhatnagar, S. (2004). *E-Government: From vision to implementation*. New Delhi: SAGE Publications.
3. Carayon, P., Hoonakker, P., & Smith, M. J. (2012). Human factors in organizational design and management. In G. Salvendy (Ed.), *Handbook of human factors and ergonomics* (4th ed., pp. 534–552). New Jersey, N.J.: Wiley.
4. Chaffey, D., & White, G. (2011). *Business information management: Improving performance using information systems*. Harlow: Financial Times Prentice Hall.
5. Crozier, M., & Friedberg, E. (1980). *Actors and systems*. Chicago, I.L.: University of Chicago Press.
6. Czaja, S. J., & Nair, S. N. (2012). Human factors engineering and systems design. In G. Salvendy (Ed.), *Handbook of human factors and ergonomics* (4th ed., pp. 38–56). New Jersey, N.J.: Wiley.
7. Downs, A. (1964). *Inside bureaucracy*. Boston, M.A.: Little Brown.
8. Dutton, W. H. (1992). The ecology of games shaping telecommunications policy. *Communications Theory, 2*(4), 303–324.
9. Dutton, W. H., & Guthrie, K. (1991). An ecology of games: The political construction of santa monica's public electronic network. *Informatization and the Public Sector, 1*(4), 279–301.
10. Eisenhardt, K. M. (1989). Building theories from case study research. *The Academy of Management Review, 14*(4), 532–550.
11. Firestone, W. A. (1989). Educational policy as an ecology of games. *Educational Researcher, 18*(7), 18–24.
12. Gascó, M. (2003). New technologies and institutional change in public administration. *Social Science Computer Review, 21*(6), 6–14.
13. Hartley, J. (2004). Case study research. In C. Cassell and G. Symon (Eds.), *Essential guide to qualitative methods in organisational research* (pp. 323–333). London: SAGE Publications.
14. Heeks, R. (2002). Information systems and developing countries: Failure, success and local improvisations. *The Information Society, 18*(2), 101–112.
15. Heeks, R. (2003). Most eGovernment-for-development projects fail: How can the risks be reduced? *i-Government Working Paper Series,* Paper No. 14. Manchester: IDPM.
16. Jacko, J. A., Yi, J. S., Sainfort, F., & McClellan, M. (2012). Human factors and ergonomic methods. In G. Salvendy (Ed.), *Handbook of human factors and ergonomics* (4th ed., pp. 289–329). New Jersey, N.J.: Wiley.

17. Kuutti, K. (1996). Activity theory as a potential framework for human computer interaction research. In B. A. Nardi (Ed.), *Context and consciousness: Activity theory and human computer interaction* (pp. 17–44). Boston, M.A.: M.I.T. Press.
18. Lefebvre, E., & Lefebvre, L. (1996). Information and telecommunication technologies: the impact of their adoption on small and medium-sized enterprises. International Development Research Centre, [Out of Print], Available at: http://www.idrc.ca/en/ev-9303-201-1-DO_TOPIC.html (Accessed on: 10th May 2015).
19. Long, N. E. (1958). The local community as an ecology of games. *The American Journal of Sociology*, 64(3), 251–261.
20. Lugmayr, A. (2013). Brief introduction into information systems and management research in media industries. In I. E. E. E. Staff (Ed.), *2013 IEEE International Conference on Multimedia and Expo Workshops (ICMEW)* (pp. 1–6). New York, N.Y.: IEEE Publications.
21. Lugmayr, A. (2013). Issues & approach in defining a European Research Agenda on information systems and management in creative eMedia industries. In E. Stojmenova & A. Lugmayr (Eds.), *Proceedings of the 1st Workshop on Defining a European Research Agenda on Information Systems and Management in eMedia Industries* (pp. 17–25). Tampere (Finland): lugYmedia Inc. for Ambient Media Organization (AMEA).
22. March, J. G. & J. P. Olsen (1989). Rediscovering institutions: The organisational basis of politics. New York, N.Y.: The Free Press.
23. McKenna, H. P., Chauncey, S. A., Arnone, M. P., Kaarst-Brown, M. L., & McKnight, L. W. (2014). Emergent learning through playful interactions and serious games when combining ambient intelligence with wireless grids. In Misc. (Eds.), *Proceedings of INTED2014 Conference* (pp. 5080–5090), March 10⁻12, 2014, Valencia (Spain).
24. Ndou, V. (2004). e-Government for developing countries: Opportunities and challenges. *The Electronic Journal on Information Systems in Developing Countries*, 18(1), 1–24.
25. Pathak, R. D. & R. S. Prasad (2005). The role of e-Government in tackling corruption: the Indian experience. In R. Ahmad (Ed.), *The role of public administration in building a harmonious society*, Selected Proceedings from the *Annual Conference of the Network of Asia-Pacific Schools and Institutes of Public Administration and Governance (NAPSIPAG)*. December 5–7 2005, pp. 343–463.
26. Pesek, M., Godec, P., Poredoš, M., Strle, G., Guna, J., Stojmenova, E., et al. (2015). The MoodStripe—An evaluation of a novel visual interface as an alternative for online response gathering. *International SERIES on Information Systems and Management in Creative eMedia* (1), 1–5.
27. Proctor, R. W., & Vu, K.-P. L. (2012). Selection and control of action. In G. Salvendy (Ed.), *Handbook of human factors and ergonomics* (4th ed., pp. 95–116). New Jersey, N.J.: Wiley.
28. Sadgopan, S. (2014). *Management information systems* (2nd ed.). New Delhi: PHI Learning Private Ltd.
29. Salvendy, G. (2012). *Handbook of human factors and ergonomics* (4th ed.). New Jersey, N.J.: Wiley.
30. Vedel, T. (1989). Télématique et configurations d'acteurs: une perspective européenne. *Réseaux*, 7(37), 9–28.
31. Virkar, S. (2011). *The politics of implementing e-Government for development: The ecology of games shaping property tax administration in Bangalore City*. Unpublished Doctoral Thesis. Oxford: University of Oxford.
32. Virkar, S. (2014). What's in a game? The politics of shaping property tax administration in Bangalore, India. In J. Bishop (Ed.), *Gamification for human factors integration: Social, educational, and psychological issues* (pp. 31–51). Hershey P.A.: IGI Global, Inc.

33. Virkar, S. (2015). The globalisation of the media: Towards new opportunities for artistic practice and cultural heterogeneity. In B. Christiansen & J. Koeman (Eds.), *Nationalism, cultural indoctrination, and economic prosperity in the digital age* (pp. 66–81). Hershey, P. A.: IGI Global Inc.
34. West, D. A. (2004). E-government and the transformation of service delivery and citizen attitudes. *Public Administration Review, 64*(1), 15–27.
35. Yin, R. K. (2003). *Case study research: Design and methods.* Applied social research methods series (Vol. 5). London: SAGE Publications.

Additional Reading

36. Asquith, A. (1998). Non-elite employees' perceptions of organizational change in english local government. *The International Journal of Public Sector Management, 11*(4), 262–280.
37. Basu, S. (2004). E-government and developing countries: An overview. *International Review of Law, Computers and Technology, 18*(1), 109–132.
38. Beinhocker, E. D. (2006). *The origin of wealth: Evolution, complexity and the radical remaking of economics.* Boston, M.A.: Harvard Business School Press.
39. Bhatnagar, S. (2003). E-government: Building a SMART administration for India's states. In S. Howes, A. Lahiri, & N. Stern (Eds.), *State-level reform in India: Towards more effective government* (pp. 257–267). New Delhi: Macmillan India Ltd.
40. Bruhat Bangalore Mahanagara Palike. (2000). *Property tax self-assessment scheme: Golden jubilee year 2000.* Mahanagara Palike Council Resolution No. 194/99-2000, Bangalore, 2000 (Handbook).
41. Bruhat Bangalore Mahanagara Palike. (2008). *Assessment and calculation of property tax under the capital value system (New SAS): 2007–2008.* Bangalore, 2007 (Unpublished Handbook).
42. De, R. (2007). Antecedents of corruption and the role of e-government systems in developing countries. In the Electronic Government 6th International Conference, EGOV 2007, *Proceedings of Ongoing Research*, Regensburg, Germany, September 3–7, 2007. Available at: http://www.iimb.ernet.in/~rahulde/CorruptionPaperEgov07_RDe.pdf. Accessed on December 5, 2013.
43. Dutton, W. H. (1999). *Society on the line: Information politics in the digital age.* Oxford: Oxford University Press.
44. Heeks, R. (2000). The approach of senior public officials to information technology related reform: Lessons from India. *Public Administration and Development, 20*(3), 97–205.
45. Heeks, R. (2006). *Implementing and managing eGovernment—An international text.* New Delhi: Vistar Publications.
46. Isaac-Henry, K. (1997). Development and change in the public sector. In K. Isaac-Henry, C. Painter, & C. Barnes (Eds.), *Management in the public sector: Challenge and change* (pp. 1–25). London: International Thomson Business Press.
47. Jha, S. N., & Mathur, P. C. (1999). *Decentralization and local politics.* New Delhi: SAGE Publications.
48. Misra, S. (2005). eGovernance: Responsive and transparent service delivery mechanism. In A. Singh (Ed.), *Administrative reforms: Towards sustainable practices* (pp. 283–302). New Delhi: SAGE Publications.
49. Ronaghan, S. A. (2002). Benchmarking e-government: A global perspective. The United Nations Division for Public Economics and Public Administration (DPEPA) Report.
50. Sinha, K. P. (1981). *Property taxation in a developing economy.* New Delhi: Puja Publications.

Author Biography

Shefali Virkar is research student at the University of Oxford (UK), currently reading for a D.Phil. in Politics at the Department of Politics and International Relations. Her doctoral research seeks to explore the growing use of Information and Communication Technologies (ICTs) to promote better governance in the developing world; with special focus on the political and institutional impacts of ICTs on local public administration reform in India.

Shefali holds an M.A. in Globalisation, Governance, and Development from the University of Warwick (UK). Her Master's dissertation analysed the concept of the Digital Divide within the context of a globalising world, its impact on developing countries, and the ensuing implications for public policy formation therein. At Oxford, Shefali is a member of Keble College.

Part II
Management, Marketing, Business Aspects and Strategic Importance of IT and IS&M in Creative eMedia Industries

The Strategic Role of Communication Standards for Media Companies

Thomas Hess, Antonia Köster and Christian Matt

Abstract Standards setting has gone from being a technical concern for individual companies to being a factor with important strategic implications for cooperation and competition among market players. The strategic issues raised by this development include the formation of competitive advantages by promoting standards or preventing their diffusion. In Sect. 1 of this chapter, we discuss the economic interpretation of standards from a descriptive perspective by drawing on the closely related issue of positive network effects, which induce a self-enhancing cycle and lead to a widespread adoption of the standard. In Sect. 2, we highlight standards setting as a competitive weapon for media companies. Standards act not only as a precondition for compatibility across technologies and systems, but can also be used to generate incompatibility and customer lock-in effects. Thus, we examine standardization strategies and tactics for horizontal competitors in the digital media industry. In Sect. 3, we view standards as a strategic instrument for cost reduction in media companies by describing a normative decision model for the economic selection of standards, referred to as the standardization problem.

1 Standards and Digital Communication

Communication requires standards—information exchange is only possible if both communication partners use a shared rule for communication. Technical communication standards played a minor role for media companies in the traditional print world; anyone could read a book, a newspaper or a magazine. This has changed with the availability of broadcasting technologies, which require the usage of standards for content processing and presentation. With the emergence of the Internet as a medium, standards have become increasingly important for media companies, because the Internet has led to a convergence of media. Most traditional media types—including print, music and movies—are being redefined or reshaped

T. Hess · A. Köster (✉) · C. Matt
LMU Munich, Munich, Germany
e-mail: koester@bwl.lmu.de

© Springer International Publishing AG 2016
A. Lugmayr et al. (eds.), *Information Systems and Management in Media and Entertainment Industries*, International Series on Computer Entertainment and Media Technology, DOI 10.1007/978-3-319-49407-4_4

by the Internet [1]. Digital content can now be distributed and consumed via only one channel. As a result of this development, media companies can reach customers only via their end-devices, which—in turn—depend on content in standardized digital forms. Therefore, standards have far-reaching strategic implications and are a key issue for media companies, defined as organizers of public, media-based communication. Today, they operate as content providers, as platform operators, or in hybrid forms in the digital world [2].

In the following, we examine the question how media companies can deal with standards. For this purpose, we first introduce key terms related to standardization and explain the economic foundations of standards. In Sect 3, we take a market-based perspective and explain how a media company can engage in three different forms of competition. We also illustrate these competition strategies with current case studies from the media industry. Following this, we describe a formal model that can be used by a central decision-making entity (usually a company) or actors to calculate cost and to achieve cost reduction via the implementation of standards. Finally, we summarize our considerations.

Standardization describes the process of developing and implementing *standards,* defined as an "agreed-upon specification for a way of communicating or performing actions" [3]. A *de jure standard* is one developed and approved by official organizations, such as public companies or regulatory authorities (e.g. ISO standards). De facto *standards* typically emerge from processes of informal self-organization or achieve acceptance through the market (e.g. MS Windows) [4]. Therefore, standards setting has gone from being the technical concern of a single company to a factor with important implications for competition. On the supply side, standards can be described as *closed* (proprietary) or *open. Proprietary standards* exist when companies intentionally decide to design incompatible elements (e.g. videogame platforms). If the access to a standard is open to any company without major restrictions, we refer to it as *open standard* (e.g. Linux). The more open the standard is, the easier it is to substitute or exchange individual elements. In general, it would be possible for the industry to define standards in such a way that any kind of hardware could work with any type of system software and application software, which—in turn—could handle any content format.

2   The Economics of Standards

The analysis of standardization is largely based on the theory of positive network effects [5]. *Network effects* are positive externalities that occur if "the utility that a given user derives from the product depends upon the number of other users who are in the same network as he or she" [6]. Research on network externalities is based on the assumption that consumers care about the network benefits they will receive over the product lifecycle. Some models of standardization formalize the users' benefits from adopting products that are used by the majority of users and are

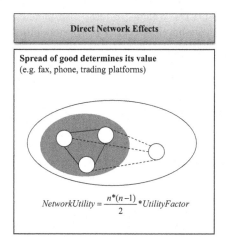

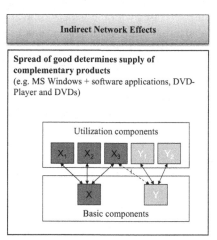

Fig. 1 Two versions of network effects

therefore based solely on the size of the existing network [5], while other studies have emphasized how companies attempt to influence consumer expectations [6].

Many digital media products and services exhibit network effects, which means that the value of adopting a technology increases either with the number of other users adopting the same technology (*direct network effects*) or with the number of complementary products and services available (*indirect network effects*). Figure 1 illustrates these two versions of network effects. Network externalities have an impact on the adoption of new products [7] and can also create significant user reluctance to switch to an alternative technology or network [8]. However, adopting a product or service used by many others can not only facilitate communication and information exchange, but also increases customer benefits by providing a fundamental knowledge repository or a large amount of complementary products and services [9, 10].

Direct network effects arise from the fact that, by employing the same standards or technologies, users can communicate with each other more easily and therefore more cost-effectively. The classic example of direct network effects is the telephone: the more people own one, the more beneficial it is for users. The same principle applies to communication technologies, such as peer-to-peer IP telephony, which becomes more useful, the greater the number of people using it. According to Metcalfe's law, the value of such a network (V) is proportional to the square of the number of users connected to the system (n): $V = n^2 - n/2$. In light of this effect, it is understandable why analysts often assign very high values to the customer basis of telecommunication and Internet companies. In contrast, indirect network effects arise from the interdependency between the consumption of a basic product and the consumption of complementary components. A widespread use of a standard can be expected to lead to an increased supply of complementary products. Therefore, the wide adoption of a product generates a broader range of associated products and services, which enhances the basic product's utility. For instance, a DVD player's value increases with the variety of available DVDs, which—in turn—can increase the adoption of the DVD player. Studies indicate that indirect network externalities create a feedback effect that can drive a market towards standardization [11].

Whether a new business model based on a new standard will be accepted by the market depends not only on its technical utility, but also on its ability to gain a critical mass of customers in a short period. Once a technology has reached a certain installed base, it becomes difficult for competitors to conquer the market. This *critical mass* is the point when diffusion becomes self-sustaining and the diffusion process no longer relies on the heterogeneity of consumers, and is accompanied by price decreases and/or quality increases [12]. Critical mass is not exactly predictable in theory or in practice. Its magnitude depends on the market size, the average value of participation, and alternative options available in the market.

Nowadays, media companies pursue various strategies to reach a critical mass of customers, such as selling the basic version of a service or product at low prices or even giving it away for free to increase the number of participants and customer loyalty. These pricing strategies are often rewarding and enable entrant companies, such as small media companies or startups, to gain an early foothold in the market or to take market share from an established competitor. This explains why we see so many free access offers in the digital media industry [13]. For instance, Music as a Service (MaaS) providers, which offer music via streaming over the Internet, have employed so-called *freemium* revenue models. Their services can be used for free or with a paid subscription to obtain premium content with value-added functions. However, MaaS providers struggle to make profits because earnings from adverts and premium users might not be sufficient to finance the free basic version of music streaming [14]. Other examples, which rely on network effects and profit from network size, are software downloads, information and communication applications, or peer-to-peer networks.

The likelihood of economic success increase when companies manage to exceed critical mass and have a growing customer base that derives value from participation. However, network effects can create *switching costs* for customers. The existence of these switching costs may impede the diffusion of new innovations [15]. Even in the presence of a superior technology, the coordination costs of changing to a new technology may outweigh the advantage of a new technology (this is referred to as *excess inertia*). The discrepancy between individual and collective benefits leads to coordination problems, since no individual is willing to bear the risk of being the first adopter of a standard if all other individuals decide to adopt another standard. This *startup problem* can inhibit the adoption and diffusion of standards [16]. An example of lock-in owing to switching costs is a customer's investment in a particular videogame console. Changing to a game console from another provider does not merely lead to a substitution of the platform, but also of the related games, since the games are usually not compatible with other providers' consoles owing to proprietary standards. Even though media companies lure customers with initial free offers, they can later accumulate revenues via advertising, access fees to partners, the distribution of complementary products and services, the sale of premium versions, or through providing fee-based updates to the customer.

In some cases, these business models are stable, but in others they will vanish into thin air because companies were unable to establish a de facto standard in their market.

Besen and Farrell [5] remark that multiple incompatible technologies rarely coexist in network markets and that the 'tip' towards one technological platform occurs suddenly, leading to winner-takes-all markets. There is a tradeoff between the customer's value of increasing network size through for instance compatible communication or increasing number of applications for a particular end-device and detrimental effects such as increased customer lock-in owing to high switching costs. These network effects are the primary reason why inefficient standards or technologies could persist or why they can cause a lockout of superior products with higher technical quality. This argumentation leads to the question whether all network effects lead to a positive and ever-increasing virtuous cycle or whether they can also have negative effects that can lead to a vicious cycle.

3   Standards as a Competitive Instrument

Having explained the fundamental concepts related to standards, we now introduce three basic market scenarios with related strategies that can be pursued by a media company that is engaging in a standards battle [5]. These strategies reflect the horizontal compatibility efforts of each company and apply if two media companies are involved. When more than two companies participate in a standards battle, particular mechanisms are effective; we explain these at the end of this part.

Suppose that there are market conditions that lead to three scenarios (Fig. 2). In each scenario, the company can decide to choose a strategy of compatibility or incompatibility with the competitor's standard [5].

Fig. 2 Overview of the three market-based scenarios

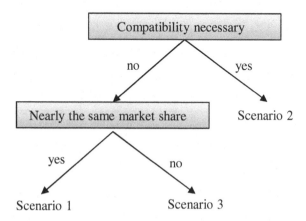

- Scenario 1: If compatibility of standards is not necessary for market success and both companies have nearly the same market share, both companies prefer to compete to determine the technology standard.
- Scenario 2: If compatibility of standards is necessary for market success, both companies would prefer to choose a compatibility strategy.
- Scenario 3: If compatibility of standards is not necessary and both companies have unequal market shares, a consensus on strategic choices is unlikely. The dominant company prefers to maintain its standard while the smaller, less established company prefers to join the competitor's standard.

Figure 3 contains an overview of the compatibility strategies and competitive tactics that can be used in each scenario.

The scenario 1, *Tweedledum and Tweedledee*, occurs when an emerging standards battle would not mitigate the new technology's diffusion and when intra-technology competition would be detrimental to profits. The prerequisite for this incompatibility strategy is that both competing companies need to be similar in their resource endowments, i.e. both players have nearly the same market share and have symmetrical technological positions. In a standards battle, the overall objective is to eliminate the competitor and to determine the industry standard. According to Besen and Farrell [5], four tactics can be applied to win an inter-technology competition. First, the competing companies should try to build an early lead in terms of customer base size in order to reach critical mass. This becomes even more important if the installed base (e.g. sales figures) is observable by consumers [5]. A market share increase can be achieved for instance by implementing aggressive pricing strategies, such as penetration pricing [17]. Second, each of the two competitors should support the supply of complementary products and services to increase the value of its proprietary product. A considerable amount of complementary products can lead to increased user adoption [18]. However, whether a third-party supplier decides to produce complements for a proprietary product also depends on the supplier's expectation to

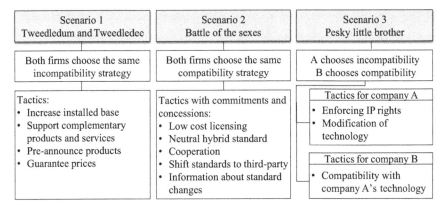

Fig. 3 Overview of the strategies and tactics of horizontal competition [5]

face a great demand and, therefore, on the size of the installed base [5]. Third, companies should pre-announce their products to create expectations and to discourage potential consumers to buy a rival's product. In addition, product pre-announcements can intimidate competitors. However, this tactic involves the danger of generating an undesired negative effect on sales, referred to as the *Osborne effect*, because pre-announcements encourage potential customers to wait instead of buying the available product [5]. Companies should also adhere to pre-announcements to prevent negative effects on the company's credibility owing to undelivered promises [19]. Fourth, long-term price commitments are another tactic to attempt to convince potential customers. However, owing to uncertainty regarding the production costs, such obligations can be risky.

A recent example of companies pursuing *Tweedledum and Tweedledee* scenario tactics are Microsoft and Sony in the videogame console market. Microsoft's Xbox One and Sony's PlayStation 4 (PS4) feature similar hardware specifications, and the products launched within one week of each other (see Table 1).

Both companies applied tactics similar to the ones mentioned above. First, both were trying to establish a customer base early on (tactic 1: increase installed base) either by applying a relatively low introductory price (Sony: US$399) or bundling its hardware with additional components to make the system more attractive and valuable to customers (e.g. Microsoft: Kinect). By setting a significantly lower price than its rival, Sony took into account a smaller profit margin, knowing that a proprietary network would stimulate future software sales [21, 22]. Moreover, a two-sided market characterizes the videogames industry. In the case of the videogame sector, this means that hardware producers such as Sony and Microsoft not only benefit from hardware and self-produced software sales, but also from charging videogame developers fixed fees and per-unit royalties [22]. In terms of attracting these software developers (tactic 2: support complements), both companies sought to get as many system-exclusive titles as possible. To date, the PS4 has 12 confirmed or released exclusive titles and the Xbox One 11 [23]. Sony and Microsoft also pre-announced their products to convince potential customers of their own product's superiority (tactic 3: pre-announce product). In 2013, both

Table 1 Comparison of hardware features: PS4 versus Xbox one [20]

Feature	PlayStation 4	Xbox one
Price	US$399.99	US$499.99
Release date	US: 11.15.2013; EU: 11.29.2013	11.22.2013
Optical drive	Blu-ray/DVD	Blu-ray/DVD
RAM	8 GB GDDR5	8 GB DDR3
GPU	AMD Radeon Graphics Core Next engine with 1152 shaders	853 MHz AMD Radeon GPU with 768 shaders
Storage	500 GB 5400 RPM SATA II hard drive	500 GB hard drive
Subscription service	PlayStation Plus	Xbox Live
Colors	Black	Black

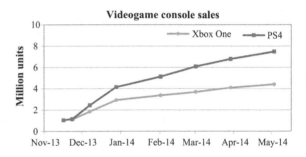

Fig. 4 Cumulated worldwide console sales [26]

companies held press conferences at the Electronic Entertainment Expo (E3). Microsoft triggered serious concerns about the Xbox One's DRM, online requirements, and Kinect functionality, while Sony used the occasion to announce that there will not be any always-on requirements or sharing restrictions [24]. Furthermore, Microsoft recently announced a lower price (US$399) for its Xbox One and the unbundling of the Kinect accessory [25], perhaps as a reaction to underwhelming sales (tactic 4: guarantee prices). Although the battle has only recently begun, it seems that both proprietary systems will have their customer base and that both systems will be able to co-exist (see Fig. 4).

Scenario 2, *battle of the sexes*, applies when compatibility is important for market success. Both companies agree that competition within a standard is preferable. Until both companies agree on a standard, there is little expected market demand for incompatible standards. Furthermore, dissipation of profits would be the result of a standards battle. If both companies insist on using their own technology, tactics of commitments and concessions must be implemented to persuade the other party to change sides in order to reach a mutual agreement. Such commitments can be either positive or negative for a company's profit. Concessions include actions that make one player more attractive to the other player. Concessions such as low-cost licensing (second-sourcing) allow one company to make an exact copy of another company's product, resulting in a loss of customers for the proprietor but also in a market growth by attracting additional suppliers. A second concession type would be the integration of two rival technologies into a third, neutral hybrid standard. Thus, on the one hand, a possible advantage of one company's technology is revealed to the other company; on the other hand, both companies are able to profit from these advantages and strengthen their own market position. A third concession type that can be utilized is an agreement of both companies to engage in future joint developments or ventures. Cooperation can yield such benefits as "reduced cost and improved quality of purchased materials, reduced product development time, and improved access to and application of technology" [27]. However, it also involves intra-organizational risks and difficulties, such as the resistance to share proprietary information, and not-invented-here syndrome. Other concessions are the shifting of standards development to third-parties and the promise to provide timely information about changes in the standards, giving others the opportunity to adapt their products accordingly [27]. These activities help to establish trust and attract rivals to a company's network.

A prominent example of the *battle of the sexes* scenario is the race between two high-definition optical disc formats, namely Sony's Blu-ray format and Toshiba's HD-DVD format, which started in the early 2000s. In February 2002, a consortium of nine electronic manufacturers founded the Blu-ray Disc Association (BDA), headed by Sony. In June 2004, the DVD Forum, a consortium including among others Sony and Toshiba officially selected the HD-DVD format, which was already introduced to the DVD Forum by Toshiba in January 2002, as the successor to DVD. As a result, Toshiba founded the HD-DVD consortium in December 2004 with the involvement of other companies such as NEC and Microsoft. Thus, there were now two opposing conglomerates, consisting of many diverse manufacturers, using incompatible technologies. As a result, both parties entered negotiations in 2005 to find a uniform solution and a common standard. However, they were unable to come to an arrangement, since neither party was willing to make concessions that would satisfy the opponent. The first HD-DVD player was released in March 2006, followed shortly by the Blu-ray player in June 2006 (see Fig. 5).

A key factor that was responsible for deciding this battle was the aforementioned two-sided market. Sony and Toshiba sought to influence two important *game changers* in the market (namely disc manufacturers) to support their standard, and content providers by offering exclusive deals to movies studios. The latter was the most important factor, because approximately 70 % of movies titles were released exclusively on Sony's Blu-ray format, after Sony managed to convince movie studios such as Paramount, Warner Bros. Pictures, Twentieth Century Fox, and Walt Disney to publish their content in the Blu-ray format. One could argue that movie studios could produce content for both mediums, but they feared increasing manufacturing costs and inventory problems when simultaneously supporting the two formats. Another success factor for Sony was the decision to integrate a Blu-ray player into its PlayStation 3, boosting the demand on the consumer side [29]. As a result, Sony won the format war, and HD-DVD products were pulled from the market in 2008.

In contrast to the two aforementioned scenarios, the key players in scenario 3, *pesky little brother*, are companies that differ significantly regarding their market share, their technological capability or their reputation for setting standards. Owing

Fig. 5 Format war: Blu-Ray versus HD-DVD [28]

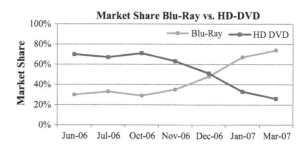

to this initial asymmetric situation, the objectives and compatibility strategies are largely dependent on the companies' positions in the market. The superior company (company A), *big brother*, is more likely to prefer incompatibility and a standard battle than the less established inferior company (company B). Company B is the *pesky little brother*, who acknowledges the superior company's dominance and seeks only to get a slice of the cake. Therefore, company B's tactic is to adopt company A's standard and to reach compatibility, while company A seeks to counteract this kind of free-riding by either enforcing intellectual property (IP) rights or frequently modifying its technology. As long as strict patent and copyright laws are present, it is likely that company A's intention to protect its IP is sustained by the courts [5] and even leads to an increasing likelihood of company B being technologically locked out [18]. Microsoft tried to prevent access to important information about the interoperability of devices by demanding excessive prices for license fees. However, in 2004, Microsoft was charged with keeping certain interoperability information from its competitors [30]. Another possibility for company A is to frequently alter its technology to inhibit compatibility. However, this tactic is much more difficult to pursue, since a dominant design often arises from long-established production methods and is accompanied by a large installed base. Thus, company A is somewhat committed to the technology it has deployed, because a change could mean abandoning its customer base, which is detrimental in network effect markets [5]. If company A cannot apply any of these tactics, it is powerless in deterring company B from following and achieving compatibility.

A suitable example of an incumbent company who wishes to protect its dominant market position is Apple and its DRM system, called FairPlay. Content providers generally establish a DRM system to protect their digital assets and to control their distribution and usage [31]. Apple's FairPlay copy protection was introduced along with the start of the iTunes store in April 2003. With this DRM system, Apple originally intended to limit the portability of songs purchased from the iTunes store to digital music players (e.g. the iPod) that support its FairPlay standard [32]. In the following years, Apple refused to license its technology to third-parties, which induced VirginMega, Virgin's French music retail subsidiary, to file a complaint with the French Competition Council. However, the French court ruled that Apple could not be forced to reveal its technology to its competitors. Nevertheless, other critics followed, such as Mitch Bainwol, chairman and chief executive of the Recording Industry Association of America, who in 2007 argued that Apple should open up its anti-piracy technology [33]. This behavior can clearly be interpreted as a *pesky little brother* attitude and as an attempt to establish compatibility in order to profit from the big brother's large network. Apple voluntarily changed its strategy by agreeing to remove the encryption technology in 2009, at least for the music titles distributed via the iTunes store, in favor of implementing a new pricing structure [34].

As mentioned at the start of this section, the three scenarios and the respective compatibility strategies and tactics apply if only two companies are involved in a conflict. But with an increasing number of players in the market, competition is likely to shift to a more vertical dimension. Therefore, relatively new approaches seek to explain the processes of applying suitable strategies in these so-called *business ecosystems* [35, 36]. Moore [35] defines such ecosystems as the number of companies "co-evolving capabilities around a new innovation by working cooperatively and competitively to support new products, satisfy customer needs, and eventually incorporate the next round of innovations". Every company functions as a player in a business ecosystem and leverages other companies to make their business more beneficial. In the PS4 versus Xbox One case, both Sony and Microsoft must deal with a number of other players in the market such as suppliers (e.g. AMD), software developers and publishers, and retailers. Therefore, it can be helpful for these companies to subdivide a complex ecosystem into a number of business domains in order to ensure that every one of these domains that is crucial for product provision remains intact and does not undermine the ecosystem's performance. For this purpose, Iansiti and Levien [36] identified three critical measures of the health of an ecosystem. The first is productivity, which is the ability to transform innovation-related input factors into new products [36]. Second, robustness must exist in order to be ready to deal with environmental changes such as the emergence of disruptive technologies. The third measure is niche creation, which is the capability to create a meaningful diversity by implementing valuable new functions [36]. However, especially niche creation can be dangerous, since established companies may be able to utilize the developmental work of others by replicating their ideas and distributing them across a wider market [35]. Owing to the numerous interrelations within and beyond an ecosystem's boundaries, companies implement strategies and tactics to remain competitive and to outsmart rivals.

4 Standards as a Cost-Reduction Instrument

In the previous section, we looked at the strategic level and described market-based effects that occur if companies pursue standard battles. However, the use of standards can also be beneficial for internal communication purposes, since network effects can allow for more cost-efficient information transfers between communication partners. An example is the usage of the *eXtensible Markup Language* (XML) for media-neutral processing and the exchange of content within a media company. The question arises whether an investment in XML is profitable, since standards can reduce costs but usually also require upfront investments. This decision problem is generally referred to as the *standardization problem* and addresses the interdependencies owing to positive network effects [5]. In this section, we examine how actors (typically in a company) decide on the selection of standards from an economic perspective and illustrate this investment decision in a graph model [37]. Thus, the model attempts to provide implications of whether or not the implementation of a standard is cost-effective. Decision-makers in media companies can also derive practical implications regarding the usefulness of communication standards from the graph model. For illustration purposes, we draw on the example of a standard document type definition (DTD) for the exchange of written content between parties.

A DTD defines the XML document structure with a list of elements and attributes. A valid XML document conforms to the rules of a DTD based on XML syntax. An XML schema is an alternative to DTD and describes the structure of an XML document, just like a DTD. With a DTD, independent parties can agree on a standard DTD for interchanging data. Consequently, the processing of XML-based languages with common tools (e.g. parser, APIs) is possible and users can specify the semantics according to their own needs [38]. We assume that a communication standard, such as in the model proposed by Arthur [39], offers a media company both a standalone utility and a utility that increases with the network's size. Standards are implemented in the nodes (e.g. exchange partners), and the network edges represent the communications relationships.

The node (i) represents the costs of standardization (K_i), while the exchange cost along the edge from node (i) to node (j) is termed (c_{ij}). These costs of content exchange (c_{ij}) consist of direct costs of exchange (e.g. costs of manual processing and transmission of documents) and opportunity costs of inferior decisions, which arise on account of non-use of standards (friction cost). The sending node (i) pays the cost of exchange (c_{ij}) to the recipient node (j). Cost reductions owing to standardization can be realized only when both actors (nodes i and j) implement a common standard such as a DTD for the exchange of text files (see Fig. 6). The media company perceives a tradeoff between the node-related costs of a standard implementation and the edge-related costs savings. If node (i) implements the DTD, it must pay the standardization costs (Ki). These standardization cost occur independently from the decision of the partner node (j). However, if node (j) also implements the DTD, the exchange costs (c_{ij}) can be saved. This does not mean that a common standard reduces these content transfer costs to zero. Rather, (c_{ij}) can be interpreted as the difference between the exchange costs without and with a common standard. Thus, to determine the benefits of implementing a DTD for each node (i), the costs of standardization (K_i) must be compared to the savings (c_{ij}). Only if the savings are greater than the costs, implementing a common standard will be advantageous owing to a positive net utility. Accordingly, the value of variable (x_i) in the formula is 1

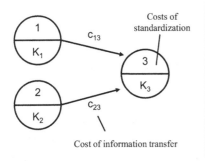

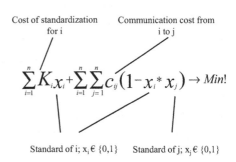

$$\sum_{i=1}^{n} K_i x_i + \sum_{i=1}^{n}\sum_{j=1}^{n} c_{ij}\left(1 - x_i * x_j\right) \rightarrow Min!$$

Cost of standardization for i   Communication cost from i to j

Standard of i; $x_i \in \{0,1\}$ Standard of j; $x_j \in \{0,1\}$

Costs of standardization

Cost of information transfer

Fig. 6 Costs of nodes and edges [37]

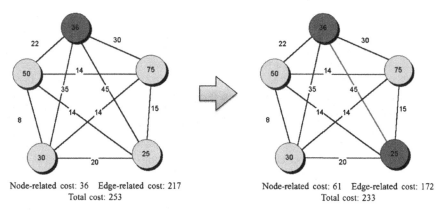

Node-related cost: 36   Edge-related cost: 217   Node-related cost: 61   Edge-related cost: 172
              Total cost: 253   Total cost: 233

Fig. 7 A simple example illustrating the standardization problem [40]

when node (i) is standardized and 0 otherwise. The standardization costs (K_i) occur if $x_i = 1$. The communication costs (c_{ij}) are equal to 0 in the simplified model and can be saved if both nodes (i) and (j) exchange XML documents based on a common DTD ($x_i = x_j = 1$). The tradeoff between the node-related costs and edge-related costs can be illustrated in a simple example (see Fig. 7).

There is only one implemented standard in the graph on the left side, which is represented with the red node. The use of a standard in only one node does not support content exchange. The node-related costs of 36 monetary units and the edge-related cost of 217 monetary units must be considered, which results in a total costs of 253 monetary units. If nodes 3 and 5 adopt a common DTD, then 61 (36 + 25) monetary units occur as standardization cost. However, the edge-related cost of 45 monetary units between these two nodes can be saved, resulting in a total cost of only 233 monetary units [40].

The decision model provides the basis for determining an optimal underlying standard for each system component focusing solely on the internal perspective and ignoring any external effects on the standardization decision. The model is based on the assumption that standards already exist. Therefore, the development or definition of standards is not discussed. In addition, the model refers to positive externalities of communication standards and does not consider negative effects. To estimate the cost of information, friction costs, which are not easy to quantify, must be considered. These limitations weaken the applicability of the decision model to real standardization problems.

5   Conclusion and Outlook

Standards are more than technical formats used at the operational level in media companies. They can have additional implications on business outcomes and can play an increasingly important role in external strategic competition (market-based perspective) and internal cost reduction (actor-based perspective). By definition, a market standard is available to actors in a market-based relationship. Three basic forms of horizontal competition can be differentiated according to market conditions. By using a selection of current, practical examples, we have shown how these standards setting strategies and tactics can be applied to standards battles in today's media industry. Moreover, taking a more internal perspective, we have described the economic selection of standards for actors (typically in a company) controlled by a central entity or actors, which have realized that business is possible only on the basis of standards. Thereby, we examined the standardization decision and addressed the tradeoff between the cost of investing in a standard and the cost-reduction potential of a standardized communication and exchange process. We provided an example to illustrate the investment decision of media companies implementing a DTD for content exchange. Companies can draw on this model for cost reduction in order to determine whether implementing a standard for communication and data exchange is profitable.

We have shown that standards can be used not only as technical basis, but also as a competitive instrument and cost reduction tool in media companies. However, standards can become less important owing to technological developments. Applications for different operating systems make it is possible to receive content on different end-devices. An example of compatibility created by an application is Spotify, which uses its own music streaming format for many reasons such as DRM and internal management. The development of platform-independent solutions reduces the need for technical standards and facilitates compatibility.

References

1. Lugmayr, A. (2013). Brief introduction into information systems & management research in media industries. Paper Presented at the Multimedia and Expo Workshops (ICMEW), International Conference on IEEE, July 15–19, 2013.
2. Hess, T. (2014). What is a media company? A reconceptualization for the online world. *International Journal on Media Management, 16*(1), 3–8.
3. David, P. A., & Greenstein, S. (1990). The economics of compatibility standards: An introduction to recent research. *Economics of Innovation and New Technology, 1*(1–2), 3–41.
4. Stango, V. (2004). The economics of standards wars. *Review of Network Economics, 3*(1), 1–19.
5. Besen, S. M., & Farrell, J. (1994). Choosing how to compete: Strategies and tactics in standardization. *Journal of Economic Perspectives, 8*(2), 117–131.
6. Katz, M. L., & Shapiro, C. (1985). Network externalities, competition, and compatibility. *The American Economic Review, 75*(3), 424–440.
7. Majumdar, S. K., & Venkataraman, S. (1998). Network effects and the adoption of new technology: Evidence from the U.S. telecommunications industry. *Strategic Management Journal, 19*(11), 1045–1062.
8. Shapiro, C., & Varian, H. (1998). *Information rules: A strategic guide to the network economy.* Boston: Harvard Business School Press.
9. Lee, D., & Mendelson, H. (2007). Adoption of information technology under network effects. *Information Systems Research, 18*(4), 395–413.
10. Liu, P., Raahemi, B., & Benyoucef, M. (2011). Knowledge sharing in dynamic virtual enterprises: A socio-technological perspective. *Knowledge-Based Systems, 24*(3), 427–443.

11. Church, J., & Gandal, N. (1992). Network effects, software provision, and standardization. *The Journal of Industrial Economics, 40*(1), 85–103.
12. Rogers, E. M. (1983). *Diffusion of innovations*. New York: Free Press.
13. Berger, B., & Hess, T. (2013) Das paid-content-problem (The paid-content problem). MedienWirtschaft-Zeitschrift für Medienmanagement und Kommunikationsökonomie 10(3), 54–58.
14. Wagner, T. M., Benlian, A., & Hess, T. (2013). The advertising effect of free-do free basic versions promote premium versions within the freemium business model of music services? Paper Presented at the 46th Hawaii International Conference on System Sciences (HICSS), January 7–10, 2013.
15. Farrell, J., & Klemperer, P. (2007). Coordination and lock-in: Competition with switching costs and network effects. *Handbook of Industrial Organization, 3*, 1967–2072.
16. Weitzel, T., Beimborn, D., & König, W. (2006). A unified economic model of standard diffusion: the impact of standardization cost, network effects, and network topology. *MIS Quarterly, 30*(Special Issue), 489–514.
17. Katz, M. L., & Shapiro, C. (1986). Technology adoption in the presence of network externalities. *The Journal of Political Economy, 94*(4), 822–841.
18. Schilling, M. A. (1998). Technological lockout: An integrative model of the economic and strategic factors driving technology success and failure. *Academy of Management Review, 23* (2), 267–284.
19. Sorescu, A., Shankar, V., & Kushwaha, T. (2007). New product preannouncements and shareholder value: Don't make promises you can't keep. *Journal of Marketing Research, 44* (3), 468–489.
20. IGN. (2014). *PS4 vs. Xbox One vs. Wii U comparison chart IGN*. http://www.ign.com/wikis/xbox-one/PS4_vs._Xbox_One_vs._Wii_U_Comparison_Chart. Accessed August 4, 2015.
21. Katz, M. L., & Shapiro, C. (1994). Systems competition and network effects. *Journal of Economic Perspectives, 8*(2), 93–115.
22. Rochet, J. C., & Tirole, J. (2003). Platform competition in two-sided markets. *Journal of the European Economic Association, 1*(4), 990–1029.
23. IGN. (2014). *PS4 games vs Xbox One games*. http://www.ign.com/wikis/xbox-one/PS4_Games_vs_Xbox_One_Games. Accessed August 4, 2015.
24. IGN. (2014). *Microsoft at E3 2013*. http://www.ign.com/wikis/e3/Microsoft_at_E3_2013. Accessed August 4, 2015.
25. Spencer, P. (2014). *Xbox wire: Delivering more choices for fans*. http://news.xbox.com/2014/05/xbox-delivering-more-choices. Accessed August 4, 2015.
26. VGChartz. (2014). *Game platforms*. VGChartz. http://www.vgchartz.com/platforms/. Accessed August 4, 2015.
27. Ragatz, G. L., Handfield, R. B., & Scannell, T. V. (1997). Success factors for integrating suppliers into new product development. *Journal of Product Innovation Management, 14*(3), 190–202.
28. Drawbaugh, B. (2008). *Two years of battle between HD DVD and Blu-ray: A retrospective. Engadget*. http://www.engadget.com/2008/02/20/two-years-of-battle-between-hd-dvd-and-blu-ray-a-retrospective/. Accessed August 4, 2015.
29. Daidj, N., Grazia, C., & Hammoudi, A. (2010). Introduction to the non-cooperative approach to coalition formation: The case of the Blu-Ray/HD-DVD standards' war. *Journal of Media Economics, 23*(4), 192–215.
30. European Commission. (2004). *Commission concludes on Microsoft investigation, imposes conduct remedies and a fine*. Press Release. http://europa.eu/rapid/press-release_IP-04-382_en.htm?locale=en. Accessed August 4, 2015.
31. Liu, Q., Safavi-Naini, R., & Sheppard, N. P. (2003). Digital rights management for content distribution. In: Proceedings of the Australasian Information Security Workshop Conference on ACSW Frontiers, Darlinghurst, Australia, January 2003.
32. George, C., & Chandak, N. (2006). Issues and challenges in securing interoperability of DRM systems in the digital music market. *International Review of Law Computers & Technology, 20*(3), 271–285.

33. Veiga, A. (2007). Music industry fires back at Apple. *NBC News*. http://www.nbcnews.com/id/17033428/ns/technology_and_science-tech_and_gadgets#.U60uyLHaU40. Accessed August 4, 2015.
34. BBC. (2009). Apple to end music restrictions. *BBC News*. http://news.bbc.co.uk/2/hi/technology/7813527.stm. Accessed August 4, 2015.
35. Moore, J. F. (1993). Predators and prey: A new ecology of competition. *Harvard Business Review, 71*(3), 75–86.
36. Iansiti, M., & Levien, R. (2004). Strategy as ecology. *Harvard Business Review, 82*(3), 68–81.
37. Buxmann, P., Weitzel, T., Westarp, F., König, W. (1999). The standardization problem—An economic analysis of standards in information systems. Paper Presented at the SIIT'99—Proceedings of the 1st IEEE Conference on Standardisation and Innovation in Information Technology University of Aachen, September 15–16, 1999.
38. Bray, T., Paoli, J., Sperberg-McQueen, C. M., Maler, E., & Yergeau, F. (1998). *Extensible markup language (XML)*. http://www.w3.org/XML/. Accessed August 1, 2015.
39. Arthur, W. B. (1989). Competing technologies, increasing returns, and lock-in by historical events. *The Economic Journal, 99*(394), 116–131.
40. Buxmann, P., & König, W. (1998). Das Standardisierungsproblem: zur ökonomischen Auswahl von Standards in Informationssystemen (The standardization problem - an economic analysis of standards in information systems). *Wirtschaftsinformatik, 40*(2), 122–129.

Author Biographies

Thomas Hess After his diploma studies in Business Informatics at Darmstadt University of Technology, Thomas Hess earned his Doctorate at St. Gallen University (Switzerland) in 1995 and has been a full professor at the Ludwig-Maximilians-Universität (LMU Munich) since 2001. At the LMU, he is among others director of the Institute for Information Systems and New Media. His research focuses on digital business models and digital management systems, digital transformation processes and methods and the management of IT, Internet and Media Companies.

Antonia Köster received her Bachelor of Science in Business Administration from the LMU Munich in 2012. She has been a research assistant and Doctoral candidate at the Institute for Information Systems and New Media (LMU) since 2013. Her research interests lie in the area of social sharing, with a focus on personal communication tools.

Christian Matt is Assistant Professor at the Institute for Information Systems and New Media at LMU Munich. He also holds a Ph.D. in Management from the LMU Munich and Master's degrees in Computer Science (University of Colorado at Boulder) and in Management (LMU Munich/EM Lyon). His current research focuses on digitization, both from the corporate and individual perspectives. Other research interests include recommender systems and digital value chains.

"Own-It": Managing Intellectual Property Processes via the Activity Table in Creative Industries

Dolores Modic and Nadja Damij

Abstract The focal idea of this paper is to use the Activity table in order to increase the efficiency of the intellectual property protection by individual businesses inside the creative industries. The creative businesses—generally being identified as businesses with activities which have a potential for wealth and job creation through the generation and exploitation of intellectual property—are especially susceptible to the issues of IP management and IP processes. This is also coupled with the fact that they operate in a world of fast adaptations and short innovation cycles. Generally, the aim of the activity table technique is to select specific business processes within the organization and tabularly show only those that are considered to be the basis for business processes improvement; here focusing on the intellectual property processes. The idea is hence putting the focus on the IP creation and IP management enhancing the concept of "own-it" in regards to the intellectual property and trough that enriching the possibilities of increased revenues from intellectual property.

1 Introduction

In the world of today, companies do not innovate anymore in isolation from other actors, but are entering into (innovation) relationships with other actors. Furthermore, actors' ideas are quickly combined with other ideas and/or re-used.

The outcome of this kind of environment is characterized by a large percentage of adaptations; a situation welcomed by authors of innovation policies. However, views of individual companies greatly differentiate from them, mostly due to their own appropriative aspirations.

Mechanisms for intellectual property (IP) protection may be distinguished to formal (patents, models, designs, trademarks etc.) and informal mechanisms (trade

D. Modic (✉)
Faculty of Information Studies, Novo Mesto, Slovenia
e-mail: dolores.modic@fis.unm.si

N. Damij
Newcastle Business School, Northumbria University, Newcastle upon Tyne, UK

© Springer International Publishing AG 2016
A. Lugmayr et al. (eds.), *Information Systems and Management in Media and Entertainment Industries*, International Series on Computer Entertainment and Media Technology, DOI 10.1007/978-3-319-49407-4_5

101

secrets, first on the market, complementary goods etc.) [17, 38]. It is hardly surprising, looking at the definition of creative industries, that these would generate most of their IP on their own. However, what comes as a surprise is they in general seem to use more formal mechanisms as is usually the case (see the comparison between Levin et al. [28] and Tang [42]).

The formal (legal) mechanism being preferred is logically the copyright, which is mostly not seen as providing a solid protection against infringement. But companies encounter the problem of the low effectiveness of all (formal and informal) mechanisms [10, 28]. The accompanying issue is hence also that of the appropriability of intellectual property in the sense of possibilities of protecting the intellectual property from (unlicensed) imitation and of reaping profits from these. Creative industries, where the level of adaptation is even faster as in other industries and has high levels of piracy present, are in this sense especially vulnerable.

When talking about intellectual property rights mechanisms (especially smaller) companies often also do not possess sufficient knowledge to use them as efficiently as possible [6, 21, 26]. This is also true inside creative industries. It is not surprising that Tang [42] has discovered that electronic publishers not only do not patent, but that the majority does not know that software-based applications could even be patented. Furthermore, intellectual property rights are often labeled as ineffective, partly due to their sub-optimal use by the companies—for example due to their use in cases, in which for this type of protection mechanism is clearly not suitable. In addition, one must bear in mind that the initial treatment of innovations (which we consider as the preparation phase) conditions the success of subsequent phases.

Throughout last decades, fields of business process modeling and consequently business process renovation have been gaining recognition and acceptance. Reasons for such evolution are found in literature, academic publications and research studies that deal with the theme, as well as in an increasing involvement of consultancy and software development companies [13]. Both business process modeling and business process renovation are based on the fact that a business process is a key element of the analysis of the organization. Business processes come within our scope in that they potentially add value to the organization and as such are attracting attention (examples given in [1, 8, 18, 35]; Hammer and Champy [19]; Davenport and Short [15] and so forth). Consequently, business process modeling and improvement is on the increase as only a thorough comprehension of the business processes within the organizations can lead to effective, efficient and value-adding systems. According to [3], it is the business processes that are the key element when integrating an enterprise.

In this paper we are offering a model of dealing with the IP processes via the activity table; in order to allow the increase of revenues from intellectual property rights and royalties. The creative industries seem to have a trap in-built. There is a continuous cycle of development in which many creative businesses are perpetually dependent on "the next job" paralleled with trimmed profits; one way out of this trap seems to be the so-called "own-it" principle (expression is adopted from [37]). Hence only quality IP creation (not having in mind the original "spark", but rather the continuation of the path to the stage of commercialization) and good IP management may provide sufficient basis for successful exploitation of the IP rights in the creative industries.

2　Ex Ante: The Dubious Relationship Between Intellectual Property and Creative Industries

Innovation seems to differ substantially across sectors in terms of "characteristics, sources, actors involved, the boundaries of the process, and the organization of innovative activities" (Malerba [34], p. 380). Though not always defined unilaterally, the creative industries are regarded often as those activities which have a potential for wealth and job creation through the generation and exploitation of intellectual property (see for an early example DCMS [11]; or for a more recent example [43]). Lugmayr [29] divides them into Core eMedia Industries (such as music, advertising or publishing), Wider Creative eMedia Industries (such as clothing and footwear, crafts or theatre) and Industries Applying eMedia Technology (such as gastronomy, jewelery or musical instruments).

However, some argue that different attitudes towards intellectual property are the basis for further taxonometry inside the creative industries. Dividing them to creative service providers (devoting their intellectual property to other businesses, such as advertising agencies, architecture companies, new media agencies etc.); creative content producers (who produce copyright-protected intellectual property which they distribute to costumers, such as film, television, fashion or (electronic) publishers); creative experience providers (who sell the right for consumers to experience activities and performances, such as theatre, opera, live music organizers) and creative original producers (involved in the creation, manufacture and sale of physical artefacts, such as craft makers, visual artists and design makers) [37, pp. 54–55].

We need to keep in mind some anomalies inside the realm of creative industries; that of the fashion industry being the most interesting one. Unlike many other creative industries, such as movie, music and commercial publishing industries—which have pushed for broad IP protections for their works—fashion enjoys a low degree of IP protection (see also [40]). All forms of IPR protection—copyright, design, trademark, and patent—provide only a very limited protection for fashion designs. The fashion industry is also one of the industries where reverse engineering is fast and simple; and the innovation cycles seem to be above average short. Much of the intellectual property of the creative industries also consists of know-how, is often uncodified and tacit [24] and is in many cases also (at least seen as) unprotectable by formal protection mechanisms [20, p. 37].

However it would still seem that in general intellectual property rights play an important role in the development of creative industries—promoting creativity and culture—while helping to retain the gains of the work by the creators and enable them to appropriate those gains. But improvements lie in developing new business models for dealing with intellectual property. Some leading experts such as Shapiro or Varian in this tradition contend that in industries—such for example the electronic publishing—the aim of businesses should be in maximizing the value of their IP and not just in protecting the IP (see also [42]).

We thus see the issue of IP management as the core question in the creative industry, which is dominated by low IP protection possibilities. As was already discussed in NESTA [37, p. 39] some companies are managing to overcome these challenges by developing innovative new approaches and business models, and there are opportunities for such models to be adopted more widely.

Here the processes of intellectual property protection are chosen as the focal processes that are to be the subject of improvement. During the improvement of individual processes it is necessary, that companies are offered standardized (typical) processes and their individual elements, so they are able—taking into account the differences between them—to identify elements that are in need of improvement.

3   Intermezzo: Briefly on Information Systems and Management in Creative eMedia Industries

Traditional media industries face the challenge of transforming themselves towards the 21st century fully digital companies. The main challenge for them, is in adapting new (digital) ways of working, introducing digital technologies into their daily lives and adapting organizational models to cope with the challenge of "digital" [30]. Also, various new forms of media have emerged—media industry developed from mass media towards smart media environments utilizing technologies to personalize content [31]. These are also still exploring possibilities and potentials of latest technology in search of new business models. In general, information management and systems deal with information on several management levels of an organizations perusing the goals of the particular organizational level (Lugmayr [29]). Inside media organizations, the basic dilemma is how management can adopt new practices and lead their firms into the digital future [30].

More in particular—looking at the IS across business functions and activities—we see that the Digital Rights Management (DRM) deals with the protection of content across the media supply chain according to Lugmayr [29], who also warns that many models did not work out in reality. We however warn that the term protection of intellectual property should be understood widely; and be directed not only towards "protection", but especially towards efficient utilization of companies IP(R)s. Looking at some of the suggested research areas we can also find workflow and asset Management inside eMedia industries [30], which is the area in which we try to make a contribution with the present article.

4 Business Process Modelling and the Idea of the Activity Table

The recent literature offers various definitions of and the extent of a process or process modelling. Throughout the last decades, the fields of business process modelling and consequently business process renovation have been gaining recognition and acceptance. The reasons for such evolution are found in the literature, academic publications and research studies that deal with the theme, as well as in the increasing involvement of consultancy and software development companies. A comparative study that closely examined 25 methodologies, 72 techniques and 102 tools was conducted [22]. Furthermore, business process modelling is one of the requirements of the ISO 9000 international standard for quality management and assurance [39], as well as being one of the key questions when implementing the majority of information systems such as Workflow Management Systems, Enterprise Resource Planning and E-Business. Both business process modelling and business process renovation are based on the fact that a business process is the key element in the analysis of the organisation.

Business processes come within our scope in that they potentially add value to the organisation and as such are attracting attention (examples given in [8, 18, 35]; Aguilar-Saven 1999; and so forth). Consequently, business process modelling is on the increase as only a thorough comprehension of the business processes within the organisations can lead to effective, efficient and value-adding systems. It is the business processes that are the key element when integrating an enterprise [3]. Furthermore, conceptual modelling of business processes is deployed on a large scale to facilitate the development of software that supports the business processes, and to permit the analysis and re-engineering or improvement of them [2]. For the purpose of this paper, the latter use of business process modelling and improvement will be considered.

To elaborate on the definition of a process referred to above, the following one is added. A process is defined as structured, measured sets of activities designed to produce a specified output for a particular customer or market [14]. Hence, a process converts inputs by summing their value through various activities into outputs. A business process is a collection of activities that takes one or more kinds of input and creates an output that is of a value to the customer [18]. However, other stressed that a business process is related to the enterprise, as it defines the way in which the goals of the enterprise are achieved [2].

The input and output, and the entry and exit points determine the process boundaries within which the relationship between the process and its environment is created through the inputs and outputs. Besides the inputs and outputs, the process architecture also includes four other main features: the flow units, the network of activities and buffers, the resources, and the information structure [4]. The flow units are the temporary entities that flow through diverse activities in order to exit as a completed output. A process is described as a network of activities and buffers through which the flow units have to pass in order to be transformed from inputs to outputs [25]. To sufficiently define a process, firstly the process activities need to be identified, and then the sequence order of the identified activities needs to be established. Resources are origins of supply, material assets required to activate process activities and are consequently twofold; capital assets and labour [25]. They are exploited within the process but not consumed. As a last feature the information structure determines the availability of necessary information for implementing the activities in the process.

As stated earlier, successful business process modelling depends on the appropriate selection of available modelling methods, techniques or process flow analyses. There are many techniques or analyses used in this field, such as general process charts, process activity charts, flowcharts, dataflow diagrams, quality function deployment, the integrated definition of function modelling, coloured Petri-nets, object-oriented methods, seven management and planning tools and so forth.

Activity table ensures that the presented process model is in fact the true likeness of the real-life business process. The concept of activity table was developed in [13]. As previously mentioned, the aim of the Activity table technique is to select specific business processes within the organization and tabularly show only those that considered to be a base for business processes improvement. The new element in the Activity table is the inclusion of the property table parameters. As such the Activity table presents a complete process system.

In order to develop a process model that represents a true likeness of the existing reality of the process, the state of the art of the process should be first discovered and understood [13]. The process model represented by the Activity Table is developed. This table consists of two parts. The first part provides information about each activity of the process by defining a number of parameters that describe the activities listed. The second part is a tabular-graphical representation of the process discussed.

To develop the activity table, information about process functioning should be gained during interviews that are organized with knowledgeable employees. This is done using the following two steps.

Activity Parameters

In the columns of part 1 of the Activity Table one or more of the following parameters are defined for each activity(i), where i ranges from 1 to the number of activities.

- Description. A short and precise description of what exactly is the work carried out by the activity defined in row(i) of the table.
- Time. The expected duration needed for activity(i) to be processed and accomplished.
- Rule. One or more constraints or rules that must be satisfied in order for activity (i) to be performed.

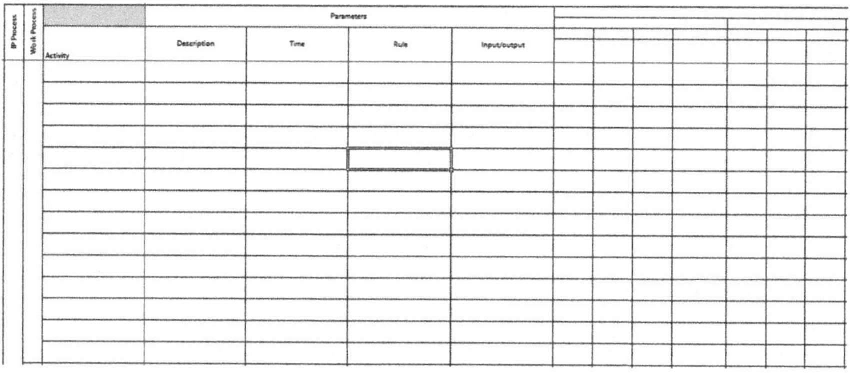

Fig. 1 The Activity table. *Source* Authors' interpretation

- Input/Output. Input(s) and output(s) of activity(i).
- Other parameters can be added if necessary.

Business Process

The process modeling starts by identifying the behavior of the business processes identified. For each process, we create a new Activity Table, which represents its "as-is" model of the process. Thus, the name of the process selected is written in the first column of the Activity Table, see Fig. 1.

If the process is large and complex, then it may be partitioned into a set of sub-processes, which are in this case listed in the second column of the Activity Table.

As was mentioned before, each process consists of a number of work processes, which are defined in the Work Process column of the Activity Table. This column is usually the second one in which all work processes of the process discussed are listed.

In addition, for each work process defined, we write in the first row of the table the name of the department in which the work process is performed, see Fig. 1. A work process is a process that consists of a set of activities performed within a certain department. To identify these activities, further interviews are organized with the employees of this department.

An activity is a micro-process that represents well-defined work performed by one resource [12]. For each work process listed in the Work Process column, we have to identify all activities that are performed within the framework of the work process discussed. These activities are listed in the Activity column, which is usually the third column in the table.

For each activity, we have to identify:

(a) The resource that executes the activity and indicate it in a certain column of the second row under the department in which the work process is defined;
(b) The predecessor and successor activities of the current activity and connect it to these activities by vertical arrows.

The Activity Table technique uses a small set of flowchart symbols to model a process, such as: ○, •, □, ◇, |, →, ←, ↓, ↑. These symbols have the following meanings [12]:

- Symbol ○ indicates the starting point of a process;
- Symbol • indicates the end point of a process or a certain path of the process;
- Symbol □ in cell(i,j) of the table means that resource(j) performs activity(i), where j ranges from 1 to the number of resources and i ranges from 1 to the number of activities;
- Symbol ◇ in cell(i,j) means that activity(i) is a decision activity;
- Horizontal arrows →, ← are used to connect the activities horizontally;
- Vertical arrows ↓, ↑ are used to link the activities vertically;
- Symbol * in cell(i,j) and cell(i,k) mean that activity(i) could be performed by resource(j) or resource(k).

5   Process of Intellectual Property Management

Innovation and entrepreneurship are tightly interconnected, hence it is required that innovation be organized as a systematic activity [16, p. xv]. Today the revised strategies of patenting and the increase of strategic handling of intellectual property [36, 38] (Cohen et al. 2000) underline the rise of intellectual property applications.

The selection of a specific mechanism is crucial for all subsequent processes related to the protection of the intellectual property. It is believed that a dual approach, which comprises of combining formal and informal mechanisms, is the most used and the most effective [23, 28] (Cohen et al. 2000). Especially for formal intellectual property mechanisms, we must point out that some authors claim that intellectual property rights today may be seen more in terms of playing the role of innovation barriers for the competition as an innovation enabler [7, 33, 44]. Furthermore, usual criticism is directed toward their costliness, low effectiveness and lengthiness [5, 10, 28].

Protection of intellectual property and the use of different mechanisms can be characterized as fluid, depending on the rapidly changing market situation and taking into account the complementarity of various protection mechanisms. The process of IP creation and management is in whole divided into three phases which are interrelated and integrated: the preparation phase, the exploitation phase and the violation elimination phase. The preparation face is stemming from the so-called creation of the IP (exploration) and the latter two the IP management (exploitation) phase. This paper deals with the preparation stage. Only efficient preparation phase leads to efficient exploitation phase.

The existence of an appropriate innovation is a necessary pre-condition. It is interactively connected with the identification of appropriate innovations for IP protection processes. This includes the characteristics of the innovation itself; market needs identification and the distinction of the necessary characteristics for protection. Hence, the beginning of our process is set at a somewhat latter stage and does not include—although very important—phase of innovation creation.

We can see three kinds of processes in the IP protection (preparation) process: those that are related to the identification, those related to the selection and those related to the registration (if needed). Furthermore, the identification process in general includes several work processes: identification of appropriate innovation, identification of protection goals, identification of existing protection mechanisms, selection of the exploitation mode, selection of protection mechanisms and the registration (or non-registration procedures).

The goal of the IP protection (preparation) process is to obtain exploitation and protection ready innovations or in other words to choose an appropriate innovation (intellectual property) protection mechanism. It also gives the answer to the question whether to use a formal or informal protection mechanism. The process may be more or less formalized, but later stages tend to demand at least a certain level of formality in order to allow sufficient codification of knowledge. This tends to be especially problematic in creative industries, where most are highly dependent on the available know-how and informal relationships and processes [41].

Let us see some general properties of the exploitation phase and the violation elimination phase, whereas the latter one is an optional one—providing the company (or other actor) has detected a violation, which seems to be a particular problem in the creative industries (see for example [42]). The primary mode of exploitation is the goods market; the IP market and strategical use are secondary. Companies may gain profit also via cross-licensing, participation in patent-pools etc., where the profits are not direct. Despite this the collateralization or the securitization of intellectual property (IP) rights, it is increasingly becoming a more viable option for financing creative industry ventures [43, p. 87].

One of the general problems of formal intellectual property rights is the link between profitability and the IPR use seems to be lacking and the IPRs may be described as probabilistic at best [9, 27]. This fact furthers our notion that the intellectual property protection processes need to be systematic, carefully designed and thoroughly thought trough. Thus, it is of utmost importance that the preparation phase and the processes therein are carried out and designed as diligently as possible.

6 The Use of the Activity Table as a Tool of Innovation Property Protection Processes' Optimization in Creative Industries

In the following section we depict standardized (model) processes and other characteristics of the Activity Table for the needs of the optimization of the intellectual property protection inside the creative industries. These standardized (model) processes help companies to identify the inefficiencies of existing processes while using the Activity Table in order to re-model and improve the processes of intellectual property protection.

In order to use the Activity Table the following model parameters need to be defined: business process, work processes and defining activities and activity parameters (description, time, rule, input/output). To develop the activity table in the field of intellectual property, information about process functioning should be gained during interviews that are organized with knowledgeable employees. These are especially (but not exclusively): innovators, R&D department heads, marketing and/or sales department employees, finance and management/director, the legal department and/or patent attorney (if existing). Inside many creative industries the art director should also be consulted (sometimes *in lieu* of the R&D department employees). But there tends to be a lack of IP protection related knowledge [6, 21, 36]. This would seem to suggest including perhaps an even wider variety of included respondents.

The business process is the intellectual property process in its narrower sense or what we may see in Fig. 2 as preparation phase processes. As seen above the processes are related to three steps: those related to the identification, those related to the selection and those related to the registration (if needed).

The preparation process includes six work processes: identification of appropriate innovation, identification of protection goals, identification of existing protection mechanisms, selection of the exploitation mode, selection of protection mechanisms and registration or non-registration formation.

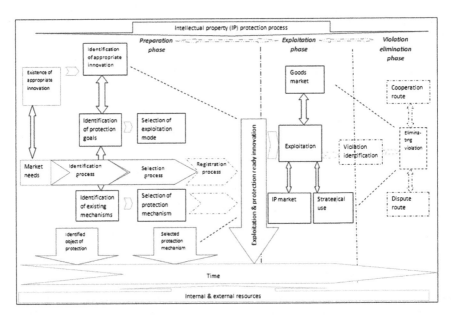

Fig. 2 Overview of a standardized intellectual property protection process. *Source* Authors' interpretation

The identification of appropriate innovation includes the following: collecting the innovations (at this stage it would be more accurate to call them invention, however we use this more generally used term), the identification of characteristics of the innovation and market needs identification, identification of active/not active IP protection and possible making of the prototype (and a decision to take over the innovation). The first activity may be organized in several different ways; weekly staff meetings, innovation forms, "innovation black-boxes" etc., the second can be organized as a meeting, the third as a written analysis/statement of market potential. Next, we have the possible making of the prototype (by inventor and/or art department, and/or research (R&D) department or an external actor altogether). This "prototype" is inside the creative industries many times in the form of "creative artifact" itself (for example inside the fashion industry an example would be the first model of a dress). It is to be noted, that for the IP protection processes, the viability of the innovation, is *pro forma* practically unimportant (here one can have in mind for example the patentability conditions), however from the point of view of making profit, this treat is of utmost importance. Furthermore, the decision to pursue active protection is done as a written or oral statement. Lastly, we have the agreement with the inventor(s) to take over a work-related innovation, which should take place to avoid any future problems. Involved employees are hence the innovator(s) and research head (also possible an innovation commission if in existence and in many creative industries the art departments), marketing and sales department employees (together with financial department employees); legal department; management representative; or in other words those included in the innovation identification team. The outputs are: description of the innovation (preferably on a form), short market and sales analysis/statement, decision to pursue/not pursue active protection of an individual innovation and a working prototype (the creative artifact) constructed. The latter is also followed up by the decision to take over the work-related innovation and possible signing of a non-disclosure agreement.

The work process of protection goals identification includes the identification of strategic goals related to intellectual property protection processes in general and the definition of specific goals of protection for the selected innovation object. Involved are: the innovator(s), the management representative, legal department, sales department representatives (in other words: the strategical team). The outputs are (ad minimum) a devised strategy for IP protection and a statement on specific goals for the selected innovation.

Identification of existing protection mechanisms process includes the creation of the analysis for potential protection mechanisms (both formal as well as informal) and the devising the viability of individual protection mechanisms. Involved employees are the innovator or R&D head, management representative, financial department and the legal department. The outputs are: an analysis of potential (viable) protection mechanisms and a viability study/statement of individual protection mechanisms.

Selection of the exploitation mode includes reaching the decision on the exploitation mode (goods market, IP market, strategic use), since the next steps are dependent on this decision. The selection of the exploitation should include the participation of the innovator, R&D department head, sales department head and management head. The output is the decision on the exploitation mode.

The work process of the selection of protection mechanisms includes the decision to use a specific formal or informal protection mechanism. It is selected in light of the characteristics of the innovation, the goal of intellectual property protection, cost and available funds, competition, as well as the desired timeframe. Furthermore, the decision must be made on which sub-option of a certain protection mechanism should be used (for example: to apply for national, European or PCT patent, to apply for a domestic or foreign design). Involved employees are the management, legal department and alternatively also the intellectual property attorney. Outputs are the decision on the selection of the protection mechanism and a (re-written) draft of innovation characteristics as relevant to the selected protection mechanism.

We are faced with distinct activities dependent on whether we have chosen protection via formal or protection via informal mechanisms; hence, either a registration procedure must be undertaken or not. The distinction must be drawn between the patents, designs and trademarks on one hand and the copyright on the other. First three require a registration process; the last does not require one. For example the US has had a registration procedure for copyright up until 1987. Although now the registration is not obligatory, it still provides legal advantages for registering works of U.S. origin.

In case of protection via formal mechanism the involved individuals in this step depend on whether there is a cooperation with an (outside) intellectual property attorney or if the application is done on its own. The first presumes an active participation of the intellectual property attorney, the other the active participation of either the legal department (if existing) or the management (especially in smaller companies, where several functions are carried out by the management). The activities involve: turning the draft into the application (in case of registrable formal IPRs)—in case of international application also the translation(s) of the application (or part thereof); sending the application to the IP office; communication with the IP office; possible corrections demanded by the IP office; and payment of the registration fee(s). In case of non-formal protection mechanisms, still some steps need to be taken. Special considerations and actions must take place when using the mechanism of technical protection mechanisms; that have come in the forefront after the rise of piracy in creative industries.

Due to the lack of relevant data on IP, we see as important to at least offer an outline of work processes, activities and other parameters of intellectual property protection processes, hence allowing an easier potential use of the Activity table for upgrading, re-modeling and improving intellectual property protection processes.

Figure 3 shows a possible outline of the Activity table for the work process of innovation identification. We see the defined activities, description, time (which would in real world usually follow after the flowchart completion), rule, output and involved employees (in our example the financial department is subsumed under the sales/marketing departments).

Business process	Work process	Activity				Department team R&D department Employees			Department Sales marketing departments Employees		Department team Management legal departments Employees		
		Description	Time	Rule	Input/output	innovator	R&D dep head	R&D team	Marketing employee	Sales employee	R&D director	General director	Employ Legal dept
IP protection (preparation) process / identification of appropriate innovation		Collecting the innovations	Overview of innovation forms	10 min	No suggestions	Description of the innovations collected							
		Identification of characteristics of the innovations	Analysis of innovation forms meeting	1h	Lack of needed knowledge	Innovation characteristics identified							
		Market needs identification	Preliminary analysis of market potential	1h	Lack of data on market potential	Written analysis statement of market potential							
		Making of the prototype	Prototype construction or innovation viability check	n.a.	Prototype not viable	Prototype or viability check							
		Identification of active/not active IP protection	Decision-making n whether to pursue or not pursue active IP protection	15 min	No agreement	Written or oral statement							
		Decision to take over the innovation	Decision-making and agreement with the inventor to take over or not to take over the invention	1 week	No consent from the inventor	Written statement, written & signed agreement with the inventor							

Fig. 3 An outline of the activity table for work process innovation identification (1). *Source* Authors' interpretation

Business process	Work process	Activity					Department/team R&D department/Art department Employees			Department/team Sales/marketing departments Employees		Department/team Management/legal departments Employees		
			Description	Time	Rule	Input/output	Innovator	R&D dep. head	R&D team	Marketing employee	Sales employee	R&D director	General director	Employ. Legal dept.
IP protection (preparation) process	Identification of appropriate innovation	Collecting the innovations	Overview of innovation forms	10 min	No suggestions	Description of the innovations collected								
		Identification of characteristics of the innovations	Analysis of innovation forms meeting	1h	Lack of needed knowledge	Innovation characteristics identified								
		Market needs identification	Preliminary analysis of market potential	1h	Lack of data on market potential	Written analysis statement of market potential								
		Making of the prototype	Prototype construction or innovation viability check	n.a.	Prototype not viable	Prototype or viability check								
		Identification of active/not active IP protection	Decision-making n whether to pursue or not pursue active IP protection	15 min	No agreement	Written or oral statement								
		Decision to take over the innovation	Decision-making and agreement with the inventor to take over or not to take over the invention	1 week	No consent from the inventor	Written statement, written & signed agreement with the inventor								

Fig. 4 An outline of the activity table for work process innovation identification (2). *Source* Authors' interpretation

Next step is to put in the flowchart the set of flowchart symbols as have been defined above in order to model the process. Once this is done the flowchart allows us to see the bottle-necks and inconsistencies; both by analyzing the individual parts of the flowchart, taking into account suggestions and comments as made in this article as well as consulting other literature or existing good practices (Fig. 4).

7   Conclusion: "Own-It"?

As said, there seems to be a shift toward a more strategic approach to intellectual property and intellectual property protection. Especially in the creative industry this could also be seen as the proliferation of the "own-it" principle; meaning the improvement in the IP creation and IP management processes.

Looking at some of the suggested research areas, we could find that workflow and asset Management inside eMedia Industries is one of often mentioned areas, hence we tried to make a contribution with the present article to this area.

This article presents a way in which the Activity table technique may be a useful, comprehensive, holistic, but still relatively simple way intellectual property protection processes' improvement; finding bottle-necks and finding ways to avoid them as well as include a systematic element into processes usually riddled by informality and accompanied with high level of uncertainty.

The ratio of the idea is—in its final result—to improve or re-design intellectual property protection processes, which allow for a more effective exploitation of innovations and in the end, contribute to higher companies' profits.

Acknowledgments   Work is supported by Creative Core FISNM-3330-13-500033 'Simulations' project funded by the European Union, The European Regional Development Fund. The operation is carried out within the framework of the Operational Programme for Strengthening Regional Development Potentials for the period 2007–2013, Development Priority 1: Competitiveness and research excellence, Priority Guideline 1.1: Improving the competitive skills and research excellence.

References

1. Aguilar-Saven, R. (2001). *Business process modelling techniques and tools*. Department of Production Economics, WP291 Linkoping Sweden.
2. Aguilar-Saven, R. (2003). Business process modeling. Review and framework. *Internatinal Journal of Production Economics, 90*(2), 129–149.
3. Aguilar-Saven, R., & Olhager, J. (2002). Integration of product, process and functional orientations. Principles and a case study. Preprints of the International Conference on Advanced Production Management Systems, APMS 2002 IFIP, The Netherlands, September 2002.
4. Anapindi, R., Chopra, S., Deshmukh, S. D., van Mieghem, J. A., & Zemel, E. (1999). *Managing business process flows*. Upper Saddle River, NJ: Prentice Hall.
5. Blackburn, R. A. (2007). Small firms, innovation and intellectual property management: The context and research agenda. In: R. A. Blackburn (Ed.), *Intellectual property and innovation management in small firms* (pp. 4–15). London: Routledge.
6. Blackburn, R. A. (Ed.). (2007). *Intellectual property and innovation management in small firms*. London: Routledge.
7. Boldrin, M., & Levine, D. K. (2008). *Against intellectual monopoly*. Cambridge: Cambridge University Press.
8. Chan, M. (2002). A framework to develop an enterprise information portal for contract manufacturing. *International Journal of Production Economics, 75*(1–2), 113–126.

9. Chou, T., & Haller, H. (2008). *Reasonable royalty and the division of profit for probabilistic patents*. ASLEA 2008 papers. http://www.en.kyushu-u.ac.jp/aslea/apapers/AsLEA-2008-TeyuChou.pdf. Accessed May 15, 2014.

10. Cohen, W. M., Nelson, R. R., & Walsh, J. P. (2000). Protecting their intellectual assets: Appropriability conditions and why U.S. manufacturing firms patent (or not). NBER Working Paper 7552. Cambridge: National Bureau of Economic Research.

11. DCMS. (1998). Creative industries mapping document, Department for Culture, Media & Sport, April 1998. Retrieved from https://www.gov.uk/government/publications/creative-industries-mapping-documents-1998.

12. Damij, N., & Damij, T. (2014). *Process management. A multi-disciplinary guide to theory, modeling, and methodology*. Berlin: Springer.

13. Damij, N., Damij, T., Grad, J., & Jelenc, F. (2008). A methodology for business process improvement and IS development. *Information and Software Technology, 50*, 1127–1141.

14. Davenport, T. H. (1993). *Process innovation: Reengineering work through information technology*. Boston: Harvard Business School Press.

15. Davenport, T. H., & Short, J. (1990). The new industrial engineering: Information technology and business process redesign. *Sloan Management Review, 31*(4), 11–27.

16. Drucker, P. F. (2010). *Innovation and entrepreneurship*. Oxford: Elsevier.

17. Hall, B., Helmers, C., Rogers, M., & Sena, V. (2014). The choice between formal and informal intellectual property protection: A review. *Journal of Economic Literature*. http://eml.berkeley.edu/~bhhall/papers/HHRS13_IP_choice_lit_survey.pdf. Accessed March 4, 2014.

18. Hammer, M. (1990). Reengineering work: Don't automate, obliterate. *Harvard Business Review, 68*(4), 104–112.

19. Hammer, M., & Champy, J. (1993). *Reengineering the corporation, a manifesto for business revolution*. New York: HarperCollins.

20. Henry, C. (2007). *Entrepreneurship in the creative industries: An international perspective*. London: Edward Elgar Publishing.

21. Holgersson, M. (2013). Patent management in entrepreneurial SMEs: A literature review and an empirical study of innovation appropriation, patent propensity, and motives. *R&D Management, 43*(1), 21–36.

22. Kettinger, W. J., Teng, J. T. C., & Guha, S. (1997). Business process change: A study of methodologies, techniques and tools. *MIS Quarterly, 21*, 55–80.

23. Kitching, J., & Blackburn, R. A. (2007). Innovation, intellectual property and informality: Evidence from a study of small enterprises and some implications for policy. In: R. A. Blackburn (Ed.), *Intellectual property and innovation management in small firms* (pp. 16–34). London: Routledge.

24. Kong, L. (2005). The sociality of cultural industries. *International Journal of Cultural Policy, 11*(1), 61–76.

25. Laguna, M., & Marklund, J. (2005). *Business process modeling, simulation, and design*. Upper Saddle River, NJ: Pearson Education Inc.

26. Lanjouw, J. O., & Schankerman, M. (2004). Protecting intellectual property rights: Are small firms handicapped? *Journal of Law and Economics, 47*(1), 45–74.

27. Lemley, M. A., & Shapiro, C. (2005). Probabilistic patents. *Journal of Economic Perspectives, 19*(2), 75–98.

28. Levin, R. C., Klevorick, A. K., Nelson, R. R., & Winter, S. G. (1987). Appropriating the returns from industrial research and development. *Brookings Papers on Economic Activity, 3*, 783–831.

29. Lugmayr, A. (2013a) Research themes in information systems & management research in creative eMedia industries. In: Proceeding Academic MindTrek'13, Proceedings of International Conference on Making Sense of Converging Media (pp. 329–330). New York, NY: ACM.

30. Lugmayr, A. (2013b). Brief introduction into information systems and management research in media industries. 2013 IEEE International Conference on Multimedia and Expo Workshops (ICMEW) (pp. 1–6).
31. Lugmayr, A. (2013c). Issues & approach in defining a European Research Agenda on information systems and management in creative eMedia industries. In E. Stojmenova & A. Lugmayr (Eds.), Proceedings of the 1st Workshop on Defining a European Research Agenda on Information Systems and Management in eMedia Industries (in conjunction with eBled, Bled, Slovenia) (pp. 17–25). Bled, Slovenia: Lugymedia Inc., International Ambient Media Organization (AMEA).
32. Lugmayr, A., Serral, E., Scherp, A., Pogorelc, B., & Mustaquim, M. (2013). Ambient media today and tomorrow. In *Multimedia tools and applications* (pp. 1–31).
33. Macdonald, S. (2004). When means become ends: Considering the impact of patent strategy on innovation. *Information Economics and Policy, 16*, 135–158.
34. Malerba, F. (2006). Sectoral systems: How and why innovation differs across sectors. In J. Fagerberg, D. C. Mowery & R. R. Nelson (Eds.), *The Oxford handbook of innovation*. Oxford: Oxford University Press.
35. Martinez, M., et al. (2001). Virtual enterprise—Organisation, evolution and control. *International Journal of Production Economics, 74*(1–3), 225–238.
36. Modic, D. (2013). New views on intellectual property protection in the context of innovation systems (in case of Slovenia). Dissertation, Faculty of Advanced Social Sciences.
37. NESTA. (2006). *Creating growth. How the UK can develop world class creative businesses*: Research Report. http://www.nesta.org.uk/sites/default/files/creating_growth.pdf. Accessed May 20, 2014.
38. Neuheusler, P. (2009). Formal vs. informal protection instruments and the strategic use of patents in an Expected-Utility framework. Fraunhofer ISI Discussion Papers Innovation Systems and Policy Analysis, No. 20. Karlsruhe: Fraunhofer ISI.
39. Ould, M. A. (1995). *Business processes: Modelling and analysis for re-engineering and improvement*. Chichester: Wiley.
40. Raustiala, K., & Sprigman, C. (2006). *The piracy paradox: Innovation and intellectual property in fashion design*. Research Paper No. 06-04. http://ssrn.com/abstract=878401. Accessed April 15, 2006.
41. Sawyer, K. (2007). Creativity as a process and outcome. Paper prepared for WIPO International Conference on Intellectual Property and The Creative Industries, Geneva, October 29–30, 2007.
42. Tang, P. (2007). Management of intellectual property rights by electronic publishers. In R. A. Blackburn (Ed.), *Intellectual property and innovation management in small firms*. London, New York: Routledge.
43. UNCTAD. (2013). Creative economy report 2013. Special Edition: Widening Local Development Pathways. New York: UNDP and UNESCO.
44. WIPO. (2011). *World intellectual property report 2011: The changing face of innovation*. Geneva: WIPO.

Author Biographies

Dolores Modic holds a Ph.D. in Sociology from the Faculty of Advanced Social Studies (Slovenia). Her Ph.D. and recent publications are related to the field of intellectual property rights, innovation and innovation systems. She is an Assistant Professor at the Faculty of Information studies and currently a visiting Fulbright Scholar at University of North Carolina at Chapel Hill in the U.S.

Nadja Damij holds a Ph.D. in Business Informatics from Faculty of Economics, University of Ljubljana (Slovenia). She is the (co)author of several publications in the area of process management and business process improvement, knowledge management and project management. She is currently working at Newcastle Business School at Northumbria University, United Kingdom.

Creative Co-production: The Adaption of an Open Innovation Model in Creative Industries

Kaveh Abhari and Elizabeth J. Davidson

Abstract Advanced information systems enable digital media and creative industries to use collaborative networks to boost creative co-production not only across organizational boundaries, but also across geographies. The initial success of crowdsourcing and other open-innovation strategies encourages these industries to consider creative co-production as a viable option for future development. This chapter suggests a general theoretical framework for the implementation of co-production in creative industries based on three components: co-creation environment, network coordination, and experiential communication. The proposed framework is sufficiently general yet grounded in the phenomenon to guide future research and development.

1 Introduction

Enabled by advance information systems, collaborative value creation (co-creation) can be broadly defined as the process in which more than two organizationally independent creative actors work together to co-create creative designs, media content, or innovative solutions. This process, referred to as *creative co-production* in this chapter, is a new paradigm where creative ideas from various internal and external sources are integrated in a network to generate a new creative content or solution [20]. *Co-creation networks* can be conceptualized as a knowledge-based and technology-enabled creative network, in which self-motivated and self-selected individual actors work together to co-create creative ideas or solutions [10].

Co-creation networks can provide important solutions for the complexities of the creative industries, notably the rising cost of innovation and shorter content life cycles in media industries. These networks can also address some current challenges such as

K. Abhari (✉) · E.J. Davidson
University of Hawaii at Manoa, Honolulu, USA
e-mail: abhari@hawaii.edu

© Springer International Publishing AG 2016
A. Lugmayr et al. (eds.), *Information Systems and Management in Media and Entertainment Industries*, International Series on Computer Entertainment and Media Technology, DOI 10.1007/978-3-319-49407-4_6

the quality and cost of creative content creation in a fast-paced, dynamic networked society. Built upon the collective intelligence of network participants, co-creation networks represent an alternative business model for generating new ideas and bringing them to market from the more traditional in-house media production and individual or firm-centric content generation models.

Creative industries have adopted this approach in different forms to provide useful solutions to the market. For example, companies such as crowdSPRING (creative designs), 12designer (marketplace for creative solutions), 99designs (design crowdsourcing), OpenIDEO (collaborative design platform), and Zooppa (creative marketing platform) directly involve external creative labors in their creative media design. These companies solicit new ideas for creative design then reward the winning ideas or share revenues, based on the external actors' influences on the creative production.

Co-creation networks are typically designed and implemented based on the *open innovation paradigm* [9, 20]. Despite these solid theoretical underpinnings, there is as yet no commonly accepted theoretical framework for analyzing and differentiating these networks [27, 31]. In this chapter, we begin to investigate these challenges by addressing three pivotal questions: First, what are the key components of co-creation networks? Second, what are the relationships between these components? Third, how can these components be articulated or arranged in creative co-production? This chapter first highlights theoretical and practical evidence that addresses these questions and then outlines a framework that hypothesizes the relationship between the key components.

2   Theoretical Foundations

The digital media and creative industries are facing significant challenges in utilizing information systems in cost-efficient and high quality content creation and collaborative production [17]. These challenges range from the creative content creation process to deployment and integration of new systems [18]. Creative industries are constantly adopting new collaborative information systems to address these challenges at four levels of operation, knowledge, management, and strategy. Co-creation network is one of those systems. For example, at the operation level, these systems can advance the media industries towards a smart media environments and personalized contents [19]. The collaborative nature of the new systems can enhance knowledge creation and dissemination across the industries. At the management level, these systems support managers to make informed decisions, for example on coordination, licensing, royalty management, investments, and budgeting. And finally, at the strategy level, co-creation networks open possibilities for new business models and revenue streams [17].

This following section first discusses the notion of open innovation as a theoretical foundation and justifies its adoption in creative industries. The concepts of co-creation and co-creation network are then reviewed to theorize the concept of creative co-production. Then, the important aspects of network-based value co-creation and coordination are addressed.

2.1 Open Innovation Business Model

Although the idea of dynamic innovation dates back to the early 1970s, the concept of open innovation gained prominence in 2003 with publication of Henry Chesbrough's book *Open Innovation: The New Imperative for Creating and Profiting from Technology*. Chesbourgh's paradigm suggested collaboration with external partners to develop and market creative ideas and open innovation as a business model empowered by external creative communities. Theoretical and practical evidence suggests that adopting this paradigm is unavoidable due to accelerating trends in globalization and advance information system use, increasing cost of creative production, and shortened product life cycle [4, 14]. Thus, open innovation has drawn increasing attention as a new paradigm in creative industries, given ever changing market conditions [5, 6, 20, 22].

The concepts of open innovation or co-creation as a business process are mainly rooted in von Hipple's arguments on integrating end-users into the R&D process to better understand potential needs and desire, as well as to utilize their hidden knowledge and competencies [29]. After three decades, scholars and practitioners have recognized the value of external networks in co-creation processes, and as a result, they suggested open innovation as a business model (e.g. [14]). The open innovation paradigm recommends the systematic use of purposive inflows and outflows of knowledge to accelerate internal creative production and expand the markets for external consumption [5]. Based on this paradigm, by sharing risks and rewards, creative industries can integrate internal and external resources to encourage collaborative production, evaluation, and distribution of creative ideas and new contents.

2.2 Co-creation Network

A co-creation network is a typically advanced knowledge-based information system in which actors realize value through reciprocal service exchanges [2, 24]. Creative co-production networks are characteristically creative service ecosystems, in which creative labor (e.g. by individuals, firms, community) is based on reciprocal creative service offerings. In this creative ecosystem, value is co-created through the dynamic exchange of creative ideas between the internal and external actors.

With the rapid growth and use of information system for inter-organizational communication and technology-mediated communities, open innovation relies increasingly on virtual collaboration platforms for facilitation and coordination of co-creation processes. Co-creation networks utilize virtual platforms for networking information, efficient collaboration, and fast-paced creative co-production among members from different working groups [7]. These platforms provide interactive environments, in which creative workers can learn from each other and collectively contribute to creative production process [10].

Although co-creation networks vary in terms of institutional arrangements, business model orientation, and supporting technologies, they share some key characteristics. Co-creation networks are governed by a central integrator (network coordinator) that regulates participation, communication, and contribution of participants. Typically, the process of co-creation (problem-solving) is coordinated in cooperation with independent creative participants and company-affiliated solution seekers, who use a technology-enabled platform to plan, develop, evaluate, and market new ideas. Creative co-production in these networks comprises a wide range of activities such as sharing information, using creative tools, spreading best practices, communicating experiences, combining knowledge from different sources, evaluating new concepts, and supporting commercialization. To better understand and design co-creation networks in digital media and creative industries, we must understand the key concepts underpinning value networks including coordination and structure, solution solicitation mechanisms, individual actor behaviors, co-creation patterns, and supporting information systems. We use these concepts to propose a framework for co-creation networks to guide future research on the development, implementation, and differentiation of these networks.

3   Creative Co-production

Collective action theory and the network theory suggest that collective actions in a well-organized network can facilitate achieving goals such as creative co-production [14]. Hence, creative co-production can be depicted as a series of collective actions when actors have a collective intention to co-create. Creative co-production is a form of community-based ideation and value co-creation with a wide range of applications in creative industries [16]. The process of creative co-production refers to active participation in collective processes of creative idea generation and dissemination as well as creative idea development and evaluation [33]. From the organizational perspective, creative co-production can be a systematic approach to engage various internal and external actors in generating creative solutions to enhance competitive advantages [20]. Adopting this approach, creative industries have developed their own creative co-production (co-innovation) platforms (e.g., Threadless, Zazzle, Cafepress) to engage a community in creative production processes. This interest in creative co-production led to the emergence of intermediary platforms such as crowdSpring and Jovoto, which facilitate the relationships between the external creative community and businesses. The mission of these networks is mainly to establish virtual networked teams, in which creative ideas and innovative solutions are co-developed, co-evaluated and co-disseminated through sharing and integrating operand resources such as creativity, skills, knowledge, and competencies.

In co-creation networks, all creative projects and associated communicative, collaborative, and coordinative actions can create, reproduce and transform the structures. External actors' goals, motivations, and expectations may also affect the structure or even the mission of the co-creation networks. Gloor [10] discussed features such as internal honesty, trust, transparency, and ethical principles that contribute to the formation, stability, and productivity of network structure. Since these factors depend largely on the behavioral characteristics of individual actor communities, actor characteristics to a greater degree than internal rules and protocols, can affect network structure evolution. Since co-creation networks typically have dynamic and constantly changing structures, the co-production framework cannot follow the structure of the networks. Instead, we can use (a) those characteristics that drive structure formation, (b) those that make co-creation possible within the structure, and (c) the goals of structure (network outcome), which exist ontologically independent from the structure. According to Monge and Contractor's arguments on complex system theory [21], the causes of structure are (a) rules and roles, which are collaboratively determined by the network coordinator (central integrator) and other individual contributors (resources), as well as the attributes or traits of the system such as the communication mechanisms and co-creation platform.

4   Creative Co-production Model

This section outlines an initial effort to conceptualize creative co-production with a holistic and relatively universal approach in in the media and creative industries. We model a co-creation network in creative industries using the relationship between creative co-production and four key antecedents: co-creation environment, experiential communication, network coordination and creative resources (Fig. 1).

4.1   Co-production Environment

The co-creation environment is the vehicle of creative co-production in media and creative industries. It is a virtual platform enabling the use of creative instruments to assist actors in learning and practicing creative co-production. The co-creation environment is an inimitable organizational resource offering collaboration opportunities [20] to drive value co-creation processes [8, 15]. Hacker's action theory suggests that the creative actors' contributions are associated with the quality of the environment that they experience as a platform for their actions [32]. Co-creation environment settings also support co-production by providing

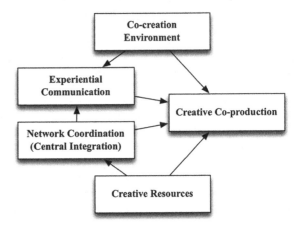

Fig. 1 A model of a creative co-production network

experience opportunities that affect creative labor behavior. These settings have determinative impacts on different aspects of co-creation such as experiencing value, accessing, adapting and integrating resources, establishing relationships, and initiating collaboration [1].

The co-production environment has three important roles: (a) facilitate creative co-production (e.g. by offering tools and interfaces), (b) motivate action (e.g. by facilitating knowledge sharing), and (c) satisfy personal needs (e.g. enabling social connection with other actors). Co-creation platforms provide an environment that can simultaneously enable creative co-production, encourage actors, and fulfill their individual desires beyond innovation. The experiential benefits of these platform (e.g. emotive, social, pragmatic, cognitive, interfacial, and materialistic benefits) can boost intention to creative co-production [12]. Therefore, we propose that:

The better the media co-creation environment design in terms of facilitating co-creation, motivating actions, and satisfying actors' creative needs, the higher levels of creative co-production among participants.

4.2 Experiential Communication

In co-production, actors need to communicate creative ideas within the network to achieve superior solutions. In addition, the interaction between the creative agents shapes the network dynamic and its outcomes. Actors' communication is primarily shaped around the network's objectives and products as well as the actors' communal motivations in performing creative co-creation tasks. Therefore, an inherent part of any co-production network is effective communication to exchange creative ideas and consummate co-production.

In creative co-production networks, experiential benefits play a significant role in determining the level and the quality of creative exchanges among the actors and between actors and the central integrator. The co-production environment can improve three components of interactions: (a) the content of communication, by providing action-oriented materials, (b) the process, by providing practical ways to interact, and (c) the actors, by informing them of events and actions. Communicative action and structures in creative co-production networks are mutually constituent, and provide a frame for sensemaking and legitimization of members' communicative and collaborative actions [25]. Füller [8] also discussed value-based communication as a critical driver of creative co-production in virtual contexts. For example, communication provides actors the opportunity to learn from their networks and allocate knowledge on issues relevant to creative tasks. This process, in addition to knowledge formation, can support knowledge dissemination across the network facilitating the creative co-production process.

Effective communication in co-production networks is competence-based communication, which refers to *experiential communication* by which an individual actor can evaluate, compare and test other actors' skill, competency, creativeness, and knowledge [11]. Experiential communication is thus a medium for collaborative interaction by which individual actors can conveniently test and anticipate other actors' competences and contributions of creative ideas or knowledge. These types of communication are driven by internal transparency and direct knowledge sharing, and work as catalysts of creative co-production. The co-creation environment provides an experiential system to enable this experience before and during collaboration. The co-creation environment also facilitates experiential communication by providing high levels of social and professional exchange among the actors. Therefore, we propose:

The effective co-creation environment design can promote higher levels of experiential communication among the participants leading to higher level of creative co-production.

As noted earlier, successful creative co-production depends on a series of productive communication exchanges between actors [8, 30]. Creative co-production can be thus stimulated when users are engaged in competence-based interactions and communication. Therefore, we propose that:

The higher the level of experiential communication at three levels of content, process, and actor, the higher the level of creative co-production.

4.3 Network Coordination

Co-production network coordinators (central integrators) are the agents responsible for establishing network goals and rules and providing a shared institutional structure for integrating key resources, motivating co-creation, and regulating the participation [13, 23]. The network coordinator pays careful attention to four coordination domains to accelerate creative co-production. First, the network coordinator manages the creative co-production processes in a way so that all individual actors have fair co-creation opportunities and their ideas are not overlooked. The processes are designed to offer the actors the possibility to ideate and collaborate in the areas of their interest based on their personal motivation and/or competencies without limitation. The network coordinator therefore facilitates communication and exchange of information, ideas, and knowledge. Second, central integrators (network coordinator) are responsible for continuous improvement of the network components such as the co-creation environment, socio-professional networking platform, or commercialization platform. Third, as a part of network governance, the central coordinator orchestrates actors' relationships and interactions based on the network structure, rules, and goals. The network coordinator manages actor relationships by facilitating communication and collaboration among actors at different levels. Without maintaining these relationships, network coordinators cannot gain insights about the community and potential markets. Finally, the network coordinator invests in virtual community building to make the business sustainable. For example, by employing various social networking tools, the network coordinator creates a socio-professional environment that not only reflects actors' backgrounds, competencies, interests and achievements but also offers means of communication for both collaboration and competition in creative co-production. It provides the members opportunities to be promoted in the community and involved at a higher level of co-production.

To model co-production coordination based on the above-discussed components, we suggest four core coordination dimensions: (a) ideation motivation, (b) idea management, (c) regulation, and (d) actor relationship management. These coordination components play important roles in orchestrating the collaboration and communication process to boost creative co-production and enhance the productivity of the network. The concept of ideation refers to encouraging creative idea proposition and distribution that can be used to generate or develop creative ideas. Network coordinators are in charge of motivating ideation to maintain the network's productivity. Creative idea management refers to knowledge acquisition, information distribution, information interpretation, and organizational memory [14]. Coordinating actor relationships is also critical for maintaining co-production performance. Lastly, network coordinators need to regulate creative co-production processes for assuring stability and productivity and enhancing the network's good standing. Therefore, we propose that:

The better the design and enactment of network coordination—in terms of ideation motivation, idea management, regulation, and actor relationship management—the higher the level of creative co-production.

The network coordinator needs to pay careful attention to the individual actors' interactions with other creative members as well as with the co-creation environment to facilitate a higher level of creative co-production. To do so, central integrators coordinate meaningful competence-based communication between actors that may lead to higher engagement and higher contribution. In order to drive these experiential communications, the network coordinator needs to co-create relationships among the actors, regulate interactions, encourage creative idea or knowledge inputs, and manage the insight distribution and applications. Therefore, we propose that:

The better the design and enactment of network coordination, the higher the level of experiential communication among actors.

4.4 Creative Resources

Creative co-production heavily relies on the integration of internal and external creative resources in collaborative production, evaluation, and distribution of creative ideas and new contents. In addition to operand resources such as technology, creative resources mainly refer to individual or institutional contributors with valuable and rare operant resources such as creativity, skills, knowledge, and competencies. To integrate the creative resources and build a creative networked enterprise, creative co-production processes should be properly designed and coordinated to engage creative external actors with different operand resources. Developing such a network requires a robust information system structure and well-coordinated processes [14].

A network coordinator typically coordinates co-production process and is in charge of resource integration. The central coordinator defines the network rules for creative resource acquisition and integration but not resource utilization. Like other co-creation systems, integrating resources is critical for the network productivity, stability, and survivability. While the network coordinator integrates resources to achieve desirable outcomes, resource utilization is spontaneously determined based on the actors' needs and goals. Hence, the success of creative co-production depends on the availability of resources as well as the capability of the central network coordinator in integrating these resources [28]. Therefore, we propose that:

Availability of creative operand resources is a key prerequisite of efficient creative co-production.

5 Conclusion

Creative co-production networks are still at an early stage of development in media and creative industries. Nonetheless, we anticipate the number of these networks will continue to increase rapidly. This review addressed the theoretical foundations of co-production and proposed a model consisting of creative resources, coordination, experiential communication, and co-creation environment. The model proposed in this chapter helps explain the relationships between key antecedents of creative co-production. Since none of the variables are associated with specific types of actors, platform owners or contents, the model is not limited to any specific network structure and therefore is widely applicable to different business models.

Future research can adopt this theoretical lens to study existing co-production networks for better theorization, classification, and comparison in creative industries. The impacts of these drivers on platform efficiency and general performance are important to be addressed by future empirical studies as well. Exploring the relationship between these components with social, technological, and network-product cortexes could be another research avenue. Future research could also address how co-production opportunities affect actor behavior and experience and ultimately influence the network outcomes. Therefore, understanding creative co-production behavior in the virtual co-creation environment is essential to realizing more value from the development and use of co-creation models in creative industries. Finally, the domain of creative labor engagement in co-production networks offers a rich agenda for future research.

References

1. Akaka, M. A., Vargo, S. L., & Lusch, R. F. (2012). An exploration of networks in value cocreation: A service-ecosystems view.
2. Allee, V. (2000). Reconfiguring the value network. *Journal of Business Strategy, 21*(4).
3. Balasubramanian, S., & Mahajan, V. (2001). The economic leverage of the virtual community. *International Journal of Electronic Commerce, 5*(1), 103–138.
4. Chesbrough, H. (2007). Business model innovation: It's not just about technology anymore. *Strategy & Leadership, 35*(6), 12–17.
5. Chesbrough, H., Vanhaverbeke, W., & West, J. (2008). *Open innovation: Researching a new Paradigm*. OUP Oxford.
6. Dawson, B. K., Young, L., Tu, C., & Chongyi, F. (2014). Co-innovation in networks of resources—A case study in the Chinese exhibition industry. *Industrial Marketing Management, 43*(3), 496–503.
7. Fan, S., Sia, C., & Zhao, J. (2012). *Towards collaboration virtualization theory. PACIS, 2012*, 1–8.
8. Füller, J. (2010). Refining virtual co-creation from a consumer perspective. *California Management Review, 52*(2), 98–122.
9. Gassmann, O., Enkel, E., & Chesbrough, H. (2010). The future of open innovation. *R&D Management, 40*(3), 213–221.
10. Gloor, P. A. (2006). *Swarm creativity: competitive advantage through collaborative innovation networks*. New York: Oxford University Press.
11. Golfetto, F. (2003). Communicating competence. An Experiential Communication approach for business markets. In *Proceedings of the 19th IMP-Conference. Lugano, Switzerland*.
12. Jeppesen, L. B., & Frederiksen, L. (2006). Why do users contribute to firm-hosted user communities? The case of computer-controlled music instruments. *Organization Science, 17* (1), 45–63.
13. Kahnert, D., Menez, R., & Blättel-Mink, B. (2012). Coordination and motivation of customer contribution as social innovation: The case of Crytek. In H. W. Franz, J. Hochgerner, & J. Howaldt (Eds.), *Challenge social innovation: Potentials for business, social entrepreneurship, welfare and civil society* (pp. 293–306). Springer.
14. Ketchen, D. J., Ireland, R. D., & Snow, C. C. (2007). Strategic entrepreneurship, collaborative innovation, and wealth creation. *Strategic Entrepreneurship Journal, 1*(3–4), 371–385.
15. Kohler, T., Fueller, J., Matzler, K., & Stieger, D. (2011). Co-creation in virtual world: The design of the user experience. *MIS Quarterly, 35*(3), 773–788.
16. Lee, G. K., & Cole, R. E. (2003). From a firm-based to a community-based model of knowledge creation: The case of the Linux Kernel development. *Organization Science, 14*, 633–649.
17. Lugmayr, A. (2013a). Brief introduction into information systems & management research in media industries. In *IEEE International Conference on Multimedia and Expo Workshops (ICMEW)* (pp. 1–6).
18. Lugmayr, A. (2013b). Issues & approach in defining a European research agenda on information systems and management in creative eMedia industries. In *Proceedings of the 1st Workshop on Defining a European Research Agenda on Information Systems and*

Management in eMedia Industries (pp. 17–25). International Ambient Media Organization (AMEA).

19. Lugmayr, A., Serral, E., Scherp A., Pogorelc, B., & Mustaquim M. (2013). Ambient media today and tomorrow. *Multimedia Tools and Applications,* 1–31.

20. Lee, S. M., Olson, D. L., & Trimi, S. (2012). Co-innovation: convergenomics, collaboration, and co-creation for organizational values. *Management Decision, 50*(5), 817–831.

21. Monge, P. R., & Contractor, N. S. (2003). *Theories of communication networks. Computer* (Vol. 91, p. 406). Oxford University Press.

22. Origho, A. O., Japheth, O., & Ukpere, W. I. (2014). Innovation through global collaboration: A new source of competitive advantage (a study of Nigerian Breweries PLC). *Mediterranean Journal of Social Sciences, 5*(1), 709–724.

23. Ritala, P., Hurmelinna-Laukkanen, P., & Nätti, S. (2012). Coordination in innovation-generating business networks—The case of Finnish Mobile TV development. *Journal of Business & Industrial Marketing, 27*(4), 324–334.

24. Romero, D., & Molina, A. (2011). Collaborative networked organisations and customer communities: value co-creation and co-innovation in the networking era. *Production Planning & Control, 22*(5–6), 447–472.

25. Sarker, S., Lau, F., & Sahay, S. (2000). Building an inductive theory of collaboration in virtual teams. In *Proceedings of the 33rd Hawaii International Conference on System Sciences* (pp. 1–10).

26. Scholten, S., & Scholten, U. (2011). Platform-based innovation management: Directing external innovational efforts in platform ecosystems. *Journal of the Knowledge Economy, 3* (2), 164–184.

27. Sorensen, E., & Torfing, J. (2011). Enhancing collaborative innovation in the public sector. *Administration & Society, 43*(8), 842–868.

28. Storbacka, K., Frow, P., Nenonen, S., & Payne, A. F. (2012). Designing business models for value co-creation. In S. L. Vargo & R. F. Lusch (Eds.), *Marketing research* (Vol. 9, pp. 51–78). Emerald Group Publishing Limited.

29. Von Hippel, E. (1978). A customer-active paradigm for industrial product idea generation. *Research Policy, 7*(3), 240–266.

30. Von Hippel, E. (2005). Democratizing innovation: The evolving phenomenon of user innovation. *Journal für Betriebswirtschaft, 55*(1), 63–78.

31. Wittke, V., & Hanekop, H. (2011). In V. Wittke & H. Hanekop (Eds.), *New forms of collaborative innovation and production: An Interdisciplinary perspective.* Göttingen: Universitätsverlag Göttingen.

32. Zijlstra, F. R. H. (1993). Efficiency in work behaviour: A design approach for modern tools. TU Delft, Delft University of Technology.

33. Zwass, V. (2010). Co-creation: Toward a taxonomy and an integrated research perspective. *International Journal of Electronic Commerce, 15*(1), 11–48.

Author Biographies

Kaveh Abhari is a lead researcher at STEMD[2] R&D Group and Information Technology Management instructor at the Shidler College of Business, University of Hawaii at Manoa. His research focuses on the adaptation and integration of social technologies to spur learning and innovation. He contributed to several interdisciplinary studies on the applications of information and communication technology in the field of education, innovation management, and business administration. Dr. Abhari has a PhD in Communication and Information Sciences with more than twelve years of professional experience as a researcher, consultant and business developer across industries.

Elizabeth J. Davidson is a professor in the Department of Information Technology Management in the Shidler College of Business, University of Hawaii at Manoa. Dr. Davidson studies how organization members identify opportunities for using information technology and orchestrate IT initiatives. She also studies how new organizational forms develop in social media platforms. A common theme in these projects is the nature of complex, collaborative knowledge work and the mediating role of IT. Dr. Davidson worked as project manager and business analyst in the information technology industry in several Fortune 250 companies in the U.S. prior to receiving her Ph.D. in Information Technologies from MIT's Sloan School of Management. She serves as Editor-in-Chief of Information and Organization. edavidso@hawaii.edu

Part III
Social Media, Consumer, Audience, Human-Computer-Interaction, and User Viewpoints

Marshall McLuhan, Affordance, Mapping, and Human Computer Interaction in Interactive Media

Robert Wellington

Abstract This chapter ties together media and human computer interaction (HCI) theories to work toward an understanding of how people interpret, gain meaning, and engage with interactive media. The concepts of media richness, social influence, and media genre proliferate the information systems literature, and in HCI a parallel can be found in the theory of affordance as it relates to the perception of material and computer 'objects'. However, little has been done to make connections between these theory sets. In this discussion, a theory developed by Marshall McLuhan is described that can be used as an explanation to make connections between these media theories and the culture to context continuum of affordance, and can help us understand how this then affects cognitive processes. Interactive media can then be thought of as having properties of materiality, beyond; representational, temporality, conceptual, and episodal. Further elaboration around the cultural and contextual aspects, of interactivity allow for a deeper exploration of the framework and the implications for ambiguity, equivocality, and emotional engagement with interactive media.

1 Human Computer Interaction (HCI) and Interactive Media

Media, at it's core, being a manifestation and simultaneously a constituent of culture, is often looked at solely from the perspective of being a cultural artefact. Understanding interactive media from an HCI perspective, where context of use is simultaneously as important as culture could be useful. In HCI the interpretation of the function of a control object does have cultural dependency, while simultaneously, often having a physical dependency. Although interactive media, and especially 'e-media' has relied mostly on cultural interpretation, there is a growing need to understand physical representation of meaning within an interactive

R. Wellington (✉)
AUT University, Auckland, New Zealand
e-mail: robert.wellington@aut.ac.nz

© Springer International Publishing AG 2016
A. Lugmayr et al. (eds.), *Information Systems and Management in Media and Entertainment Industries*, International Series on Computer Entertainment and Media Technology, DOI 10.1007/978-3-319-49407-4_7

framework. Hopefully the ideas in this chapter can help structure one perspective on how this may happen.

A paper at a conference in Australia entitled, Making sense of Electronic Communication: Media Richness, Media Genre, and Marshall McLuhan [13] presents an interesting comparison of two of the more common media theories in the Information Systems (IS) literature, namely media genre and media richness, with a third media theory developed by Marshall McLuhan that is less common. Connecting this work to the field of HCI in relation to affordance and mapping, is a useful exercise, as it allows us to apply communication theory in a field where people tend to focus on the 'tangible' technologies and physiological effects; however, at the core of the interaction between people and technology is communication, whether it be physical or conceptual. Holding a well designed hammer 'tells' you that it is comfortable and designed to be held the way it sits in your hand. Seeing a bright red button 'communicates' more significant consequence than the other, not so colourful, buttons.

Media is a very broad term, referring to any and all modes of communication, 'electric media' has been described as having a structural vacuum [10], as the formation of the message within the carrying technologies encodes no structure in and of itself. Individuals seek meaning of the message from clues within how the media has appeared to have been structured. As we move toward media as being interactive and embedded with cues and objects for manipulation, we move away from an understanding of media as being something for consumption or interpretation, toward media that is more deeply engaged with as part of a dialogue of interaction. Individuals then, have to interpret their engagement methods in relation to what they perceive in the message. Within HCI, the concepts of context and culture dually dictate the ways in which the individual makes sense of the affordance of an artefact, and rely on familiarity and enculturement respectively. These terms could apply to interactive media and are discussed later in the chapter.

2 McLuhan

Marshall McLuhan passed away well before the proliferation of computer technology; however, he was present at the dawn of our electronic awakening and has made some comments about television and other communication technologies that could be highly related to our current technological challenges, although McLuhan was of the 'electric' age rather than the electronic one. McLuhan notes that our thinking about technology must change in order to understand 'electric' media, and one might equally extend this to electronic media, based on the content of what he said. Following on from a discussion of weapons as an extension of our body in order to illustrate our changing ways of thinking McLuhan says,

> Our highly literate societies are at a loss as they encounter the new structures of opinion and feeling that result from instant and global communication. They are still in the grip of "points of view" and of habits of dealing with things one at a time. Such habits are quite crippling in any electric structure of information movement, yet they could be controlled if we recognized whence they had been acquired. But literate society thinks of its artificial visual bias as a thing natural and innate [9: 342].

And McLuhan didn't have the benefit of Twitter or Facebook on which to form these ideas, merely television and radio. On the one hand McLuhan questions the visual bias that society has developed as opposed to acoustic. McLuhan posits that western phonetic language sits in a left brain dominance of linear thinking rather than spatial cognition, whereas the suggestion is that a different hemispherical bias may be prominent in new media; however, he also suggests that electric communication is without structure, in that;

> ... there is a component in the automation story that is as basic as tactility to the TV image. It is the fact that, in any automatic machine, or galaxy of machines and functions, the generation and transmission of power is quite separate from the work operation that uses the power. The same is true in all servo-mechanist structures that involve feedback. ... Electricity has brought a strange elasticity in this matter, much as light itself illuminates a total field and does not dictate what shall be done. The same light can make possible a multiplicity of tasks, just as with electric power. Light is a nonspecialist kind of energy or power that is identical with information and knowledge. Such is also the relation of electricity to automation, since both energy and information can be applied in a great variety of ways [9: 350].

In an emergent media based interactive environment, such confining or pre arrangement that has been prominent in computer interaction, through traditional scripted software, is often not appropriate. Media genre do not exist in the media channel, but in the manifestation of culturally structured media instantiations, and this may be problematic in ad hoc interactive media methods.

Some of the ideas that came out of McLuhan's rethinking of media theory was a chart associated with different media, essentially similar to Fig. 1.

This grid was experimental and incorporated many of McLuhan's ideas including, apparently, Frances Bacon's vestigia communis, [8:150], meaning that our human senses have a vestige of commonality, sculptors gain tactility from vision, musicians can see colour in music, and dancers can create 'poetry' in motion. Unfortunately there is not a comprehensive description of the full relationships between the quadrants as McLuhan apparently never included this in a publication; however, what does exist appears to be tantalisingly significant.

Sensory closure relates to the separation of sensory impression with sensory effect, whilst structural impact was not wholly explained it seems to relate to social

Fig. 1 McLuhan's grid, from a description in Marchand [8]	High Definition	Sensory Closure
	Structural Impact	Low Definition

consequence, social objectification, or structuration, being essentially an interpretation within a culture. The terms and the chart suggest that subjective completion occurs at a learned perceptive level rather than at a contemplative level, where structural impact is the link to action, intentions, and consequence. It is here, with these two concepts that we can imagine a connection with the strong cultural and contextual elements of affordance. If we follow McLuhan's thinking we can imagine that sensory closure, subjective completion, and subsequently structural impact relate to the process arising from the physical stimuli through to the socially constructed implications of interactive media or the affordances of tangible artefacts.

To McLuhan the most resounding part of this chart was the distinction between high definition and low definition media [8:159]. The connection to media richness theory is strong; however, where media richness theory associates a level of ability to reduce uncertainty and carry social 'language', McLuhans level of 'definition' is associated with the quality of the evoked image and the amount of processing required by the eye, ear, mouth, body, and importantly the brain, in order to understand the intent. From this perspective, plain text which is considered to be a 'lean' media, or low in social presence, would also probably be considered to be 'low definition' by McLuhan and therefore require a larger amount of processing or transformation to 'find' the social information—rather than not containing the social information in the first instance. So McLuhan would suggest that there is a higher emotional engagement in a low definition/lean media as there is a greater higher function cognitive involvement in the interpretation. On the other hand there is also likely to be higher equivocality as there is a greater subject dependent interpretation. Therefore, a traditional typed novel can be emotionally engaging whilst a high definition movie may not be, a richer media does not equate to greater engagement.

3   Context

When it comes to non-interactive media, context—or context of use—is mostly subjugated by the cultural influences of the media. That is, when the media is populated by a genre of education or information exchange, or is purely for entertainment purposes, then the context of use is much less important in the analysis of the media than the culturally determined message it delivers. If the media was used for instructional purposes such as a 'how to' then we may see an incipient context of use influence. As media becomes instrumental in the interaction with a system, then context of use becomes apparent, and related to the activities of the users of the system.

Here, context will be described in relation to affordances. Context, or context of use describes the manifest physical work or activity that the interaction is involved in. Context, then, is apparent at the physical and the physiological level of the interaction. However, it is more often the case that context is prominent in the interaction of physical rather than media artefacts, although in theory both contribute to the constitution of the affordances, and if we interpret context and culture with McLuhans grid, as discussed below, they contribute to our understanding in sequence.

4   Culture

Culture is synonymous with communication, and most obvious in the concept of media and media genre. Culture could be thought of as being the knowledge a person needs to attain in order to operate successfully in a specific social group, whether that be an; ethnic, professional, occupational, organisational, or special interest group for example. Culture is not purely explicit language, it is also the combination of symbols and behaviours associated with that social group that have meaning to the other members of the group, including the use of, and engagement in, technology. Therefore, culture is most obviously important in the understanding of interactive media.

5   Affordance

Affordance has quite a history; with Gibson [5] given some credit for the original concept, and Norman [11] the popularity in HCI. Gibson promoted the ecological theory of affordance as part of social theory, later referred to in HCI as real affordance. Here, there is the concept of affordance being inter-subjective and inherent in material artefacts or natural objects.

Affordance has been taken further by other authors in the HCI area, such as Gaver [4], Hartson [6], and Turner [12]. Hartson's [6] definitions of 'cognitive, physical, sensory, and functional affordances' have been widely cited, and constitute some theory development from Norman, and some clarity between 'real' and 'perceived' affordances. However, the physical, ecological, and task focus of affordance theorising still dominate and it has been suggested it could be re-grounded using a 'socio-cultural framework' [7], and that Gibson's theory of affordance still needs to be extended to include such phenomena as 'communication, culture, and context' [7:967].

Affordance being synonymous with context [12] is a common perspective, and familiarity with the context being necessary for the understanding of affordance cues. At one end of a continuum of affordance presented in this paper, being an extension of the work in Wellington [13], you have the context (Fig. 2), this is the physical reality that represents human activity and artefacts and that dominates the literature on affordance; however, culture is not context, it is not the physical ecological view that sits well with task analysis, or work flow, it is the virtual socially constructed set of social objectifications (Berger and Luckman [2] that

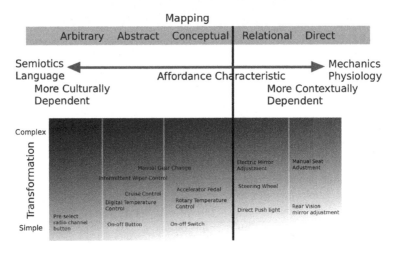

Fig. 2 A unified theory of affordance and mapping

allow us to navigate in a cultural environment. Indeed, culture at its core has meaning and is propagated through communication, and hence the human inter-action with the system, comprising of communication artefacts, is significantly cultural. There are references to affordance as communication [6:319, 1:136], but seldom are there references to communication theory. Considering that artefacts in HCI often have text labels and symbolism it is a wonder that there is not a greater connection to general language and communication theory and semiotics in the HCI literature. Communication is synonymous with culture, and indeed we can find reference to culture in the affordances literature, although it's presentation is mixed.

If we put culture at the other end of the continuum, as shown in Fig. 2, then we have culture (language/semiotics etc.) at one end and context (physical reality) at the other. Culture and context provide two useful points between which a range of research and development strategies into affordance and mapping can be designed.

Affordance theory suggests that affordance cues come from contextually and cultural sources simultaneously. Hartson [6:322] says *"To put Gibson's ecological view in HCI terms, affordances have a relational ontology: their existence as an affordance is relative to the environment of users and usage. In HCI, the user's environment is the work context plus the interaction design."* Indeed culture and context may not be practicably mutually exclusive, but conceptually able to be discriminated. More often than not, culture and context are bundled together or confused in the literature on affordances, and often elsewhere in HCI and Information Systems (IS) Literature.

As suggested above, context and culture are replete in the literature about affordance. There have been some attempts to formulate the relationship between them, such as a layered model (Turner and Turner 2002 cited in [12]), but generally they are considered as being separate influences, and some times part of a classification scheme of mutually exclusive characteristics, such as Fragoso et al. [3] representational, technical, and social affordances. More often culture is considered as a mediator to the way that 'real' affordance is perceived, and although in hindsight this has seemed to be a naïve perspective, when contemplating McLuhan's grid there may be some substance to this relationship.

McLuhan's grid has two stages that intermediate the consumption and interpretation of these cues; sensory closure, and structural impact. These in turn are effected by the relative level of definition of the media. McLuhan also uses the concept of subjective completion, that is not wholly explained but infers the transition between sensory closure and structural impact. As one matches up aspects of affordance with McLuhan's grid it helps to understand the use of common interaction conventions.

A volume control for example either rotates clockwise to increase volume, or slides up. If you ask a roomful of people why, they indicate that as the volume increases it goes 'up', and that is the most sensible and self referential explanation. Higher is more. Similarly, concepts such as 'forward in time' or 'turning on a tap' are so strongly embedded in our culture that they appear to be contextual rather than cultural. When you realise that in China there are vertical references to past and future, before and after noon is above and below noon, or if you go to a Muslim country and find they use a left hand thread on soda bottles, you begin to realise the arbitrariness of many of our deeply embedded cultural norms. McLuhan's grid can allow us to investigate the points at which affordance cues are processed in our navigation of the world, and the implications of changing them.

Sensory closure can be considered to be at the physical/physiological end of the process, where such phenomena as gestalt theory are relevant. Whereas structural impact implies greater cultural significance in interpretation. Physical contextual cues will be subject to some subjective completion, variance in levels of effort of interpretation in sensory closure are likely to impact on subconscious cognitive processes, most of which will not have much impact on emotional and attitudinal associations. Although there are some specific known exceptions to this, for example the difference in minor and major scales in music. In affordance theory, the ecological perspective of Gibson most directly relates to sensory closure, being objective and being of physical properties of things—objective and inherent.

Structural impact on the other hand is responsible for a great deal more emotional and attitudinal variance of interpretation. Learned and habituated response to sensory cues, and the cultural significances of them relate to Norman's perceived affordance and to the body of work of social constructionism. Far from being totally subjective, structural impact relates to social objectifications. However, in the affordance literature these extremes are discussed as opposing theories, but in McLuhan's grid they are stages within a process. In this theory of affordance and mapping below they are treated as being dually influential in the understanding of what a control does, but the continuum distinguishes the range of influence within the process.

The impact of culture and communication on affordance, especially in computing and in media is very important. Taking two different cultures for example, encapsulated in New Zealand English, and Mandarin Chinese can give us some perspective on McLuhans grid. Mandarin Chinese is spoken and written, ostensibly in quite different forms. There are two forms of intermediate versions of Mandarin that incorporate phonetic or tonal properties; Pin yin, and Zhuyin fuhao, both of which were invented for foreigners struggling with the complex relationship between written and spoken Chinese. The way that humans utilise these very different language systems has a very large effect on the way that the human brain works in interacting with technology. Translation between languages is completely imperfect and evidence of the significance of the effect of culture on interaction. Having struggled with an air-conditioning remote control in a Chinese hotel, and having a dictionary and a beginners level of Mandarin, I can most adamantly say that a direct translation of the characters, the symbols, and the functionality was not possible.

6 Mapping

Donald Norman [11] talked about mapping in his seminal book "The Design of Everyday Things" and the concept occurs often in text books on HCI. However, the references to mapping are often quite simple, and the authors will often say that there needs to be 'good mapping' or 'natural mapping'. Wikipedia even uses Norman's example of a stove top from the book. The problem then arises as to how do you define good mapping and what sorts of issues can there be with it, when the treatment in the literature is so simplistic. In comparison with other HCI phenomena there has been very little theory on mapping. Affordance has seen more attention in the literature, with; Gibson, Norman, Hartson, and many others all contributing to a better understanding of it. Prima facie, a theory of mapping cannot ignore the concepts of affordance, as it is this theory that helps us understand how someone might perceive that there is any mapping in a control at all. Similarly, one could argue that mapping is perceived in the interpretation of the control in relation to it's function, which would naturally be defined as affordance. In this way we could very easily conceive of mapping as being a characteristic of affordance.

The model of mapping here is constructed using the terms already used to describe it in the literature. Norman refers to 'arbitrary' mapping, and 'natural' mapping, and often the term that crops up frequently is the 'relationship', as in the relationship between the real world and the control. Where Norman uses the term natural mapping he says that it relates to 'physical analogies' and 'cultural standards' [11], and in the model in this paper this concept is quite literary split in half by an important distinction related to these different categories and then elaborated in relation to communication and social constructionist concepts.

7 Communication Theory and Social Constructionism

Media genre could be considered context in communication, it has some cross-cultural propagation, but is still culturally dependent, and it transcends specific communication channels [13], much as context transcends cultural boundaries and technological platforms in the HCI field. The core of Social Constructionism is communication [2], and similarly many of the tools we use in computer interaction are socially constructed [12:791, 793] and gain legitimacy through communication within a culture {talking about them}, and furthermore, in that the meaning (purpose, utility, what it 'offers' [6:316]) of the tools is communicated through affordance, the tools themselves are communication artefacts. The labeling and referencing through language creates social objectifications, and so it is with HCI tangible and intangible interaction elements. As such, semiotics, denotation, connotation, ambiguity, equivocality, are concepts that are all applicable in the study of HCI, and material artefacts.

Even though affordance is often considered from a social constructionist perspective, there is not generally an incorporation of both ecology and culture in the design and communication of what affordances offer. Creating a continuum from culturally dependent communication cues of affordance to context dependent communication cues could provide a framework to understand affordance better and aid in design choices for interactive media.

8 Mapping as a Characteristic of Affordance

Using a descriminated continuum of affordance to explain different types of mapping is useful at this point, shown graphically in Fig. 2. As was stated in the introduction, the premise here is that mapping and affordance are linked very closely, if not being aspects of the same thing, here it is explained that affordance is the parent concept and mapping a characteristic of it. You can't have mapping without affordance, but you can have affordance without mapping. Although the intention here is to discuss interactive media, it is much easier to develop an understanding of these concepts with physical artefacts, so this explanation revolves around controls in a car, being familiar to most readers.

8.1 Arbitrary Mapping

Working along the continuum from the left hand side, we could consider Berger and Luckmans [2:111] concepts of 'incipient', and 'referential' legitimacy as a move toward the conceptually derived affordance, but to start with, we have the artefacts that have yet to achieve any cultural significance and that are seemingly divorced from context. In this case we call could call the interaction as arbitrary. One might also infer that since no useful information is communicated, then no affordance or mapping exists according to some of the literature. Consider the example in the model of 'pre-select radio channel button'. The car audio unit has a few numbered pre-select buttons, but looking at the buttons, there is nothing that tells you what they do, and the labels are just numbers and the go from left to right, so within the English speaking cultural context it may just look like someone was counting buttons, and they give you very little indication of the exact action that will occur. This category is linked with the basic language and symbolism in the culture. Although it could be argued that arrows on buttons, for example, fall into the next category, and the buttons of 'rewind', 'play', and 'fast forward' on many media devices go beyond arbitrariness. The key test of whether the mapping is arbitrary is whether the language or symbolism have any meaning external to the control itself in relation to the context of use, or whether it simply identifies the control as being unique. At the very end of the spectrum the control is completely disconnected and has no association with the context of use. Media that have no—apparent—interactive properties belong at the far left of this continuum.

8.2   Abstract Mapping

Using the 'pre-select radio channel buttons' again, consider a user that has a partner, and they programme the pre-select buttons so that at one end of the buttons they suit the users preferences, and at the other they suit his/her partners preferences. There is a level of abstract ordering being used to organise the meaning of the buttons, but this is now based on the specific culture evident in that particular vehicle.

Abstract mapping could also relate to culturally created categories or groupings, for example the distinction between what goes into the file menu as opposed to the format menu could be considered to be an abstract mapping. This category is then linked with ontologies, or what Berger and Luckman call, social objectifications, or Norman's reference to 'cultural standards', that would all also extend into the next category 'conceptual mapping'. The abstract mapping may very well relate to a feature of media interaction that needs to be learned in relation to a specific instantiation.

8.3   Conceptual Mapping

When the user can begin to interpret the function of a control based on physical analogies then you at least have conceptual mapping. Relating a control to 'turning on a tap' to increase the volume or rate of activity relates to conceptual mapping. We could also think of clicking on a mouse button to activate an object as conceptual mapping. I have included the 'accelerator pedal' in the conceptual category as there is not an immediate relationship between the movement of your foot and acceleration. Acceleration would be intermediated by a range of factors including the current rpm of the engine, and the demands on the vehicle (load, gradient). The experienced driver uses the accelerator pedal in sympathy with the state of the engine, and the concept of accelerating a car appropriately becomes in itself a well developed conceptually mapped phenomena. To a novice it may still be arbitrary or abstract, and of course that is just one of their problems.

In a media environment such as a video game, conceptual mapping might relate to connections between auditory output and volume control, or playback controls. The concepts of audio and video playback hardware is a strongly formed set of control concepts that the bulk of the audience can relate to. There are strong conceptual models in a variety of media environments, gaming for example offers many concepts that are reinforced constantly, such as the way a car racing game is controlled, or how you navigate in a 'first person shooter' game.

8.4 Relational Mapping

Some of the early conceptions of mapping in HCI were related to a predominantly 'PC' based environment, and so the conception of 'physical analogies' is now pushed a little as much computing is coming out of the box, as it were, and rather than being analogous to physical actions, are actual physical interactions with the actual controls. Being stimulated by driving controls, this theory has a natural physical component, and so the intention of the relational mapping category was that it related to actual physical movements. However, with mapping we cannot constrain the model entirely in the spatial realm. Relational mapping, or any of the other mapping categories for that matter, may relate to sound (pitch, tone), pressure, time, taste, etc. The best way to describe how a control could be considered to have relational mapping is to determine whether the mapping is implicit within the context of use. For example, a wheel control on a train is unlikely to map to steering. Scissors may be considered to have relational mapping, whilst a knife would quite obviously be 'direct'. I see Norman's category of 'physical analogies' being split between the conceptual and the relational mapping categories in my model. Opening or closing a window with a manual winder is just as obvious an interaction with a control in this model as using a rocker button to operate an electric window motor. Whereas, the winder converts a rotational manipulation into a vertical movement, the electronic button uses concepts of 'up' and 'down' to activate movement of one or the other, so where the manual system is relational, the electric one is conceptual. One might argue that the physical displacement of the manual winder, and the translation from rotary to linear, increases transformation complexity more than the tradeoff of introducing the concept of 'up' and 'down'. However, if the rocker switch is placed out of alignment with the direction of the motion of the window, then this could increase it's transformation complexity to make it a worse choice. We find relational mapping in the navigation of 3D virtual immersive environments, in some of these environments with something such as a 'Treadport' the user can 'walk' within the environment as there is a relationship between the walking motion and the virtual environment 'scrolling'.

8.5 Direct Mapping

Direct mapping may also be considered as not having any mapping at all, although that would be at the very end of the spectrum where the control was entirely integral with the context of use. Hitting someone with a stick could be considered to be at the extreme end, and also using a knife to cut something as described in the previous example. Slightly off the end of the spectrum you have examples where you manipulate a control that directly operates something, such as a slide bolt, or perhaps bicycle handlebars. One could imagine that direct mapping could never be problematic, but the ingenuity of designers can sometimes be astounding, and excessive transformation complexity can ruin anyone's day. There is also an opportunity to mimic direct manipulation through the technology. One can imagine that if it appears that the user is directly controlling something even though it is being intermediated by a complex system, then you would still have direct mapping. I had an opportunity to sit in the pilot seat of a relatively old (but still in service) military passenger aircraft whilst I was interviewing the pilots about controls. This aircraft used 'old school' cable technology to operate the control surfaces, and whilst there was most probably a significant collection of apparatus between the yoke and the wing, it felt as though there was none at all. It was as 'smooth as butter' as they say and felt as though you had immediate and direct control with no mediating 'relationship' between the operation of the yoke and the movement of the control surface. You would also feel the air flow and turbulence directly through the controls when flying. In the world of media and immersive technologies, using motion capture and physical motion a user can navigate through a virtual world through directly mapped motion.

8.6 Transformation Complexity

Consider a sliding bolt to secure a cupboard or a door, perhaps a toilet door in an office building. If the bolt has a knob directly fixed to it, and all you do is slide it across to lock the door, then that would be a simple mapping with no transformation in the action, and for all intents and purposes this is the same as an affordance. Whereas, if the latch was fitted with a rotating knob, engaged into the sliding bolt with a gear, then the rotation of the knob would then translate into the sliding motion; however, the knob needs to be rotated in the opposite direction if it is under the bolt as opposed to over it. This would suggest one transformation in the mapping, although you could say it is still a directly mapped action. You can also see in the model that 'steering wheel' is considered to have some level of transformation in the action, where the vehicle direction has a relationship with the degree of rotation of the wheel; however, the relationships transform through the speed of the vehicle, the steering ratio, and the level of steering 'assist' from the steering booster system. There are also occasions where you could assert that the transformation complexity was in flux. Two examples come to mind, one an excavator, the other, the indicators/turn signals on the steering wheel of Ferrari's Italia 458. I have had the pleasure of driving one of these, but unfortunately it wasn't the Ferrari. A common design for an excavator is to have a tracked base on top of which sits the rotating body complete with driver, excavator arm, etc. The driver has two levers available to move the tracks (although the first time you sit in one of these you'll have no idea which of the many levers to use) and you push them away from yourself to operate the two sets of tracks to go forward. Push them together and you go in a relatively straight line, push the left, and you go to the right, etc. However, and this is a big 'however', if you happen to have rotated 180° on the base unit, the levers will have the reverse consequence, and you could drive over something you were particularly fond of, or your bosses car. On the other hand, the Ferrari Italia 458 has indicators/turn signals on the steering wheel, either side of the central boss. This is all very well when you are indicating an intended turn from a straight road, but if you are attempting to indicate a turn off a roundabout then you'll find that the left indicator is no longer on the left of the steering wheel, and quite possibly pointing right or at some obscure angle. Where the Ferrari's indicator problem is only momentary, and once the steering wheel is re-centred the transformation complexity disappears through the perception of the correct orientation of the steering wheel, the problem with the excavator is likely to continue, as the operator has limited affordance in the control itself, but has to work out in their head the transformations by seeing which way the base is pointing, and then determining which way to push or pull the controls. In fact, an excavator parked outside my office, as shown in Fig. 3, shows that this can be so problematic that some people (or manufacturers) have painted arrows on the track units to show the operator which way they go. There are some opportunities to screw up transformations with media, certainly navigating through media within which you can rotate and stretch could affect the relations, concepts, or abstractions of mapping.

9 Using McLuhan's Grid to Interpret Interactive Media

If we take an example of interaction from interactive media, such as a menu navigation using both visual and auditory media objects, we can explore McLuhan's theory of media interpretation, and the theories of affordance and mapping above, in relation to the interaction.

A colleague was working on a game design for both visually impaired and sighted users. Using a tablet and relying on swiping motions, the player can

Fig. 3 Directional indicator

navigate spatially throughout the game. Part of this navigation is through the menu system itself. The menu system can be thought of as being visual and auditory media, you visually navigate from one side to the other of the menu 'swatches', or for the visually impaired, you navigate through a soundscape, where the sounds travel binaurally across space. A problem had arisen, where the swiping motion to travel aurally, was in conflict with the visual representation of the menu movement in relation to the swiping motion. It wasn't possible to reverse the menu order for sighted individuals as this would then run in the opposite direction to the sounds, and it was considered important that sighted users had the same sound experience as the non-sighted, and also that the design needed to accommodate varying degrees of visual impairment, meaning that some individuals may only rely on the visual cues partially. The two media channels needed to match, and the navigation needed to synchronise. One option was to consider the swiping motion as moving liquid from one menu swatch to the next, therefore selecting it. It was considered too much work at that point to implement that alternative, and in hindsight, without the visual information, visually impaired users might get confused if the liquid analogy was propagated into the auditory channel. I suggested that they use a 'target' icon, the swiping of the finger moves the target to the next menu swatch and selects it, it then moves into focus at the centre of the screen. This was considered 'not very zen' by one of the other project participants.

This is a non-trivial problem, and the context and culture of the different users overlaps, but has significant differences within the technological platform being employed. The culture and the context that the player appropriates is in relation to the entire game, that which is experienced, but also the cues that are evident in explicit labels and in marketing and promotional material. The media may be navigated separately, or entwined. The cues that exist in each of the media need to be sympathetic to each other and also have the entirety of the meaning that is associated with either, substantively as individual cues as well. Someone that is going to play a single person puzzle game will have different interaction expectations than someone who is going to 'play' in a group creativity activity, but there is an expectation that they will be married by the menu system, and the interaction in different game genre will be sympathetic to the menu interaction method.

Visually the institutionalised design practice in negotiating a menu is to have the menu stationary and the user selects an element within it. Because the game is designed with the intent of being solely navigable/playable in an auditory way as well, the menu needs to reflect the movement of sounds, and macro gestures on the screen. If I swipe my finger on the screen from the left to the right then I am selecting a sound on the right, and apparently this is a cultural convention. Whereas the menu needs to visually move left.

If we use physical analogy in the affordance of the menu function then we would be reinforcing a stronger involvement in sensory closure, and lesser in structural impact. There may be less equivocality and therefore better 'usability', but potentially less emotional and attitudinal involvement, less fun. If you take McLuhans grid and the models above for affordance and mapping as useful and accurate, then there is not any real chance that the designers could create an interaction method across the two media that gave the same experience. Prima facie, as the media change, the experience must do as well. The mapping of the controls with their functional effect cannot be perfectly matched across the different methods of interaction. However, the interaction through a touch screen, using a combination of gesture inputs, has cultural properties that are weakly institutionalised, and therefore could be re-learned. Much as the 'natural' scrolling direction in a mouse wheel has recently changed in Mac OSX.

Ultimately, in designing a solution for the auditory and visual menu navigation it is important to develop an understanding of both the context of use—the activities and physical flow representations of the artifact, and of the cultures of the different users—in this case, sighted and visually impaired users. It is only with this knowledge that you can determine a design that provides appropriate affordances and mapping that provides the right level of cognitive involvement. Where in some instances you are trying to minimise equivocality, in others you are comfortable with lower definition media that has a higher level of interpretive involvement from the user.

References

1. Bardone, E. (2010). Affordances as abductive anchors. In L. Magnani et al. (Eds.), *Model-based reasoning in science and technology, SCI 314* (pp. 135–157).
2. Berger, P. L., & Luckmann, T. (1967). *The social construction of reality: A treatise in the sociology of knowledge*. Anchor Books.

3. Fragoso, S., Rebs, R., & Barth, D. (2012). Interface affordances and social practices in online communication systems. In *Proceedings of advanced visual interfaces, AVI'12, Italy* (pp. 50–57).
4. Gaver, W. W. (1991). Technology affordances. In *CHI'91 conference proceedings, ACM* (pp. 79–84).
5. Gibson, J. J. (1979). *The ecological approach to visual perception.* Boston: Houghten Mifflin.
6. Hartson, H. R. (2003). Cognitive, physical, sensory, and functional affordances in interaction design. *Behaviour & Information Technology, 22*(5), 315–338.
7. Kaptelinin, V., & Nardi, B. (2012) Affordances in HCI: Toward a mediated action perspective. In *CHI'12 conference proceedings, ACM.*
8. Marchand, P. (1989). *Marshall McLuhan: The medium and the messenger.* Mass: The MIT Press.
9. McLuhan, M. (1964). *Understanding media: The extensions of man.* London: Routledge.
10. McLuhan, M., Fiore, Q., & Agel, J. (1967). *The medium is the massage: An inventory of effects.* New York: Bantam.
11. Norman, D. A. (1988). *The design of everyday things, basic books.*
12. Turner, P. (2005). Affordance as context. *Interacting with Computers, 17*, 787–800.
13. Wellington, R. J. (2005). Making sense of electronic communication: Media Richness, Media Genre, and Marshall McLuhan. In *16th Australasian conference on information systems, Sydney.*

Author Biography

Dr Robert Wellington Robert is a social anthropologist who started his academic career researching communication technology with an interest in decision making and politics. He slowly moved into HCI (Human Computer Interaction) and has been teaching and researching in this field for about 12 years. He enjoys teaching computer science students about people, it is something that they often don't know much about. Robert developed and delivers HCI papers at the undergraduate final year and post graduate levels. Robert teaches in Hangzhou, China, two weeks each year. He also has experience of commercial video and audio production. His hobbies include horticultural pursuits, martial arts, carpentry, bread making, and being a dad.

Towards a Personalised and Context-Dependent User Experience in Multimedia and Information Systems

Matevž Pesek, Gregor Strle, Jože Guna, Emilija Stojmenova, Matevž Pogačnik and Matija Marolt

Abstract Advances in multimedia and information systems have shifted the focus from general content repositories towards personalized systems. Much effort has been put into modeling and integration of affective states with the purpose of improving overall user experience and functionality of the system. In this chapter, we present a multi-modal dataset of users' emotional and visual (color) responses to music, with accompanying personal and demographic profiles, which may serve as the knowledge basis for such improvement. Results show that emotional mediation of users' perceptive states can significantly improve user experience in terms of context-dependent personalization in multimedia and information systems.

M. Pesek (✉) · M. Marolt
Faculty of Computer and Information Science, University of Ljubljana, Ljubljana, Slovenia
e-mail: matevz.pesek@fri.uni-lj.si

M. Marolt
e-mail: matija.marolt@fri.uni-lj.si

G. Strle
Scientific Research Centre of the Slovenian Academy of Sciences and Arts, Institute of Ethnomusicology, Ljubljana, Slovenia
e-mail: gregor.strle@zrc-sazu.si

J. Guna · E. Stojmenova · M. Pogačnik
University of Ljubljana, Faculty of Electrical Engineering, Ljubljana, Slovenia
e-mail: joze.guna@fe.uni-lj.si

E. Stojmenova
e-mail: emilija.stojmenova@fe.uni-lj.si

M. Pogačnik
e-mail: matevz.pogacnik@fe.uni-lj.si

© Springer International Publishing AG 2016
A. Lugmayr et al. (eds.), *Information Systems and Management in Media and Entertainment Industries*, International Series on Computer Entertainment and Media Technology, DOI 10.1007/978-3-319-49407-4_8

149

1 Introduction

Research on emotional processing of audio-visual information is an interdisciplinary effort, comprising fields of psychology, cognitive science, human-computer interaction, machine learning and music information retrieval among others. Studies range from theoretical and experimental research on music cognition [1], to practical applications in music information retrieval (MIR) [2–4]. Music cognition is a particularly emotional experience, affected by individual's personal traits, music preferences, temporary mood and emotions, as well as individual's demographic background (age, gender, education). Current MIR research aims to integrate these parameters into the development of algorithms for computational analysis of music and music-related context. From the perspective of human-computer interaction (HCI), the main challenge is to reduce the complexity of interactions between audio-visual modalities and tailor user-specific parameters into the functionality of a system.

In this chapter, we present our findings and discuss possible applications towards a multi-modal and context-dependent personalization in multimedia and information systems. Our overall aim is to provide a multi-modal dataset of mood dependent emotional and color responses to music by capturing a variety of personal aspects, which, concurrently or as long-term features, influence users' perception of music and colors. For this purpose, we introduce a methodology and novel interfaces for modeling emotional and multi-modal interactions, as well as user feedback. We explore these interactions and discuss how our findings could be extended to a multi-modal and context-dependent personalization of multimedia and information systems.

The chapter is structured as follows: Sect. 2 presents related work on this interdisciplinary topic. The methodology and novel interfaces for gathering users' responses are presented in Sect. 3, while Sect. 4 discusses the results of preliminary analysis of the dataset. Possible applications of our findings are discussed in Sect. 5 along with an application of machine learning exploring the connection between the visual and emotional modality. Section 6 concludes the chapter with ideas for future work.

2 Related Work

Due to the interdisciplinary nature of the topic, the chapter presents viewpoints from several fields of research. We start by an overview of music information retrieval research, specifically in domain of audio mood estimation for purpose of music recommendation. Next, we discuss the user-oriented approach to music visualization. Finally, we investigate the general applicability of our research in domains of information and multimedia systems, focusing on human computer interaction for the purpose of improving user experience and personalization of the system.

2.1 Applications in Music Information Retrieval

Music information retrieval (MIR) deals, among others, with two generalised tasks of observing information in music: feature extraction for music recommendation, and music visualization for music analysis.

2.1.1 Audio Mood Estimation

The topic of mood estimation links MIR to research in psychology and music cognition. The goal of audio mood estimation is to find algorithms that can extract (usually the perceived) mood from a given audio recording. Mood and emotions are generally modeled in two ways: as discrete (modelling emotions as discrete categories) or as dimensional (modelling emotions as set of non-discrete and overlapping dimensions). Perhaps the most known and used emotion model is Russell's Circumplex model of affect [5]. This is a two dimensional model, where mood and emotions can be rated along the two dimensional coordinate space of *valence* and *arousal*. Variations of Russell's model have been used in several music-related studies, for example [6–9]. For evaluation of the algorithms, authors usually use annotated datasets (the *ground truth*), which are commonly derived from a survey involving a number of annotators. Several mood datasets have been collected over the years. Eerola et al. [10] gathered an annotated dataset of 361 film music clips with a single average emotional rating within a three-dimensional valence-arousal-tension space. The Mood Swings Turk Dataset contains on average 17 valence-arousal ratings for a set of 240 popular music audio clips [11]. The Cal500 dataset provides mood labels for 500 western popular songs [12], with three annotations per song. The MTV Music Dataset contains 5 bipolar valence-arousal ratings for 192 popular songs [13] from the MTV channel playlists. Using the GEMS-9 model, Aljanaki et al. [14] gathered over 8000 responses by 1778 participants on a set of 400 excerpts of classical, rock, pop and electronic music. The All Music Guide (AMG) 5 mood clusters were proposed by Hu and Downie in 2007, to "reduce the diverse mood space into a tangible set of categories" [15]. Several studies used the proposed approach in a variety of task-specific applications, e.g. [7, 9]. For comparison of dimensional and discrete emotion models Eerola et al. [10] gathered a dataset of 110 film music excerpts annotated by 116 non-musicians.

2.1.2 Music Visualization

User-oriented research on music visualization has been largely neglected in the past [16], but recent attempts (e.g., the Grand challenge at Mirex evaluation exchange initiative[1]) indicate a growing interest in this domain. There are numerous attempts of providing visualizations for a variety of music and audio features, from low-level spectral features to high-level music patterns and music meta data [17]. There are two main categories of music visualizations: visualizations of music parameters (e.g. harmonies, temporal patterns and other music entities) [18–21], and visualizations of virtual spaces representing relationships among different music pieces. The latter are more suitable for music recommendation systems and for systems using data exploration in general. Examples include a visualization of musical pieces in a form of thumbnail images by Yoshii and Goto [22], a visualization for a personal library information system [23], and a visualization of the information system for exploration of collections, especially designed for small-screen devices [24, 25]. Julia and Jorda [26] developed the visualization for exploring large collections of music in tabletop applications, extending user interaction beyond the standard keyboard/mouse interface, whereas Lamere and Eck [27] developed the visualization for three-dimensional space.

Nevertheless, visualizations in most existing music information systems are generally not based on any formal set reflecting 'real world' color-music associations, as the research on interactions between audio-visual modalities is still in its initial stage. General limitations of proposed music information systems exist due to a lack of systematic analysis and integration of cognitive processes related to music. Existing MIR datasets are limited both in the scope (e.g., number of music excerpts and variety of genres) and user context (music experience and preferences), as well as in the number of annotations per music excerpt. Moreover, more complex approaches to music research, aimed at integrating different perceptual modalities, which could give us additional insight into human music processing, are yet to be explored.

2.2 Information and Multimedia Systems

In the following part we briefly describe the state of the art. The future predictions regarding information and multimedia systems are included. We briefly describe the state of the art in the first subsection, and later focus on the human computer interaction aspect as one of the leading fields in multi-modal applications.

2.2.1 Perspectives

According to [28] there are five distinct perspectives on information systems and management in media industries: technological perspective, information perspective, human perspective, organizational perspective, and management. We will

---

[1]http://www.music-ir.org/mirex/wiki/2014:GC14UX.

shortly discuss the impact of the first three. Technological perspective deals with the development of software, hardware, algorithms and information networks, to handle information. Information perspective sees the latter as the core asset and strategic resource of an information system. Human perspective investigates conditions related to human processing of information and interaction with the system, integrating system usability with design aspects, knowledge management and representation. All three perspectives converge.

"The medium is the message! And the message was literacy, media democracy and music charts. Mostly one single distinguishable medium such as TV, the Web, the radio, or books transmitted the message. Now in the age of ubiquitous and pervasive computing, where information flows through a plethora of distributed interlinked media—what is the message ambient media will tell us?" state the authors in [29].

With the rapid evolution of multimedia and Internet technologies, the evolution of networked multimedia platforms followed by a convergence towards digital information representation and conveyance. For example, digital television is the manifestation of the trend, evolving from the passive and rigid medium towards a fully interactive environment supporting a plethora of innovative service schemes. The possibilities of a digital environment extend far beyond the rigid service space of analogue appliances enabling the combination of audio-visual information and interactive services, traditionally perceived as foreign to physical media.

Two of the trends, which are especially apparent in the digital environment, are social and collaborative interactive communication in convergence with the Internet as the information, communication and collaboration media [30]. Thus, the importance of human perspective cannot be overlooked in a digital world. How people deal with digital technologies has a significant influence on the design and development of multimedia and information systems. Regardless of all the other aspects, when designing an application, a service, a product, the integration of a human aspect into interactive modalities (e.g. user interface and interaction) of the system is one of the crucial factors of success or failure. Not only in terms of usability and overall user experience, but also in terms of the survival of the system.

2.2.2 Human Computer Interaction

The concept of Human Computer Interaction (HCI) first came into existence with the development of interfaces needed to interact with modern day computers. HCI focuses on functionality, usability and user experience and requires the integration of three core aspects: the human aspect, the system (technological aspect) and the interaction procedure/mode between them. The field is rapidly evolving towards the design of multi-modal architectures,—multi-modal human-computer interaction (MMHCI) [31]—and connecting different areas of HCI, computer vision and signal processing, psychology, cognitive science and artificial intelligence, among many others. In future, computing will move to the background, weaving itself into the fabric of our everyday living spaces and projecting the user into the foreground. To realize this prediction, next-generation computing should develop anticipatory user interfaces which are human-centered and based on naturally occurring multi-modal human interaction with the world. These interfaces will transcend the traditional keyboard and mouse metaphor and have the capacity to understand and emulate human communicative intentions as expressed through language and behavioural cues, including affective and social signals [32].

The capability to understand, not only the purely functional and logical part of human-computer interaction, but also the subtle (and sometimes illusive and illogical) emotional part of human communication, is becoming one of the most researched topics in HCI, commonly termed 'affective computing' [33]. The aim of affective computing [34] is to simulate human emotional (cap)abilities by computational means, by observing, interpreting and generating affect features involved in human information processing. This strong interest is driven by a wide spectrum of promising applications in many areas, such as virtual reality, smart surveillance, multi-modal interfaces, wearable computing, etc., with the overall aim to provide an improved, more intuitive and pleasant human-computer interaction.

3 Methodology

In order to evaluate interactions in emotional processing of color and music, we performed an online survey and gathered over 7000 user responses on a set of emotional labels, colors and music excerpts. Additionally, users' demographic and background information (e.g.: age, music experience and genre preference), as well as their current mood, have been recorded. To our knowledge, there is no comparable dataset offering user ratings on emotion-color-music associations.

This section discusses the methodological procedure. Firstly, we elaborate on the preliminary survey for selection of emotion labels used in the survey, and introduce two novel user interfaces for gathering user feedback, MoodStripe and MoodGraph. Next, we present the structure of the survey. Finally, we present the evaluation of overall user experience, and separately, the evaluation of MoodStripe and MoodGraph interfaces in comparison with traditional approaches to gathering user responses.

3.1 Preliminary Survey

As the main focus of our study is on emotional processing, our first step was to define sets of emotion labels to be used in the survey. We have conducted a comparative analysis on emotion label sets used in psychology and music research literature. We found there are no universally accepted sets of labels, beyond the set of basic emotions proposed by [35]. Thus, preliminary survey was conducted in order to establish a relevant set of emotion labels.

Initially, a large set of emotion labels was used in order to determine their relevance and select a subset that best describes participants' perception of individual emotions. In the preliminary survey, 63 participants were asked to describe their current emotional state through a set of 48 emotion labels, each graded with the Likert intensity-scale from 1 (inactive/completely absent) to 7 (significantly expressed). The principal component analysis of the gathered data revealed the first three components explained more than 64 % of the variance in the dataset. We chose 17 emotion labels that strongly correlated with the first three components, for our basic set of emotions, the rest of the labels were discarded.

Similar approach was used to gather a set of colors that best describes individual emotions. The participants were asked to choose colors on a continuous color wheel. The results indicated that the continuous color wheel was too complex for some participants. Thus, we adapted the color-choosing procedure and introduced a modified discrete-scale color wheel, with a set of 49 colors displayed as large tiles. Our goal was to provide good balance between the complexity of the full continuous color wheel and limitations of a smaller subset of colors.

An important finding of preliminary survey was users' feedback on emotional model. Traditional Likert scale presented an additional task load, as each emotion had to be rated within separate scale. To avoid the complexity and task load, we developed two novel graphical user interfaces for gathering mood and emotion ratings, the MoodStripe and the MoodGraph, described further on.

3.2 Main Survey

The findings from preliminary survey were implemented into the on-line survey. The survey is divided into three parts. The first part contains basic demographic questions, including questions regarding participant's musical experience. The second part focuses on participants' current mood and their perception of emotions and associated colors. The third part focuses on emotional processing of music and color associations.

3.2.1 Demographic Data

To evaluate how participants' personal characteristics influence their perception of emotions, colors and music, the participants were asked a set of questions, shown in Table 1. The set contains three demographic-oriented questions, two questions related to participants' musical background, and two questions inquiring about medications and drug use (we considered them necessary in order to detect possible discrepancies).

We intentionally avoided the use of a larger set, as the focus of the survey is on perception of emotions, colors and music, a very demanding task in itself. We aimed for an average total length of 15 min.

Table 1 Part 1: Demographic questions. Each question is provided with a set of possible answers (2nd column) and optional comments (3rd column)

Question	Range	Comments
Age	[5, 99]	In years
Gender	{Male, Female}	
Area of living	{City, rural area}	
Music school attendance	[0, 20]	In years, 0—meaning not attending
Instrument playing or singing	[0, 20]	In years, 0—meaning not attending
Usage of drugs	{Yes, no}	Is participant using drugs
Influence of drugs	{Yes, no}	Is participant under the influence of drugs when filling the survey
Genre preference	{Classical, Opera, Country, Folk, Latin, Dance/Disco, Electronic, RnB/Soul, Hip Hop/Rap, Reggae, Pop, Rock, Alternative, Metal, Blues, Jazz, Vocal, Easy Listening, New Age, Punk}	Up to three preferred genres (at least one) can be selected starting with the most preferred genre
Time listening to the music	{Less than 1, 1–2, 2–3, more than 3}	In hours per day

The responses provide some background information about the participant's music experience and preferences

3.2.2 Part 2: Gathering Participant's Ratings of Mood, Emotions and Colors

The second part of the survey is designed to capture information about the participants' current mood, their perception of emotions and colors associated with individual emotions. Both mood and emotions are being rated along the two-dimensional valence-arousal space. The structure is outlined in Table 2.

Firstly, the participants were asked to describe their current mood and emotions by placing a point in the valence-arousal space (Fig. 1). The same approach was used for self-estimation in the MoodStripe interface.

The questions two and five refer to a color wheel, shown in Fig. 2. The participants were asked to choose the best-matching color for particular emotion. The color wheel contains a set of 49 colors.

The question three was designed to assess how participants perceive the pleasantness and activeness of individual emotions in the valence-arousal space. The participants were asked to rate a set of ten emotion labels in the MoodGraph (Fig. 3), according to their perception of pleasantness and activeness of individual emotions.

Table 2 Second part of the survey: mood, emotions and colors

Question	Range	Comments
Current mood	Valence-arousal space	Participant selects their mood in a 2 dimensional space according to the pleasantness and activeness of the mood—see Fig. 1
Color of the mood	Color wheel	participant chooses the color tone most reflecting her current mood—see Fig. 2
Perception of emotions	{Fear, energetic, angry, relaxed, happiness, sadness, liveliness, joy, disappointment, discontent}	Participant places the set of emotions onto valence-arousal space—see Fig. 3
Emotional state	{Active, wide awake, drowsy, inactive, miserable, discontent, disappointment, relaxed, happiness, cheerful, joyous, satisfied, sleepy, sad, calm, angry}	Participant places all emotions onto a stripe with a continuous scale ranging from unexpressed to highly expressed —see Fig. 4
Colors of emotions	{Energetic, discontent, sad, disappointed, relaxed, angry, fearful, happy, joyous, lively}	For each word in a set, participant selects a color most resembling the described emotion

The fourth question is visually divided into three blocks, with six, six and five emotions in each block. The fifth question is presented to the participant in a combination of a word describing the mood and a color wheel for user input (see Fig. 2)

Fig. 1 The valence-arousal space. The graph axes are marked *Unpleasant* and *Pleasant* for the abscissa, and *Passive* and *Active* for the ordinate values

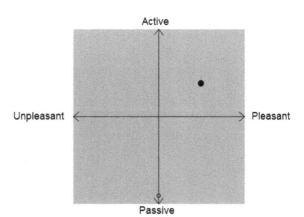

The fourth question was designed to capture participants' current emotional state, by annotating 17 emotions on a scale from unexpressed to highly expressed. To make the task more intuitive and keep in line with the overall user experience of the survey, we designed the MoodStripe interface (Fig. 4). As in the MoodGraph, the participant drags emotion labels onto a space representing activation of individual emotion. To ensure the ease of positioning, the emotions are divided into three separate *MoodStripes*.

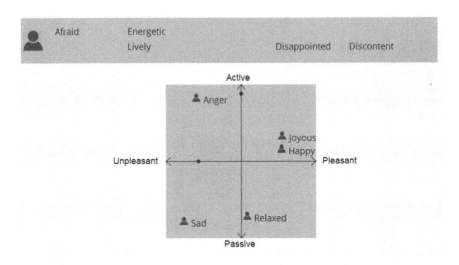

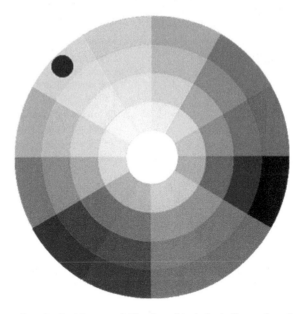

Fig. 2 Discrete color wheel with a set of 49 colors (*black dot* indicates the selected color)

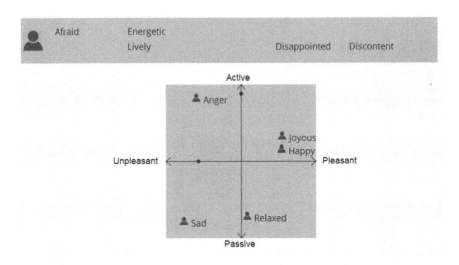

Fig. 3 The MoodGraph: emotions are dragged from the container above the graph onto the valence-arousal space. *Blue dots* indicate the position of the selected emotion in the valence-arousal space

Both novel user interfaces, the MoodGraph and MoodStripe, could be replaced by a set of ordinal Likert scales, implemented as radio button sets for each emotion. An optional feedback form was provided to participants who finished the survey, with the

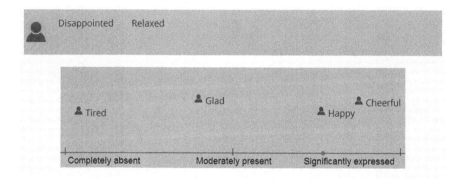

Fig. 4 The MoodStripe: activation rating of individual emotions on continuous scale, from unexpressed on the left to highly expressed on the right (areas of the scale are marked from *left absent* over *present* in the *middle*, to *expressed* on the *right*)

aim to compare and evaluate user traditional and proposed interfaces. User feedback revealed that concurrent rating of emotions in the MoodGraph and MoodStripe interfaces is more intuitive, as well as more efficient in reducing the task load. The empirical evaluation of user experience for both interfaces is discussed in Sect. 3.3.

3.2.3 Part Three: Gathering Participants' Ratings on Emotions and Colors in Music

In the third part of the survey, the participants are asked to complete two tasks related to the emotional processing of music. Each participant is presented with a set of ten randomly selected 15-second long music excerpts. After listening to a single music excerpt, the participant is first asked to choose best matching color for the excerpt (Fig. 2). Next, the participant is asked to place a set of emotion labels in the MoodGraph, according to two separate emotional categories: emotions evoked in the listener (induced emotions) and emotions expressed by music (perceived emotions). The category of induced emotion labels is marked with a person icon, whereas perceived emotion labels are represented with a note icon. The participant may place any number (but at least one from each category) of emotions in the MoodGraph. An example is shown in Fig. 5. Distinguishing between the two tasks is a complex process, but as results of analysis showed [36] the participants were able to rate both categories independently.

3.3 Evaluation of Survey and Interfaces

We conducted a post-survey analysis and evaluation of the survey, with focus on the MoodStripe and MoodGraph interfaces. The evaluation study involved

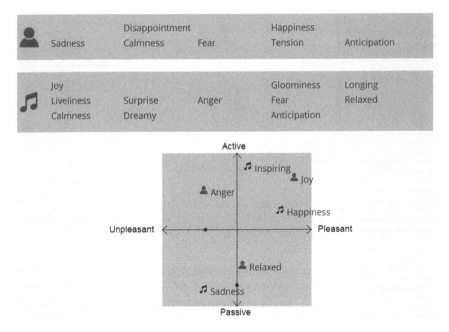

Fig. 5 An example of two-category MoodGraph. Induced emotions are marked with a person icon, perceived emotions with a note icon

participants of the survey. The participants were asked to evaluate several aspects of the survey: user experience (UX) [37], complexity of the questionnaire and both interfaces. Our goal was to determine the functionality and user-friendliness of both interfaces, compared to the standard approaches of gathering participants' ratings. The user interface evaluation followed a subset of the NASA load task index [38] evaluation survey and a set of questionnaire-specific questions. The questions are presented in Table 3. The results are presented in Sect. 3.3.1.

The evaluation was performed in Slovenian language in order to avoid potential misunderstanding of English expressions. The questions in Table 3 are translations of original questions.

The evaluation study presented in Sect. 3.3 was filled-in by 125 participants. This number is sufficient to draw conclusions on various aspects of the survey. Although responses to the first question show balanced mental difficulty of the survey (1), the physical difficulty seems to be more uniformly distributed across participants (2). Thus, it can be speculated that the listening part of the survey represents a physical challenge to a significant number of participants. A subset of participants experienced some frustration when solving the questionnaire (12). The majority spent 11–15 min or even more than 15 min completing the survey (11). However, the cumulative responses show the overall experience of a balanced survey (3), in context of the estimated time spent completing the survey.

Table 3 The structure of the evaluation survey

No.	Question	Comments
1	Mental difficulty of solving the questionnaire	1—simple, 7—extremely complex
2	Physical difficulty of solving the questionnaire	1—simple, 7—extremely complex
3	Time complexity of solving the questionnaire	1—extremely brief, 7—extremely time consuming
4	Intuitiveness of the *MoodGraph* interface	1—not intuitive at all, 7—extremely intuitive
5	Time complexity of the *MoodGraph* interface	1—extremely brief, 7—extremely complex
6	Number of available emotions in categories	1—categories are lacking emotions, 7—categories include too many emotions
7	Intuitiveness of the *MoodStripe* interface	1—not intuitive at all, 7—extremely intuitive
8	Intuitiveness of the *MoodStripe* interface compared to a radio group	1—radio group is far more intuitive, 7—MoodStripe is far more intuitive
9	Time complexity of the *MoodStripe* interface compared to a radio group	1—radio group is faster by far, 7—MoodStripe is faster by far
10	Number of color tones on the color wheel interface	1—Color wheel lacks colors, 7—color wheel includes too many colors
11	Time spent while solving the questionnaire	time spent in minutes – {<3, 3–5, 5–7, 7–9, 9–11, 11–15, >15}
12	Frustration induced while solving the questionnaire	1—extremely frustrating, 7—not frustrating at all

The participant was presented with an image of the MoodGraph (Fig. 5) before the 4th question, images of the MoodStripe (Fig. 4) and a radio group before the 7th question, and an image representing a color wheel before the 10th question

3.3.1 Evaluation of MoodStripe and MoodGraph Interfaces

The *MoodGraph* interface was rated as quite intuitive (4), however, it was also time demanding (5). Considering the complexity of tasks (e.g., distinguishing and rating emotions from two conceptually separate emotion categories) and task load (e.g. number of emotions involved), such feedback was expected. The participants suggested the number of emotions in *MoodGraph* categories is slightly unbalanced (6), and we plan to review and extend both categories in future. The *MoodStripe* interface represents a significant improvement over a variation of the Likert scale (a group of radio buttons), both in intuitiveness (7, 8) and time complexity (9). The participants also indicated that the set of 49 colors may not be large enough, so we will consider expanding the existing set.

The results of the evaluation demonstrate the usefulness of the proposed MoodGraph and MoodStripe interfaces. The key advantages, compared to the standard input types, are the reduced time complexity and task load, and an increased intuitiveness of the interfaces, resulting in a lower mental difficulty and frustration of participants. At the same time, the participants' comments give some useful future directions for improving current methodology.

4 Analysis

4.1 Demographic Data

The data presented here involves 741 participants who completed the entire survey. From 741 participants, 247 were men (33 %) and 494 were women (67 %). The youngest participant was 15 years old, the oldest 64 years old. More than 75 % of participants were 30 years old or younger (Q3 = 28.45 years). This is probably due to the use of the Internet for conducting the survey and the use of social media and public student associations channels for promotion and dissemination of the survey.

Here, we present some general findings. Age significantly correlates with gender ($r = -0.078$, $p = 0.03$), place of living ($r = -0.158$, >0.000) and with the arousal component of valence-arousal space in the current mood ($r = 0.108$, $p = 0.003$). Gender significantly correlates with the amount of years of formal music education ($r = 0.128$; $p > 0.000$) as well as with the use of drugs ($r = 0.096$; $p = 0.009$). Almost 60 % of male participants never attended music school, amongst women this percentage is smaller; just over 44 % of women never attended music school. Almost 12 % of women and just 6 % of men finished primary music education which is a standardised 6-year programme in Slovenia. Music education is also strongly correlated with years of playing an instrument or singing ($r = 0.652$; $p > 0.000$). The most popular music genre is rock, which was chosen as the favorite genre by 31 % of participants. It was followed by pop which is the favourite genre of 17 % of participants. More than 5 % of participants voted for alternative and classical music as their favourite genres. Other genres received significantly less than 5 % of the votes. As a second favourite genre, 20 % of participants chose rock, whereas pop received 14 % of votes. There is higher variance between the genres in the second-favourite genre group. Classical music was the most chosen genre as the third-favourite (13 %). It was followed by rock (12 %) and pop (10 %). The choice of the first-favourite genre is correlated with age (Spearman rho = -0.094, $p = 0.011$), and the time a participant spends listening to music (Spearman rho = -0.111, $p = 0.002$). First, second and third choices of preferred genre also negatively correlate amongst each other as a logical consequence of mutual exclusion of the selection.

4.2   Analysis: Music, Colors and Emotions

In what follows, we present some general findings on the interplay between emotions, colors and music, gathered from the analysis of the Moodo dataset.

4.2.1   Emotional Mediation of Color and Music

One important aspect of context-dependent user experience and interaction is how various modalities are being represented and integrated in the system. In the field of MIR recommender systems much emphasis is typically given to the system focus design and development of algorithms that rely on the data within music, much less so on the data about users and their perception and use of music. The aim of the Moodo dataset is the latter: to study interactions between auditory and visual (color) modalities and the effects emotions have on both. For example, we know from the previous studies on multi-modal perception that associations between music and colors use emotional mediation as an underlying mechanism [39, 40]. Furthermore, results show that abstract musical dimensions (e.g. mode) are associated with specific color hues as well as changes in saturation and lightness, whereas emotional mediation is also evident in color ratings along happy-sad or energetic-relaxed emotional dimensions [40]. Further evidence for direct emotional mediation of both modalities is given by [36] and in the following analysis.

The results of a two-part study show a strong contrast between valence-arousal ratings of individual emotions and their color associations in non-music context (emotion-color associations) and in music context (emotion-color-music associations), as shown in Figs. 6 and 7 respectively. Note that the data is taken from the

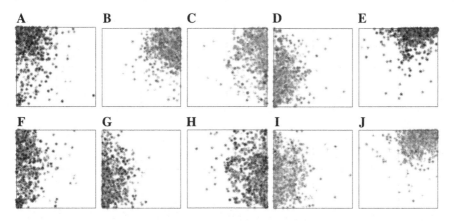

Fig. 6 User ratings of emotions and associated colors for the 10 emotion labels in the valence-arousal space (without music): *A* Anger, *B* Joy, *C* Happiness, *D* Disappointment, *E* Energetic, *F* Fear, *G* Sadness, *H* Relaxation, *I* Discontent, and *J* Liveliness. This set refers to the second part of the survey

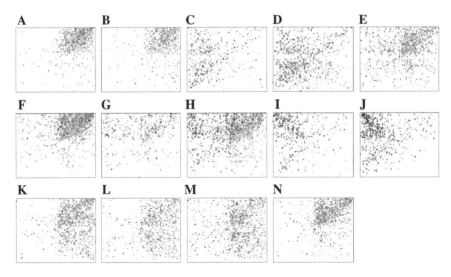

Fig. 7 User ratings of emotional and color perception of music for each of the 14 emotion labels in the valence-arousal space: *A* Joy, *B* Happiness, *C* Sadness, *D* Gloominess, *E* Longing, *F* Liveliness, *G* Surprise, *H* Anticipation, *I* Anger, *J* Fear, *K* Relaxed, *L* Calmness, *M* Dreamy, and *N* Inspiring. This set refers to the third part of the survey

second and third part of the survey by gathering users' valence-arousal ratings of emotions and their color associations in the second part, and in the third part, by asking users to associate color and then select and rate emotions expressed by individual music excerpts in the valence-arousal space. Slightly different emotion label sets were used in each part (the decision taken based on the previous studies [41]), where researchers found some emotion labels are more relevant in music context than others.

Figure 6 shows color associations for individual emotions, without music. The results are generally in line with the previous research [40, 42], with light green hues for happiness (C) and more vibrant red-yellow-green hues for joy and liveliness (B and J), with strong red hues typically associated with emotions characteristic for high activity, such as energetic (D). Negative emotions, such as anger, fear and sadness (A, F and G) are associated with more hues, such as blue, violet and black. Positions of the individual emotions in the valence-arousal space are in agreement with how they are usually modeled (e.g. compare anger (A) and sadness (G): both are characterized as unpleasant, but differ in their activity). There are a few noticeable exceptions in regard to color. For example, bright red-green-yellow hues for disappointment (D) and discontent (I) do not match its characterization as an unpleasant emotion and its position in valence-arousal space. On the other hand, relaxation (H) is occupying the positive position on the valence dimension, but with dark blue-violet-black hues characteristic of negative emotions.

In music context (Fig. 7) emotion-color associations change considerably. Here, emotions occupy a more central position in the valence-arousal space, compared to the emotion-color ratings in the non-music context from Fig. 6. The distribution of individual ratings is also significantly larger (e.g. distribution of sadness (C) over positive part of valence-arousal space), and hues associated with individual emotions are also different. Red hues prevail over dark blue-violet-black hues in negative emotions (e.g. anger (I) and fear (J)), and also over green-yellow hues in positive emotions of joy (A) and happiness (B). Green dominates in pleasant emotions of relaxation, calmness and dreaminess (K, L and M).

The results from both Figures are only a glance into the emotional mediation of both modalities, but can nevertheless give us an important insight: emotions and colors are being perceived differently depending on the context. For example, even sad music can sometimes be perceived as pleasant, and negative emotions in music are generally attributed to brighter hues.

4.3   Applying Machine Learning

To show the overall usefulness of our multi-modal dataset for information and multimedia systems, we present a machine learning approach to evaluate interdependencies between emotions and different modalities. Similar approach could be incorporated into any multimedia system, making use of the computational procedures presented in the following two experiments. In our first experiment we used the dataset for computational mood estimation. We analysed three different yet related spectral feature types, of which two types (chroma feature vector and Mel-frequency cepstral coefficients), are commonly used for audio signal analysis. In the second experiment, we estimated the emotional state of an audio excerpt based on the color associations provided by survey participants. Both experiments analyzed the emotional processing and interactions between the auditory and visual modalities presented in previous sections, and the results show significant improvement towards user experience and personalization.

4.3.1   Mood Estimation

Similar to [43], we tested the dataset for audio mood estimation. The goal is to estimate mood of a music excerpt based on the features calculated from the audio signal. We evaluated multiple feature sets and compared the results: the Mel-frequency cepstral coefficients (MFCC), the chroma features and the features of the compositional hierarchical model [44]. The dataset was divided into the training (70 %) and testing (30 %) sets, and regression with least squares [45] selected as the machine learning method. The model was trained to predict the mean perceived valence-arousal values (averaged over all participants' responses) for each music excerpt.

The results show that prediction is successful—the average distance between the estimated and actual mean valence-arousal value is around 0.2 (0.5 std. deviations),

Table 4 Results in prediction of valence and arousal values from audio using regression

Feature	Avg. distance	Nearest point	Avg. distance in standard deviation
MFCC chroma	0.2060	0.0595	0.4870
	0.2215	0.0614	0.4993
CHM chroma	0.1862	0.0719	0.4459

Measures represent average distance to the target value, distance to the nearest user response and average distance measured as a multiple of standard deviation of all responses

which given the high volatility of participants' responses, is good. The results in Table 4 also show that the compositional hierarchical model's features give the best results.

4.3.2 Predicting Associations Between Colors and Emotions in the Valence-Arousal Space

This experiment is based on participants' color associations for perceived emotions. We analyzed a subset of our dataset, consisting of participants' annotations of music excerpts, where a single perceived emotion label was chosen and placed in the valence-arousal space. 2950 responses or roughly 41 % of the dataset corresponds to these conditions. We define these *single perceived emotion per excerpt* responses as *typical* responses. Each response contains the best-matching color for the music excerpt, as chosen by the participant. Our goal was to find correspondences between chosen colors and locations of perceived emotions in the valence-arousal space, by training a regression algorithm to predict the valence-arousal values from the hue-saturation-value (HSV) color representation. We tested two different valence-arousal representations: an Euclidean space and polar coordinates. Results presented in Table 5 indicate similar accuracy, compared with previous experiment where audio features were used for valence-arousal prediction. Moreover, in the subsequent tests, we discovered that the whole process can be reversed to predict color associations from valence-arousal responses. This opens up further possibilities for improving prediction of emotional responses by combining both modalities as inputs, as well as by using emotional responses for finding appropriate color schemes and visualizations.

Table 5 Estimation of valence-arousal values for music excerpts from HSV representation of excerpt's associated color

Source features	Valence-arousal Euclidean distance	Valence-arousal spherical distance
HSV	V: 0.208	ϕ: 0.118
	A: 0.135	r: 0.328

The first column corresponds to estimation in Euclidean space, while the second column provides estimation using polar coordinates

5 Applications in Multimedia and Information Systems

Modeling users' affective state, perception of emotions and interactions between audio-visual modalities expands the possibilities for a more user oriented and personal human computer interaction. Just knowing users' music and colour preferences, and combining these elements with emotional processing, provides a small but important step in this direction. The presented analysis shows that significant improvements towards user experience and personalization can be achieved by investigating multi-modal interactions and uncovering general patterns. Given the comprehensiveness of the Moodo dataset, the preliminary findings look especially promising.

Two primary applications, based on the research of the Moodo dataset, are mood and colour enhanced music visualization and recommendation systems. It has been shown, that there is a strong relationship between mood and colour perception for various music genres. The authors [46] investigated the relationship between mood and colour in connection to musical preference. The results showed that both mood and colour are affected by different combinations of two factors, the preferred genre and the music genre presented. Consequently, the feelings of someone listening to music can be enhanced by colour, e.g. by matching the colour of the ambient illumination to the mood evoked by the music played, after the listener's preferred musical genre and the genre of the music presented are considered. The music, whole albums, particular songs or even parts of songs, can be presented in a condensed, yet cognitively undemanding way, by using personalized colour schemes. In this way, instead of the comprehensive and usually complex list of music items, a simple colour bar or a list of colour geometrical shapes could be used to represent dozens of recommended personalized music items at once, corresponding to the current mood if the user, without increasing the cognitive load of the user, providing a better and more enjoyable user experience [47]. Closely related with the music visualization is the contextual music information retrieval and recommendation. The survey in [48] illustrates various tools and techniques that can be used for addressing research challenges posed by context-aware music retrieval and recommendation. The authors cover a broad range of topics, starting from classical music information retrieval (MIR) and recommendation system (RS), and then focusing on context-aware music applications as well as the newer trends of affective and social computing applied to the music domain.

Beside the visual modality, the auditory modality represents an important communication channel in the human-computer relationship, which can take the role of primary modality for needs of visually-impaired users [49]. The purely auditory oriented interfaces, or a combination of auditory and visual interfaces, can be applied to other domains, for example for the use in vehicles [47]. The emotion and colour enhanced versions could provide improved user experience, and possibly contribute towards better efficiency, as well as safety.

Finally, important outcome of the presented study are innovative user interface elements. The MoodGraph and MoodStripe provide a condensed, yet cognitively undemanding way of gathering a variety of different measures in a single component and user task, and both were shown to be better than the traditional approach using Likert scale matrices.

6 Conclusions and Future Work

The aim of this chapter was to provide an insight into several aspects of affective MIR by analyzing correlations between emotions, colors and music. We performed a large-scale user study on emotional and color responses to music, based on two novel interfaces for modeling emotions, the MoodStripe and MoodGraph. The results show that context is very important when analyzing interactions between multiple modalities and should be more tightly integrated into MIR. Using the machine learning approach for mood estimation on audio and color features showed we can improve predictions of emotional responses by combining both modalities as inputs, as well as by using emotional responses for finding appropriate color schemes and visualizations. These findings are not limited to MIR, but extend to all types of multimedia systems that integrate visual and auditory modalities. In this context, the presented Moodo dataset is an important step towards personalised and context-dependent user experience.

In future, our goal is to develop a personalised multimedia recommendation system for music and video, by integrating various modalities into a situation-dependent decision model.

References

1. Juslin, P. N., & Västfjäll, D. (2008). Emotional responses to music: The need to consider underlying mechanisms. *Behavioral and Brain Sciences, 31*(5), 559–575.
2. Kim, Y. E., Schmidt, E. M., Migneco, R., Morton, B. G., Richardson, P., Scott, J., et al. (2010). Music emotion recognition: A state of the art review. In *Proceedings of the international conference on music information retrieval (ISMIR)* (pp. 255–266), Utrecht.
3. Laurier, C., Meyers, O., Serrà, J., Blech, M., Herrera, P., & Serra, X. (2009). Indexing music by mood: design and integration of an automatic content-based annotator. *Multimedia Tools and Applications, 48*(1), 161–184.
4. Song, Y., Dixon, S., & Pearce, M. (2012). A survey of music recommendation systems and future perspectives. In *Proceedings of the 9th international symposium on computer music modelling and retrieval (CMMR)* (pp. 395–410), London.
5. Russell, J. A. (1980). A circumplex model of affect. *Journal of Personality and Social Psychology, 39*(6), 1161–1178.
6. Barthet, M., Marston, D., Baume, C., Fazekas, G., & Sandler, M. (2013). Design and evaluation of semantic mood models for music recommendation using editorial tags. In *Proceedings of the international conference on music information retrieval (ISMIR)*, Curitiba.
7. Laurier, C., Sordo, M., Serrà, J., & Herrera, P. (2009). Music mood representations from social tags. In *Proceedings of the international conference on music information retrieval (ISMIR)* (pp. 381–386).

8. Mcvicar, M., Freeman, T., & De Bie, T. (2011). Mining the correlation between lyrical and audio features and the emergence of mood. In *Proceedings of the international conference on music information retrieval* (*ISMIR*) (pp. 783–788), Miami.
9. Yang, Y.-H., & Chen, H. H. (2012). Machine recognition of music emotion.
10. Eerola, T., & Vuoskoski, J. K. (2010). A comparison of the discrete and dimensional models of emotion in music. *Psychology of Music, 39*(1), 18–49.
11. Schmidt, E. M., & Kim, Y. E. (2011). Modeling musical emotion dynamics with conditional random fields. In *ISMIR* (pp. 777–782).
12. Turnbull, D., Barrington, L., Torres, D., & Lanckriet, G. (2008). Semantic annotation and retrieval of music and sound effects. *IEEE Transactions on Audio, Speech, and Language Processing, 16*(2), 467–476.
13. Schuller, B., Hage, C., Schuller, D., & Rigoll, G. (2010). 'Mister DJ, Cheer Me Up!': Musical and textual features for automatic mood classification. *Journal of New Music Research, 39*(1), 13–34.
14. Aljanaki, A., Bountouridis, D., Burgoyne, J. A., van Balen, J., Wiering, F., Honing, H., & Veltkamp, R. C. (2014). Designing games with a purpose for data collection in music research. Emotify and Hooked: Two case studies. *Lecture Notes in Computer Science*.
15. Hu, X., & Downie, J. S. (2007). Exploring mood metadata: relationships with genre, artist and usage metadata. In *Proceedings of the international conference on music information retrieval* (*ISMIR*), Vienna.
16. Schedl, M., Flexer, A., & Urbano, J. (2013). The neglected user in music information retrieval research. *Journal of Intelligent Information Systems, 41*(3), 523–539.
17. Donaldson, J., & Lamere, P. (2009). Using visualizations for music discovery. In *Proceedings of the international conference on music information retrieval* (*ISMIR*), Tutorial.
18. Grohganz, H., Clausen, M., Jiang, N., & Mueller, M. (2013). Converting path structures into block structures using eigenvalue decompositions of self-similarity matrices. In *Proceedings of the international conference on music information retrieval* (*ISMIR*), Curitiba.
19. Isaacson, E. (2005). What you see is what you get: On visualizing music. In *Proceedings of the international conference on music information retrieval* (*ISMIR*) (pp. 389–395), London.
20. Jiang, N., & Mueller, M. (2013). Automated methods for analyzing music recordings in sonata form. In *Proceedings of the international conference on music information retrieval* (*ISMIR*), Curitiba.
21. Mardirossian, A., & Chew, E. (2007). Visualizing music: Tonal progressions and distributions. In *Proceedings of the international conference on music information retrieval* (*ISMIR*) (pp. 189–194), Vienna.
22. Yoshii, K., & Goto, M. (2008). Music thumbnailer: Visualizing musical pieces in thumbnail images based on acoustic features. In *Proceedings of the international conference on music information retrieval* (*ISMIR*) (pp. 211–216), Philadelphia.
23. Torrens, M., Hertzog, P., & Arcos, J. L. (2004). Visualizing and exploring personal music libraries. In *Proceedings of the international conference on music information retrieval* (*ISMIR*), Barcelona.
24. Van Gulik, R., & Vignoli, F. (2005). Visual playlist generation on the artist map. In *Proceedings of the international conference on music information retrieval* (*ISMIR*), London.
25. Van Gulik, R., Vignoli, F., & Van de Wetering, H. (2004). Mapping music in the palm of your hand, explore and discover your collection. In *Proceedings of the international conference on music information retrieval* (*ISMIR*), Barcelona.
26. Julia, C. F., & Jorda, S. (2009). SongExplorer: A tabletop application for exploring large collections of songs. In *Proceedings of the international conference on music information retrieval* (*ISMIR*) (pp. 675–680), Kobe.
27. Lamere, P., & Eck, D. (2007). Using 3D visualizations to explore and discover music. In *Proceedings of the international conference on music information retrieval* (*ISMIR*) (pp. 173–174).

28. Lugmayr, A. (2013). Brief introduction into information systems & management research in media industries. In *2013 IEEE international conference on multimedia and expo workshops (ICMEW)* (pp. 1–6). IEEE.
29. Lugmayr, A., Risse, T., Stockleben, B., Laurila, K., & Kaario, J. (2009). Semantic ambient media—An introduction. *Multimedia Tools and Applications, 44*(3), 337–359.
30. Bachmayer, S., Lugmayr, A., & Kotsis, G. (2010). Convergence of collaborative web approaches and interactive TV program formats. *International Journal of Web Information Systems, 6*(1), 74–94.
31. Jose, P. T., Miglani, S., & Yadav, S. (2014). Human computer interaction: Analysis and journey through eras. *International Journal of Computer Science and Mobile Computing, 3* (4), 653–650.
32. Pantic, M., Nijholt, A., Pentland, A., & Huanag, T. S. (2008). Human-centred intelligent human? Computer interaction (HCI^2): How far are we from attaining it? *International Journal of Autonomous and Adaptive Communications Systems, 1*(2), 168–187.
33. Picard, R. W. (2000). Toward computers that recognize and respond to user emotion. *IBM Systems Journal, 39*, 705–719.
34. Tao, J., & Tan, T. (2005). *Affective computing: A review* (Vol. 1). Berlin, Heidelberg: Springer.
35. Ekman, P. (1992). An argument for basic emotions. *Cognition and Emotion, 6*, 169–200.
36. Pesek, M., Godec, P., Poredos, M., Strle, G., Guna, J., Stojmenova, E., et al. (2014). Introducing a dataset of emotional and color responses to music. In *Proceedings of the international conference on music information retrieval (ISMIR)* (pp. 355–360), Taipei.
37. Albert, W., & Tullis, T. (2013). *Measuring the user experience: Collecting, analyzing, and presenting usability metrics (Google eBook)*. Newnes.
38. Hart, S. G. (2006). Nasa-task load index (NASA-TLX); 20 years later. *Proceedings of the Human Factors and Ergonomics Society Annual Meeting, 50*(9), 904–908.
39. Griscom, W. S., & Palmer, S. E. (2012). The color of musical sounds: Color associates of harmony and timbre in non-synesthetes. *Journal of Vision, 12*(9), 74–74.
40. Palmer, S. E., Schloss, K. B., Zoe, X., & Prado-León, L. R. (2013). Music-color associations are mediated by emotion. *Proceedings of the National Academy of Sciences, 110*(22), 8836–8841.
41. Juslin, P. N., & Sloboda, J. A. (2001). *Music and emotion: Theory and research*. Oxford University Press.
42. Ou, L.-C., Luo, M. R., Woodcock, A., & Wright, A. (2004). A study of colour emotion and colour preference. Part I: Colour emotions for single colours. *Color Research & Application, 29*(3), 232–240.
43. Schmidt, E. M., & Kim, Y. E. (2009). Projection of acoustic features to continuous valence-arousal mood labels via regression. In *10th international society for music information retrieval conference. ISMIR*.
44. Pesek, M., Leonardis, A., & Marolt, M. (2014). A compositional hierarchical model for music information retrieval. In *Proceedings of the international conference on music information retrieval (ISMIR)* (pp. 131–136), Taipei.
45. Abdi, H. (2007). The method of least squares. *Encyclopedia of measurement and statistics*. CA, USA: Thousand Oaks.
46. Moon, C. B., Kim, L., Lee, H. A., & Kim, B. M. (2013). Analysis of relationships between mood and color for different musical preferences. *Color Research & Application, 39*(4), 413–423.
47. Peter, C., & Beale, R. (2008). *Affect and emotion in human-computer interaction: From theory to applications*. Springer.
48. Kaminskas, M., & Ricci, F. (2012). Contextual music information retrieval and recommendation: State of the art and challenges. *Computer Science Review, 6*(2–3), 89–119.
49. Sodnik, J., Jakus, G., & Tomažič, S. (2011). Multiple spatial sounds in hierarchical menu navigation for visually impaired computer users. *International Journal of Human-Computer Studies, 69*(1–2), 100–112.

Author Biographies

Matevž Pesek is a doctoral student at the Faculty of Computer and Information Science, University of Ljubljana. He received his B.Sc. in computer science in 2012, where he is currently working on his Ph.D. and has been working as a teaching assistant since. He is a member of the Laboratory of Computer Graphics and Multimedia since 2009. His research interests are biologically-inspired models, deep architectures including compositional hierarchical modelling and music multi-modal perception, including human-computer interaction, and visualization for audio analysis and music generation.

Dr. Gregor Strle is a research assistant at the Research Centre of the Slovenian Academy of Sciences and Arts. His works in the field of cognitive science, auditory cognition, conceptualization models, and computer semantics.

Dr. Jože Guna graduated in 2002, defended his master's thesis in 2005 and his Ph.D. thesis in 2014, all at the Faculty of Electrical Engineering, University of Ljubljana. His area of research focuses on Internet technologies, multimedia technologies and IPTV systems with special emphasis on user centred design, user interaction modalities and designing the user experience, including gamification and flow aspects. Currently he is involved in a number of projects focusing on the development of intuitive user interfaces for elderly users of eHealth application and interactive multimedia HBBTV application. He is an expert in Internet, ICT and IPTV technologies and holds several industrial certificates from CISCO, Comptia and Apple, including trainer licenses from Cisco and Apple. He is an active member of the IEEE organization.

Dr. Emilija Stojmenova is a researcher at the Laboratory for Telecommunications within the Faculty of electrical engineering, University of Ljubljana, where she is involved in various research and development projects. She received her Ph.D. in Electrical engineering in 2013 for her doctoral thesis "User-centered Design for Multi-screen e-HealthApplications for Elderly People". One of the major dissertation contributions was the proposal for improving an existing standard (ISO9241-210:2010), demonstrating the practical application of the results in an industrial standard. Her research work focuses mainly in the fields of user centred design and methodologies for evaluating user experience and usability for specific groups of users, such as: elderly people, children and people with disabilities. Previously, she was employed at Iskratel, Ltd. as a user experience manager, where she was responsible for the overall user experience in the company. She is "World Usability Day Slovenia" conference chair, IEEE Women in engineering (WIE) Slovenia section chair and an active member of IEEE, ACM UxPA, IxDA. Since September 2013, she is actively involved in the Demola Network as the head of RAZ:UM, Demola Slovenia operator. In Demola project ideas and needs come from the project partners, companies and organizations or international Demola Network partners.

Dr. Matevž Pogačnik is working as an associate professor at the University of Ljubljana. He is very active in the field of interactive multimedia services development, mores specifically in the fields of mobile applications, IPTV/smartTV applications and digital TV services. His recent research work has been mostly focused on improvement of user experience and introduction of new interaction modalities. He is also a member of the international organisation IEEE.

Dr. Matija Marolt is assistant professor with Faculty of Computer and Information Science, University of Ljubljana, where he has been working since 1995. He is head of Laboratory for Computer Graphics and Multimedia, where his research interests include music information retrieval, specifically semantic description and understanding of audio signals, retrieval and organization in music archives and human-computer interaction.

Using Social Media as a Mechanism to Consolidate the Organizational Memory—Insights from the Attention Based View of the Firm Theory

Victor F.A. Barros and Isabel Ramos

Abstract Increasingly, organizations are aware that the knowledge generated in the organization over time is a primary factor to remain competitive in the market. This leads organizations to seek strategies that preserve this knowledge generated over time and create mechanisms to encourage its employees to use part of this accumulated knowledge, in the generation of innovative products and strategies, on solving problems as well as in decision-making. In this potentiating process, the Organizational Memory (OM) comes in the interim as a way of conceptualizing how is this process of creation, storage and dissemination of knowledge in the organization over time and how the knowledge accumulated by members of an organization can influence the actions and decisions, both in the present and the future of the organization. For this development of OM to be effective and harmonious, it is necessary that the attention of individuals to be targeted and aligned, noticing the stimuli from the environment, and directing organizational time and cognitive effort towards the decisions to be made in the organization. In this scenario, in an attempt to improve our understanding of theoretical concepts taking into account the influence of Social Media in organizations, we raise the following question: How Social Media can be used to guide the attention of decision makers towards better creation, storage, dissemination and application of knowledge in the organization? Therefore this research is an important first step to understand the potential of Social Media in the organizational setting as a means of focusing the attention of policy makers on the development of OM. Adopting an interpretative approach to the literature review, the paper provides a discussion of 22 case studies found in the literature that were analyzed using the Attention-Based View of the Firm as a guiding lens. This analysis shows some evidence and relevant implications of the use of Social Media in the organizational context as well as a first

V.F.A. Barros (✉) · I. Ramos
Information Systems Department, School of Engineering,
University of Minho, Azurém, Guimarães, Portugal
e-mail: vfbarros@dsi.uminho.pt

I. Ramos
e-mail: iramos@dsi.uminho.pt

© Springer International Publishing AG 2016
A. Lugmayr et al. (eds.), *Information Systems and Management in Media
and Entertainment Industries*, International Series on Computer Entertainment
and Media Technology, DOI 10.1007/978-3-319-49407-4_9

173

theoretical description of how the focus of attention of decision makers influence the development of OM.

1 Introduction

In an increasingly globalized world, where information is increasingly available and the barriers of communication and collaboration between individuals are increasingly narrow, it is an undeniable fact that we "live in a world where people have opportunities to connect, communicate, and collaborate in ways that were once inconceivable." [1, p. A69].

It is also known that organizations are aware that the knowledge generated in the organization over time is one of the primary factors to remain competitive on the market. "That organizations need to know what they already know to use that knowledge in present collective and individual decisions and actions and also in projections of the future." [2, p. 1].

This causes organizations to seek strategies and tools that preserve this knowledge generated over time and create mechanisms to stimulate and empower its professionals to share knowledge and use part of this accumulated knowledge to support improvements and innovation in the organization [3], whether in the generation of new products [4–6], in solving problems [7, 8] and also in decision-making [9–11].

Thus, the Organizational Memory (OM)—as a theoretical concept—enters in the interim as a way to help understanding how these processes of creation, storage, dissemination and application of knowledge in the organization unfold over time [12–15] and how the accumulated knowledge can influence the present and future actions and decisions of the organization [16–18].

OM has exists from the first moment a group of individuals begins to work and interact to achieve common goals and respond to stimuli perceived as coming from the organization's environment, in order to ensure the success of the business activity. Throughout the existence of the organization, OM keeps developing as the members of the organization collect information from outside and inside, are faced with common challenges, learn, share knowledge, and develop solutions.

In order to this development of OM be effective and harmonious, it is necessary that the individuals' attention is directed and aligned so that they perceive the relevant stimuli from the organizational environment and effectively use their time and cognitive effort to perform the actions or decisions that provide the best possible answers to the perceived stimuli [19]. Additionally, it is necessary that the technological tools be planned in this scenario.

The triad composed of the alignment of the attention in the organization, the effective development of OM and the support of technological tools, should allow for making the information capture and processing more effective; enhancing communication, interaction and the action of the members of the organization; and facilitating the sharing and dissemination of individual experience. With the evolution of technologies, one of the technological tools that have been increasingly incorporated in organizations are the Social Media [20].

With Social Media, organizations gain a set of tools that align perfectly in different actions, strategies and functions in the organization, whether they are in project management [21], relationship with customers [22], dissemination of corporate information [23], on learning of individuals is at the individual level, organizational or team [24], or even on the decentralization of work in General in the Organization [25, 26]. All this in order to provide an environment conducive for information and experience sharing by strengthening the construction of open communication [23, 27–30], and an organizational culture of collaboration and trust [23, 30, 31].

The Social Media can be considered relatively easy and cheap to be introduced within the organizational scenario [32]. However, due to its diversity, both in scope and functionality—which implies a set of attributes, features and varied resources—, certain aspects and adjustments are necessary in order to effectively meet the goals and strategic needs of the organization [29, 30]. These arrangements can potentially provide a rich environment to expand and benefit the organization, as well as enable greater understanding within the organization about how Social Media could be used in different contexts and environments.

In addition, despite this growing importance of Social Media technologies and insertion of the organizational context, it is noted that there are few studies in this area assessing the role of Social Media as a tool to guide organizational attention in promoting the creation, storage, dissemination and application of knowledge, which highlights the need for more research in this area. Moreover, there are several case studies and practical analyses of the use of Social Media in organizations without previous efforts to ground the use of this new technological trend on a sound theoretical basis in order to obtain a more effective understanding of this phenomenon.

The study described in this paper is a first attempt to answer the research question: How Social Media can be used to guide the attention of decision makers towards better creation, storage, dissemination and application of knowledge in the organization?

Therefore, this investigation is an important step towards understanding the potential of Social Media in the organizational context as focusing instruments of the decision-makers' attention to the creation, sharing and application of organizational knowledge required to develop of the Organizational Memory.

This analysis shows some positive evidence for the implications of the use of Social Media in organizations, and allows greater familiarity and awareness of the theoretical constructs underlying the role of organizational attention in the development of OM.

The structure of this paper is as follows. Section 2 describes the approaches and methods supporting this study. Then, Sect. 3 describes the theoretical basis necessary for the analysis proposed in this paper. Section 4 compares and contrasts the case studies with the literature review seeking to elicit the effects of the use of Social Media in different organizational contexts. Section 5 discusses the theoretical implications of our research results by identifying some theoretical assumptions listed in Sect. 4. Finally, Sect. 6 concludes with some implications about this study, its limitations and some implications for future studies.

2 Materials and Methods

This paper is part of an ongoing research aimed at analyzing how the Social Media guide the organization in the construction of knowledge, focusing on the process that starts with the creation/capture till knowledge is institutionalized in the organization.

In this paper, we seek to perceive how Social Media can be used to guide the attention of decision-makers along the process of developing OM. A systematic review of the literature was performed, making it possible to identify, assess and interpret the relevant of papers addressing the relevant topics.

The selection of literature was performed in two steps. The first step (Etp_01) corresponds to a selection of scientific papers related to the central research themes to elucidate the reader on two main theoretical perspectives guiding the research—Organizational Memory and Attention-Based View of the Firm—and the relationship of these theoretical perspectives with the information systems' field, more specifically the use of Social Media in the organizational scenario.

In order to find as many papers related to the subject of the research as possible. The search was carried out in some main international scientific databases, namely: Scopus, Web of Science and AIS Electronic Library (AISeL). These databases were chosen because of their great prestige among the scientific community in general and, especially, because they hold a substantial number of scientific publications in the information systems area.

The second stage (Etp_02) corresponds to a selection of case studies evaluating, in its most varied aspects, the use of Social Media in the organizational scenario in order to empirically investigate the main theoretical perspectives used in our research. It was carried out a systematic collection of relevant case studies on Scopus, Web of Science and recent AISeL scientific bases, from the last five years (2009–2013) referring, whether in the title, abstract or keyword, the terms "Case Study Research" or "Multiple Case Study Research", and "Social Media" within the organizational scenario.

On the basis of this Boolean search, with clusters of keywords mentioned above, 172 scientific papers were accessed, 20 of these being indexed in more than one base, totaling 152 papers. Table 1 describes this result.

The titles, keywords and abstracts of the 152 selected papers were analyzed to verify the relevance of the study, being selected only papers citing and detailing the case study and/or that propose a certain relationship between Social Media and the organizational memory and/or that focus the decision maker's attention in the organization.

Table 1 Number of publications in the Scopus, web of science and AISeL databases related to papers with case studies of social media from the last five years (2009–2013)

Database	Organizational scenario				
	Year				
	2009 [7]	2010 [12]	2011 [27]	2012 [44]	2013 [82]
Scopus [122]	01	09	18	32	62
Web of science [24]	–	01	05	05	13
AISeL [26]	06	02	04	07	07

We identified that most of these papers were focused on case studies related to very specific matters, such the use of Social Media in education, its benefits and harms in the teaching-learning process [33–43]; customer' satisfaction and/or their interaction with the organization mediated by the use of Social Media [29, 44–53]; movements and political decisions about social and environmental issues in Social Media [54–63]; studies of networks and monitoring of data generated from the organizations' exposure in Social Media [64–68]; analysis of the opportunities and risks of the use of Social Media in the well-being and health promotion in the community [69–72]; among other topics relevant to this study.

Based on the focus of the collected papers, and taking into account the alignment of the paper's topic with the purpose of our research, 40 papers that clearly specified the study of Social Media within an organizational setting in the title, abstract and/or keywords were selected.

From these papers were selected 22 cases for further analysis. The choice of these cases is due to the high degree of detailed research and extensive description of the use of Social Media in the organizational setting. It may stressed that these delimiters were necessary so that we could maintain the focus and purpose of the study but also minimize a set of publications from other areas and other approaches that could deviate us from the scope of our research.

Thus, these 22 selected cases were analyzed, interpreted and summarized so that better an understanding of the role that Social Media plays in guiding decision making and the co-creation of organizational knowledge. The relationship and the description of the selected case studies can be viewed in Table 2.

3 Theoretical Foundation

In order to explore how the Social Media guide the attention of organizational actors and the development of effective organizational memory, this literature review focused studies that address three central themes—Social Media, Organizational Memory and the Attention-Based View of the Firm.

Table 2 Cases selected for further analysis

Id	Year	Journal	SJR
C01	2013	Int. Journal of Voluntary and Nonprofit Organizations	–
C02	2013	Int. Journal of Voluntary and Nonprofit Organizations	–
C03	2013	Journal of the American Society for Information Science and Technology	Q1
C04	2013	International Journal of Information Management	Q1
C05	2013	Information & Management	Q1
C06	2013	Information & Management	Q1
C07	2013	Information & Management	Q1
C08	2013	Journal of Org. Computing and Electronic Commerce	Q2
C09	2011	International Journal of Information Management	Q1
C10	2013	Zeitschrift fur Personalforschung	Q2
C11	2013	Zeitschrift fur Personalforschung	Q2
C12	2013	Information and Organization	Q1
C13	2013	Information Systems Journal	Q1
C14	2011	MIS Quarterly Executive	Q1
C15	2013	Journal of Computer-Mediated Communication	Q1
C16	2010	Learning Organization	Q2
C17	2013	Journal of Knowledge Management	Q1
C18	2013	Journal of Product & Brand Management	Q2
C19	2013	Journal of Organizational Computing and Electronic Commerce	Q3
C20	2011	Negotiation Journal	Q2
C21	2013	Public Relations Review	Q1
C22	2013	Development in Practice	Q2

3.1 Information Technologies as Enhancers of Knowledge: The Social Media

For Information Systems to support the effective management of organizational knowledge, they must be flexible, robust and reliable in relation to a variety of situations and decisions in the organization. The organizational perspective deals with the issues of business functions, workflows, processes, training, among many others [73, p. 2]. For this, the Information Systems should be capable of efficiently and effectively dealing with unexpected situations, connecting knowledge sources and providing information as required for complex decisions and/or solving a given problem [74].

The Social Media is playing a growing role in the creation, dissemination and application of information, supporting cooperation and the sharing of individual experience [1, 74–76].

The use of Social Media is being in many different contexts and for different purposes. In the organizational context, Social Media seem to play a particularly important and significant role in addressing organizational agents' attention, stimulate collaboration and sharing of knowledge and experiences between individuals in the organization [74, 75, 77].

The Social Media allow creating collaborative environments supporting collective knowledge generation required to solve problems and face challenges. Furthermore, this knowledge can be applied in the organization, leading to benefits for the development of new projects, products and services as well as in decision-making. Therefore, studying the use of existing Social Media can help understanding the distributed nature of knowledge development (in particular, explicit knowledge) and of collaborative actions in the organizational environment.

A research conducted by Larcker et al. [78] with representatives of top management such as CEOs, senior executives and Board and Management members, has analyzed how the use of Social Media influenced the practices and strategies of their organizations. According to the survey, the use of Social Media represents a consistent medium of direct interaction, improving collaboration and communication in the organization, both internally between members of the organization and externally with customers, suppliers, shareholders and other stakeholders.

In addition, other advantages were listed such as: ability of the companies to collect market information about stakeholders, competitors and industries; quick disclosure of the company, its products, services and activities; source of information on how customers, employees, suppliers, shareholders, and others see the company, its products, services and activities [79].

"Different initiatives emphasize different types of content collaboration and different types of content, be it informative, creative or communicative" [80, p. 9]. Social Media enable the creation, modification, improvement or discussion of contents directed and developed according to own organization's guidelines. Wikis, blogs, social networks, business networks and many other Social Media are the most common examples of these highly popular collaborative applications and are of high impact in organizations.

In a research conducted by Anderson [81], authors stressed the importance of these new collaborative mechanisms for the organization and showed the role of Wikipedia, Blogs, micro blogs and social networks—the current Social Media phenomena used in the organizational context—played in creation of knowledge. The study identified significant benefits to the organization brought by Social Media, both for business processes and decision-making. The paper concludes that Social Media effectively support collaboration required for giving rise to several innovative business models that challenge the already established organizations and generate value for organizations that know how to exploit them to their own favor.

Proper use of Social Media in organizations as resources facilitators and effective supporters of decision-making throughout the organization can, if well thought-out, optimize resources, services and operations in organizations. For this, the main challenge for the organization is "in adapting new digital ways of working, introducing digital technologies into their daily lives, as well as adapting the organizational model to cope with the challenge of 'digital'" [82, p. 18].

3.2 The Organizational Memory (OM)

Increasingly, organizations are aware that the knowledge generated over time is one of the key factors to remain competitive on the market. However, most of this knowledge is not absorbed by the organization because it is retained in the individuals or is lost over time [83].

Once the knowledge generated in the organization over time is one of the primary factors to remain competitive in the market, it is important that organizations are aware of and seek mechanisms and strategies that enable to keep this accumulated knowledge in the organization [84]. This set of accumulated knowledge accumulated being preserved through time is called organizational memory (OM).

The OM allows this knowledge to be accumulated over time, distributed and applied within the organization.

> Organizational Memory (OM) may be thought of as comprising stocks of data, information, and knowledge (the memories) that have been accumulated by an organization over its history. When an individual accesses OM, he performs an act of interpretation on the memory(ies) that is(are) accessed and may or may not act on it(them) [85, p. 1].

One of the earliest accepted models of organizational memory was proposed by Walsh and Ungson [17] that, from a synthesis of several studies and past achievements, have viewed OM as the process of obtaining, retaining and retrieving information, therefore bringing information from the past to be applied in the present. This is a static conception of how knowledge is shared and focuses solely on the information generated in the organization to enhance decision-making.

Although this model proposed by Walsh and Ungson [17] can distinguish the kinds of knowledge that can be retained in Organizational Memory, these "retention bins" of knowledge generated by the organization are not independent, i.e. there is an interrelation between them making them flexible, integrated and dynamic. Therefore, it was proposed a functional view of OM in which the structure initially proposed by Walsh and Ungson [17] evolved to include the continuous interactions between the members of the organization, supported by artifacts that support the memory processes [86].

In this approach, the OM involves all activities of the organization at all levels of influence, including policies, standards, communication, culture, size, resources, technologies, giving rise to the organizational identity [3, 87–91].

Despite the wide literature on OM, the scientific knowledge produced about organizational memory is fragmented [92, 93] without holistic methodological tools to support managers in the diagnosis of OM [94, 95]. To address problem, a new model of OM is being developed at the University of Minho that uses the human memory model—discussed in areas such as cognitive psychology and neuroscience—as a reference metaphor to conceptualize how organizations retains knowledge in a distributed way in all organizational activities [2]. This model shows the OM as a distributed component and active in the organization, which accumulates knowledge and facilitates its use in actions and decision-making in the organization.

According to the human memory model proposed by Baddeley et al. [96], human memory is composed of three types of memory: sensory memory (i), (ii) short-term memory and (iii) the long term memory, which when associated with them allow human beings adapt to their environment, reaching goals, integrating knowledge and recognizing various patterns that allow the interpretation of new events on the basis of past experience.

Similarly, in accordance with the model proposed by Ramos [2] the organizational memory is composed of:

(i)   Sensory Memory, which consists in the encoding of information so that it can become useful to the organization. This step registers and collect impressions of the environment, whether internal or external, which in turn is activated whenever the organization has to respond to these stimuli and support in decision-making [97, 98]. The attention and interest of individuals in generating and sharing information are of great importance in this step;

(ii) Communicative Memory, which concerns daily interactions needed to perform the negotiation and decision-making activities in the organization, achieving goals and meet the mission and goals of the organization [90]. This step consists of the storage of this information in the organization through the stabilization and consolidation of this information. This storage occurs when there is an environment that encourages the creation of information, whether it internal or external, so that this information can be present to be used in the organization. We are talking here of the way that this information created is accumulated in the organization over time; and

(iii) Cultural memory, which carries the identity of the organization built on years of experience with shared meanings and institutionalized by the organization. This step is the result of the institutionalization of processes and practices that occurred in communicative memory, routines, and standards actions of the organization, i.e., everything that actively influence and consolidate this information created in the organization.

Moreover, it is added the concept of Political Memory. Seen it as crossing sensory, communicative and cultural memory, the political memory is created and recreated in negotiation processes, which include statements of interest, exercises of power and formation of coalitions [18, 90]. Figure 1 shows the Organizational Memory model presented by Ramos and Levine [99].

As represented in the model, the organizational knowledge is created and shared in the exercise of individual activities, the interactions of these individuals with group or in the context of organizational practices. The members of the organization in the exercise of their activities, either in groups or individually, interact within and with the environment of the organization. Through the exchanges with the environment, individuals and groups form impressions about the external environment and integrate them into an experience, either individually or in group, to be preserved in the organization, which should be recognized as important and then

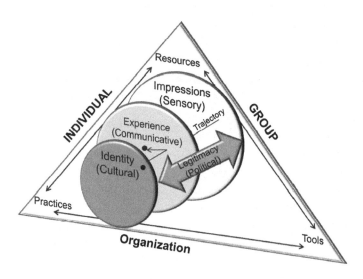

Fig. 1 Organizational memory model. *Source* Taken from [99]

integrated into the organization through technologies and organizational processes [2, 99].

To validate this model, the authors describe a set of theories that are organized according to the way that knowledge is created and moves to integrate in the organization up to their institutionalization. These theories, which are recognized by the high explanatory power and proven usefulness in various fields of study, directly or indirectly, discuss knowledge as primary resource for organizations, seeking to understand the organizational phenomena and trying to explain the processes that guide this trajectory of knowledge.

In accordance with the purpose of this paper, Sect. 3.3 describes one of these theories, the Attention-Based View of the Firm, which justifies the prospect that the behavior of individuals is directly related to how organizations allocate, distribute and regulate their makers 'attention on a particular organizational context.

3.3 The Attention Focus and Its Influence on the Decision-Making Process

An abundance of information are placed daily for individuals in the organizations, leading to high levels of attention deficit [100–102]. Individuals can focus only on a limited amount of information at each moment; thus mechanisms and strategies are needed that allow the individuals' attention is guided to the most necessary and relevant information to the performed activities and decisions.

The Attention-Based View of the Firm explains that the behavior of individuals in organizations is directly related to how organizations allocate, distribute and regulate the attention of their decision-makers. "At the level of individual cognition, attention processes focus the energy, effort, and mindfulness of organizational decision-makers on a limited set of elements that enter into consciousness at any given time." [103, p. 190].

In this sense, it is necessary that the decision makers focus their energy, effort and attention on a limited number of aspects in order to achieve a sustained strategic performance. This energy and effort, because they are limited resources, should be directed to aspects that are most relevant to ensure the success of organizations [100, 103–108].

According to the theory, any decision has a focus, a context, and a structure constraint. Therefore, in order to ensure success in their decisions, three factors must be taken into account when designing work systems: (i) the focus of attention; (ii) the context in which the attention is aimed; and (iii) the conditioning structure that involves this attention.

The focus of attention is directly related to the interest of decision-makers. This interest will orientate their attention to a particular set of issues and solutions determined by their decision environment. The elements contained in this set of issues are related to the problems, opportunities and existing threats that the decision-makers must focus their attention to make a decision. The solutions are sets of possible actions and decisions to be taken in the organization; solutions may be proposals, projects, programs, routines and procedures [103]. It is in this subset of issues and solutions that decision-makers concentrate all their efforts, energy and attention, influencing directly their action.

By limiting this attention to this subset, the understanding and action of the issues and activities become clearer and, on the other hand, the perception and action of the remaining issues and activities are inhibited.

> But the focusing of attention by organizational decision-makers allows for enhanced accuracy, speed, and maintenance of information-processing activities, facilitating perception and action for those activities attended to [103, p. 204].

This context in which the attention is intended is related to the decision-making environment to which these individuals are. It is in this environment where decision-makers act, communicate, interact, and take their decisions, that is, it is here where the decision-makers direct, intended and shape in a structured way the attention in organizational scenario [103]. In this dimension there is a set of rules; symbols; beliefs; environmental, social and cultural factors; artifacts; narratives and resources that affect and shape the attention of the decision-makers. Therefore, it is in this step that evaluates the communication both internally and externally, relationships and existing interactions, as well as the involvement of the individual within the organizational scenario.

Finally, in order to ensure that the decision is effective and goals achieved, the theory defines that the distribution of the decision-makers' attention should be structured within the organization. Namely, this factor focuses on the stable

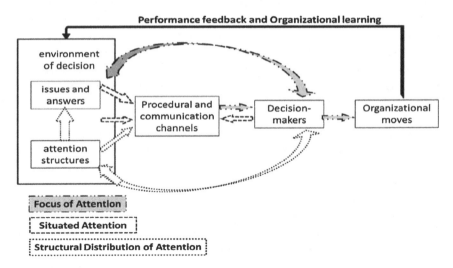

Fig. 2 Attention-based organizational theory proposed by Ocasio [103]. *Source* taken from [104]

organizational structures that influence/guide the attention, including, for example, actions, situations, communication channels, routines and procedures in the organization. Figure 2 illustrates the model created by Ocasio [103] to understand how attention can explain organizational behavior.

Thus, to understand the organization requires more than understanding the focus of attention for the individuals in the organization; it includes also understanding the contextual and structural factors, as well as a series of decisions and actions taken in the organization over time, both individual and organizational level [104].

Based on these principles, as illustrated in Fig. 2, some constructs and mechanisms describe how the processing of attention at the individual, cognitive, social, and organizational levels interact to shape the behavior and attention of individuals in the organization [103]. The relevant constructs are:

A. The decision-making environment that involves social, cultural factors, both internal and external to the organization, and which gives meaning to any decision-making activity. The decision-making environment includes economic and financial markets (competitors, customers and suppliers), tradable resources (raw materials, labor and capital), technology and institutional rules (laws and Government regulations, professional standards, among others), including the results of previous decisions and measures. It is in this environment that all movements required for decision-making happen;

B. The structures of attention that include the resources, structure and rules. These structures govern the allocation and distribution of attention of decision-makers;

C. A set of issues and solutions that constrain decision makers to respond or ignore problems, opportunities, threats and environmental stimuli of the organization.

This set of questions and solutions direct the attention of decision-makers and also shape their actions within the organization. These actions or responses can be expressed in the form of projects, programs, routines, and procedures;

D. Procedural and communication channels that are responsible for the established interactions and communications and that induce the decision maker to the set of issues and solutions considered relevant, limit the attention structures of the organization; they may include meetings, reports, protocols, satisfaction surveys, among others. These channels can display a spatial dimension represented by the physical location, sites and structures of work spaces, equipment, materials and written documents; the temporal dimension, represented by the time in which a meeting was held, its duration and its temporal proximity with other meetings; and the procedural dimension including the schedule of meetings, the formal structure, the voting rules and the formal and informal rules that govern the duties and responsibilities of decision makers in the organization;

E. The decision-makers themselves who jointly participate in any specific procedural and communication channel. Decision-makers are part of the action and environment by applying selective attention, building mental models that result in specific actions and decisions; and

F. Organizational actions that are the consequences of the formal and informal procedures defined and executed as a result of the intentional actions individuals performed to comply with the rules, achieve defined goals and implement organizational strategy emerging from the decision-making processes.

The importance of attention in decision-making and problem-solving has been noticed by scholars for many years. Examples of this research include an analysis of how effective targeting of attention has led to an institutional change in the chemical industry [109]; verification of how collaborative participation brought more attention to the possibilities of formation of strategic alliances within the organization [110]; the analysis of how attention to external events was shaped by threats to the image and identity of the industry [111]; among others.

A common point of understanding among these studies is that attention is considered a valuable resource for organizations and, like human and intellectual capital, it is a scarce resource that must be well managed to ensure greater responsiveness to strategic issues [100, 104, 108, 112], innovative and technological capabilities front to competitors [113, 114]. Not only the individual but also the environment and interactions between these individuals interfere in knowledge sharing within the organization and this shaped the attention by the organization's structure, i.e. the formal structure, rules, culture, political leadership and resources [103, 105, 107, 115].

Other studies such as [116] where it was found that companies could be more prone to an expansive strategy when they paid attention to various elements in their internal and external environment; [117] that studied how the effects of the labor division and the hierarchy in organizational units changed the attention focus and direction of the actions and decisions in the organization; [118] that examined how cognitive guidance combined with environmental stimuli shaped attention, interpretation and rapid response to competition in the air sector; and the analysis reported in [119] to understand how the effective targeting of attention led to changes in institutional logics.

These studies stress the current concern in analyzing how individuals' attention can bring benefits to the organization. In general, the authors say that decision-makers are flooded by stimuli and concerns that should be directed to all decisions and actions are carried out in the organization. Evidence of this can be found in [104] where authors talk about the decisions that managers must make and the major changes that occurred within the organization during times of crisis; or in [100] where the authors point out the importance of this theory in the area of information systems (SI), more specifically in the definition of the interface of electronic brainstorming.

For all actions, analyses or strategies created by the organization that can contribute effectively in productivity and in the decisions of the organization, you must create an environment that prioritize and cultivate ideas and experiences of those involved in the organization starting from policies or guidelines that intended to attention of these individuals to a limited set of concerns and problems thereby minimizing, perch of knowledge in the organizational environment.

4   Case Studies Analysis

This section summarizes 22 selected cases analyzed in order to gather evidence for the role Social Media may play in directing the decision-makers' attention. To achieve this goal, the Attention-Based View of the Firm was used as the theoretical lens to interpret the selected case studies.

In each case examined, the strategy underlying the adoption of Social Media and/or their actual use were analyzed. In order to synthesize the findings, Appendix shows a conceptual framework with the organizational demographics, actions and/or strategies cited in the analyzed case studies, grouped the light of Attention-Based view of the Firm theory.

It is worth mentioning that this reading of the papers is interpretive. Specifically, we seek to understand how the attention devoted, located and structured, move in order to establish an environment conducive to the creation and capture of knowledge in the organization.

Therefore, as a way of letting this research more clear and concise at the same time with the conceptual/theoretical part, the following subsections advances come theoretical assumptions and used the selected cases to discuss them.

4.1 Social Media as an Enhancer of the Focus of Attention and a Mechanism for the Creation, Storage, Dissemination and Application of Knowledge in the Organization

According to [99], the way that organizations provide and distribute the necessary attention to its employees helps organizations achieve maximum performance possible and with that, meet the objectives and strategies of the organization. When using Social Media, organizations access to new ways, mechanisms and strategies for individuals to direct their attention to the information necessary to assist them in decision making.

This attention is better focused when the professionals feel engaged and involved in activities (T01) and more than just directing their attention to the activities being performed they also tune and involve other professionals in a active and integrated communication effort (T07), thus becoming more effective in the sharing of ideas and experiences across the organizational setting required to effective decision-making.

In this way, the organization can not only perform better the usual activities but becomes more effective in developing new solutions and experiences (T02, T12); For example, by producing descriptions of decisions that are independent of a specific industry or position in the organization, therefore making them easier to reuse in other situations in the organization (T04, T05); in recognition of the organization's members for their decision taken through comments, compliments and suggestions (T06, T09); and in a greater confidence of the organization's members for their actions and decisions taken (T01, T07).

4.2 Social Media as an Effective Facilitator Mechanisms for Organizational Communication and for Guiding Attention to the Environmental Aspects Regarded as Relevant for the Success of Organization

Beyond the strategies and actions that stimulate the focus of attention in organizations, it is important to understand the environment and context that situate this attention. Attention is always situated and understanding the local influences on attention is essential to be able to create the circumstances for effective decision-making.

The decision's environment integrate the set of rules; symbols; beliefs; environmental, social and cultural factors; artifacts; narratives and others that affect and shape the attention of individuals. The Social Media in this interim emerges as a communication channel that provides that these sets of factors are disseminated by the organization.

A collaborative arrangement of work can be leveraged by Social Media that can play a significant role as an enhancer of attention and communication. "[…] domain experts, project managers and community leaders are all encouraged to utilize the intranet by using the participative features of Social Media as a means of engaging and communicating" [20, p. 118].

To provide an effective transmission of knowledge in the organization, a set of rules and factors in the organization must be directly aligned to an open and collaborative movement provided by Social Media (T10). To achieve this movement, the knowledge generated can be transmitted throughout the organization and can be reused in order to bring better benefits to both the individual and the organization itself.

Thus, content transformations, suggestions, comments created by Social Media can be used as knowledge to the organization itself (T12); to the generation of behavioral changes as much external as internal organization (T10); to information sharing and exchange of experiences, regardless of hierarchical position of the organization (T03); to even on its offer of targeted and specialized services to the needs of its customers (T02, T14). All this makes it clear that the stimuli generated by the organization associated with the Social Media allow connecting people and sharing experiences, ideas and practices throughout the organization, facilitating the perception and collective action needed to solve problems, make decisions and take advantage of opportunities.

4.3 Social Media as Effective Mechanisms of Institutionalization of Experiences and Meanings in Stable Structures that the Effective Distribution of Attention in the Organization

Given the support to collaboration that Social Media typically provide by enabling integrated communication and sharing of content, the attention of individuals in the organization can be extended and guided to encompass a wider variety of possibilities as well as of communication and knowledge sharing alternatives within organizational values and strategies. Moreover, knowledge co-creation and sharing are drivers for innovation and effective decision so Social Media can also play a central role to boost organizational capacity to transform itself.

Organizational transformation supported by Social Media has a direct impact in the norms and culture of the organization and may lead to the consolidation of a new cultural identity (T11, T12, T13). Improved organizational flexibility requires changing the structures of attention (T11); extend the scope, the depth and variety of use of Social Media by individuals of this organization (T10); integrate and embed Social Media into organizational processes using them on a daily basis the organization (T13); generate greater breadth of issues and solutions to decision-makers (T07, T08, T09); reduce communication barriers (T05); flatten hierarchies (T04, T05) or even change hierarchical responsibility in the organization (T01, T14).

With the Social Media integrated, the organization can direct the attention of individuals effectively by the organization; further stimulate the use of Social Media; ensure the involvement of all members of the organization or sector-independent hierarchical level (T04); and consolidating independent business units (T12, T13). All this to allow a common environment of sharing experiences, decisions and activities held in the organization; ensure better dissemination and access of information (T07); and to generate an effective flow of knowledge in the organization.

4.4 Social Media as Favoring the Situation and Structured Distribution of Attention in Developing Effective Organizational Memory

To provide an organizational environment conducive to interaction and the sharing of knowledge, it is necessary that the focus, the situation and the distribution of attention of individuals are aligned with the mechanisms, strategies and procedures of the organization. This alignment will provide a collaborative environment making the whole process of creation, storage, and dissemination of knowledge in the organization increasingly effective over time.

The Social Media in this context plays a crucial role as an enabler for the communication and knowledge sharing in the organization. "[...] multiple types of media are often available and are used by actors, in combination, for effective communication." [20, p. 113].

Therefore, the experience gained in a particular environment/sector/organization unit becomes part of the organizational memory in order to be used by other sectors and units of the organization, increasing and making organizational learning more effective (T07).

Once this knowledge is made available through channels of communication—in particular, the Social Media—, and distributed to all members of the organization, there is the possibility of using this accumulated knowledge to draw new strategies and solutions to long time perceived problems (T12).

This accumulated knowledge is the ground over which new knowledge is then generated (T10), that will guide new actions and decisions to be taken by the organization (T08). All this knowledge being created, stored and disseminated over time in the organization ensures improved organizational performance by empower individuals building new sources of knowledge relevant to face new challenges (T07), and to be used to inform innovative actions and decisions.

Thus, the Social Media becomes a tool to reduce collective memory fragmentation, distributing this capacity evenly throughout the organization. Therefore, the organization as a whole, becomes more effective at perceiving external stimuli and providing effective answers to them, co-creating knowledge within the context of ongoing activities and integrating new acquired knowledge into in the rules, actions, conceptual models and, therefore, in the organization culture and identity, making the necessary realignments in organizational power distribution relevant for processes where the structures of meaning are negotiated.

5   Discussion

The use of Social Media is increasing in organizations, thus becoming more and more relevant to organizational communication, interaction and knowledge sharing. Social Media is gradually gaining space in organizations, leveraging the flow of knowledge and making collaboration more effective and intuitive. Social Media also makes the flow of knowledge and collaboration with external actors easier, thus promoting the endogenization of external knowledge and practices.

The case analysis reported in this paper shows that Social Media can play an important role in guiding the attention of organizational actors to the aspects they feel relevant and also highlighting unexpected issues that would pass unnoticed.

In each of the aforementioned cases, several were the actions and strategies adopted by organizations to stimulate individuals to use Social Media as a supporting tool for interaction. Moreover, these tools were also used to generate information and knowledge considered relevant for decision-making.

Large organizations are trying to use the Social Media to accelerate learning, disseminate a consistent image among its members, and promote knowledge co-creation; all this is being fostered to ensure that the decision and action of organizational members is in line with the values and strategies outlined to promote the success of the organization.

However, to effectively support decision and action it is not enough that the tools are made available; a culture of knowledge sharing must be nurtured and incentives to collaboration should be made available.

Then, the next step must be to monitor the effectiveness of Social Media to capture external information and knowledge considered relevant, to support the day-to-day decisions and actions and to promote the institutionalization of knowledge in renewed or innovative organizational routines.

The analyzed cases also show the need for changes in culture, norms, expectations, streams, practice, and confidence of individuals in order to take the maximum benefit from the investments in Social Media.

When implementing Social Media, it is important to notice that these tools encourage horizontal communication that will collide with the traditional communication practices in organizations with various levels of authority. This may, again, require important cultural changes and create initial political tensions among established power balances. Therefore, systematic efforts should be made to strengthen collaboration habits and an open communication using Social Media. Thus, Social Media may also emerge as effective transformation tools when skillfully implemented.

6 Conclusion

This paper examined how Social Media can be used to guide the focus, the context and the distribution of attention in the organization in order to promote the creation, storage, dissemination and application of knowledge in the organization. For this, an analysis was made of 22 selected case studies in the literature that examine the use of Social Media in organizations. These case studies were studied from the theoretical lens provided by the Attention-Based view of the Firm.

The case analysis reported in this paper shows that Social Media can play an important role in guiding the attention of organizational actors to the aspects they feel relevant and also highlighting unexpected issues that would pass unnoticed. The first contribution of this study is to provide an initial view of cases in the literature that address the use of Social Media in organizations, in particular regarding specific insights on the role Social Media play in guiding the attention of decision-makers and for the effective development of organizational memory.

The second contribution of this study was to list a few theoretical assumptions generated from the results of this analysis of Social Media with the central concepts of this investigation that serve to list a few deep points of analysis that can be explored and studied in further work in order to explore how this relationship between theory and practice allow bring benefits to the area of knowledge in studying the case, the information systems.

In order to understand the role of Social Media in the construction of the organizational memory, it is not enough to use secondary sources of evidence like case studies performed by other researchers doing research with different goals. However, the exploratory nature of the analysis already provided the evidence for this role and for the value of the ABV theory as the research lens.

This study comes as a starting point to show the need to identify the main challenges that organizations may face decisions that they should take, while the adoption and use of Social Media as a new channel of communication in the organization. Several other theories are related to this process of trajectory of knowledge and organizational memory. We want, in future work, present other theories, analyses them and relates them with the organizational memory and relate the importance of these concepts and procedures in the organizational context.

Acknowledgments This work has been supported by CAPES Foundation, Ministry of Education of Brazil and by FCT—Foundation for Science and Technology within the Project Scope UID/CEC/00319/2013.

Appendix: Positive Actions Applied or Expected with Implantation and Use of the Social Media in Organizations Cited in Case Studies Selected

COD	Positive actions analyzed—applied or expected—with implantation and use of the social media in organizations	Memory			
		SS	CM	CL	PL
Attention focus					
T01	Provide a confidence feeling among other members of the organizations assuring a higher involvement with all members of the organizations	X			
	"[…] social media are more effective in addressing the three knowledge-sharing challenges revealed in behavioral research: (a) they help increase employees' awareness of each other's expertise and personal interests; (b) they can motivate contribution through frequent, timely feedback and through soliciting reciprocal exchange; and (c) they can better support the development and maintenance of social capital" [120, p. 1667]				
	"While access to technical support and training will assist with developing members' skills, capabilities and confidence, a critical success factor appears to be the need for someone within Parent Support to 'champion' social media developments, that is, to mobilize the chain of resources. In both organizations, having someone to oversee planning and provide a sense of continuity amid frequent turnover of volunteers and staff will greatly improve the chances of achieving improved communication through social media" [121, p. 685]				
T02	Change the view of each organization's member as to share of information, influencing directly on behavior, attention and involvement of the individual in the organization	X			
	"One important reason why I am motivated to share on social media is that I could increase my visibility in the organization by interacting with others on the platform. For example, some worldwide colleagues who I don't work with can recognize me by following my blog" [120, p. 1665]				
	"There are a growing number of domain experts, project managers and community leaders who have been using blogs and wikis to position themselves as an active voice in the organization, across regions and functions. As stated by one of the users (a team leader), we have 'a very active blogosphere … some teams are spread all over the world and use wikis to work collaboratively'" [20, p. 117]				

(continued)

(continued)

COD	Positive actions analyzed—applied or expected—with implantation and use of the social media in organizations		Memory			
			SS	CM	CL	PL
T03	Motivate and stimulate the initiative by own members in sharing information and making decisions in the organization individually/collectively	"Hence, this kind of low-level communication strengthens the aspect of sociability that is important for collaborative work such as co-creation and contributes to knowledge sharing without the need to be involved in long-lasting conversations" [122, p. 38]	X			
		"[…] a recent on-going discussion on the intranet has focused on organizational restructuring, with messages from senior management, project leaders and employees, all of whom are interested in voicing their concerns and suggestions" [20, p. 117]				
		"[…] more than half of internal social media users interviewed think the increased social capital associated with social media use increases their motivation for sharing expertise with one another" [120, p. 1664]				
T04	Become herself/himself available and open to transmit details of the rationale process behind each decision in the organization in order to re-use that knowledge in the organization	"By examining screenshots (for anonymity they are omitted from this paper), it became evident that some of the senior managers have used their blogs to outline the rationale behind some of their decisions (for instance, to enter a new market in South America or the selection of a new venturing partner)" [20, p. 117]	X			
		"Blogs can help to focus an individual's own thinking about his/her work, providing an additional tool for reflective practice. In addition to the individual focus, publishing this thinking on a blog makes one's thinking easier to share and can lend itself to creating a small 'community of practice' if others comment on the author's posts […]" [123, p. 458]				

(continued)

(continued)

COD	Positive actions analyzed—applied or expected—with implantation and use of the social media in organizations	Memory			PL
		SS	CM	CL	
Situation of the attention					
T05	Provide the share of ideas, information and experiences among the members freely and with no barriers, no great interventions, no hierarchy or sectorization, so that to generate an environment suitable for discussion of the problems and concerns in the organization, for the exchange of information in order to suggest solutions and propose innovation	"All news stories can be commented upon and rated. There's no censoring at all. People are very happy to comment and have very candid comments, which is very good." [20, p. 117] "Encouraging open and free participation with little or no intervention has become an important governance principle; one that has been gradually established and accepted by organizational members, many of whom are actively engaged in rhetorical practices" [20, p. 117]	X	X		
T06	Ensure the position of the professional as active voice in the organization, in all sectors and functions, providing higher valorization of this professional in the organization	"One important reason why I am motivated to share on social media is that I could increase my visibility in the organization by interacting with others on the platform. For example, some worldwide colleagues who I don't work with can recognize me by following my blog" [120, p. 1665] "Because I blog about the issues that I'm thinking about and dealing with in the course of my everyday job, I'm able to gain a wide spectrum of input and perspective on those issues, whether via comments on my posts, posts on other blogs that 'riff' off of mine, or—again—twitter conversations spun off of those same blog posts [...]" [123, p. 458]				X
T07	Provide improvements in communication and share of information both in the external and the internal environment to organization, so that to provide greater information global reach and to stimulate interactivity among the organization's individuals	"The CIO and CMO jointly are accountable for social media strategy and implementation. Performance evaluations, compensation and incentives are based on mutual performance and deliverance of shared objectives and goals. The social media goals and objectives of marketing are aligned with other organizational social media objectives through IT" [124, p. 193]	X	X	X	

(continued)

(continued)

COD	Positive actions analyzed—applied or expected—with implantation and use of the social media in organizations	Memory			
		SS	CM	CL	PL
T08	Guarantee the follow up permanent of views, suggestions and comments exposed from responsible professionals in the organization	"Our findings suggest that the use of social media had become part of the social fabric of BX. Blogs, wikis and commenting were no longer a novelty and are accepted as a normal feature of the intranet by employees. Open and participative communication is the default mode of BX's communication culture, and is representative of a shift in the role of employees from 'audience' to active 'rhetors' in the organization's on-line environment. Monitoring feedback and engaging in discussions regarding certain strategies and decisions is now a feature of the day-to-day life of senior management" [20, p. 119]		X		
Structured distribution of the attention					
T09	Disseminate the organization's values simply and integrate such values to actions and decisions in the organization	"In this context, DX's intranet is perceived as the most important medium for internal communication, not just because of its wide reach globally, but also because of its capacity to broadcast a unified voice to communicate and reinforce corporate values and strategy" [20, p. 118]			X	
T10	Facilitate better adaptation, whether by training, handbooks and guidelines, in effective use of the technologies adopted by part of the organization in order to make easy the organization's internal and external communication	"Organizations must provide training and role definition that maintains a balance between autonomy, flexibility, and the identified responsibilities and expectations" [125, p. 78]	X	X	X?	

(continued)

(continued)

COD	Positive actions analyzed—applied or expected—with implantation and use of the social media in organizations	Memory			
		SS	CM	CL	PL
T11	Produce new organizational structures and models considered useful for the making-decision from the permanent follow-up of the views, suggestions, problems and comments exposed by the organization	"From looking at maps that others had generated from Google Maps and posted online the author created a method for displaying the information geographically instead of in a table" [74, p. 10]		X	X
		"With wikis in place, CoP leadership will have access to training materials, organizational CoP standards, templates, and best practices in order to be truly prepared and empowered by the organization to lead his or her CoP. Providing this space for CoP leaders to post information on salient issues and building on each other's experiences and knowledge, is an important step in the continuity of training and role definition for future leaders and members of CoP" [125, p. 78]			
T12	Generate changes in the processes, strategies, routines and culture of the organization so that such changes can lead in effective restructuring, alignment and adequacy of the communication and share of information in the organization	"Specifically, we see a highly vibrant landscape where social media has been incorporated extensively into NX's organizational communication, and embedded in its day-to-day functioning." [20, p. 118]		X	X
		"Social media adoption is less about the tools but rather the strategies and the attitudes of the people and the community driving it. Part of the objective of the BlueBI Campaign is to develop a coherent platform which can be used to nurture a community" [126, p. 508]			
		"Implementing the guidelines using SM has implications for resource allocation and change in organizational culture. Organizations must allocate the appropriate resources for training and support of these communities. Perhaps most noteworthy is the change in culture required at all levels of the organization. Upper management and its employees must change perceptions of the role of the CoP and their importance to the organization. Striking a balance between alignment with organization structure and strategy as well as the emergent and informal nature of the CoP is also essential" [125, p. 79]			

(continued)

(continued)

COD	Positive actions analyzed—applied or expected—with implantation and use of the social media in organizations	Memory			
		SS	CM	CL	PL
T13	Strengthening of organizational standards in order to allow an open, bidirectional and interactive communication				X
	"Clear guidelines should be provided to help employees handle the "sticky" aspects of earlier tools. In the absence of such guidelines, employees may go in different directions, which may create more difficulties for knowledge sharing" [120, p. 1667]				
	"Creating and maintaining norms that promoted engagement seems to have played a significant role in encouraging employees to establish two-way communication in this organization. Interactivity is enabled by a sense of openness of communication that is unconstrained by hierarchy [...]" [20, p. 117]				
T14	Ensure a positive and functional corporative image, increasing the reputation not only of the organization, but also their employees				X
	"[...] the internal social media platform makes it so easy to share" [120, p. 1665]				
	"Some of these blogs have received extensive comment from employees, ranging from the positive to the extremely negative. Some request clarification regarding, or even questioning, NX's strategy moving forward. What is insightful is the amount of effort that the various bloggers spend in responding to comments and concerns" [20, p. 117]				

Legend
SS Sensorial memory
CM Communicative memory
CL Cultural memory
PL Political memory

References

1. Everson, M., Gundlach, E., & Miller, J. (2013). Social media and the introductory statistics course. *Computers in Human Behavior, 29*(5), A69–A81.
2. Ramos, I. (2011). Organizational memory : A neuroscience-based comprehensive model. In *Proceedings of the 7th organization science winter conference (OSWC-XVII) on organizational memory* (pp. 1–5).
3. Barnier, A. J., Sutton, J., Harris, C. B., & Wilson, R. A. (2008). A conceptual and empirical framework for the social distribution of cognition: The case of memory. *Cognitive Systems Research, 9*(1), 33–51.
4. Wang, C. L., & Ahmed, P. K. (2003). *Organisational memory, knowledge sharing, learning and innovation: An integrated model.* Telford, Shropshire, WP006/03.
5. Kim, N., Im, S., & Slater, S. F. (2013). Impact of knowledge type and strategic orientation on new product creativity and advantage in high-technology firms. *Journal of Product Innovation Management, 30*(1), 136–153.
6. Olivera, F. (2000). Memory systems in organizations: an empirical investigation of mechanisms for knowledge collection, storage and access. *Journal of Management Studies, 37*(6), 811–832.
7. Hamid, N. A. A., & Salim, J. (2010). Exploring the role of transactive memory system (TMS) for knowledge transfer processes in Malaysia E-government IT outsourcing. In *International conference on information retrieval & knowledge management, CAMP'2010* (pp. 303–309).
8. Dorasamy, M., Raman, M., & Kaliannan, M. (2013). Knowledge management systems in support of disasters management : A two decade review. *Technological Forecasting and Social Change, 20.*
9. Allahawiah, S., Al-Mobaideen, H., & Al Nawaiseh, K. (2012). The impact of information technology on knowledge management processes—An empirical study in the Arab Potash Company. *International Business Review, 6*(1), 235–252.
10. Toulabi, Z., Dehghani, M., & Al Taha, H. R. (2012). A survey of the relationship between organizational memory and organizational learning in public organizations of Kerman. *International Business Review, 6*(1), 90–96.
11. McCaughey, D., & Bruning, N. S. (2010). Rationality versus reality: The challenges of evidence-based decision making for health policy makers. *Implementation Science, 5,* 39.
12. Alavi, M., & Leidner, D. (2001). Review: Knowledge management and knowledge management systems: Conceptual foundations and research issues. *MIS Quarterly, 25*(1), 107–136.
13. Stein, E. W., & Zwass, V. (1995). Actualizing organizational memory with information systems. *Information Systems Research, 6*(2), 85–117.
14. Ackerman, M. S. (1994). Augmenting organizational memory: A field study of answer garden. In *Proceedings of the ACM conference on computer-supported cooperative work, CSCW-94* (pp. 243–252).
15. Abecker, A., Bernardi, A., Hinkelmann, K., Kühn, O., & Sintek, M. (1998). Toward a technology for organizational memories. *IEEE Intelligent Systems,* 40–48.
16. Chang, D. R., & Cho, H. (2008). Organizational memory influences new product success. *Journal of Business Research, 61*(1), 13–23.
17. Walsh, J. P., & Ungson, G. R. (1991). Organizational memory. *Academy of Management Review, 16*(1), 57–91.
18. Rowlinson, M., Booth, C., Clark, P., Delahaye, A., & Procter, S. (2010). Social remembering and organizational memory. *Organization Studies, 31*(1), 69–87.
19. Barros, V. F. A., & Ramos, I. (2015). Using social media as organizational memory consolidation mechanism according to attention based view theory. In *Proceedings of the twenty-first Americas conference on information systems, AMCIS* (pp. 1–22).

20. Huang, J., Baptista, J., & Galliers, R. D. (2013). Reconceptualizing rhetorical practices in organizations: The impact of social media on internal communications. *Information & Management, 50*(2–3), 112–124.

21. Böhringer, M., Richter, A., & Koch, M. (2009). Awareness 2.0—Ein Anwenderbeispiel von Microblogging im Unternehmen. *Information Wissenschaft & Praxis, 60,* 275–279.

22. Bughin, J., Byers, A. H., & Chui, M. (2011). How social technologies are extending the organization. *McKinsey Quarterly,* 1–10.

23. Smith, S., & Harwood, P. (2011). Social media and its impact on employers and trade unions.

24. King, K. P. (2011). Professional learning in unlikely spaces: Social media and virtual communities as professional development. *International Journal of Emerging Technologies in Learning, 6*(4), 40–46.

25. Kohler, T., Fueller, J., Matzler, K., & Stieger, D. (2011). Co-creation in virtual worlds: The design of the user experience. *MIS Quarterly, 35*(3), 773–788.

26. McAfee, A. P. (2006). Enterprise 2.0: The dawn of emergent collaboration. *MIT Sloan Management Review, 47*(3), 20–29.

27. Kaplan, A. M., & Haenlein, M. (2010). Users of the world, unite! The challenges and opportunities of social media. *Business Horizons, 53*(1), 59–68.

28. Duane, A., & Finnegan, P. (2003). Managing empowerment and control in an intranet environment. *Information Systems Journal, 12,* 133–158.

29. Hanna, R., Rohm, A., & Crittenden, V. L. (2011). We're all connected: The power of the social media ecosystem. *Business Horizons, 54*(3), 265–273.

30. Fournier, S., & Avery, J. (2011). The uninvited brand. *Business Horizons, 54*(3), 193–207.

31. Jackson, A., Yates, J., & Orlikowski, W. (2007). Corporate blogging: Building community through persistent digital talk. In *40th Hawaii international conference on system sciences* (pp. 1–10).

32. Davenport, T. H. (2011). Rethinking knowledge work: A strategic approach. *McKinsey Quarterly,* 1–11.

33. Balayeva, J., & Quan-Haase, A. (2009). Virtual office hours as cyberinfrastructure: The case study of instant messaging. *Learning Inquiry, 3*(3), 115–130.

34. Berkovich, I. (2011). No we won't! Teachers' resistance to educational reform. *Journal of Educational Administration, 49*(5), 563–578.

35. Hatakka, M., Andersson, A., & Grönlund, Å. (2013). Students' use of one to one laptops: A capability approach analysis. *Information Technology & People, 26*(1), 94–112.

36. Hargreaves, T. (2011). Pro-environmental interaction: Engaging Goffman on pro-environmental behaviour change. *Working Papers, Centre for Social and Economic Research on the Global Environment, 1,* 1–20.

37. Lantz-Andersson, A., Vigmo, S., & Bowen, R. (2013). Crossing boundaries in Facebook: Students' framing of language learning activities as extended spaces. *International Journal of Computer-Supported Collaborative Learning, 8*(3), 293–312.

38. LaRue, E. M. (2012). Using Facebook as course management software: A case study. *Teaching and Learning in Nursing, 7*(1), 17–22.

39. Mackness, J., Waite, M., Roberts, G., & Lovegrove, E. (2013). Learning in a small, task-oriented, connectivist MOOC: Pedagogical issues and implications for higher education. *International Review of Research in Open and Distance Learning, 14*(4), 140–159.

40. Menkhoff, T., & Bengtsson, M. L. (2012). Engaging students in higher education through mobile learning: Lessons learnt in a Chinese entrepreneurship course. *Educational Research for Policy and Practice, 11*(3), 225–242.

41. Nández, G., & Borrego, A. (2013). Use of social networks for academic purposes: A case study. *Electron Libre, 31*(6), 781–791.

42. Potter, J., & Banaji, S. (2012). Social media and self-curatorship: Reflections on identity and pedagogy through blogging on a masters module. *Comunicar, 19*(38), 83–91.

43. Schejter, A. M., & Tirosh, N. (2012). Social media new and old in the Al-'Arakeeb conflict: A case study. *The Information Society, 28*(5), 304–315.

44. Zhang, D., & Yue, W. T. (2013). Big data and social media use in commerce, work, and social life. *Decision Support Systems*, 7–8.
45. Wikström, P., & Ellonen, H.-K. (2012). The impact of social media features on print media firms' online business models. *Journal of Media Business Studies, 9*(3), 63–80.
46. Culnan, M. J., McHugh, P. J., & Zubillaga, J. I. (2010). How large U.S. companies can use twitter and other social media to gain business value. *MIS Quarterly Executive, 9*(4), 243–259.
47. Shirazi, F. (2013). Social media and the social movements in the Middle East and North Africa: A critical discourse analysis. *Information Technology & People, 26*(1), 28–49.
48. Unsworth, K., & Townes, A. (2012). Social media and E-Government: A case study assessing Twitter use in the implementation of the open government directive. *Proceedings of the American Society for Information Science and Technology, 49*(1), 1–3.
49. Cai, K., Spangler, S., Chen, Y., & Zhang, L. (2008). Leveraging sentiment analysis for topic detection. *Web Intelligence and Agent Systems*, 265–271.
50. Chauhan, K., & Pillai, A. (2013). Role of content strategy in social media brand communities: A case of higher education institutes in India. *Journal of Product & Brand Management, 22*(1), 40–51.
51. Hopkins, J. L. (2012). Can Facebook be an effective mechanism for generating growth and value in small businesses? *Journal of Systems and Information Technology, 14*(2), 131–141.
52. O'Shea, M., & Alonso, A. D. (2013). Fan moderation of professional sports organisations' social media content: Strategic brilliance or pending disaster? *International Journal of Web Based Communities, 9*(4), 554–570.
53. O'Shea, M., & Alonso, A. D. (2011). Opportunity or obstacle? A preliminary study of professional sport organisations in the age of social media. *International Journal of Sport Management and Marketing, 10*(3–4), 196–212.
54. Bernardo, T. M., Rajic, A., Young, I., Robiadek, K., Pham, M. T., & Funk, J. A. (2013). Scoping review on search queries and social media for disease surveillance: A chronology of innovation. *Journal of Medical Internet Research, 15*(7), e147.
55. Vicari, S. (2013). Public reasoning around social contention: A case study of Twitter use in the Italian mobilization for global change. *Current Sociology, 61*(4), 474–490.
56. Wolfsfeld, G., Segev, E., & Sheafer, T. (2013). Social media and the arab spring: Politics comes first. *The International Journal of Press/Politics, 18*(2), 115–137.
57. Holmberg, T. (2013). Trans-species urban politics: Stories from a beach. *SP Culture, 16*(1), 28–42.
58. Hvass, K. A. (2013). Tourism social media and crisis communication: An erupting trend. *Tourism Social Science Series, 18*, 177–191.
59. Luoma-aho, V., Tirkkonen, P., & Vos, M. (2013). Monitoring the issue arenas of the swine-flu discussion. *Journal of Communication Management, 17*(3), 239–251.
60. Martyn, H., & Gallant, L. M. (2012). Over 50 and wired: Web-based stakeholder communication. *First Monday, 17*(6).
61. Näkki, P., Bäck, A., Ropponen, T., Kronqvist, J., Hintikka, K. A., Harju, A., et al. (2011). Social media for citizen participation report on the somus project. *VTT Publications, 755*, 1–131.
62. Schwarz, A. (2012). How publics use social media to respond to blame games in crisis communication: The love parade tragedy in Duisburg 2010. *Public Relations Review, 38*(3), 430–437.
63. Segaard, S. B., & Nielsen, J. A. (2013). Local election blogs: Networking among the political elite. *Information Polity, 18*(4), 299–313.
64. Tufekci, Z. (2013). 'Not this one': Social movements, the attention economy, and microcelebrity networked activism. *American Behavioral Scientist, 57*(7), 848–870.
65. Sykora, M. (2011). Web 2.0: Common uses and potential applications: An interdisciplinary study of social media with case studies of applications and some methodology improvements. *International Journal of Interdisciplinary Social Sciences, 5*(10), 411–450.

66. Stocker, A., & Mayer, H. (2012). Unternehmen und soziale Medien—wie passt das zusammen? [Enterprises and social media—How to get this to work?]. *Elektrotechnik und Informationstechnik, 129*(2), 72–75.
67. Chua, A. Y. K., & Banerjee, S. (2013). Customer knowledge management via social media: The case of Starbucks. *Journal of Knowledge Management, 17*(2), 237–249.
68. Bygstad, B., & Presthus, W. (2013). Social media as CRM? How two airline companies used facebook during the 'ash crisis' in 2010. *Scandinavian Journal of Information Systems, 25* (1), 51–71.
69. Betton, V., & Tomlinson, V. (2013). Social media can help in recovery—But are mental health practitioners up to speed? *Mental Health and Social Inclusion, 17*(4), 215–219.
70. Gupta, A., Tyagi, M., & Sharma, D. (2013). Use of social media marketing in healthcare. *Journal of Health Management, 15*(2), 293–302.
71. Mitra, S., & Padman, R. (2012). Privacy and security concerns in adopting social media for personal health management: A health plan case study. *Journal of Cases on Information Technology, 14*(4), 12–26.
72. Neiger, B. L., Thackeray, R., Burton, S. H., Giraud-Carrier, C. G., & Fagen, M. C. (2013). Evaluating social media's capacity to develop engaged audiences in health promotion settings: Use of Twitter metrics as a case study. *Health Promotion Practice, 14*(2), 157–162.
73. Lugmayr, A. (2013). Brief introduction into information systems & management research in media industries. In *2013 IEEE international conference on multimedia and expo workshops (ICMEW)* (pp. 1–6).
74. Yates, D., & Paquette, S. (2011). Emergency knowledge management and social media technologies: A case study of the 2010 Haitian earthquake. *International Journal of Information Management, 31*(1), 6–13.
75. Yates, D., Wagner, C., & Majchrzak, A. (2010). Factors affecting shapers of organizational wikis. *Journal of the Association for Information Science and Technology, 61*(3), 543–554.
76. Kietzmann, J. H., Hermkens, K., McCarthy, I. P., & Silvestre, B. S. (2011). Social media? Get serious! Understanding the functional building blocks of social media. *Business Horizons, 54*(3), 241–251.
77. Metter, E., Gyster, V., Lamson, R., & Perrin, T. (2008). Enterprise 2.0 and HR: realizing the potential. *IHRIM Journal, 12*(5), 3–8.
78. Larcker, D. F., Larcker, S. M., & Tayan, B. (2012). What do corporate directors and senior managers know about social media? In *The conference board. trusted insights for business worldwide* (p. 15).
79. Scott, P. R., & Jacka, J. M. (2011). *Auditing social media: A governance and risk guide.* Hoboken, New Jersey: John Wiley & Sons, Inc.
80. Ala-Mutka, K. (2008). *Social computing: Study on the use and impacts of collaborative content.* Seville, Spain, EUR 23572 EN.
81. Anderson, E. (2010). *Social media marketing: game theory and the emergence of collaboration.* Heidelberg, Germany: Springer.
82. Lugmayr, A. (2013). Issues & approach in defining a european research agenda on information systems and management in creative eMedia industries. In *Proceedings of the 1st workshop on defining a european research agenda on information systems and management in eMedia industries*, 2013, (pp. 17–25).
83. Meyer, M. H., & Marion, T. J. (2013). Preserving the integrity of knowledge and information in R&D. *Business Horizons, 56*(1), 51–61.
84. Barros, V. F. A., Ramos, I., & Perez, G. (2015). Information systems and organizational memory: A literature review. *Journal of Information Systems and Technology Management, 12*(1), 45–64.
85. Cegarra-Navarro, J.-G., & Sánchez-Polo, M. T. (2011). Influence of the open-mindedness culture on organizational memory: An empirical investigation of Spanish SMEs. *International Journal of Human Resource Management, 22*(1), 1–18.

86. Hofmann, D. A., & Morgeson, F. P. (1999). Safety-related behavior as a social exchange: The role of perceived organizational support and leader-member exchange. *Journal of Applied Psychology, 84*(2), 286–296.

87. Assmann, J., & Czaplicka, J. (1995). Collective memory and cultural identity. *New German Critique*, 125–133.

88. Coman, A., Brown, A. D., Koppel, J., & Hirst, W. (2009). Collective memory from a psychological perspective. *International Journal of Politics, Culture, and Society*, 125–141.

89. Halbwachs, M. (1992). *On collective memory*. Chicago: University of Chicago Press.

90. Hirst, W., & Manier, D. (2008). Towards a psychology of collective memory. *Memory, 16* (3), 183–200.

91. Ricoeur, P. (2004). *Memory, history, forgetting* (Vol. 225). Chicago: University of Chicago Press.

92. Ackerman, M. S., & Halverson, C. (2004). Organizational memory as objects, processes, and trajectories: An examination of organizational memory in use. *Computer Supported Cooperative Work, 13*(2), 155–189.

93. Lehner, F., & Maier, R. K. (2000). How can organizational memory theories contribute to organizational memory systems? *Information Systems Frontiers, 2*(3/4), 277–298.

94. Casey, A., & Olivera, F. (2003). Learning from the past: A review of the organizational memory literature. In *The proceedings of organizational learning and knowledge, 5th international conference* (pp. 1–27).

95. Nevo, D., Furneaux, B., & Wand, Y. (2008). Towards an evolution framework for knowledge management systems. *Information Technology and Management, 9*(4), 233–249.

96. Baddeley, A. D., Eysenck, M., & Anderson, M. C. (2009). *Memory*. Hove: Psychology Press.

97. Greening, D. W., & Gray, B. (1994). Testing a model of organizational response to social and political issues. *Academy of Management Journal, 37*(3), 467–498.

98. Lambert, D. M., & Cooper, M. C. (2000). Issues in supply Chain Management. *Industrial Marketing Management, 29*(1), 65–83.

99. Ramos, I., & Levine, L. (2012). Organizational memory : A preliminary model based on insights from neuroscience. In *Gmunden retreat on NeuroIS 2012 proceedings*.

100. Javadi, E., Mahoney, J., & Gebauer, J. (2013). The impact of user interface design on idea integration in electronic brainstorming: An attention-based view. *Journal of the Association for Information Systems, 14*(1), 1–21.

101. Briggs, R. O. (2004). On theory-driven design of collaboration technology and process. In G.-J. de Vreede, L. A. Guerrero, & G. M. Raventós (Eds.), *Groupware: Design, implementation, and use* (pp. 1–15). Berlin: Springer-Verlag Berlin Heidelberg.

102. de Vreede, G.-J., & Dickson, G. W. (2000). Using GSS to design organizational processes and information systems: An action research study on collaborative business engineering. *Group Decision and Negotiation, 9*(2000), 161–183.

103. Ocasio, W. (1997). Towards an attention-based view of the firm. *Strategic Management Journal, 18*(Summer Special), 187–206.

104. Ekelund, L., & Räisänen, C. (2011). Re-organizing for innovation: Top management attention as a driver of strategic renewal. In *International society for professional innovation management symposium, XXII ISPIM'2011*.

105. Ocasio, W. (1999). Institutionalized action and corporate governance: The reliance on rules of CEO succession. *Administrative Science Quarterly, 44*, 384–416.

106. Ocasio, W., & Joseph, J. (2008). Rise and fall—or transformation? The evolution of strategic planning at the general electric company, 1940–2006. *Long Range Planning, 41*(3), 248–272.

107. Gavetti, G., Greve, H. R., Levinthal, D. A., & Ocasio, W. (2012). The behavioral theory of the firm: Assessment and prospects. *Academy of Management Annals, 6*(1), 1–40.

108. Sullivan, B. N. (2010). Competition and beyond: problems and attention allocation in the organizational rulemaking process. *Organization Science, 21*(2), 432–450.
109. Hoffman, A. J. (1999). Institutional evolution and change: Environmentalism and the U.S. chemical industry. *Academy of Management Journal, 42*(4), 351–371.
110. Rosenkopf, L., & Nerkar, A. (2001). Beyond local search: Boundary-spanning, exploration, and impact in the optical disk industry. *Strategic Management Journal, 22,* 287–306.
111. Hoffman, A. J., & Ocasio, W. (2001). Not all events are attended equally: Toward a middle-range theory of industry attention to external events. *Organization Science, 12*(4), 414–434.
112. Davenport, E., & Hall, H. (2002). Organizational knowledge and communities of practice. *Annual Review of Information Science and Technology, 36*(1), 170–227.
113. Kaplan, S. (2008). Cognition, capabilities, and incentives: Assessing firm response to the fiber-optic revolution. *Academy of Management Journal, 51*(4), 672–695.
114. Eggers, J. P., & Kaplan, S. (2009). Cognition and renewal: Comparing CEO and organizational effects on incumbent adaptation to technical change. *Organization Science, 20*(2), 461–477.
115. Barnett, M. L. (2008). An attention-based view of real options reasoning. *Academy of Management Review, 33*(3), 606–628.
116. Levy, O. (2005). The influence of top management team attention patterns on global strategic posture of firms. *Journal of Organizational Behavior, 26*(7), 797–819.
117. Jacobides, M. G. (2007). The inherent limits of organizational structure and the unfulfilled role of hierarchy: Lessons from a near-war. *Organization Science, 18*(3), 455–477.
118. Marcel, J. J., Barr, P. S., & Duhaime, I. M. (2011). The influence of executive cognition on competitive dynamics. *Strategic Management Journal, 32,* 115–138.
119. Nigam, A., & Ocasio, W. (2010). Event attention, environmental sensemaking, and change in institutional logics: An inductive analysis of the effects of public attention to Clinton's health care reform initiative. *Organization Science, 21*(4), 823–841.
120. Yuan, Y. C., Zhao, X., Liao, Q., & Chi, C. (2013). The use of different information and communication technologies to support knowledge sharing in organizations: From e-mail to micro-blogging. *Journal of the Association for Information Science and Technology, 64*(8), 1659–1670.
121. Zorn, T. E., Grant, S., & Henderson, A. (2013). Strengthening resource mobilization chains: Developing the social media competencies of community and voluntary organizations in New Zealand. *International Journal of Voluntary and Nonprofit Organizations, 24*(3), 666–687.
122. Hauptmann, S., & Steger, T. (2013). 'A brave new (Digital) world'? Effects of in-house social media on HRM ['A brave new (Digital) world'? Konsequenzen von in-house Social Media für das Personalmanagement]. *Zeitschrift für Personalforschung, 27*(1), 26–46.
123. Denskus, T., & Papan, A. S. (2013). Reflexive engagements: The international development blogging evolution and its challenges [Engagements basés sur la réflexion: L'évolution des blogs consacrés au développement international et les défis qu'elle présente]. *Development in Practice, 23*(4), 455–467.
124. Candance Deans, P. (2011). The impact of social media on C-level roles. *MIS Quarterly Executive, 10*(4), 187–200.
125. Annabi, H., & McGann, S. T. (2013). Social media as the missing link: Connecting communities of practice to business strategy. *Journal of Organizational Computing & Electronic Commerce, 23*(1–2), 56–83.
126. Fernando, I. (2010). Community creation by means of a social media paradigm. *The Learning Organization, 17*(6), 500–514.

Author Biographies

Victor Freitas de Azeredo Barros is Researcher at Algoritmi Centre of the University of Minho, Portugal. He is Vice-President of the Brazilian Chapter of the Association for Information Systems (AIS) and the Executive Secretary of the Science and Education Research Council (COPEC). He is Editor-in-Chief of the Brazilian Journal of Education, Technology and Society; Associate Editor of the Directory of Open Access Journals (DOAJ) and Member of Editorial Board of the Journal of Information Systems and Technology Management (JISTEM). Victor Barros is certificate as "International Engineering Educator" by International Society for Engineering Pedagogy (IGIP), Austria. He is member of several research groups, in particular: Information Systems and Technologies for the Transformation of Organizations and Society (ISTTOS) of the Algoritmi Centre of the University of Minho, Portugal; Labour Market Observatory for Information and Documentation of the University of São Paulo (USP), Brazil; Competitive Intelligence and Strategies for Innovation of the Mackenzie University, Brazil; Digital Media, Design, Interactivity and Usability of the Paulista State University (UNESP), Brazil; and in Applied Computing of the Catarinense Federal Institute (IFC), Brazil. He has more than 60 scientific papers published in Portuguese, Spanish and English in several journals, books and international congresses and he has organized more than 30 congresses around the world. He was professor at Goiás Federal Institute (IFG); Researcher and Consultant to Government of the State of Goiás; Researcher and Professor at Advanced Center for Continuing Education of Teachers of Basic Education (FORMA/IFG); and Professor at e-learning center E-PROINFO/MEC/UFG that belong to Brazilian government.

Isabel Ramos is Associate Professor (Ph.D., Habilitation) at the Department of Information Systems of the University of Minho in Portugal. She has a Ph.D. in Information Technologies and Systems, specialization in Information Systems Engineering and Management, since 2001. Isabel Ramos is Director of the Doctoral Programme in Information Systems and Technologies and President of the Portuguese Association for Information Systems. Isabel Ramos is President of the Portuguese Chapter of the Association for Information Systems and the Secretary of the Technical Committee 8 (Information Systems) of IFIP—International Federation for Information Systems, as well as the Portuguese representative. She is member of the AIS Communications Committee and the AIS LEO award Committee. She was awarded the IFIP Outstanding Service Award and IFIP Silver Core Award. Isabel Ramos coordinates the research group Information Systems and Technologies for the Transformation of Organizations and Society (ISTTOS) and the Thematic Research Stream Resilience and Agility of Organizations of the Algoritmi centre of the University of Minho. She advises several Ph.D. and Master dissertations in the areas of Knowledge and Innovation Management and IST for Organizational Resilience. She is the principal researcher in several projects in partnership with Portuguese companies and governmental agencies as well as in European funded projects. She is author and co-author of 9 books and more than 100 scientific and technical papers.

Part IV
Technology Perspective of the Usage of Media in IS&M in Media Industry and the Application of Media in IS&M across Domains: Technology, Processes, Workflows, Infrastructures and Global Production Pipelines

Systems Analysis as a Basis for Designing IT in the Media Industry

Svenja Hagenhoff

Abstract Systems analysis is the basis for decisions relating to the design and implementation of information technologies in companies. However, in many companies in the media industry systems analysis and modelling of functional and non-functional requirements are not very widespread. No domain-specific reference model exists which could help to conceptualise basic structures and processes. For this reason, objective recommendations for action and development cannot be made, and sustainable and feasible infrastructures cannot be established. The objective of this paper is to determine the current state of research regarding designing IT in the media industry and to introduce a theoretical overview of the instrument of systems analysis based on an example from the publishing industry.

1 Introduction

Technology is becoming ever more important in the media industry. It is present in value creation in the form of application systems for supporting business processes, for realising business models of social media platforms such as Goodreads or Pinterest and in the form of hardware (for example TV studios or printing lines). Technology is also an integral part of media products as a large quantity of media are not just electronic but also digital. Information technology as general purpose technology [8] is of particular significance. IT is becoming a critical resource, as media companies need IT to support basic operational processes efficiently and to create new product forms or offer complex services, for example providing specialist information on demand (e.g. [20]).

IT must be recognised by media companies as a resource which needs to be designed and structured actively. In its various forms IT must fulfil requirements which have to be specified and documented to support rational investment decisions. In many industries, it is common practice to use systems analysis to document and

S. Hagenhoff (✉)
Friedrich-Alexander-Universität Erlangen-Nürnberg (FAU),
Institute for the Study of the Book, Erlangen, Germany
e-mail: svenja.hagenhoff@fau.de

© Springer International Publishing AG 2016

A. Lugmayr et al. (eds.), *Information Systems and Management in Media and Entertainment Industries*, International Series on Computer Entertainment and Media Technology, DOI 10.1007/978-3-319-49407-4_10

analyse the current situation which will be supported by IT or considered in an IT-based solution offered to the customer. For established media companies, this approach is relatively uncommon and is still in its infancy with regard to the required expertise and acceptance. It is also noteworthy that studies on technology in the media industry usually focus on the opportunities or risks of digitalisation for product characteristics, modes of use or reception or media-supported communication processes rather than concentrating on the complex area of systems analysis.

This area is addressed in this paper which introduces the process of systems analysis, an instrument established in the software industry for designing and structuring IT as a resource. As part of this, the next chapter will name and investigate areas of analysis and design in relation to IT. Subsequently, the third chapter includes a literature review of IT in the domain of the media industry. This is followed by a review of processes and instruments for designing and structuring IT. Systems analysis is defined as a central task, data and process modelling is described as a central part of this analysis and the construct of reference modelling is discussed. Chapters "This area is addressed in this paper which introduces the process of systems analysis, an instrument established in the software industry for designing and structuring IT as a resource. As part of this, the next section IT as basic infrastructure in the digital world will name and investigate areas of analysis and design in relation to IT. Subsequently, the third section IT as a research focus in the domain of the media industry includes a literature review of IT in the domain of the media industry. This is followed by a review of processes and instruments for designing and structuring IT. Systems analysis is defined as a central task, data and process modelling is described as a central part of this analysis and the construct of reference modelling is discussed. Section Systems analysis and modelling based on an example from a rights and licensing department at a book publishing company presents the results of an actual systems analysis and modelling process in the rights and licensing department at a book publishing company. This example can be interpreted as an initial attempt to devise a reference model for this functional area. presents the results of an actual systems analysis and modelling process in the rights and licensing department at a book publishing company. This example can be interpreted as an initial attempt to devise a reference model for this functional area.

2   IT as Basic Infrastructure in the Digital World

Information technology (IT) is used as a collective term for digital information and data processing using applications. Applications provide functions that support specialist tasks ([17], p. 86.) In this sense, applications are tools. The functions of an application are applied to data, which can be entered, manipulated or deleted. An example of this is generating an author contract in which data relating to the author as the publisher's contractual partner including name, address, manuscript title and exploitation rights for the manuscript are collated and consolidated in a single document. As tools, applications always need data to work with.

Ideally, applications are designed to facilitate an entire business process and work with data from a centralised database (for other views on the topic see e.g. the editor's own contributions: [14, 15]. It is important to make a distinction between primary value-added processes and processes consisting of supporting activities. While applications for the latter form of processes are not industry-specific in their basic function, applications involved in primary value-added activities are always industry and even company-specific. Content management systems or social reading platforms are examples of such applications in the media industry. Applications in primary value-added processes are important for working efficiently, however they can also generate strategic advantages where they contribute to unique selling points or excellent service. Applications can be classified as standard software and customised software. Customised software is designed to meet the needs of a business and has been especially developed for this purpose either by the company or service provider. Standard software is developed for a mass-market and is designed to meet the standard requirements of the target user group ([3], p. 4). For applications to support tasks and processes adequately, organisations, processes and the required data must be analysed and requirements must be formulated in the software specification based on this systems analysis.

Data is understood as formal representations (constructs of characters) of facts and thoughts in a machine-processable form. Conventional data processing in companies typically focuses on data that represent business service processes and management of these processes. They represent real entities of an application domain and can be related to one another (for example reader X clicked article Y). The data required and processed in these processes is usually structured data. Data is characterised by clear semantic content and can be uniquely identified. Data can be classified as reference data (master data, inventory data) or transaction data (including financial transaction data and audit data).

For unstructured data, the meaning of individual elements is not defined or specified or this must be added individually in a much more granular way for a large collection of data. An example of this is adding content tags and jump links to sections of a video. These types of data are often highly complex and storage intensive [19].

Companies in the media industry are characterised as having products which consist of data: the content (facts and thoughts) is represented by data in different forms (for example static: text and images, or dynamic: audio and video). Data in companies in the media industry are therefore a material asset which is used to produce the final product. These data represent real entities of the organisation and its environment and describe the business service processes and the generated products. The management of data in media companies is not limited to the aspects of conventional business data processing; data is a core means of production based on the codification of thoughts (for example through writing) and the consolidation of assets for works in varying forms (printed book, blog article). The following figure illustrates the data structure of a book consisting of two chapters. While the title, the author's name, headlines and captions are structured data, the cover image, the figures and the body of the text are unstructured data. All of these data are included in the generated book.

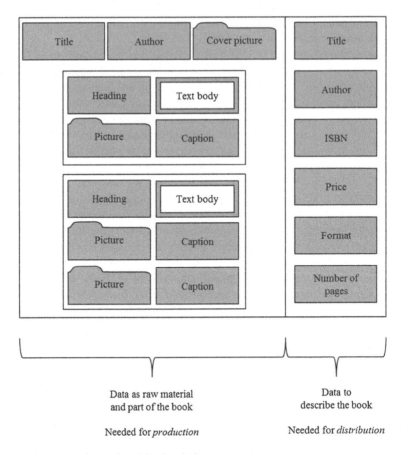

Fig. 1 Data as part of a book and its description

Title, author's name, price, format, ISBN and number of pages are product metadata which describe the generated product. Metadata are needed in the distribution process in printed or electronic catalogues and directories (Fig. 1).

For a long time, technology was only relevant for media companies at the value creation level of print production but not for collating, editing and consolidating content which are traditionally considered as intellectual activities. Today technology is a key part of all value-added stages in the publishing industry [13, 9, 12]. Information technology as a general-purpose technology [8] is needed to create and edit content, to package and format content (especially in the area of individual reader content services), to reproduce content (print and digital), to distribute content (warehousing and logistics) and to access and use content. Applications and the ability to organise data using technology have become some of the most critical resources in the media industry. Adequate IT infrastructures are required to ensure the sustainable support of business and production processes and realise business models.

3   IT as a Research Focus in the Domain of the Media Industry

The appended table (research from August 2015) shows an overview of studies related to information technology in the media industry. It is a result of continuous monitoring of publications submitted to conferences and magazines in German and English. The following organisations in the disciplines of information systems, computer science and media economics were monitored: *Business & Information Systems Engineering, European Journal of Information Systems, Journal of Management Information Systems, Journal of Information Technology, Informatik Spektrum, Americas Conference on Information Systems (AMCIS), European Conference on Information Systems (ECIS), International Conference on Information Systems (ICIS), Hawaii International Conference on System Sciences (HICCS), Jahrestagung Wirtschaftsinformatik (WI), Multikonferenz Wirtschaftsinformatik (MKWI), Publishing Research Quarterly, The Journal of Electronic Publishing, The Journal of Media Innovations, The International Journal on Media Management, International Journal of the Book, Journal of Digital Media Management, Journal of Media Business Studies, MedienWirtschaft —Zeitschrift für Medienmanagement und Medienökonomie.* Regular research was also conducted in the Springerlink, WisoNet and EBSCO databases.

The table attached shows the state of current research according to the areas of application software, workflow and workflow management, data and data management, and reference models in the media industry. The publications were selected strictly by relevance to these areas, as there is a plethora of publications with unspecific topics such as media and technology or digitalisation which are not of sufficient relevance to current research. It is difficult to classify the relevance of new technologies or prototypical solutions for the design of specific digital information products such as a travel guide with ambient intelligence components or new library services based on semantic web technologies. These studies have provided useful insights into the areas focused on in this research such as data structures and data management and logic functions for processing data. However, publications of this type, especially in the field of computer science and library and information science, are too numerous to count. A common characteristic among studies is that they showcase specific solutions and it is difficult to draw generalised findings in relation to designing infrastructures in the media industry. For this reason, these types of studies were not included in the summary.

The analysis of the current state of research shows that the media industry is not often chosen as a domain for evaluating the analysis and design of IT. This can be compared to the conclusions of Meyer et al. [16]. The listed studies were published from the year 2000 which is connected to the Internet and e-business boom at the end of the 1990s. At this time, research began to focus on the media, telecommunications and IT industries (for example [18, 21] as their processes can be completely digitalised. A fragmentary element is notable in the analysis of applications. Individual systems (such as content management systems, digital rights management systems) are described without reference to system landscapes and the interfaces required for integrated data processing. There is also a deficit in process analysis required for the design of applications. Of the eight studies in this area, only a minority include specific process descriptions. Only the study by Berliner Werkstatt Herstellung [1] led by Helmut von Berg included specific processes, however these are limited to the functional area of production. There was a similar finding for the management of data as a core resource. There is a lack of studies which formulate domain-specific data structures beyond individual functions and processes as well as research which contributes to adapting key terminology such as reference data, control data and metadata to the specifics of the domain. Reference models have been and will be published for many domain [4] with the purpose of publishing a conceptual framework which is not related to specific scenarios. However, there are hardly any examples of such research in relation to the media industry. The available research handles specific phenomena. This results in a lack of established concepts with regards to elementary structures and processes which are massively affected by digitalisation such as primary value-added processes and business model logic. As such, objective recommendations for action and development cannot be made, and sustainable and feasible infrastructures cannot be established.

4   Processes and Instruments for Designing IT

4.1   Systems Analysis as a Central Task

IT infrastructures and application systems do not exist by themselves, they support business process or other specific task within companies. Therefore it is important to collect and analyse specific requirements of technological solutions and document them in a suitable form. This process is known as *systems analysis*, *specification* or *requirements engineering* and is separate from *construction* and *design*. It covers the specific implementation of requirements in an application system or a technological solution. Without a good specification, companies will not be able to develop a system themselves or be capable of choosing an adequate solution from applications which are already available on the market. For the development of application systems, Brooks had already recognised the significance of the specification in 1987: "The hardest single part of building a software system is deciding precisely what to build. No other part of the conceptual work is as difficult as establishing the detailed technical requirements, including all the interfaces to people, to machines, and to other software systems. No other part of the work so cripples the resulting system if done wrong. No other part is more difficult to rectify later" (cf. [2], 8).

For the sake of differentiation in the requirements engineering phase, it is important to make a distinction between functional requirements, non-functional requirements and framework conditions. Functional requirements specify what an application system must do. They are based on tasks which diverse users are expected to perform. In the case of a content management system, the functional requirements might specify if the system will support electronic and print media as well as media-neutral work and if chief editors should have different permissions to editors. Non-functional requirements focus on the behaviour of the application system and additional characteristics which are not related to specific tasks. This includes performance, usability or reliability. A platform which users can upload images to must be able to support several thousand simultaneous transactions without affecting performance. Beyond this, there are framework conditions which are derived from the environment that the solution will be implemented in. This includes existing hardware an application system must run on or the required interfaces to other systems. For example, an application system which manages fees and licenses must have an interface to the accounting system.

4.2 Data and Process Modelling Are an Essential Part of Systems Analysis

A significant part of systems analysis is analysing processes which take place within a company and which should be supported by technological solutions—for example an application system—and analysing data which is used in a company. Several graphical representations based on complex analytical and modelling concepts have been established for modelling data and processes. The basic principles of data and process modelling are outlined below using Unified Modelling Language (UML) by way of example. For different perspectives of the system being analysed there are numerous diagrams available; this paper briefly explains three of these which are of key relevance from a functional perspective.

The *use case diagram* shows the relations between the application system and the stakeholders which interact with the system. Stakeholders can be people who use the system or application systems which are connected to the system via interfaces. A use case is a number of activities within a system which is always initiated by a stakeholder and which has a clear outcome. Use cases represent the typical interaction between users and the system. Examples for use cases in a content management system include an author writing an article or an editor publishing an article.

The *activity diagram* represents business processes and the sequence of individual activities. It defines where a workflow begins (process trigger), where it ends (process result), which activities occur in the workflow, which order the activities occur in and which stakeholders or organisation units are responsible for individual tasks. In a content management system, the article is written by the author, checked by an editor and any changes required by the editor are communicated to the author and implemented by the author. The correction and checking stages loop until the article is approved. When this occurs, the article is published online and archived.

The *class diagram* describes the static structure of an application system. A class represents specific objects of the company being analysed in abstract form. Classes initially consist of attributes which describe the real values of the represented objects. An author can be described with the attributes name, date of birth and address; an article could have the attributes title, number of pages and publication date. The specific attribute values (title: designing and structuring the IT landscape in media companies, number of pages: 17, publication date: 28 August 2015) are examples of the final data which an application system works with. Furthermore, classes include operations or functions which perform operations on data and cause data to be processed or an action to be carried out with a specific object. For example, an article can be released for publication on an online platform. Classes have a quantifiable relationship to one another. As such, an article can have one or many authors and an author can write one or many articles. A volume must consist of several articles but an article can only be published in one volume. A clean quantification of class relationships is the basis for a company to maintain high quality data which is fit for purpose.

4.3 Reference Models as an Instrument

For many domains, reference models for system architectures and process design were developed to establish generalised solutions and concepts [4]. Models represent specific characteristics and aspects of relevant real world scenarios. Models are usually used in developing and customising applications in the scope of systems analysis and requirement specifications. This process defines an actual/target relation between the organisation and IT. This does not relate to the actual organisation. Instead all relevant information about the organisation is abstracted within the model. An IT system or system landscape is developed and implemented according to information from the model (next figure from Horstmann [11], p. 80) (Fig. 2).

Reference models are a specific form of model. They can be understood as a conceptual framework which can be used as a blueprint or a model pattern to conceptualise a specific solution. The most important characteristic of reference models is that they can be, or at least are intended to be, re-used [6, 7, 10]. From a descriptive perspective, a reference model describes the shared characteristics of a class of models. From a prescriptive perspective, a reference model is a proposal of

Fig. 2 Relations between the organisation, model and IT system

how a class of models can be represented [5]. In relation to information technology, it is useful to create reference models for processes, data, applications, and system landscapes and use this to map the primary and secondary processes for an entire domain.

Various advantages and disadvantages are associated with reference models. Standardisation effects within a specific industry are a key benefit. These can achieve reductions in time, costs and uncertainties but also reduce competitive potential. These reference models can be used effectively where characteristics of products and manifestations of processes represent hygiene factors. If companies in the media industry compete based on content, information technology can be classified as a hygiene factor. This factor must function efficiently and sustainably across the entire industry. Reference models can make an important contribution to this.

5 Systems Analysis and Modelling Based on an Example from a Rights and Licensing Department at a Book Publishing Company

Based on the example of rights and licensing management at a book publication company, the parts of the functional specification are modelled using UML. The following figure demonstrates the relations between the acquisition and exploitation of rights in the form of licenses (Fig. 3).

The simplified *use case diagram* shows that the rights and licensing department has four use cases: first the rights to content must be acquired from the copyright holder (1). This work is first performed by editors who seek contact to potential authors and acquire suitable manuscripts for the publisher, while the rights and licensing department supervises the legal side of the transaction which is formally concluded by the directors and the copyright holder. For existing content, specific licenses can be assigned to the licensee (2). This could include a license for the hardcover edition of a paperback license or merchandising products for characters in a novel. This application involves the rights and licensing department and the directors and the licensee for concluding the contractual agreement. The licenses assigned and

Fig. 3 Relations between the acquisition of rights and exploiting licenses

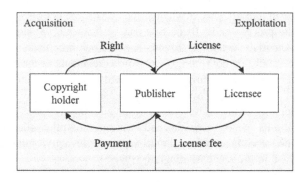

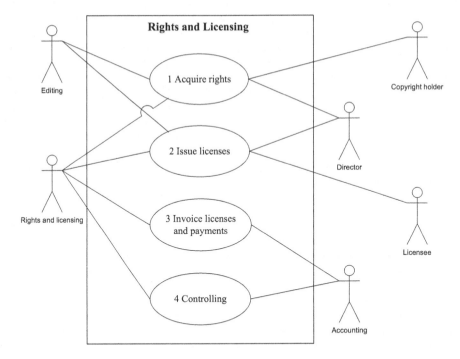

Fig. 4 Use case diagram

the payments must be invoiced (3). These transactions are forwarded to the accounts department. All activities must be monitored (4) by the rights and licensing department and the accounts department. This includes monitoring contracts which are due to expire soon, incoming payments and outstanding payments (Fig. 4).

The *activity diagram* shows the business processes which are involved in the use case 'issue license' in a simplified form. Participants include the editing team, the rights and licensing department and the directors as internal stakeholders and the licensee as an external stakeholder which are represented in so-called swim lanes. The business process can be triggered by three events: the editing team acquires a new title, the rights and licensing department determine that an existing license has expired or an existing licensee returns a license. The rights and licensing department initially checks whether the title can be licensed. If the title cannot be licensed, the process ends. If the title can be licensed, an acquisition attempt is made. If a potential licensee is found, negotiations are made until these either end unsuccessfully or both parties reach an agreement. In the latter case, the conditions are recorded in a contract, the generated contract is signed and subsequently archived. A correlation between the use case diagram and the activity diagram can be identified: the activity diagram details the use cases by dividing a rough use case into its specific activities and information on the order of the activities. In addition, the same stakeholders should appear in the activity diagram as in the associated use case in the use case diagram (Fig. 5).

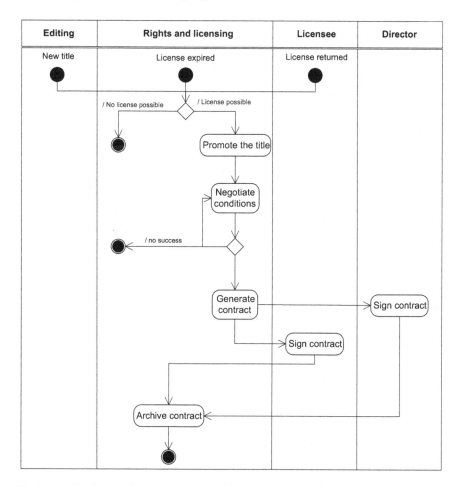

Fig. 5 Activity diagram for the license acquisition use case

While the use case and activity diagrams represent dynamic perspectives of the systems analysed, a *class diagram* represents the static relationships between different real world constructs. The middle section of each class shows the attributes; the lower section shows some of the functions which operate on the attribute values (data). The classes are related to one another. It should be noted that one license is related to exactly one title or vice versa (not verbalised) a title can be exploited in no or many licenses. A licensee holds one or many licenses while a specific license is held by exactly one licensee. Again the relations between the different diagrams are evident: the example of the license agreement class shows that the operation 'generate contract' is modelled in the activity diagram as an activity on this object (Fig. 6).

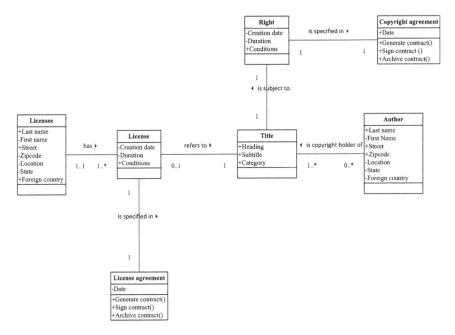

Fig. 6 Class diagram

6 Summary and Outlook

This paper has considered the instruments of systems analysis and modelling as a
basis for making informed decisions when designing IT-based solutions for business processes or products. Based on the example of a rights and licensing
department at a book publishing company, unified modelling language was used to
present extracts of systems analysis and modelling. Through use case, activity and
class diagrams, a functional representation of actual processes, data and their
relationships were presented from a section of this company.

Reference models are useful for establishing concepts in a domain and they are
becoming standard in many industries through the mass implementation of software. The media industry lacks reference models with regards to processes and
technology-based products or services and key terminology such as usage data,
control data or metadata has not yet been adapted to the specifics of the domain. In
particular for small and medium sized companies, reference models are helpful to
avoid re-inventing the wheel which is resource-intensive and to avoid misunderstandings in communication with IT service providers. An important objective for
further research in the media and creative industries is therefore establishing
domain-specific reference models.

Appendix

Title	Authors	Year	Published in/as	Topic
Application systems				
IT in der Medienindustrie. Trends und Anforderungen	Hartert	2001	Buhl et al.: (Hrsg.): Information Age Economy. Heidelberg 2001, P. 43–54	IT in the media industry in general
Present state and emerging scenarios of Digital Rights Management systems	Fetscherin	2002	Journal of Media Management 4 (2002), 3, P. 164–171	Digital rights management
Systeme für das Management digitaler Rechte	Hess/Ünlü	2004	Wirtschaftsinformatik 46 (2004) 4, P. 273–280	Digital rights management
IT-Verhalten und Defizite in KMU	Meyer/Tirpitz/ Koepe	2010	Monograph (Köln)	IT in SME publishing houses
Softwareunterstützung für die Bereitstellung klassischer Medienprodukte und -dienstleistungen	Hess/Dörr	2012	Working paper (München)	Description of selected application software
The Inevitable Shift to Cloud-Based Book Publishing	Hill	2012	Publishing Research Quarterly 28 (2012) 1, P. 1–7	Necessity of specific software
Mission Possible. Über die Einführung von Unternehmens-software in der Film- und TV-Branche	Knaf/ Hünemörder	2012	Becker et al. (Hrsg.) Management kreativitäts-intensiver Prozesse. Berlin 2012, P. 88–98	Implementation of ERP software in movie and TV companies
Der Einsatz von Content-Management-Systemen beim crossmedialen Publizieren in Fachverlagen: Ergebnisse einer Erhebung	Hagenhoff/ Pfahler	2013	Alt/Franczyk (Hrsg.): Proceedings of the 11th International Conference on Wirtschafts-informatik (WI2013) 2013, P. 359–374	Special interest publishers and content management systems
Reference models				
Referenzmodellierung für Buchverlage	Tzouvaras	2003	Monograph (Göttingen)	Book publishers
Generische Bücher—ein graphentheoretisches Modell zur logischen Strukturierung von Büchern in on-Demand-Publikationsprozessen	Kreulich	2002	Monograph (Chemnitz)	Structure of books
Konstruktion eines Referenzmodells für das Online Content Syndication auf Basis einer Geschäftsmodellanalyse	Pankratz, G.; Benlian, A.	2004	Becker/Delfmann (Hrsg.): Referenz-modellierung 2004, P. 125–149	Online content syndication
Referenzmodell für technische und organisatorische Abläufe bei der international verteilten Medienproduktion	Engelbach/Delp	2006	Working paper (Stuttgart)	Media engineering in interantional media networks
Ein Referenzmodell für die Herstellung von Fachmedien-produkten.	Delp	2006	Monograph (Heimsheim)	Specialist media production

(continued)

(continued)

Title	Authors	Year	Published in/as	Topic
Referenzmodellierung technologischer Hauptprozesse der grafischen Industrie	Reiche	2008	Monograph (Chemnitz)	Processes at printing industry
Erstellung eines Metamodells zur Entwicklung einer kolla-borationsplattform für die kundeninduzierte Orchestrierung komplexer Dienstleistungen in der Druckbranche	Eine/Stelzer	2014	Kundisch/Suhl/Beckmann (Hrsg.): Tagungsband Multikonferenz Wirtschaftsinformatik 2014 (MKWI 2014). Paderborn 2014, P. 1808–1820	Web services for the printing industry
Data and Data management				
Identifikation und technische Bewertung von integrierten Datenverteilungsvarianten für eine effiziente Mehr-fachnutzung multimedialer Medieninhalte	Benlian	2004	Working paper (München)	Data integration
Verbreitung, Anwendungsfelder und Wirtschaftlichkeit von XML in Verlagen. Eine empirische Untersuchung	Benlian et al.	2005	Ferstl et al. (Ed.): Wirtschaftsinformatik 2005. Heidelberg 2005, P. 209–228	Diffusion & usage of XML
Semantic Web Technologies for content reutilization strategies in publishing companies	Andreakis et al.	2006	Proceedings of the International Conference on Web Information Systems and Technologies 2006, P. 491–494	Content tagging and modularization
Aufbau eines Data Warehouse für ein Verlags-Controlling	Bücker/Ross	2010	Gleich/Klein (Hrsg.): Controlling von Dienst-leistungen. Freiburg, Berlin, München 2010, P. 181–204	Data warehouse in publishing houses
XML-basierte Anreicherung von Texten: Potentiale für Verlage	Haußer	2014	Working Paper (Erlangen)	XML as data technology in publishing houses
Datenlizenzierung als Diversifikationstreiber in der Medien-industrie	Pellegrini	2014	Rau (Hrsg.): Digitale Dämmerung. Die Entma-te-rialisierung der Medienwirtschaft. Baden-Baden 2014, P. 267–280	Data licensing
Workflows and workflow management				
Book-On-Demand: Entwicklung eines Konzepts zur Integration der Buchweiterverarbeitung in einen digitalen Workflow	Thielen	2003	Monograph (Chemnitz)	Books on demand
Koordination—Digitaler Workflow in Print-Unternehmen	Friedrichsen	2006	Scholz (Hrsg.): Handbuch Medienmanage-ment. Berlin, Heidelberg 2006, P. 377–391	Digital workflow in publishing houses
Do process standardization and automation mediate or moderate the performance effects of XML?	Benlian/Hess	2009	Proceed. of the 13th Pacific Asia Confe-rence on	process standardization and automation

(continued)

(continued)

Title	Authors	Year	Published in/as	Topic
			Information Systems 2009, Paper 12	
IT Standard Implementation and Business Process Outcomes—An Empirical Analysis of XML in the Publishing Industry	Benlian/Hess	2010	Proceed. of the 31st International Confe-rence on Information Systems 2010, Paper 50	Standard software
Change Management in Fachverlagen: Am Beispiel der Ein-führung eines Redaktionssystems	Heinold/ Hagenhoff	2010	Brancheninformationen der Deutschen Fachpresse	Specialist media publishers, content management
Die Standardworkflow-Elemente. Berliner Werkstatt Herstellung— Ergebnisse 2010	Berliner Werkstatt Herstellung	2011	Working paper (Berlin)	Workflows in publishing houses
Instituting an XML-First Workflow	Rech	2012	Publishing Research Quarterly 28 (2012) 3, P. 192–196	XML as basic technology
Management kreativitätsintensiver Prozesse: Theorien, Methoden, Software und deren Anwendung in der Fernsehindustrie	Becker/ Schwaderlapp/ Seidel	2012	Monograph (Berlin)	Management of creativity based processes
Process-Oriented Business Modeling—An Application in the Printing Industry	Malsbender et al.	2014	Zelm et al. (Ed.):Enterprise Interoperability 2014, P. 47–54	Printing industry

References

1. Berliner Werkstatt Herstellung (Ed.). (2011). *Die Standardworkflow-Elemente. Berliner Werkstatt Herstellung—Ergebnisse 2010*. Berlin.
2. Brooks, F., Jr. (1987). No silver bullet: Essence and accidents of software engineering. *Computer, 20*(4), 10–19.
3. Buxmann, P., Diefenbach, H., & Hess, T. (2013). *The software industry*. Berlin.
4. Fettke, P., & Loos, P. (2003). Classification of reference models—A methodology and its application. *Information Systems and e-Business Management, 1*(1), 35–53.
5. Fettke, P., & vom Brocke, J. (2013). Referenzmodell. In: K. Kurbel, J. Becker, N. Gronau, E. SInz, & L. Suhl (Eds.), *Online-Enzyklopädie der Wirtschaftsinformatik*. Munich.
6. Fowler, M. (1997). *Analysis patterns: Reusable object models*. Menlo Park.
7. Fowler, M. (2003). *Patterns of enterprise application architecture*. Boston.
8. Helpman, E. (1998). *General purpose technologies and economic growth*. Cambridge.
9. Hill, T. (2012). The inevitable shift to cloud-based book publishing: The next step in the digital transformation of book publishing may be closer than you think. *Publishing Research Quarterly, 28*(1), 1–7.
10. Hohpe, G., & Woolf, B. (2003). *Enterprise integration patterns: Designing, building, and deploying messaging solutions*. Boston et al.
11. Horstmann, C. (2011). *Integration und Flexibilität der Organisation durch Informationstechnologie*. Wiesbaden.

12. Knaf, J., & Hünemörder, C. (2012). Mission possible—Über die Einführung von Unternehmens-software in der Film—und TV-Branche (pp. 87–98). In: J. Becker, W. Schwaderlapp, & S. Seidel (Eds.), *Management kreativitätsintensiver Prozesse*. Berlin.
13. Koblinger, D. (2003). Die Verlagsbranche im Wandel.*Ein empirischer Forschungsbericht*. München.
14. Lugmayr, A. (2013a). Issues & approach in defining a European research agenda on information systems and management in creative eMedia industries. In: E. Stojmenova & A. Lugmayr (Eds.), *Proceedings of the 1st Workshop on Defining a European Research Agenda on Information Systems and Management in eMedia Industries* (in conjuction with eBled, Bled, Slovenia) (pp. 17–25). Bled, Slovenia.
15. Lugmayr, A. (2013b). Brief introduction into information systems and management research in media industries. In: *IEEE International Conference on Multimedia and Expo Workshops (ICMEW)* (pp. 1–6).
16. Meyer, J.-A., Tirpitz, A., & Koepe, C. (2010). *IT-Verhalten und -Defizite in KMU*. Cologne: Lohmar.
17. Schumann, M., Hess, T., & Hagenhoff, S. (2014). Grundfragen der Medienwirtschaft. Eine betriebswirtschaftliche Einführung. 5. Ed. Berlin.
18. Shapiro, C., Varian, H. R. (1999). *Information rules. A strategic guide to the network economy*. Boston, Mass.
19. Somani, A., Choy, D., & Kleewein, J. (2002). Bringing together content and data management systems: Challenges and opportunities. In: *IBM Systems Journal 41*(4), 686–696.
20. Viljakainen, A., & Toivonen, M. (2014). The futures of magazine publishing: Servitization and co-creation of customer value. *Futures, 64*, 19–28.
21. Zerdick, A., Picot, A., Schrape, K., Burgelman, J.-C., Silverstone, R., Feldman, V. (2000). *E-conomics*. Berlin, New York.

Author Biography

Svenja Hagenhoff is professor in Erlangen since 2011. Previously, she was director of the Research Institute of Media Economy at the St. Pölten University of Applied Sciences (Austria), and leader of a research group at the University of Goettingen. She had research and teaching stays at universities in Hildesheim, Los Angeles and Lübeck. She did her Ph.D thesis (2001) as well as her Habilitation (2007) in the fields of Information Systems and Business Administration. Her research and teaching topics in Erlangen are the media industry with a focus on written media as well as application-oriented technology aspects in this domain.

Digital Production Pipeline for Virtual Cultural Heritage Applications Using Interactive Storytelling

Luka Pavlič, Selma Rizvić and Domen Mongus

Abstract Preserving the past within the collective memories of people is one of the ultimate goals of creative industries. Virtual cultural heritage applications recreate history by inviting users to travel back in time. One of the more popular approaches for enhancing the immersion of time-travellers within virtual environments is interactive digital story-telling, which enables users to learn while exploring. While the process of developing interactive digital story-telling applications is still complex, involving professionals from various artistic and scientific disciplines, significant technological advances have recently been made towards improving content production. Namely, advanced Earth observation systems are capable of capturing hundreds of thousands of points within a second, thus creating extremely accurate representations of artefacts such as cultural sites. Usually mounted on mobile and airborne platforms, they produce high-resolution point-clouds with densities ranging up to several hundred points per square meter. However, the lack of topology, huge data sizes, and the contained noise, requires new data processing, storage, and management approaches before these data can be successfully utilized. This chapter introduces an advanced pipeline for creating virtual worlds as environments for interactive digital story-telling applications. By considering the challenges and issues arising during this process, recent developments in content creation, warehousing, editing, and postproduction will be demonstrated through the usage scenario of the implemented end-user application.

L. Pavlič (✉) · D. Mongus
Faculty of Electrical Engineering and Computer Science,
University of Maribor, Maribor, Slovenia
e-mail: luka.pavlic@um.si

D. Mongus
e-mail: domen.mongus@um.si

S. Rizvić
Faculty of Electrical Engineering, University of Sarajevo, Sarajevo
Bosnia and Herzegovina
e-mail: srizvic@etf.unsa.ba

© Springer International Publishing AG 2016
A. Lugmayr et al. (eds.), *Information Systems and Management in Media
and Entertainment Industries*, International Series on Computer Entertainment
and Media Technology, DOI 10.1007/978-3-319-49407-4_11

223

1   Introduction

The digital era is changing our perception of the world, offering us advanced technologies in every segment of our lives. The history of mankind is a very important aspect for understanding the present. Cultural heritage is one of the tools for preserving collective memory. Today, using the new media and creative industries, we can perceive cultural heritage in a completely new and exciting way. We can travel to the past through interactive virtual cultural heritage applications and see the objects that are currently only remnants of what they once were. These applications are produced using a number of different techniques (3D modelling, computer animation, digital storytelling, video production, compositing, web programming) and by inter-disciplinary teams from different fields (ICT, e-media, archaeology, history, sociology). The production pipeline (e.g. producing cultural heritage applications) is therefore quite complex and can be improved. We will present some ideas and proven concept improvements for this process.

The chapter is structured as follows: in this section we will introduce the motivation for introducing improvements in the digital storytelling pipeline. The most closely related works will also be presented. Section two presents approaches for capturing 3D data from the environment and preparing extracted 3D objects and metadata for storing in our repository (called 3D Storage). The third section focuses on enriching metadata and effectively storing 3D content and metadata in the (explained in great detail) 3D Storage. Section four presents the utilization of stored models and metadata in real production. Creating a cultural heritage application with an improved pipeline is presented as a case study. The chapter is concluded in last section, where improvements are further elaborated upon and some more potential areas for improvement are identified.

1.1   Motivation

A typical production process for an interactive storytelling application, such as a virtual cultural heritage storytelling application consists of: collecting data, 3D object modelling, characters and environments, exporting them to interactive web technologies, preparing digital stories from materials containing live and rendered sequences, recording narrations, animating the avatars and then completing the final editing and postproduction. In the end, all the elements are combined and implemented online or on-site using different kinds of digital installations (Keys to Rome exhibition [1]. The proposed process is focusing mainly on knowledge level of information systems in media, as described in "Brief introduction into information systems and management research in media industries" [2].

This process includes several opportunities for optimization. We want to introduce improvements in content creation, warehousing, editing, searching, and postproduction. Those will be demonstrated through the implementation of the

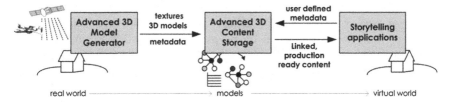

Fig. 1 A bird's-eye view of the presented digital storytelling pipeline

end-user application. We are developing automatic approaches regarding the generation of 3D models from Earth observation data, together with advanced storage and organization of 3D content, thus providing a holistic overview of information management within digital story-telling.

The core of our motivation for making improvements in the whole digital storytelling process, while making the process simpler, is presented in Fig. 1. The first component in the pipeline is "Advanced 3D Model Generator" (shorter: "3D Generator"), which enables the automatic acquisition of 3D surface and objects on one hand, and generating metadata on the other hand. Metadata and content are stored, linked and further described in an "Advanced 3D Content Storage" (shorter: "3D Storage") component, which is the main entry point for the third component "Storytelling applications". It enables easy searching (keywords, categories), proposing (in terms of "see-also", "is-related-to" etc.) and extracting appropriate content for connected applications (via industry-proven REST endpoint). In addition to component-to-component communication in terms of inserting content to storage component, we have also prepared a simple, proof-of-concept web application to interact with 3D Storage components. All components and approaches will be described in detail in subsequent sections.

1.2 Related Work

The use of digital media in the presentation and preservation of cultural heritage is becoming more and more frequent. In this chapter, we will mention some important projects that use digital storytelling and digital media in creating immersive and interactive virtual cultural heritage applications. In order to enhance the understanding of presented artefacts and improve the experience of museum visitors, they are either standalone online or incorporated in museum exhibitions.

The Virtual Museum Trans-national Network [3] defines a virtual museum (VM) with the following statement: "A virtual museum, in a real or virtual space, exists if there is a focus on tangible or intangible heritage, real or virtual, linked by a communication system, and is used in various forms of interactivity and immersion, by the public for the purpose of education, research, enjoyment, enhancement of visitor experience or promotion," Ferdani, et al. [4]. The following are the various implementations of virtual cultural heritage applications and virtual museums.

In the virtual world of Eternal Egypt, as described by Tolva and Martin [5], visitors are offered different multimedia features for exploring, such as: a collection of high-resolution zoomable pictures, virtual recreations of famous Egyptian sites, 3D views of artefacts, 360 degree interactive panoramic views of locations in Egypt, animations helping to illustrate and explain artefacts, and web cameras providing up-to-date interactive views from certain locations in Egypt.

The Virtual Hampson Museum offers a range of 3D presentations of artefacts available for download in VRML, 3D PDF and OBJ formats in both high and low resolutions [6]. The VR museum of Inuit culture, see Ivory [7], contains 2D images, 3D artefacts viewable in 360 degrees in QuickTime Virtual Reality (QTVR), video clips including archival film footage about how the exhibits were produced and used, video conversations with elders, narrations and transcriptions.

Some of the darkest events in human history and the sites where they occurred can also be presented using digital media. The State Museum of Auschwitz-Birkenau offers a virtual tour of Auschwitz/Birkenau [8] via either QTVR or Flash panoramas, with a textual explanation provided on the side. This website is an example of darker tourism VMs [9]. The "Siege of Sarajevo: Interactive chronology project" represents an "interactive timeline that depicts the most important events, experiences, personal stories and developments that occurred during the Siege of Sarajevo between March 1992 and March 1996" [10]. The Srebrenica-mapping genocide project [11] is another example of the use of digital storytelling and multimedia in presenting horrific war events in Bosnia and Herzegovina, particularly the genocide perpetrated upon Bosniak Muslims in Srebrenica in July 1995, when over 8000 civilians were executed in the UN protected zone. The project contains 17 animated maps. The maps are organized in chronological order and are in line with the methodologies adopted by institutions collecting and archiving documents related to the Srebrenica genocide and genocide in general—as identified by the number of respectable studies. Each map has key points containing particular evidence (text files, photos, video clips). The authors of the project call this form of digital storytelling "a documentary animation." The Sarajevo Survival Tools project presents a story-guided virtual museum of objects that the citizens of Sarajevo were creating and using in order to survive 3.5 years under siege [12].

In order to extend and evolve their relationship with visitors, museums need to develop a holistic view of the audience's journey across both the physical and virtual spheres [13]. Different forms of media (audio and visual) in virtual environments can increase the users' feeling of presence and make them more involved and interested in exploration [14–16].

The research project "Virtual Heritage Tours: Developing Interactive Narrative-Based Environments for Historical Sites" is about Nottingham's cultural heritage [17]. Users can choose the road they will take and they feel as though they are a part of the examined environment and not just a passive audience. They can move around, view the action and sometimes interact with it. The story is not linear although a narrative coherence still exists. The narratives are triggered as the users approach an object. In [18] a virtual environment was created from Giotto's scene "The Rule Confirmation." This scene is presented in 3D. Characters in the scene are mapped by Giotto's original fresco models.

In most of the mentioned projects, the digital storytelling production pipeline consists of materials collection, rendering computer generated scenes, editing and postproduction. The 3D models are created using classic modelling techniques, without laser scanning of photogrammetry. There was no reuse or sharing of the digital content. The creators of many interactive cultural heritage projects, particularly those containing digital storytelling, have been considering the improvement of the production pipeline. In [19] the authors discuss how to effectively manage and exploit 3D assets handling them with a cross-media approach. The same authors propose collecting, sharing and reusing geo and time-variant 3D models of the City of Bologna [20]. An open source pipeline in creation of 3D computer graphics short films for communicating cultural heritage is presented in [21]. In the following sections we will demonstrate how our proposed methodology could solve the observed problems and optimize the pipeline for creation of interactive virtual cultural heritage applications.

Digital storytelling is an very tangible application in the creative eMedia industries. In this paper we focus mainly on technological part of the information systems in eMedia stack (see [2]). However, our work do not only upgrade existing results in research area and introduce novel approaches. It also fits well into research agenda for creative eMedia industries, as described by Lugmayr [22].

2 Data Capturing and Processing

We have recently begun witnessing a paradigm shift in data capturing and processing that started at the beginning of the 21st century. Data acquisition is increasingly faster, continuous, and changing in diversity and complexity, while analytics is being shifted towards cloud computing. This Big Data phenomenon is becoming ever more apparent in remote sensing, where advanced data capturing systems are capable of rapidly recording extensive geographic areas with resolutions greater than a single decimetre and accuracies within a range of a few millimetres. By creating digital replicas of the real world with virtually forensic precision, the immense potential for the production of media content is becoming ever more evident.

This section provides an overview of recent advances in data acquisition technologies that promise to reshape the traditional pipelines in media production and expose key challenges facing creative industries when trying to embrace them. Since these are inevitably related to the Big Data phenomenon, we will provide an in-depth view into advanced methodologies in remote sensing data analytics for the extraction of meaningful information for content creation. Finally, we will focus on automatic 3D reconstruction for the automated generation of digital models of environments and objects.

2.1 Data Capturing

While data acquisition for production of media content traditionally relies on passive sensor-like analogue or digital cameras, active remote sensing systems have only recently started to garner attention. As passive sensors can only record natural radiation that is emitted or reflected from their surroundings, the acquired data is inevitably limited in dimensionality and the information it contains. Active systems, on the other hand, emit energy when capturing targeted objects and are capable of providing additional information by analysing the radiation that is reflected or backscattered from the targets [23]. RADAR (radio detection and ranging) and LiDAR (light detection and ranging) are well recognised examples of these technologies. Although they utilize radiation of different wavelengths, they both rely on the same underlying principle for capturing information from distant objects. Namely, by measuring the time-delay between the emission of an electromagnetic pulse and detection of its reflection, they are capable of estimating the distance from the targeted object and, thus, essentially providing a 3D image of the recorded scene [24]. Moreover, when measurements are performed at different wavelengths, detailed information about the properties of the materials and textures are obtained. These technologies are also known as multi- or hyper-spectral imaging, depending on the number of frequency bands being recorded [25].

While close-range laser scanning technologies are already attracting wide-spread interest from creative industries (especially in the area of cultural heritage, as reported yearly by the International Society of Photogrammetry and Remote Sensing [26], middle- and long-range data acquisition technologies have only recently become recognised for their cost efficiency, reliability, and promptness of data acquisition at large scales. Airborne LiDAR systems are among the most obvious example of contemporary state-of-the-art. They are capable of executing over 100,000 measurements per second [27] and acquiring several tens of points per square metre with beyond-decimetre accuracies. Moreover, by detecting multiple reflections from a single laser pulse, these systems are able to detect objects and terrain beneath the vegetation. With the increasing effort to acquire high-resolution 3D datasets at the national and regional level (some of the countries that have already acquired national LiDAR datasets include: Denmark, Finland, the Netherlands, Poland, Slovenia, Spain, Sweden, Switzerland, USA, and England), immense potential is available for the creation of media content and the development of various creative applications. Gaming, digital storytelling, architecture, augmented reality, video and 3D animation are just some of the many applications where these huge pools of information are expected to become valuable resources to build on the growth and innovation potential of creative industries. However, challenges imposed by huge point-clouds that often contain several tens of millions of topologically unstructured 3D points with linked scalar values, require remodelling of traditional digital production pipelines and the introduction of efficient Big Data analytics for the extraction of meaningful geometric patterns.

2.2 Data Processing

Based on the above, there is an obvious need to achieve a common representation of heterogeneous remote sensing data types, capable of combining complementary information contained within them. This so-called data fusion (or data integration) is not only intended to combine the data source by superimposing them, but focuses on extracting complementary information in order to enrich the output dataset with metadata and attributes about the contained patterns. In the early years of data fusion, the Joint Directors of Laboratories (JDL) data fusion subpanel within the US Department of Defence defined the JDL Data Fusion Framework for assistance in the development of military applications. Although several of the JDL model's drawbacks have become apparent over the years, especially with regard to its inability to represent human interaction within the data integration, it is still one of the most widely used frameworks for the implementation of information fusion. In that regard, the Data Fusion Information Group (DFIG) model [28] is the most recent attempt to revise JDL model by introducing an additional level of data fusion for the user refinement of processes. Thus, the DFIG model describes following six levels at which data fusion is achieved. While higher levels of DFIG data fusion model are application-specific, lower-levels are intended to provide the necessary information structuring and management support for adding value to the data. In continuation, we therefore concentrated on the latter (Fig. 2).

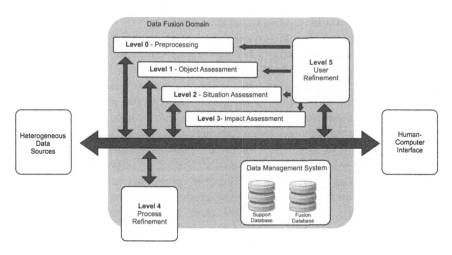

Fig. 2 JDL/DFIG data fusion framework

We are currently witnessing an immense degree of progress towards the development of an in-depth understanding of underlying structures of geometric patterns, which was enabled by an algebraic formalization of the mathematical morphology. This provides fundamental rules of quantitative arithmetic of shapes on the basis of concepts derived from set theory, lattice theory, and topology [29]. In the theory of mathematical morphology, data are considered as sets of points in arbitrary dimensions with established mutual topological relations (e.g. a grid), where a partial order between points and sets is induced by a discrete function (e.g. intensity values in case of an image or point-heights in the case of LiDAR data). Therefore, the same set of tools can be applied in the analysis of 1D time queues, 2D or 2.5D images, 3D point clouds, and multi-dimensional vector spaces as long as the topological structure between points is ensured [30]. This, together with common representation achieved at data fusion level 0, allows for the efficient changing of analytics tools and methods for data segmentation and object recognition in heterogeneous data sources. Recently developed morphological and attribute profiles are an important example, which have proven to be especially efficient when processing Earth observation data [31–34]. Based on the observation that morphological filters remove features that correspond to their shape and size, differential profiles effectively provide a data decomposition framework for the estimation of geometric [31, 32] and shape [34] attributes of the analysed geometric patterns. This is achieved by progressively filtering the data at increasing filtering scale and measuring the responses to each particular filter (i.e. the differences between the data before and after filtering). Consequently, while data is being decomposed in this way, segments are simultaneously attributed in an automatic manner. This has proven to be a powerful concept and is being adopted by numerous methods for object extraction either from airborne or spaceborne images [32] or 3D point-clouds [35]. The latter is particularly important in the context of media information production as it is a critical step in the creation of 3D models for creative applications.

When consider 3D Earth observation data (either LiDAR data or point-clouds generated from stereo-paired images), detection of ground points for the generation of digital terrain model (DTM) is a key step of object detection and reconstruction processes. The terrain is by itself an essential element for the creation of virtual worlds, while it can additionally be considered as a background for the recognition of objects above the surface [33]. Consequently, the detection of ground points has been in focus of the research over the last decade and a number of solutions have been proposed for this purpose. By considering the ground as a smooth continuous surface [36], an obvious solution for the detection of ground points is to filter features by thresholding them based on the heights of responses estimated by differential morphological attributes. However, protruding terrain features, like mountain peaks and sharp ridges, may produce higher responses than low non-ground objects. Thus, currently the most accurate approach proposed by Mongus et al. [35] has been adopted for the purposes of this study, where the sizes of the features are considered in addition to their heights by using the linear definition of the threshold function. In addition, the geometric attributes of the filtered features estimated during this process have proven to be essential for the recognition of objects as well. Namely, Zhang et al. [37] demonstrated that buildings are often filtered at larger scales than most other objects, while Mongus et al. [35, 38] proposed supplementing geometric and shape attributes with a surface analysis. In our case, the latter was achieved by locally fitted surfaces (LoFS) and the extracted geometry of segments was integrated with information obtained by the wavelet transformation [39] of orthophoto images. In this way, the essential geometric, shape, and texture attributes of the objects contained within the heterogeneous data types was obtained and stored within so-called feature vectors. Data fusion at a semantic level is thus achieved by their concatenation, leading to a significant increase in the accuracy of object recognition. In more simple cases, like the recognition of buildings and vegetation, object recognition was achieved by straightforward thresholding of features, while supervised machine learning algorithms were used for the recognition of objects with complex geometry, as proposed by several authors, expected maximisation, Bayes classifier, support vector machines [40], self-organising maps [41], and decision trees [42].

In the final step, the recognised geometric features were supplemented with the definitions of surfaces achieved by so-called object reconstruction. The purpose of this step is to achieve sufficient data structuring for object representation in a 3D environment. This includes texture mapping, shading and shadow casting. A raw surface topology, as used for object recognition, is triangulated in this step where surface-normals are defined. The removal of noise is achieved by surface smoothing and any possible unwanted holes on the surface are repaired during this step, as well [43]. Further details on reconstruction algorithms can be found in [43, 44], while it is worth mentioning that due to imperfect data and errors introduced in object extraction, reconstruction is in practice still labour intensive and requires a significant amount of human interaction. In any case, the output of the data processing was a set of objects defined by their geometry (set of points) and topological relations (set of edges and faces), together with liked attributes like sizes, shape factors, frequency spectre and textures.

2.3 3D Model Generation

3D data acquisition, processing and providing end-user usable 3D models is implemented in the 3D Generator component. In addition to the presented operation, the component also provides metadata about the generated 3D model. The metadata is automatically generated and prepared for direct inserting into the 3D Storage component (introduced in detail later in this chapter).

Since 3D Storage enables communication via HTTP-based REST endpoint in terms of JSON (JavaScript Object Notation) formatted data, the 3D Generator component also uses JSON as a data exchange format. The metadata is also persistently stored in addition to the 3D binary model. It is also further enhanced in order to link models and enable rich searching facilities. Below, an example of automatically generated metadata in JSON format about White Baston (a cultural heritage monument located in Bosnia and Herzegovina) is shown:

```
{
"id":"11267F3",
"object_type":"3DModel",
"object_type":"Interactive",
"content": [

{"key":"11267F3_1.jpg", "size":67002,

"type":"image/jpeg", "width":1024, "height":1024,
"resolution":"96dpi"},

{"key":"11267F3_2.max", "size":45223936,

"type":"application/x-3ds"}

],
"tags": ["building", "3dmodel"],
"spatial_reference_system":"UMT33",
"gps_time":"37084.0654",
"position": ["436818931","13993714"],
"area":"8543",
"height":"38.52",
"volume":"224634.13",
"shape_factor":"8.1312",
"texture_spectre":[".0834",".1834",".2456",".0145",".0010"]
}
```

The 3D Generator to 3D Storage communication is straightforward. All generated binary files are sent to the 3D Storage component with the HTTP POST method, returning a 3D Storage generated identifier. At the time of uploading, 3D Storage also generates some trivial metadata (such as file sizes, types, timestamps etc.). Additional HTTP POST invocations are used for inserting 3D Generator prepared metadata about already uploaded files. The provided metadata is automatically appended to already generated metadata. Further management and usage scenarios are the responsibility of the 3D Storage component, presented in the next section.

3 Data Storage and Integration

Data storage and integration is one of the fundamental elements in the digital production pipeline. In addition to persistently storing and linking 3D models with the critical metadata, prepared for interactive storytelling applications, the data storage system also plays an important role in enabling not only easy access to 3D content, but also, and more importantly, to enable smart searching, connecting and classifying 3D content. A potentially high volume of data, a lot of data retrievals and other performance-related concerns means that decisions made on used components for data storage are crucial. In this chapter we propose the component for efficient storing, retrieving and smart searching within the collections of 3D content and related data.

3.1 Advanced 3D Content Storage System, 3D Content and Metadata

Since the nature of the content, used in digital storytelling is so diverse (e.g. 3D models, images, media in terms of videos, music etc.), an appropriate data storage system should be selected. At first glance, established relational databases would seem to be a promising choice. They are well established, tried-out, proven in practice, and have few known problems. They also enable the storing of all kinds of data and metadata, including high volume binary content; they enable easy data relations, data consistency is guaranteed through transactions.

However, the nature of the data and required functionalities imply that at the end of the day, the potentials of relational databases are not really needed in our domain. They are actually a kind of disability for us (slow transactions, data locking, etc.) What is actually needed, is the ability to efficiently store a lot of data with small latency times, the ability to easily grow as data grows, and to provide the most efficient way of storing binary data on one hand and metadata for easy searching and data retrieval on the other. 3D Storage should always be available. On the other hand, we really do not consider it to be problematic, if certain 3D content is not available instantly after insertion. A second or two for propagating data changes in the system is not critical in our case. We would trade transactions, pessimistic data locking, conservative column-row data model etc. for higher performance, high availability and freedom in terms of modelling data. This is why the NoSql data storage approach is used in our 3D Storage.

NoSql was coined to unify numerous products, that enable data persistence and access in rather different ways, as it is done in relational databases. This movement is mostly driven by modern web- and sensor-related applications, which have to cope with high volumes of data, typically very diverse and stored in geographically separated systems. ACID transactions (Atomic, Consistent, Isolated and Durable transactions), data organization in terms of tables, primary keys, references etc. and enforcing references and integrity, etc. are not advantages in this context; they are an obstacle. For data with different structures, which is typically (but not by requirement) in large volumes, and could be replicated in an environment with growth in mind (replicas, shards etc.), the term BASE was introduced. Derived from the CAP theorem (also known as Brewer's theorem) (distributed data could only be guaranteed available or consistent at the same time; but not both), BASE is property of all NoSql products [45].

The authors managed to find similarities between diverse NoSql products in terms of data structure, which is supported by the database. One product typically supports one particular data model (e.g. MongoDB is a document-oriented database), there are also exceptions, where one database can accept several different data models (e.g. some authors consider Apache Cassandra to be both big-table storage and key-value storage). Four identified dominant data models are [46]:

- key-value (KV),
- document based,
- big-table (or wide-column) and
- graph.

In the case of our 3D Storage, we identified two types of data to be persistently stored. The most obvious, binary 3D content, is stored in the KV database. Metadata about binary 3D content, on the other hand, is stored in the document oriented database. The KV database for binary content is a quite natural and straightforward selection, since data (point clouds, textures and likes) will be stored in a database with easy and fast accessing in mind. All processing of this data will be done by a 3D Model Generator component before being persistently stored in 3D Storage.

Storing metadata, on the other hand, could be done within different data models. We find graph or wide-column options to be unsuitable for our needs, since metadata for particular 3D content will be structured on one hand, but a set of metadata will not be fixed. We do not want to invent limitations on describing content, but on the other hand we would like to do searching also in terms of aggregating 3D content that shares similar attributes (in terms of location, time span, etc.) We also require tagging metadata with user-defined categories and linking metadata in terms of "is similar" or "see also" relations. This is why the document oriented database was chosen, and why we used the industry-recognized and proven Mongo DB. It enables the storing of documents in the form of JSON (JavaScript Object Notation) with relatively free structure and possibilities of well supported searching in a document base. Changing documents is also well supported, which is required for adding user-defined metadata.

As demonstrated in Fig. 3, we propose and present a 3D Storage that is built on top of three infrastructural elements:

- the application server for hosting business and web components (we use Java EE Application Server, namely WildFly; other more lightweight ones such

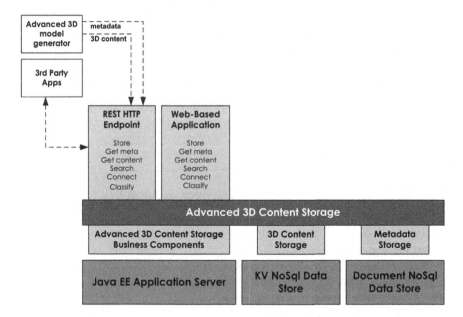

Fig. 3 Elements in advanced 3D content storage component (3D storage)

as Apache Tomcat or full-profile Java EE Servers such as GlassFish etc. could also be used without important changes);

- a specialized NoSql data store for efficiently handling high volume binary data (NoSql KV data storage system; at testing stages we used flat-file implementations, Redis and Oracle NoSql database, other KV solutions could also be used with little changes regarding the chosen product requirements);
- specialized NoSql data store for efficiently handling (freely) structured metadata about binary content and their relationships (document-based NoSql data storage system; we use Mongo DB).

We exposed our 3D Storage system with REST (Representational state) [47] Endpoint, which makes it possible to have a natural and easy system usage via HTTP protocol. It is quite a natural selection, since the endpoint will have to accept and provide several data structures that will also change over time. The REST Endpoint also makes it easier to accept and provide data to several qualified data users. They include desktop, mobile and web applications, and other systems as well—including the 3D Generator, presented in the previous section. The basic functionalities exposed via REST endpoint are:

- Storing and updating single (or a set of) binary 3D content and metadata,
- Providing additional user-defined metadata to existing 3D content,
- Linking 3D content (in terms of "see-also" and "is similar" links),
- Classifying content (in terms of folksonomies—tagging content),
- Retrieving particular 3D content or metadata, based on identifiers,

- Retrieving 3D content and metadata, based on keyword-search method,
- Retrieving 3D content and metadata, based on an advanced (criteria-based) search method.

For human users we also provide an out-of-the-box web application as part of our 3D Storage system. The web application enables user-friendly interaction with the system. It offers the same set of functionalities as offered by the REST endpoint (e.g. uploading new 3D content, browsing and searching in the 3D Store, downloading 3D content, etc.)

3.2   Advanced Data Storage and Access Approaches

The primary role of the 3D Store component is to persistently store 3D content and related metadata. Data is pushed to the component automatically, using the REST endpoint. However, other data sources could also be used in order to insert content and metadata. With an appropriate implementation, virtually any existing 3D content repositories could be naturally attached to the 3D Storage component.

In addition to providing persistent storage for the 3D Generator component, the 3D Storage component also enables some advanced data storage approaches. These include:

- updating and linking 3D content by end-users in an "as-you-go" fashion,
- classifying 3D content,
- searching 3D content, based on any metadata element,
- proposing candidate 3D content, to be used with already used 3D content.

We enable users to insert additional metadata to 3D content. Editing metadata do not only enable them to provide additional information on 3D content, but also, and more importantly, enables them to connect similar content.

Access to 3D Storage content is possible with the REST endpoint, making it possible to access them with virtually any HTTP-enabled software (including web browsers or other third party tools and libraries). The REST endpoint would, of course, also be accessed by other components—we see higher added value of the component in terms that other components will access content in the component and provide it to end users. However, as a proof-of-concept, we have prepared user interfaces on the web. They enable all REST operations in a user friendly manner. We are providing just a few screenshots, which demonstrate the possibility of inserting new content and/or metadata (3D Generator components use the same endpoint operation) (see Fig. 4), searching and navigating the 3D Storage content (see Fig. 5). The 3D Storage component is not only limited to automatically generated content by the component 3D Generator. In addition to this component, virtually any binary content (video, audio and other) can be inserted, managed and provided to users, that create virtual worlds.

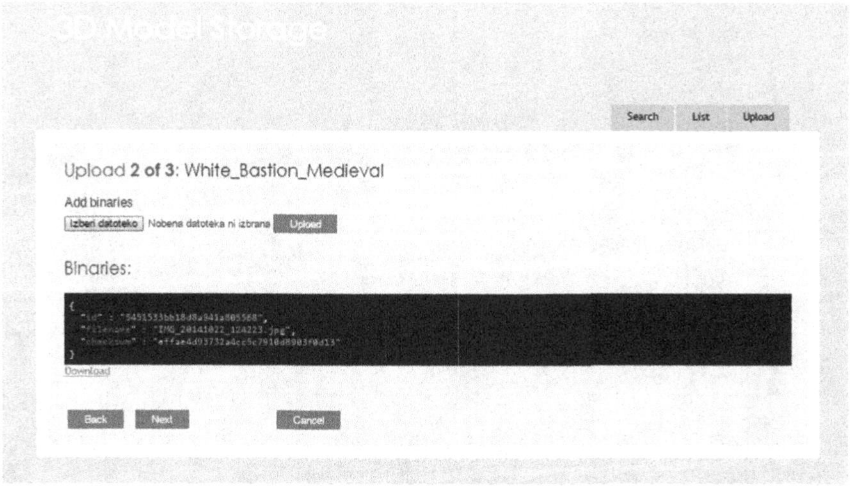

Fig. 4 Manually inserting new 3D content

Fig. 5 Proof-of-concept web view on REST interface for searching and navigating

4 Application: Organizing and Querying 3D Content

In a proof of concept, a case study, the proposed pipeline as a whole, will be the visualization of the White Bastion fortress in Sarajevo. The fortification known as the "White Bastion" is one of the most impressive and important historical sites in Sarajevo, Bosnia and Herzegovina. It is located on the southeast outskirts of the city, with an overview of the city valley (see Fig. 6). Throughout history it had a very significant and strategic position. The fortification is part of the dominant defence walls that surrounded the old city of "Vratnik".

Fig. 6 Bijela tabija (White bastion) fortress, Sarajevo, Bosnia and Herzegovina

The value of this historical site rests in its various strata, starting from medieval times until the present. During excavations, archaeologists found remnants from a medieval fortification from the 14th century, and from the Ottoman period (17th century) when the fortification was expanded and some new objects were built. During Austro-Hungarian rule (19th century) part of the fortification and the objects inside the walls were demolished and destroyed and a new cluster of objects was built. During the early excavation, a significant number of artefacts were found, registered and conserved for the purpose of an exhibition hosted in the Museum of Sarajevo.

The goal of this case study was to evaluate the proposed pipeline by creating an interactive virtual cultural heritage application based on high quality 3D models of the fortress (from the medieval, Ottoman and Austrian Hungarian period) combined with interactive digital stories as demonstrated in Fig. 7.

The application is based on interactive video methodology, where in a digital story video file at certain key moments links appear, leading to sub-stories or interactive 3D models. The concept is recursive, as both sub-stories and interactive 3D models can contain links to self-similar kinds of digital content. Interactive 3D models' parts can be clickable, offering links to digital stories about those parts (in our case the mosque, the ammunition room, etc.), or high quality detailed 3D models of objects that used to be in places and are found during the archaeological excavations of the site (weapons, coins, pottery etc.). Those detailed 3D models can again contain digital stories about their historical period, purpose of use or characters that were known for using them.

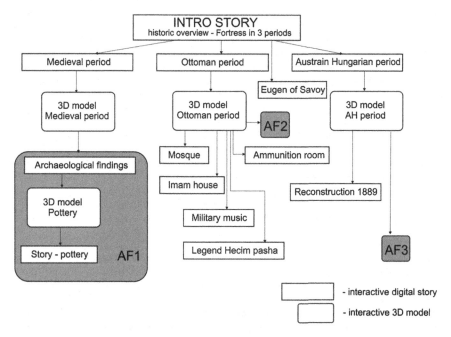

Fig. 7 Interactive digital storytelling application structure

The production process consisted of the following steps:

1. Laser scanning the site and archaeological findings,
2. Creating 3D models of the artefacts found on the site using photogrammetry,
3. 3D modelling of White bastion,
4. Creating interactive digital stories,
5. Design and development of the interactive digital storytelling application,
6. User evaluation of the project.

From the developer of digital storytelling application view, we can observe several improvements in the process of building such applications. With the proposed pipeline, the whole complex set of operations (including 3D scanning, processing data, creating 3D objects, moving them to a shared repository, finding relevant objects while developing, including objects to application) is dramatically simplified. More importantly—the operations until the object is literally ready to be used in an application are automatized and transparent. As an example we can observe several improvements in the process of the White Bastion application development in the following ways:

- Automatic reconstruction of 3D geometry from laser scanned data can significantly speed up the modelling process and add to the accuracy of the obtained high quality 3D models.

- Models of 3 fortress appearances can be based on some existing typical constructions found in the 3D data warehouse and those elements can be combined in the final 3D geometry.
- The transition of 3D models from the scanning phase to the repository is done automatically, important data about them is also presented in the repository.
- The requested model elements can be located in the data storage using a meta-data search, related models (in terms of similar location, etc.) could easily be located in the repository.
- Elements needed for digital stories such as images, videos, 3D geometry elements can be found using the proposed smart search and proposing algorithms.

5 Conclusion

In this chapter we presented and explained some important aspects in the process of transforming the real world into a virtual one. We did this from the storyteller's perspective, who wishes to have appropriate tools and approaches during the whole process. Relevant technological solutions were presented and demonstrated. When combined, these components enable users to have the whole complex process covered. The steps in this process are scanning real world with state-of-the-art technologies, identifying relevant objects from scanned point clouds, managing and storing 3D objects, having metadata support while browsing and searching for appropriate 3D objects, and easy content extraction from the repository in order to include it in a scene in the virtual world.

Our proof-of-concept implementations and case study show that the presented pipeline not only addresses all organisational and technological aspects that are necessary in order to enable the successful construction of virtual worlds, but also simplifies the current activities that storytellers have to perform.

However, we also see some potential for improvement, since the content transition from 3D Storage to end application (namely Cinema 4D) could also be automatized. The development of a plug-in for popular software in this area could be the next logical step. This is how all advanced functionalities could be available directly while modelling virtual worlds. The effort invested in such a plug-in would not be large, since the 3D Storage component exposes the REST interface, which is the de facto industry standard for simple component to component communication. Another improvement could also be done on the input side. In cases where one is using several 3D models repositories during the creation of virtual worlds, and our pipeline is just one of them, developers should use their existing repositories as well. It would be quite a straightforward operation in order to integrate these repositories.

At the moment we are promoting digital storytellers to use our tools and approaches. This is how we will be able to be sure about the benefits and obstacles for end users and will have the opportunity to improve. However, current user responses are promising.

References

1. Keys to Rome exhibition. (2014). International multimedia exhibition "Keys to Rome", Rome, Sarajevo, Amsterdam, Alexandria, 2014, www.keys2rome.eu
2. Lugmayr, A. (2013). Brief introduction into information systems and management research in media industries. In *2013 IEEE International Conference on Multimedia and Expo Workshops* (ICMEW), pp. 1–6.
3. V-MUST.NET. (2013). Virtual Museum Transnational Network Project, www.v-must.net
4. Ferdani, D., Sartini, M., Vigliarolo, P., Denard, H., Prescott, A., Pescarin, S., et al. (2013). State of the art on Virtual Museums in Europe and outside Europe, V-Must.net Deliverable report. http://v-must.net/sites/default/files/D2.3b_StateOfArt_VirtualMuseums_final.pdf
5. Tolva, J., & Martin, J. (2004). Making the transition from documentation to experience: The eternal Egypt project. In *ICHIM 04—Digital Culture and Heritage/Patrimoine & Culture Numrique, International*.
6. Smallwood, C., Payne, A., Simon, K., Goodmaster, C., Limp, F., & Cothren, J. (2006). Lighting systems in three dimensional non-contact digitizing: A view from the virtual Hampson museum project. In *3DPVT06—In Proceedings of Computer Applications and Quantitative Methods in Archaeology CAA* (pp. 954–961).
7. IVORY. (2010). Virtual museum of Inuit culture. http://www.rom.on.ca/exhibits/ivory/index.html
8. Auschwitz. (2010). State Museum of Auschwitz/Birkenau. http://en.auschwitz.org/z/index.php?option=com_content&task=view&id=6&Itemid=8
9. Kaelber, L. (2007). A memorial as virtual traumascape: Darkest tourism in 3d and cyber-space to the gas chambers of Auschwitz, e-Review of Tourism Research 5, 2 (June) (pp. 24–33).
10. Fama Collection. (2005). The siege: interactive chronology. http://www.famacollection.org/eng/fama-collection/the-siege-interactive-chronology/index.html
11. Srebrenica: Mapping Genocide. (2012). http://www.srebrenica-mappinggenocide.com
12. Rizvic, S., Sadzak, A., Hulusic, V., & Karahasanovic, A. (2012). Interactive digital storytelling in the Sarajevo survival tools virtual environment. In *SCCG '12 Proceedings of the 28th Spring Conference on Computer Graphics* (pp. 109–116). ACM New York, NY, USA ©2012, ISBN 978-1-4503-1977-5
13. Barry, A. (2006). Creating a virtuous circle between a museums on-line and physical spaces. In Proceedings of Museums and the Web 2006.
14. Murphy, D., & Pitt, I. J. (2001). Spatial sound enhancing virtual storytelling. In *Proceedings of International Conference on Virtual Storytelling* (pp. 20–29).
15. Brown, S., Ladeira, I., Winterbottom, C., & Blake, E. H. (2002). An investigation on the effects of mediation in a storytelling virtual environment. Tech. Rep. CS02-08-00, Department of Computer Science, University of Cape Town.
16. Walker, H. Q. N., Song, C., Kobayashii, A., & Hodges, L. F. (1999). Evaluating the importance of multisensory input on memory and the sense of presence in virtual environments. In *Proceedings of the IEEE Virtual Reality* (pp. 222–228).
17. Tuck, D., & Kuksa, I. (2009). Virtual heritage tours: Developing interactive narrative-based environments for historical Sites. In *Second Joint International Conference on Interactive Digital Storytelling—ICIDS* (Vol. 5915, pp. 336–339), Portugal.

18. Pietroni, E., & Antinucci, F. (2010). "The Approval of the Franciscan Rule"—Virtual experience among the characters of Giotto's work. In *Proceedings of The 11th International Symposium on Virtual Reality, Archaeology and Intelligent Cultural Heritage*.
19. Guidazzoli, A., Baglivo, A., De Luca, D., Imboden, S., Liguori, M. C., & Rivalta, A. (2014). Crossmedia integration of 3D contents for cultural communication. In *Proceedings of 3DTV-Conference: The True Vision—Capture, Transmission and Display of 3D Video (3DTV-CON)*, 2014.
20. Guidazzoli, A., Liguori, M. C., & Felicori, M. (2012). Collecting, sharing, reusing geo and time-variant 3D models of the City of Bologna: An open project. In *Proceedings of Virtual Systems and Multimedia (VSMM)* (pp. 611–614) (Casalecchio di Reno).
21. Ponti, F. D., De Luca, D., Guidazzoli, A., Imboden, S., & Liguori, M. C. (2013). 3D computer graphics short films for communicating cultural heritage: An open source pipeline, Digital Heritage International Congress (DigitalHeritage), (Volume: 2) (Casalecchio di Reno).
22. Lugmayr, A. (2013). Issues & Approach in Defining a European Research Agenda on Information Systems and Management in Creative eMedia Industries. In E. Stojmenova & A. Lugmayr (Eds.), *Proceedings of the 1st Workshop on Defining a European Research Agenda on Information Systems and Management in eMedia Industries (in conjunction with eBled, Bled, Slovenia)*. Bled, Slovenia: lugymedia Inc., International Ambient Media Organization (AMEA) (pp. 17–25).
23. Shan, J., & Toth, C. K. (Eds.). (2008). *Topographic laser ranging and scanning: principles and processing*. CRC Press.
24. Vosselman, G., & Maas, H.-G. (Eds.). (2010). *Airborne and terrestrial laser scanning*. Whittles.
25. Liang, Haida. (2012). Advances in multispectral and hyperspectral imaging for archaeology and art conservation. *Applied Physics A, 106*(2), 309–323.
26. ISPRS. (2011). Annual report. Available at: http://www.isprs.org/news/newsletter/2012-01/
27. Maune, D. F. (2008). Aerial mapping and surveying. In S. O. Dewberry & L. N. Rauenzahn (Eds.), *Land development hand-book* (3 ed., pp. 877–910). McGraw-Hill Professional.
28. Blasch, E., Bosse, E., & Lambert, D. A. (Eds.). (2012). *High-level information fusion management and systems design*. Artech House.
29. Najman, L., & Talbot, H. (Eds.). (2013). *Mathematical morphology*. New York: Wiley.
30. Salembier, C., Philippe, J., & Wilkinson, M. (2010). Connected operators: A review of region-based morphological image processing techniques.
31. Pesaresi, M., & Benediktsson, J. A. (2001). A new approach for the morphological segmentation of high-resolution satellite imagery. *IEEE Transactions on Geoscience and Remote Sensing, 39*(2), 1940–1949.
32. Ouzounis, G. K., Pesaresi, M., & Soille, P. (2012). Differential area profiles: Decomposition properties and efficient computation. *IEEE Transactions on Pattern Analysis and Machine Intelligence, 32*(8), 1533–1548.
33. Mongus, D., & Žalik, Borut. (2012). Parameter-free ground filtering of LiDAR data for automatic DTM generation. *ISPRS Journal of Photogrammetry and Remote Sensing, 67*, 1–12.
34. Mongus, D., & Žalik, B. (2014). Computationally efficient method for the generation of a digital terrain model from airborne LiDAR data using connected operators. *IEEE Journal of Selected Topics in Applied Earth Observations and Remote Sensing, 7*(1), 340–351.
35. Mongus, D., Lukač, N., & Žalik, B. (2014). Ground and building extraction from LiDAR data based on differential morphological profiles and locally fitted surfaces. *ISPRS Journal of Photogrammetry and Remote Sensing*.
36. Haugerud, R. A., & Harding, D. J. (2001). Some algorithms for virtual deforestation (VDF) of LiDAR topographic survey data. The International Archives of the Photogrammetry, Remote Sensing and Spatial Information Sciences (34(Part 3/ W4), pp. 211–218).
37. Zhang, K., Yan, J., & Chen, S. C. (2006). Automatic construction of building footprints from airborne LiDAR data. *IEEE Transactions on Geoscience and Remote Sensing, 44*(9), 2523–2533.

38. Mongus, D., Lukac, N., Obrul, D., & Žalik, B. (2013). Detection of planar points for building extraction from LiDAR data based on differential morphological and attribute profiles. In *ISPRS Annals of the Photogrammetry, Remote Sensing and Spatial Information Sciences* (II-3 W 1, pp. 21–26).

39. Choi, M., Young Kim, R., Nam, M. -R., & Oh Kim, H. (2005). Fusion of multispectral and panchromatic satellite images using the curvelet transform. *Geoscience and Remote Sensing Letters, IEEE,* 2(2), 136–140.

40. Mallet, C., Bretar, F., & Soergel, U. (2008). Analysis of full-waveform LiDAR data for classification of urban areas. *Photogrammetrie Fernerkundung Geoinformation,* 5, 337–349.

41. Salah, M., Trinder, J., & Shaker, A. (2009). Evaluation of the self-organizing map classifier for building detection from LiDAR data and multispectral aerial images. *Journal of Spatial Science,* 54(2), 15–34.

42. Hermosilla, T., Ruiz, L. A., Recio, J. A., & Estornell, J. (2011). Evaluation of automatic building detection approaches combining high resolution images and LiDAR data. *Remote Sensing,* 3(6), 1188–1210.

43. Repnik, B., & Žalik, B. (2012). A fast algorithm for approximate surface reconstruction from sampled points. *Advances in Engineering Software,* 53, 72–78.

44. Mullen, P., Goes, F. D., Desbrun, M., Cohen-Steiner, D., & Alliez, P. (2010). Signing the unsigned: robust surface reconstruction from raw pointsets. *Comput Graph Forum,* 29(5), 1733–41.

45. Fox, A., & Brewer, E. (1999). Harvest, yield and scalable tolerant systems. In *Proceedings of 7th Workshop Hot Topics in Operating Systems (HotOS 99)* (pp. 174–178), IEEE CS, 1999.

46. Hecht, R., & Jablonski, S. (2011). NoSQL evaluation: A use case oriented survey. In *Proceedings of the 2011 International Conference on Cloud and Service Computing.* IEEE Computer Society.

47. Fielding, R. T., & Taylor, Richard N. (2002). Principled design of the modern web architecture. *ACM Transactions on Internet Technology,* 2(2), 115–150.

Author Biographies

Luka Pavlič received his Ph.D. degree in computer science in 2009 from the University of Maribor, Slovenia. He is currently a senior researcher with the Institute of Informatics, FERI, at the University of Maribor. His main research interests include all aspects of IS development, reuse in software engineering, object orientation, information system architecture, Java, UML and XML-related technologies, semantic technologies, intelligent systems, big data and nosql. He has appeared as an author and co-author in several peer-reviewed scientific journals. He has also presented his work at a number of international conferences. In addition, he has participated in many national and international research projects.

Dr. Selma Rizvic is Associate Professor at the Faculty of Electrical Engineering Sarajevo and founder of Sarajevo Graphics Group. She also works as visual artist and Head of Broadcast Design Department at BH Radio Television. Her scientific interests are Computer Graphics, Computer Animation, Broadcast Graphics, Virtual Heritage and Digital Storytelling. Presently is involved in several EU and local projects. Sarajevo Graphics group was a partner of EU FP7 Network of Excellence "Virtual Museum Transnational Network V-MusT.net" which organized the largest European multimedia exhibition Keys to Rome in Amsterdam, Rome, Alexandria and Sarajevo in 2014. She and her colleagues from Sarajevo Graphics Group created many virtual cultural heritage projects in Bosnia and Herzegovina, most famous of them Sarajevo Survival Tools, virtual museum of Sarajevo siege. More details at http://people. etf.unsa.ba/ ~ srizvic/.

Domen Mongus received the Ph.D. degree in computer science in 2012. Since 2013, he has been an Assistant Professor of computer science at the Faculty of Electrical Engineering and Computer Science at the University of Maribor, Maribor, Slovenia. He was a member of Management Board of ACM Slovenia from 2008 to 2012, while he is currently a member of Executive Committee of European Umbrella Organisation for Geographic Information (EUROGI). A great majority of his work is related to the LiDAR data processing. His other research interests include mathematical morphology, pattern recognition, computational geometry, and data compression.

Automated Augmented Reality Content Creation for Print Media

Rocco Raso, Sebastian Cucerca, Dirk Werth and Peter Loos

Abstract The widespread diffusion of mobile technologies enables to reach a multitude of virtual contents, which crowd the infinite space of the internet: a huge extension that could not be transferred into a paper-based medium. Nowadays, traditional print media must face the growing diffusion of internet-based media. An opportunity to face the decreasing trade of paper-based media is provided by Augmented Reality (AR). The creation of Mixed Reality (MR) environments seems to offer the possibility to build a bridge between real and virtual, between print media and internet-based media. However, the integration of AR and print media still needs to deal with the issue of the automated content creation. In this paper we bring into focus the problem of the lack of automation in hybrid media and we propose a different paradigm, which results useful to design new editorial models. Furthermore, the system that we defined enables the creation of individualized reading experiences through the integration of a recommender system. By means of the definition of the domain ontology of the system, we have been able to define a prototypical implementation of the described automated AR content creation process, in order to demonstrate the feasibility of the proposed approach.

1 Introduction

The increasing market of internet-based media gives a hard time to the market of traditional print media. The large diffusion of smartphones enables the possibility to reach the wide-spreading space of the internet, with rapidity and simplicity. The finite space of print media appears sentenced to a definitive decline and the possibility to define a connection between internet-based contents and print medium represents an engaging challenge. Smartphone users are getting more familiar with the concept of virtuality, notion that on the screen of a mobile device seems to be

R. Raso (✉) · S. Cucerca · D. Werth · P. Loos
Institute for Information Systems (IWi), German Research Center
for Artificial Intelligence (DFKI), Saarbrücken, Germany
e-mail: rocco.raso@dfki.de

© Springer International Publishing AG 2016
A. Lugmayr et al. (eds.), *Information Systems and Management in Media
and Entertainment Industries*, International Series on Computer Entertainment
and Media Technology, DOI 10.1007/978-3-319-49407-4_12

even tangible. The definition of a mixed reality environment for print media through the integration of AR tools offers an interesting perspective to shape the concept of hybrid media as a possible "third way" in the duality internet-based media/print media. However, hybrid media systems must be further investigated in order to face specific research questions.

1.1 Motivation

One of the main challenges regarding the integration of AR systems into print media is represented by the lack of standardization. The absence of univocal AR browsers doesn't deal with the need of automated content creation processes for hybrid media. If the effort to reach the standardization of AR browsers seems to require a big player with a consistent critical mass [1], on the other hand the possibility to define automated processes for the AR contents creation represents an affordable research question. The development of MR environments for print media may guarantee to the users new reading experiences and a high degree of immersion in the reading [2]. This aspect ensures a real and tangible advantage for the publishing companies in terms of feedback and impact on the costumer. Aimed by the generalized lack of automation and standardization of traditional AR systems for print media, in this paper we present a system which is useful to generate automated AR contents by means of the integration of a recommender system. Furthermore, the recommender system enables the generation of individualized recommendations, which are able to provide a consistent added value to the presented MR system.

1.2 Methodology and Paper Structure

The contributions of the paper can be summarized as follows:

- Introduction of our concept and motivation of the need to consider new hybrid editorial systems, which are able to perform a persistent modification of the modalities of use of print media. The automated content creation process that we show enables the detection of relevant virtual contents, which are necessary to generate an up-to-date AR app for every release of a print medium. Specific user related recommendations are then integrated into the AR system in order to enable an individualized reading experience.
- Brief exploration of the status quo of AR based hybrid media. We introduce examples of integration of AR tools in print media and we present some of the possible technical modalities to integrate virtual contents in paper-based systems with mobile devices.

- Description of the architecture of the system. The framework that we defined is oriented to the creation of an AR app, which is based on our concept and integrates an individualized recommender system. The recommender system suggests relevant editorial contents but it also works as a search engine: it has the task to suggest appropriate contents and to detect relevant virtual contents, which may become AR contents.
- Presentation of the implementation design. Our work has been developed according to a specific knowledge framework derived from the domain ontology that we developed for the specific MR environment of the system. We examined different use cases to describe the knowledge framework of the hybrid media model that we present and we point out the specific use case related to editorial articles. In this way we can show the automated and individualized content generation process that we defined.
- Presentation of the prototypical implementation and evaluation of the artifact.
- The paper concludes with the synthesis of the achieved results, a short outlook and a discussion of future work.

According to a design science research approach [3], our research has to follow seven guidelines to be rigorous and relevant. The automated recommender system, which is integrated into the described hybrid media system to detect and create AR contents represents the innovative and purposeful artifact (Guideline 1) and it finds its expression in this chapter. The introduction chapter specifies the relevance of the research problem and the problem domain (Guideline 2). The aspects concerning the evaluation of the artifact (Guideline 3) are considered in Chapters "Issues of e-Collaboration and Knowledge Management in Media Industries", "Model-Driven Design of eMedia: Virtual Technology Transfer Office", "The Impact of Fluid Publishing on Media Information Management—A Survey of Latest Journalistic Trends as Data-Driven Journalism, Journalism as Process and Metrics-Driven Journalism" and "Determining the Benefit of Interactive Videos in the Health Sector: Validating a Custom Measurement Instrument". Moreover, we dedicated a chapter to the description of a first prototypal implementation of the presented system, in order to show the feasibility of the system and its innovative strength (Guideline 4). Chapter "Multi-screen Viewing and Contents: Understanding Connected TV" shows the respect of a rigorous methodological research approach, which reflects the coherence and the consistence of the artifact (Guideline 5). Considering the design science as a search process (Guideline 6), in Chapters "The Role of Standards in the Digital Media Industry", ""Own-it": Managing Intellectual Property Processes via the Activity Table in Creative Industries", and "Creative Co-production in eMedia and Creative Industries" we show that the presented approach considers the relevance of previous related work. The purpose to permit the communication of the research (Guideline 7) is expressed by our intention to publish this paper.

2 Related Work

2.1 Augmented Reality and Print Media

One of the first examples of integration of an AR system into a print medium is represented by the "MagicBook" [4]. The MagicBook is a prototype of an AR book that permits a reader with HMD to explore 3D models during the reading of a print medium. Although this AR system has a considerable importance in terms of research, it also presents some limits: the use of HMD reduces its diffusion in large scale and the use of AR markers as trigger entities limits the printing area of the text, aspects that reduce considerably its business potential. Other examples of integration of virtual reality and print medium consider with a forward-looking vision the use of mobile technology. The German magazine "Süddeutsche Zeitung Magazin" [5] created one of the first AR apps useful to integrate a release of the newspaper with virtual contents. The reader can experience the enhancement of contents of some selected printed images just scanning the print medium with a smartphone. The success of this example of AR tool for print media was, in terms of downloaded apps, really high [6] and similar experiences have been performed by other editorial companies (e.g., "Stern" [7], "Auto Bild" [8], "Welt der Wunder" [9], "Rheinische Post" [10], etc.). Relevant examples of paper-based AR applications stand out in the field of advertising. These applications are not only limited to the field of the publishing industry but they regard more in general the field of paper-based media, like for instance the packaging industry [11] and commercial leaflets [12]. An interesting research demonstrates that the average reading time of a paper-based AR advertisement is 12 s [13]. The average reading time of a traditional printed advertisement is instead 3.9 s [14]. It means that the users are generally more engaged and they are more available to pay attention to the proposed advertisements if they are involved into MR environments.

2.2 AR App Generation Tools

The use of AR technology to integrate print media is certainly dependent on the existing IT tools useful to develop AR systems. The spectrum of technical possibilities gets wider very fast and the offer of AR tools grows rapidly. Nowadays several IT tools offer the possibility to create AR applications (e.g. Metaio SDK [15], Vuforia AR SDK [16], Wikitude SDK [17], etc.). For their own nature, augmented reality and print media may be easily integrated. The necessary presence of a physical print medium useful to transmit the information enables the integration of trigger entities directly on the print medium. Images such as Matrix Barcodes (e.g., QR-Code, Aztec Code, Data Matrix, etc.), AR Markers or textured images may be easily printed on the print medium and used as trigger entities. Additionally, different typologies of trigger entities permit to access virtual contents by means of

AR applications. Trigger entities may be for instance simple physical objects, in feature detection based AR systems [18]. Moreover, innovative techniques such as OCR-tools [19], encoded paper [20] or text patch recognition [21] may be involved to create AR systems.

2.3   Research Contribution

Even if the possibilities offered by hybrid media are not confined only in the domain of augmented reality [22], mixed and augmented realities represent a key tool to permit the development of hybrid contexts and to maintain a fluid interaction between the different environments [23]. The use of AR technologies and print media results usually sporadic and does not represent a persistent modification of the typology of the offered editorial contents [24]. The use of AR tools in print media doesn't implicate the integration of virtual contents into print media. In order to integrate virtual contents into print media through the creation of specific hybrid media systems, it is necessary to provide the periodical publication with a periodical up-to-date AR app, which is realizable only through a structured and automated app creation process. To make the AR app generation process completely automated, it is necessary on one hand to define a process which enables the correct interaction of the different components of the system, in order to create the app itself and on the other hand, it is necessary to define a correct content generation process, which must be of course automated. The analysis of the literature shows the relevance of the integration of automated content generation processes for AR contents. The automated AR content generation process is in particular the result that our research wants to show in this paper.

3   Architecture of the System

We developed a specific automated process to create a hybrid media model which is tailored on the needs of an existing publishing company, in order to consider the validity of the defined paradigm of automation and to test our concept. In this chapter we shape the core building blocks of the system: publishing system, recommender system, external services, BPaaS platform, AR app (Fig. 1).

3.1   Publishing System

We proofed our concept with the editorial company "Saarländische Wochenblatt Verlagsgesellschaft mbH (Wochenspiegel)", which publishes a free of charge weekly distributed publication and it offers every week 15 different editions for the

Fig. 1 Architecture of the
system

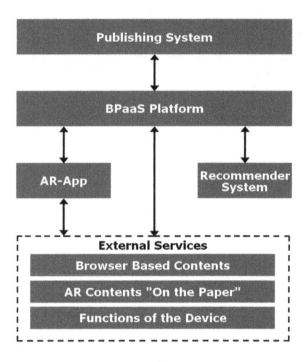

coverage of a German region. The existing editorial process can be summarized in two phases. In the first phase, all contents are created and selected for a specific issue of the newspaper. In the second phase, all selected contents are registered in the publisher system. In this way, it is possible to elaborate a large quantity of different contents. Editorial articles are archived in the publishing system through text files, image files and an XML index. Commercials are archived by image files and classified ads are archived through text files, image files, XML index and a database suitable for the online search.

3.2   Recommender System

The purpose of the recommender system is to provide appropriate suggestions to both user and actors of the publishing process. Suggestions are strict related to the profile of the user and to the editorial contents. The profile of the user is gained by implicit feedback (e.g. usage behavior) as well as explicit feedback that users can proactively submit to the app. Moreover, the recommender system has also the important role to make automated the whole AR content creation process. On this line, the recommender system works as a search engine: it detects relevant information in the text of an editorial article. This information are then elaborated and automatically elected as potential AR contents.

3.3 External Services

The app creation process determinates the selection of specific virtual contents related to printed editorial subjects. These virtual contents are available in the MR environment generated by the app, in form of AR contents. Links to external services such as the online version of the newspaper, video-sharing websites, web mapping services, social media and other URLs are directly overlaid on the newspaper. They can be virtual contents shown through the use of an internet browser, virtual contents shown as AR entities directly on the view of the print medium or they can be functions of the device, such as the possibility to call a phone number related to an editorial content. They represent a high customizable component of the architecture of the system because they are subject and release related.

3.4 BPaaS Platform

The BPaaS platform is an online based platform developed by the project partner Scheer Management. In the general context of the Business Process as a service (BPaaS), this platform permits the technical implementation of individualized IT tools for business processes. The BPaaS platform is responsible for the generation of the AR app.

3.5 AR App

The AR app is the interface through real and virtual environment. Downloading the index of every release, the AR app is always actualized. Therefore the user can experience a different modality of reading of the newspaper, which enables a real-time actualization of paper-based contents. Different typologies of recommendations are integrated in the MR environment created by the AR app. Every release has specific hybrid contents and every content permits to provide personalized recommendations according to the specificity of every reader.

4 Implementation Design

4.1 Knowledge Framework (Domain Ontology)

The knowledge model of the system has been shaped according to the definition of Reality–Virtuality Continuum [25] and it represents a concrete application of this theoretical definition. The development approach has been leaded according to the following methodological process [26]:

- Determination of the domain and scope of the ontology through the definition of specific competency questions [27].
- Enumeration of important terms in the ontological domain through a brain-storming process.
- Definition of classes and class hierarchy through a top-down development approach [28].
- Definition of the properties of the classes and the relationships between them.
- Iterative and deductive reprocessing according to the specific requirements of the system (e.g., the definition of "browser based virtual contents" reflects the requirement of the AR app to use third party contents without having direct responsibility on the contents).

The knowledge model which is the basis to define our concept is expressed by the domain ontology presented in Fig. 2. The creation of a hybrid media system requires the definition of a MR environment. A MR environment is a context where real and virtual worlds merge together to enable the coexistence and interaction of physical and digital objects [29]. The definition of a MR environment is the necessary condition to permit the creation of an AR interface for hybrid media. The hybrid media model that we present develops itself into three different environments: real environment, AR environment and virtual environment. The real environment is the tangible world of print media, which is composed by a publisher who creates a print medium, different users who read the print medium and have peculiar preferences and profiles and of course by a print medium. The difference between AR and virtual environment is defined by the presence in the AR environment of a coexistent and integrated component of tangible reality. AR environments imply a fixed reference with physical objects whereas virtual realities develop themselves through only digital objects. Reading a print medium, users will be able to deepen the editorial content just scanning it with the camera of a smartphone. Virtual links are superimposed on the real time streaming view of the camera and they enable the connection between print based contents and virtual entities. Clicking specific AR links, the users can access different virtual contents. Several typologies of contents may be included in this hybrid environment: galleries of photos, hyperlinks, videos but also individualized services like virtual recommendations.

Different scenarios represent typical editorial contents for print media. We identified the editorial articles as use case to test our concept. Every editorial article which has to be implemented with AR contents has a print based component as trigger entity to access specific AR links in an AR environment, when a user films the print medium with a smartphone. These AR links enable the user to experience virtual contents directly on the print medium (AR contents such as videos, galleries, info or 3D models embedded and visualized on the print medium). Moreover, AR

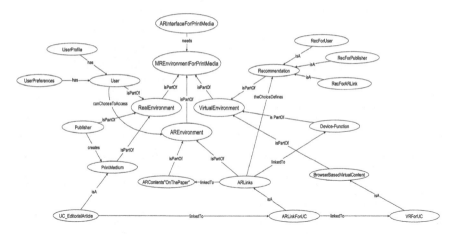

Fig. 2 Ontology of the system

links enable the direct opening of browser based virtual contents and enable to interact with functions of the mobile device.

When a user selects a particular AR link, s/he automatically expresses her/his preferences and her/his profile will be defined. According to user's profile and user's preferences, a recommender system provides appropriate and relevant recommendations about the content of every chosen scenario [30]. Specific recommendations for specific actors of the publishing company (publisher, journalist or content manager) can be provided during the phases of creation of editorial articles in order to receive suggestions and further information about different articles that may treat the same theme. These kinds of recommendations do not depend on user's profile and user's preferences but they are only defined by the content of print based editorial articles (Fig. 3).

4.2 Use Case: Editorial Articles

In our concept, we identified a use case that results useful to proof the automated AR content generation process. This use case refers to the editorial articles. As soon as the trigger entities let the augmentation of the print medium start, the user can see related AR links superimposed on the articles. Print medium and AR links are univocally correlated and filming a specific article, it is possible to detect automatically its own AR links. These links enable to access several virtual contents. AR links related to this use case are divided into two categories.

The first category is composed by the AR entities which connect to browser based virtual contents (e.g., the online article, external websites, etc.). These kinds of AR links are able to open a browser and to conduct the user to specific internet-based contents. When a user chooses to open one of these links, s/he

Real Environment   Augmented Reality
                                                              Environment

Fig. 3 Representation of the hybrid media system which links reality and virtuality through the definition of an augmented reality environment

automatically expresses her/his interest in the topic of the article. Therefore it is possible to deduce preferences and profile of the user and to provide, through the integrated recommender system, appropriate recommendations about similar editorial contents. These recommendations are shown in a context of virtual reality. The second category of AR links enables the interaction between AR interface and functions of the mobile device. For instance, the user who reads an article where it is present the date of a coming concert will see superimposed on the print medium an AR link useful to save the date on the calendar of the mobile device.

The user experiences the contemporary presence of virtual entities (VR recommendations, browser based contents and device interactions) and AR entities (AR links and virtual objects superimposed "on the paper") just using a smartphone during the reading of a print medium. In this use case, the recommender system provides specific recommendations useful to support journalists, publishers and content managers during the phase of creation of an article. These kinds of recommendations help them to detect older pertinent articles that may contain useful information during the creation of a new article.

4.3 The Recommender System as an Automated Search Engine for AR Contents

The core result of our research is the definition of an automated AR content generation process. This process is possible thanks to a correct definition of the interfaces between the different components of the system. To reach this task, the recommender system must be able to communicate with publishing system and BPaaS platform. The content generation process that we present is related to the described use case. As soon as an article has been generated by the publishing company, it is automatically added to the XML-based database of the publishing system. This database is accessible for the recommender system, in order to enable the implementation of the articles which need AR contents. Sending a request to the recommender it is possible to trigger an automated text analysis of the editorial content. This analysis enables the research of specific concepts in the text of the article, in order to detect the presence of editorial contents which may be useful for the automatic generation of AR contents. In this way, the recommender system works as a search engine. The concepts which the recommender is able to mine within the text of an editorial article are:

- *Addresses* (e.g., the address of a shop which may be described in an editorial article).
- *Dates* (e.g., the date of a concert which is the topic of an article and will take place in the future).
- *Email addresses* (e.g., the contact of the author of the editorial article).
- *Phone numbers* (e.g., the phone number of an association which is described in the article).
- *Websites/Social media* (e.g., the webpage of a theme which is treated in the editorial article).

These concepts are detected according to specific algorithms, which are based on the research of notions with comparable semantic relevance and they are derived from the presented ontological model. They are automatically extracted from the text of the editorial content in order to define relevant AR contents for the original article. From the presented items, it is possible to derive specific AR contents, which are useful to be integrated in the presented MR system through a completely automated process.

These possible AR contents are the following:

- AR link of a web mapping service, according to the extracted *address*.
- AR link of the function of the mobile device, which enables to save a *date* on the user's calendar.
- AR link of the email provider of the user to write an email to the extracted *email address*.
- AR link of the function of the mobile device, which enables to call a *phone number*.
- AR link of an internet browser, which enables to visualize the extracted *webpage*.

The described AR content generation process has a high degree of automation. The only human interventions that are needed are the upload of the editorial content and the final approval of the AR contents suggested by the recommender system.

5 Prototypical Implementation and Evaluation

We have created a prototypical implementation of the automated AR content generation system in order to demonstrate the implementability of the artifact and to show our proof-of-concept. The prototype has been created through the platform Java EE (Figs. 4 and 5).

The whole system is reachable on a server through a simple HTTP request/response scheme. It is possible to send requests to the server to interrogate the editorial content which constitutes the database. These requests trigger the automated search of defined contents in the text of an article. The process is completely automated and the request only has to be referred to a specific article-ID, which identifies a specific editorial content that has to be analyzed, in order to extract potential AR contents (Fig. 6).

According to a design-oriented methodology [3], the presented research must be evaluated against following evaluation criteria:

- *Validation of the quality of the recommendations*: validation of the relevance of the recommendations detected and proposed by the recommender system according to recall and precision [31].
- *Integration into the existing system*: evaluation of the integration of the automated AR app creation process into the existing publishing system, from the creation of the print contents to the creation of the AR app.

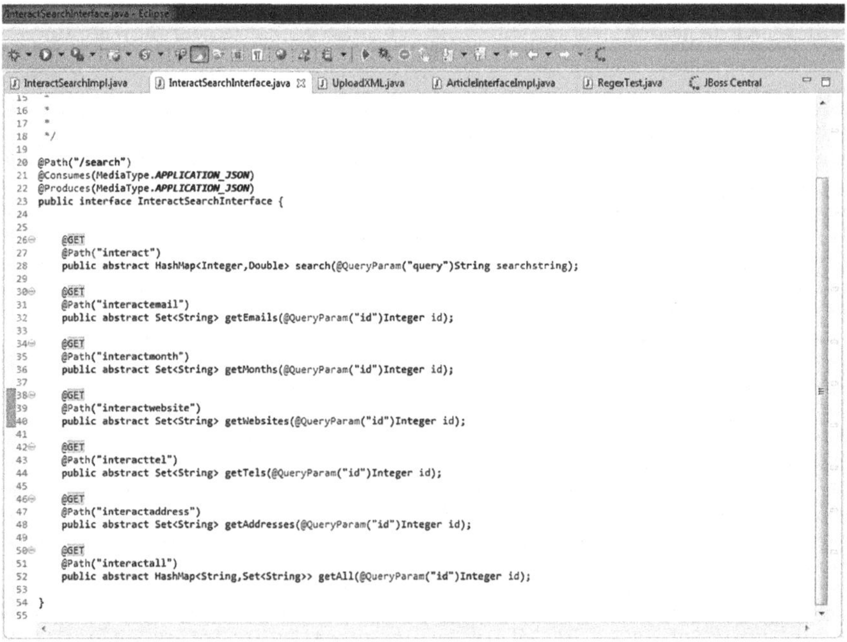

Fig. 4 Screenshot of the prototypical implementation

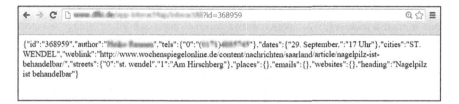

{"id":"368959","author":"████ ████","tels":{"0":"(██ █)███ █ ██"},"dates":{"29. September.":"17 Uhr"},"cities":"ST. WENDEL","weblink":"http://www.wochenspiegelonline.de/content/nachrichten/saarland/article/nagelpilz-ist-behandelbar/","streets":{"0":"st. wendel","1":"Am Hirschberg"},"places":{},"emails":{},"websites":{},"heading":"Nagelpilz ist behandelbar"}

Fig. 5 The recommender system detects potential AR contents related to a specific editorial article in order to generate AR links

Fig. 6 Screenshot of the AR interface created according to detected AR contents

- *Reliability of the extracted AR contents*: validation of the relevance of the AR contents, which are automatically extracted from the text of the print medium.

6 Conclusion and Future Work

The work presented in this publication summarizes the importance of the use and integration of information systems for the media industry. Print media must be able to face the challenges that information technology offers. New typologies of virtual contents and innovative hybrid systems are able to offer cutting-edge approaches for the media industry. This paper shows a novel approach which integrates print media and internet-based contents, by means of the definition of hybrid media systems based on MR environments. The added value of the defined approach is expressed by the definition of an automated AR content creation process which is based on the direct analysis of the editorial content through the integration of a recommender system. The integration of a recommender system enables several goals: the readers can experience a novel and individualized reading approach and the publishers are able to provide a persistent modification of the editorial offer, thanks to the integration of an automated and industrialized AR content generation process. Our research designs a structured and persistent modification of the offer of contents for print media through the definition of a MR environment.

Several aspects have large potentialities in terms of research and permit further implementations. The text analysis of editorial contents may be further refined and also extended to different kinds of metadata regarding editorial contents. Moreover, the recommender system could also integrate thematic external search engines, in order to provide more specific results for the creation of AR contents. The presented concept offers interesting outlooks to define innovative applications able to integrate AR tools in print media and even in different fields. Our concept offers results which may be easily extended to various paper-based AR systems. Other domains that use print medium (e.g., learning, advertisement, marketing and communication, etc.) may take advantage of the presented research. In terms of research, it could certainly contribute to the definition of an advanced concept of hybrid media which could shape new business models based on the use of AR technology.

Acknowledgements The research project INTeRACT 4AP has been funded by the German Federal Ministry of Education and Research (BMBF) under the framework of the KMU-Innovativ Programme for Information and Communication Technologies with the project ID 01IS13010B. Our special thanks goes also to the other involved parties in this research: Saarländische Wochenblatt Verlagsgesellschaft mbH (Wochenspiegel), Scheer Management GmbH and Landesmedienanstalt Saarland.

References

1. Siltanen, S., & Aikala, M. (2012). Augmented reality enriches hybrid media. In *Proceeding of the 16th International Academic MindTrek Conference* (ACM Press, pp. 113–116).
2. Fedorovskaya, E., & Yu, L. (2010). Investigating the effect of publishing approches using print, electronic and augmented reality media on user experience. In: *Advances in printing and media technology—Print and media research for the benefit of industry and society* (p. 39).
3. Hevner, A. R., March, S. T., Park, J., & Ram, S. (2004). Design science in information systems research. *MIS Quarterly, 28*(1), 75–105.
4. Billinghurst, M., Hirokazu, K., & Poupyrev, I. (2001) The magicbook: A transitional AR interface. *Computers and Graphics*, pp. 745–753.
5. http://www.metaio.com/press/press-release/2010/sueddeutsche-zeitung-sz-magazin/. Accessed September 19, 2015.

6. http://www.metaio.com/customers/case-studies/sueddeutsche-zeitung-sz-magazin/. Accessed September 19, 2015.
7. http://play.google.com/store/apps/details?id=com.metaio.junaio.plugin.stern_ar. Accessed September 19, 2015.
8. http://play.google.com/store/apps/details?id=de.autobild.augmentedreality. Accessed September 19, 2015.
9. http://www.wuv.de/medien/welt_der_wunder_bauer_magazin_spielt_mit_augmented_reality. Accessed September 19, 2015.
10. http://www.rp-online.de/so-funktioniert-rp-alive-vid-1.2980484. Accessed September 19, 2015.
11. Linqvist, U., Federley, M., Hakola, L., Laukkannen, M., Mensonen, A., & Viljakainen, A. (2001). Hybrid media on packages.
12. Böhmer, M., Daiber, F., Gehring, S., & Löchtefeld, M. (2013) Augmented reality—Based advertising strategies for paper leaflets. In: *Workshop on Pervasive Technologies in Retail Environment*, Zürich.
13. http://www.axelspringer-mediapilot.de/dl/16384913/DW_2014_WELTderZukunft.pdf. Accessed September 19, 2015.
14. http://de.statista.com/statistik/daten/studie/271067/umfrage/betrachtungsdauer-von-werbung-in-verschiedenen-medien/. Accessed September 19, 2015.
15. http://dev.metaio.com/content-creation/overview/. Accessed September 19, 2015.
16. http://developer.vuforia.com/resources/dev-guide/native-sdk. Accessed September 19, 2015.
17. http://www.wikitude.com/products/wikitude-sdk/. Accessed September 19, 2015.
18. Schmalstieg, D., Langlotz, T., & Billinghurst, M. (2011). Augmented reality 2.0. In G. Brunnett, S. Coquillart, & G. Welch (Eds.) *Virtual realities* (pp. 13–37). Vienna: Springer.
19. Smith, R. (2007). An overview of the tesseract OCR engine. In *Ninth International Conference on Document Analysis and Recognition*.
20. Pettersson, M., & Edsoe, T. (2001). Encoded paper for optical reading. Patent WO 2001026032 A1, Issued April 12, 2001.
21. Hull, J. J., Erol, B., Graham, J., Ke, Q. K. Q., Kishi, H., Moraleda, J., & D. G. Van Olst. (2007). Paper-based augmented reality. In *17th International Conference on Artificial Reality and Telexistence*.
22. Reiss, M., & Steffens, D. (2010). Hybrid toolboxes: Conceptual and empirical analysis for blending patterns in application of hybrid media. *Technological and Economic Development of Economy, 16*(2), 305–326.
23. Johnson, W. L., Vilhjalmsson, H., & Marsella, S. (2005). Serious games for language learning: How much game, how much AI? In *Proceedings of the 2005 Conference on Artificial Intelligence in Education: Supporting Learning through Intelligent and Socially Informed Technology* (pp. 306–313).
24. Perey, C. (2011). Print and publishing and the future of augmented reality. *Information Services and Use, 31*(1/2), 31–38.
25. Milgram, P., & Kishino, F. (1994). A taxonomy of mixed reality visual displays. *IEICE TRANSACTIONS on Information Systems, E77-D*(12), 1–15.
26. Noy, N., & McGuinness, D. (2001). Ontology development 101: A guide to creating your first ontology. *Development, 32*, 1–25.
27. Grüninger, M., Fox, M. S., & Gruninger, M. (1995). Methodology for the design and evaluation of ontologies. In *International Joint Conference on Artificial Inteligence (IJCAI95), Workshop on Basic Ontological Issues in Knowledge Sharing* (pp. 1–10).
28. Uschold, M., & Gruninger, M. (1996). Ontologies: Principles, methods and applications. *Knowledge Engineering Review, 11*, 93–136.
29. De Souza e Silva, A., & Sutko, D. M. (2009). Digital cityscapes: Merging digital and urban playspaces (pp. 205–209). Peter Lang Publishing Inc.
30. Di Valentin, D., Emrich, A., Werth, D., & Loos, P. (2014). Architecture design of a hybrid recommender system in e-learning scenarios. In *Proceedings of the 7th IADIS International Conference on Information Systems*.

31. Zaier, Z., Godin, R., & Faucher, L. (2008). Evaluating recommender systems. In *Proceedings—4th International Conference on Automated Solutions for Cross Media Content and Multi-Channel Distribution* (pp. 211–217), Axmedis.

Author Biographies

Rocco Raso is a researcher at the Institute for Information Systems (IWi) at the German Research Center for Artificial Intelligence (DFKI). He received a Master Degree in Engineering with honours from the Polytechnic University of Turin. His research activity focuses on the integration of Augmented and Virtual Reality technologies into different contexts (e.g., print media, logistics, construction and facility management, manufacturing industry), combining artificial intelligence methods and techniques, such as recommender systems and text data mining, with immersive technologies. His work resulted in a patent and several academic publications.

Sebastian Cucerca is student research assistant at the Institute for Information Systems (IWi) at the German Research Center for Artificial Intelligence (DFKI). He is currently completing his studies in Media and Computer Science at the Saarland University. His research activities include neuronal networks, deep learning and text data mining.

Dr. Dirk Werth is senior researcher and head of research group Business Integration Technologies at the Institute for Information Systems (IWi) at the German Research Center for Artificial Intelligence (DFKI). Dr. Werth holds diplomas in Business Administration and in Computer Sciences, as well as a Ph.D. in economics. His research activities comprise collaborative business processes, business integration and advanced business information systems. He wrote and edited several books and published scientific papers and articles in international journals and proceedings.

Univ.-Prof. Dr. Peter Loos is director of the Institute for Information Systems (IWi) at the German Research Center for Artificial Intelligence (DFKI) and head of the Chair of Information Systems at Saarland University. His research activities include business process management, information modelling, enterprise systems, software development as well as implementation of information systems. Prof. Loos graduated from Saarland University in 1984 with a degree in Business Administration and Information Systems (Dipl.-Kfm.) He received his PhD in Business Sciences (Dr. rer. pol.) in 1991 awarded with the Dr.-Eduard-Martin-Preis also in 1991 and his venia legendi in 1997. Prof. Loos wrote several books, contributed to 40 books and published more than 100 papers in journals and proceedings.

Part V
Methods, Approaches, and Importance of IT and Information Systems and Management in Media–Media and Content as Part of IS&M across Application Domains

Issues of e-Collaboration and Knowledge Management in Media Industries

Blaž Rodič

Abstract Globalisation of media industries in regards to sourcing and casting of artists, content, locations for filming, image, video and audio treatment has brought geo-graphically and culturally diverse teams together in projects ranging from video games and ads to major studio live-action and animated features. This new concept of teams however presents several issues as well as advantages and new opportunities. This chapter aims to present a holistic view on the issues present in e-collaboration. We introduce the field of e-collaboration and virtual teams. We propose a new categorization of e-collaboration tools. Further we examine the issues regarding culture, trust, human-computer interaction, social systems and management associated with e-collaboration and virtual teams. The perspective of knowledge management is discussed in the final section. In order to achieve optimal results from e-collaboration, companies should acknowledge and address the discussed issues in addition to organizational and technical issues.

1 Introduction

In the information age, creative or cultural industries are becoming a major part of economy in many post-industrial societies. According to Drucker [1], societies transition from an economy based on material goods to one based on knowledge. This transition has led to the creation of information societies, where the creation, distribution, use, integration and manipulation of information is a significant economic, political, and cultural activity.

Globalisation of media industries in regards to sourcing and casting of artists, content, locations for filming, image, video and audio treatment has brought geographically and culturally diverse teams together in projects ranging from video games and ads to major studio live-action and animated features. According to Lugmayr [2], media industries are the third largest spender in IT infrastructure, software, and

B. Rodič (✉)
Faculty of Information Studies, Ljubljanska cesta 31A, 8000 Novo mesto, Slovenia
e-mail: blaz.rodic@fis.unm.si

© Springer International Publishing AG 2016   265
A. Lugmayr et al. (eds.), *Information Systems and Management in Media
and Entertainment Industries*, International Series on Computer Entertainment
and Media Technology, DOI 10.1007/978-3-319-49407-4_13

hardware after banking and manufacturing industries, and utilize the latest technologies to produce, manage, and distribute their content. However, while new media companies seem to succeed well in adopting new technologies, traditional media industries such as broadcasters, publishing, or advertisement agencies seem to face the challenge of transforming their industries towards the 21st century fully digital firm.

Nevertheless, well designed technology can alleviate many remote collaboration issues, but does not substitute physical proximity, and the issues described in this chapter are present to an extent even if the users have access to the latest and best technologies. Cross-functional/departmental/geographical/etc. systems are not always compatible with differences in languages, cultural heritages, and business processes in other countries [3–5]. As noted by Lugmayr [2], issues stem from "different organizational cultures, requirements towards the creative content creation process, methods in deploying information systems on organizational level, integration of departments, legacy system integration, up to fully different non-compatible architectures on operational and strategic levels."

An important part of the information systems field is concerned with behavioural issues that arise in the development and long-term maintenance of information systems. Other behavioural disciplines contribute important concepts and methods. Sociologists study information systems with an eye toward how groups and organizations shape the development of systems and also how systems affect individuals, groups, and organizations. Psychologists study information systems with an interest in how human decision makers perceive and use formal information [6].

Issues of e-collaboration in media industry in the digital age stems from its specific product. As noted in Lugmayr [7], "The particular product in media industry is content requiring its production, processing, distribution, and management. Thus, on operational level, the core of media industry is any information architecture dealing with content alongside with other information systems (i.e. data warehousing, document management, customer management etc.) that were introduced on the basis of other than media industries." As the product of media industry is (largely) perishable and digital, the business models and workflows also differ from industries offering services and physical products.

This chapter aims to present a holistic view on the issues regarding knowledge management, culture, trust, human-computer interaction, social systems and management associated with e-collaboration and virtual teams, particularly in the media industry.

2 E-collaboration

Main goal of e-collaboration systems is to reduce the isolation of users from each other [8] by providing [9] communication support, coordination support and cooperation support. Advancing research in the area of human-computer interaction, smart environments, multi-modal interaction, ambient intelligence and ubiquitous computing nowadays is converging into the dawning era of human computing [10]. Human computing escalates the complexities of human-human and human-machine interaction in the already complex software engineering and system integration [11]. Emerging e-collaboration systems are expected to be increasingly adapted to the nature of human cognition and communication and present a quantum leap beyond modern productivity-oriented workplace technologies in which performance is the key objective and the user experience comes after business process logic and formalized workflow.

To understand the current limitations, i.e. opportunities for improvement in e-collaboration tools and concepts and possible issues, we first need to define e-collaboration itself. Kock [12] stated that e-collaboration consists of the following elements:

• The collaborative task: A task that parties can work on together. For example, jobs beyond the capacity of one organization, or jobs that require complementary skill sets;
• The e-collaboration technology: Existing or new IT infrastructure such as teleconferencing, discussion boards and instant messaging;
• The participants: Organizations that are collaborating, industry associations and government agencies. Characteristics of the participants and size of the group can also have an effect on the collaboration;
• Mental schemas of the participants: The knowledge and experience of the participants and the degree of similarity between participants. For example, expert or novice understanding of the task;
• The physical environment: The location of the participants. For example, the geographical location of the toolmakers was dispersed and therefore they needed to apply more effort to e-collaboration, whereas the IT organizations were within the same geographical area;
• The social environment: the perceptions of trust and the behaviour among the participants as well as peer pressure among participants.

E-collaboration can be categorized according to the time and space where/when the participants are present. The space dimension is discrete, while the dimension of artificiality (nature of a participant's presentation in the software) can use several different combinations of realistic and synthetic representations. We have combined the model of shared spaces proposed by Benford et al. [13], which focuses on synchronous communication with the categorization of several types of groupware tools. Our proposed categorization of groupware is shown in Table 1. This new categorization gives a better insight into the relation between the dimensions of artificiality, space, time, and the type of tools available. Several examples of tools are listed in multiple categories, as their flexibility allows usage under synchronous and asynchronous conditions and the choice of representation is left to the user.

Table 1 Proposed categorization of e-collaboration systems according to time, space and artificiality

Dimension of artificiality Synthetic (generated) physical (real/istic)	**Augmented reality**	**Virtual reality**
	Same time (synchronous)	Same time (synchronous) *e.g. virtual worlds, chat*
	Different time (asynchronous)	Different time (asynchronous) *e.g. virtual worlds, forums, wikis*
	Physical reality	**Tele-presence**
	Same time (synchronous) *e.g. e-meetings, e-voting, e-brainstorming*	Same time (synchronous) *e.g. teleconferencing, e-meetings, screen sharing, shared documents, chat*
	Different time (asynchronous) *e.g. collaborative design*	Different time (asynchronous) *e.g. workflow tools, document management systems, email, shared documents, forums*

Local (physically present) remote (represented)
Dimension of space

3 Cultural Issues

Collaboration is defined as "a method that implies working in a group of two or more to achieve a common goal, while respecting each individual's contribution to the whole" [14].

However, collaboration often does not come naturally to participants, especially in cultures that cultivate individual accountability and responsibility. Concievably, team members from cultures that regard the value of working together differently (e.g. USA vs. Japan) will have difficulties. In most companies, it is difficult to encourage employees to collaborate and even cooperate with others; they avoid sharing resources or customers on tasks with little recognition of individual input [15]. These issues are illustrated in Lugmayr [7] on the examples of differences of artistic departments and digital (web) departments in TV media houses, publishers diversifying into web content and film industry implementing HD and 3D technologies.

The cultural differences not only affect how individuals must interact with each other on a personal level but also how they have to interact in a business setting. Different cultures have different standards for business behaviour. One country's idea of proper business etiquette could be another's idea of rudeness.

A research on issues in e-collaboration in writing of technical documents [16] finds that while culture clashes were common, only one out of eleven participants had been provided with formal training on how to deal with these potential issues by his or her employer. Further, using technologies which prevent the observation of nonverbal behaviour can result in a reduced understanding of the social meanings of group member actions.

One of the main psychological issues in e-collaboration in general is the inability of people to see each other's physical cues, which is especially problematic when working remotely with people from varied cultural backgrounds because of the increased dependence on physical cues for determining intent. Especially when individuals are unfamiliar with each other's culture, nonverbal communication becomes an important method for interpreting the behaviour of group members who are not necessarily from the same culture.

Given the experience from social networks, younger generations may have fewer intercultural issues, both due to their previous intercultural experience and due to their familiarity with and adoption of the global Anglo-American culture spread by social networks and global brands. This may be part of the reason for successful integration of diverse teams of designers, web developers, programmers etc. from Europe to India in quick-rise startups such as Outfit7 (Talking Tom franchise) and Rovio (Angry Birds franchise).

4 Trust Issues

Trust develops out of the joint experience of working together. When trust is low, we usually build formal protections into these relationships. When trust is high, we are more likely to develop informal but well-understood ways of working together.

Rusman et al. [17] state that the main issues in virtual teams are: (1) Unequal distribution in time for communication (sporadic at the start of the project and overload at the end), (2) the exchange of incomplete information, (3) infrequent and unequal "spread of interaction between team members ...," (4) "...'flaming' (online name-calling), personal conflicts and enduring misunderstandings between group members," and (5) low overall group performance. Trust in virtual teams develops more slowly and is more delicate than face-to-face teams. This trust develops even more slowly when group members have even less in common due to different cultures, a common situation in virtual teams.

Trust in a virtual environment may come easier to the generations that grew up with social networks though. According to the findings of our research [18] the young people are much more willing to share personal information with acquaintances and strangers on Facebook than in the street. The respondents in our research were between 16 and 25 years of age. The main results are shown in Figs. 1 and 2.

Basic personal information (name and surname) would never be shared with an acquaintance on the street by 11 % of respondents, which is significantly more than 1 % of respondents on Facebook, and an even greater percentage of respondents would never share their birth date (29 % compared with 18 % on Facebook) and phone numbers (only 5 % would always share their number in the street, compared with 13 % who share their phone number on Facebook). Also, more than 70 % of respondents share their posts with all their Facebook "friends" and let all their "friends" post to their "wall". 67 % of respondents do not segregate their "friends" into groups, even though some of the "friends" are Facebook-only acquaintances.

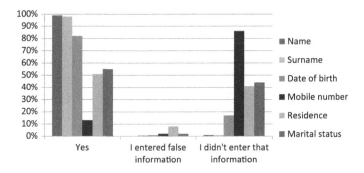

Fig. 1 What information about yourself do you disclose on Facebook?

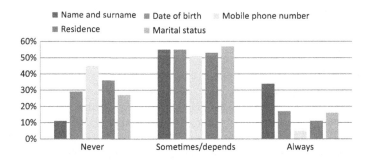

Fig. 2 What personal information would you be willing to share on the street with a stranger or a casual acquaintance?

18 % of respondents have more than 91 such "friends". These results are in sharp contrast with the low level of trust towards Facebook: only 21 % of respondents replied that they trust Facebook with their personal information [18]. We can conclude that the attitude of the respondents towards privacy is relaxed, and personal information is shared regardless of their trust towards the provider of the social network service.

However, according to Bente et al. [19], trust could be enhanced through re-inserting some sort of physical cues via the individuals' avatars providing humanlike physical properties that enable the transmission of nonverbal signals, which is discussed in the next section.

5 Human Interaction Issues

Even if the development of technologies and concepts in e-collaboration tools has been impressive, there are still aspects of human collaboration and interaction that are yet not sufficiently supported. While "ICT allows organizations to bridge time and distance barriers with once undreamed of ease" [20], it also creates new boundaries at the level of the work unit [21]. Scholars have shown that computer-mediated communication can lead to severe problems of interpreting transmitted information [22].

Most of the nonverbal cues that we take for granted in face-to-face communication are not transferred in online communications: these include spatial orientation, body posture, hand gesture, glancing, and facial expression. Furthermore, users in a virtual environment typically have a very limited awareness of others, who may silently "lurk" by remaining passive [23].

Teleconferencing does not provide body language or other spatial cues—gaze direction, spatial presence and direct or peripheral awareness of the activity of participants. Videoconferencing does not create a feeling of co-location: you can't place people in relation to one another; other than knowing that someone is looking at the camera; you cannot tell what they are looking at [24].

Facial expressions are the basic way of expressing emotion, agreement or disagreement and understanding or confusion. Glancing and eye contact are another important aspects of body language. As with body orientation, the direction of a person's gaze indicates their focus of attention: it is used for initiating, maintaining, and ending a conversation. It is also used extensively in group conversations, which require non-verbal turn-taking cues. To overcome these limitations of telecommunication, emotional icons are used extensively in text-based environments including emails, chats, forums and instant messaging to give users the ability to express emotion. Real-life communication however makes far more extensive use of non-verbal mechanisms. The social subtleties of gaze and eye contact require a strong degree of presence within a virtual environment for them to work effectively [25].

Real-time modelled human-like representations (avatars) give the potential for body language to be included as a communication channel. While the graphics of most virtual environments have generally been rather unsophisticated, studies have shown that even crude block-like forms of avatars can be useful in communicating non-verbal social cues [26]. Despite the graphic simplicity, a user's awareness of the spatial proximity and orientation of others has a strong impact on the dynamics of group communication.

A greater level of realism and support for non-verbal communication can be developed within collaborative virtual environments (CVEs), which are computer-enabled, distributed virtual spaces or places in which people can meet and interact with others, with agents and with virtual objects. CVEs vary greatly in their representational richness from 3D virtual reality to 2D and even text based environments. The main applications to date have been military and industrial team training, collaborative design and engineering, and multiplayer games.

CVEs clearly have the potential to enable innovative and effective distance teaching techniques, involving for example debate, simulation, role play, discussion groups, brainstorming, and project-based group work. Immersion in a common virtual "space" however cannot be compared to direct contact—2D environments lack engagement, and current 3D virtual technologies are too unpractical for regular business use and lack business oriented applications.

6 Social Issues

Apart from the human interaction, another area that needs to be further developed in e-collaboration systems is their support for existing socio-technical systems and their improvement. For an online environment to be successful, there have to be good reasons for people to use it. For work-driven e-collaboration, this is known to include the provision of useful collaborative tools within the environment. However for social e-collaboration, this should also include mechanisms for fostering social activity—something that has rarely been recognized in CVE research [25]. E.g. chance meetings; informal and unplanned meetings with colleagues are rarely supported in e-collaboration tools, yet they are known to be crucial to the work of many workers, particularly knowledge workers. Informal meetings are crucial to the work activities (development of a team spirit) and for a meeting to take place, a synchronous, rather than asynchronous awareness is indispensable. A meeting space does not come into being unless synchronous awareness is realized.

The technical system and the social system have to be co-optimized for the whole system to be successful. If a technical system is created or introduced at the expense of a social system, the obtained results will be sub-optimal. The main messages from the socio-technical systems discussion for e-collaboration are [27]:

- Technical systems (e-collaboration support technology) are highly embedded in social systems.
- The social and the technical subsystems should be optimized (designed) in parallel, because they influence each other.
- The goal/task of the overall system should not be forgotten—it usually is a main source for the coherence of the system.

In this context it is important to note that implementing an e-collaboration system should mean designing a complete socio-technical system, including organizational and social aspects. The technical aspect is less important that the socio-technical aspect. As many collaboration aspects are common to different e-collaboration and Web 2.0 systems, they are implemented in (sometimes freely) available components, which can be reused. Therefore it is common that a new e-collaboration is not developed from scratch and off-the-shelf components are used instead. Development therefore means selection, adaptation, integration and configuration.

7 Management Issues

Several management and organization challenges are also associated with virtualizing organization structures. Through virtualization the complexity of the organization can increase drastically, because of new barriers and inter-group interfaces [22]. Especially challenging is the management of a multi-project (e.g. matrix) organization where most employees work on several project concurrently. At the group level, new problems of information exchange and knowledge sharing arise due to the emergence of new spatial and social barriers in distributed environments [22]. In distributed work arrangements people are often left out of important decision processes (remoteness), which can cause unnecessary conflicts at the team level [28].

Moreover, in the virtualized organization people have to show social competencies and to learn to act as boundary spanners to ensure knowledge sharing [21]. From a human resource perspective further problems are posed by the control and incentive aspects of the new work settings [29]: controlling people and their work processes becomes much more challenging once traditional co-located settings are given up.

8 Knowledge Management

A firm only gains sustainable advances from what it collectively knows, how efficiently it uses what it knows, and how quickly it acquires and uses new knowledge [30]. This is especially true in creative industries, and we need to examine the relation between e-collaboration and knowledge management.

The creation and diffusion of knowledge have become increasingly important factors in competitiveness. More and more, knowledge is being thought of as a valuable commodity that is embedded in products (especially high-technology products) and embedded in the tacit knowledge of highly mobile employees. Knowledge management is the deliberate and systematic coordination of an organizations people, technology, processes, and organizational structure in order to add value through reuse and innovation. This is achieved through the promotion of creating, sharing, and applying knowledge as well as through the feeding of valuable lessons learned and best practices into corporate memory in order to foster continued organizational learning [31]. E-collaboration technologies allow companies to bring together team members from different locations, and should in theory improve the development and acquisition of new knowledge.

There are two kinds of knowledge: explicit knowledge and tacit knowledge. According to Nonaka and Konno [32] "... tacit knowledge is exchanged through joint activities—such as being together, spending time, living in the same environment—rather than through written or verbal instructions."

Explicit knowledge can be expressed in words and numbers and shared in the form of data, scientific formulae, specifications, manuals, media libraries and toolkits and the like. This kind of knowledge can be readily transmitted and shared between individuals formally and systematically. Tacit knowledge is highly personal and hard to formalize, making it difficult to communicate or share with others in and yet it can represent a major asset of a company. There are two dimensions to tacit knowledge. The first is the technical dimension, which encompasses the kind of informal personal skills or crafts often referred to as "know-how." The second is the cognitive dimension. It consists of beliefs, ideals, values, schemata, and mental models which are deeply ingrained in us and which we often take for granted. While difficult to articulate, this cognitive dimension of tacit knowledge shapes the way we perceive the world [32]. Tacit aspects of a firm's knowledge are embedded into its organizational culture (e.g. "how *we* do things") and reflect on informal standards for quality, work ethics, etc. However organizational culture takes a long time (years) to develop, meaning that ad hoc project teams in e-media projects may lack this quality.

Socialization involves the sharing of tacit knowledge between individuals. In practice, socialization involves capturing knowledge through physical proximity. The process of acquiring knowledge is largely supported through direct interaction. Disseminating tacit knowledge is another key aspect of socialization. The process of transferring one's ideas or images directly to colleagues or subordinates means to share personal knowledge and create a common place or space. This process is however markedly different if the transfer is conducted within a virtual environment.

We can conclude that the transfer of tacit knowledge in e-collaboration of virtual teams is limited by the level of immersion provided by the e-collaboration technology and the perception of shared space, as well as the duration of virtual teams. The opportunity exists, but as long as there is significant qualitative difference between direct and virtual contact, the potential remains unfulfilled.

Many executives aspire to develop knowledge-sharing cultures where knowledge is shared easily among team members through social and other networks. This aspiration is also a primary assumption behind the knowledge management literature that proposes that knowledge-sharing cultures are more conducive to knowledge creation and enhanced performance [33]. However, the development of any common culture depends heavily on the frequency and quality of direct human contact, something which is lacking withing virtual environments.

9   Conclusion

To summarize, in order to successfully implement e-collaboration systems also from the non-technical aspects, the media industry has to adapt to the new collaboration possibilities and new ways of working brought by the e-collaboration systems. We propose involving the employees as much as possible in the design of the e-collaboration system—to do a participatory design of the work systems (the whole socio-technical system including technology but also organizational and social aspects. As interpersonal communication depends strongly on cultures of persons involved, we can conclude that cultural differences further influence trust and social issues in e-collaboration, and intercultural issues must be given adequate attention in design of teams and their management as well as in selection of e-collaboration tools.

Nunamaker et al. [34] list nine principles they see as being essential for effective virtual teams: "...realigning reward structures for virtual teams", "...find new ways to focus attention on task", "...design activities that cause people to get to know each other", "...building a virtual presence", "...agree on standards and terminology", "...be more explicit", "...train teams to self-facilitate", and "...embed collaboration technology into everyday work". These principles could be applied to e-collaboration both in domestic e-collaboration and global.

Groups with high common ground (i.e. matched culture, history of collaboration, common goals) and loosely coupled work, with readiness both for collaboration and collaboration technology, have a chance at succeeding with remote work. Deviations from each of these create strain on the relationships among teammates and require changes in the work or processes of collaboration to succeed.

The companies' experience with Facebook and similar social sites shows that the user motivation to use social software is higher than using classical e-collaboration systems, and the main difference may be the possibility to "have fun". Social software is built for being a 'medium', i.e. being flexible to be used in different settings for different—not yet envisioned—tasks, while e-collaboration tools are relatively rigid, focused on the work tasks and leave users too little freedom. The potential of "social" and internet based collaboration has been recognized at least by the content generation and editing companies such as Adobe (e.g. its Creative Cloud and CQ Social Community present a major shift from a one user/one workstation/one perpetual license paradigm). This allows the implementation of "digital end-to-end workflows, where content is digitally managed from production to consumption" [2] in a virtual team.

To ensure that the co-workers still collaborate efficiently if provided with an open collaboration media a company should not restrict the possibilities, but rather by help the users to explore the possibilities and to avoid errors others have made before. Key to success is to strike the right balance between providing the right guidelines and leaving enough freedom for users to develop their own ways of using the e-collaboration tools, and monitor the evolving process in order to identify problems and good practices. Insufficient guidance might lead to an ineffective diversity, but too much guidance might kill the important "fun factor". Consequently, the guidelines should be developed in a participative approach in close cooperation with the end users.

References

1. Drucker, P. (1969). *The age of discontinuity*. London: Heinemann.
2. Lugmayr, A. (2013a). Issues and approach in defining a European research agenda on information systems and management in creative eMedia industries. In E. Stojmenova & A. Lugmayr (Eds.), *Proceedings of the 1st Workshop on Defining a European Research Agenda on Information Systems and Management in eMedia Industries* (in conjuction with eBled, Bled, Slovenia) (pp. 17–25). Bled, Slovenia: Lugymedia Inc., International Ambient Media Organization (AMEA).

3. Davison, R. (2002). Cultural complications of ERP. *Communications of the ACM, 45*(7), 2002.
4. Liang, H., Yajiong, X., Boulton, W. R., & Byrd, T. A. (2004). Why Western vendors don't dominate China's ERP market. *Communications of the ACM, 47*(7), 2004.
5. Martinsons, M. G. (2004). ERP in China: One package two profiles. *Communications of the ACM, 47*(No. 7).
6. Laudon, K. C., & Laudon, J. P. (2012). *Management information systems: Managing the digital firm* (12th ed.). Upper Saddle River, NJ: Prentice-Hall Inc.
7. Lugmayr, A. (2013b). Brief introduction into information systems and management research in media industries. In *2013 IEEE International Conference on Multimedia and Expo Workshops (ICMEW), 2013* (pp. 1–6).
8. Koch, M., & Gross, T. (2006). Computer-supported cooperative work—Concepts and trends. In *Proceedings of Conference of the Association Information and Management (AIM), Lecture Notes in Informatics (LNI) P-92*. Bonn: Koellen Verlag.
9. Sauter, C., Mühlherr, T., & Teufel, S. (1994). Sozio-kulturelle Auswirkungen von Groupware. In W. Rauch, F. Strohmeier, H. Hiller, & C. Schlögl (Eds.): Proceedings of the 4th International Symposium für Informationswissenschaft (pp. 517–526). Universitätsverlag Konstanz.
10. Pantic, M., Pentland, A., Nijholt, A., & Huang, T. (2006). Human computing and machine understanding of human behavior: A survey. In F. Kwek & Y. Yang (Eds.), *ACM SIGCHI proceedings eighth international conference on multimodal interfaces (ACM ICMI 2006), Banff, Canada* (pp. 239–248). New York: ACM.
11. Clancey, W. (1997). *Situated cognition: On human knowledge and computer representations.* Cambridge: Cambridge University Press.
12. Kock, N., "What is e-collaboration?", International Journal of e-Collaboration, Vol. 1, No. 1, pp. i-vii, 2005.
13. Benford, S., Greenhalgh, C., Reynard, G., Briwn, C., & Koleva, B. (1998). Understanding and constructing shared spaces with mixed reality boundaries. *ACM Transactions on Computer-Human Interaction (ToCHI), 5*(3), 185–223.
14. McInnerney, J., & Robert, T. S. (2004). Collaborative or cooperative learning? In T.S. Roberts (Ed.), *Online collaborative learning: Theory and practice* (pp. 203–214). Hershey, PA: IGI Global.
15. Hansen, M. T. (1999). The search-transfer problem: The role of weak ties in sharing knowledge across organization subunits. *Administrative Science Quarterly, 44*(1), 82–111.
16. Wertz, K. (2012). Study of the issues in technical writing e-collaboration and methods to enhance collaborative cooperation with a focus on global collaboration. Available at: http://www.katherinewertz.com/wp-content/uploads/2012/02/ENG-700-Paper.pdf. Accessed on November 27, 2012, 2014.
17. Rusman, E., van Bruggen, J., Sloep, P., & Koper, R. (2010). Fostering trust in virtual project teams: Towards a design framework grounded in a TrustWorthiness ANtecdents (TWAN) schema. *International Journal of Human-Computer Studies, 68*(11), 834–850.
18. Fortuna, D., & Rodič, B. (2013) Perception of privacy in social networks among youth. In Z. Levnajić (Ed.), *5th International Conference on Information Technologies and Information Society (also) ITIS 2013* (Proceedings. Novo mesto: Faculty of information studies, 2013), Dolenjske toplice, November 7–9, 2013.
19. Bente, G., Krämer, N., & Eschenburg, F. (2008). Is there anybody out there? Analyzing the effects of embodiment and nonverbal behavior in avatar-mediated communication. In E. Konijin, S. Utz, M. Tanis, & S. Barnes (Eds.), *Mediated interpersonal communication* (pp. 131–157). New York, NY: Routledge.
20. Kasper-Fuehrer, E. C., & Ashkanasy, N. M. (2001). Communicating trustworthiness and building trust in interorganizational virtual organizations. *Journal of Management Information Systems, 27*, 235–254.
21. Breu, K., & Hemingway, C. J. (2004). Making organisations virtual: The hidden cost of distributed teams. *Journal of Information Technology, 19*(3), 191–202.

22. Andres, H. P. (2002). A comparison of face-to-face and virtual software development teams. *Team Performance Management, 8*(1/2), 39–48.
23. Preece, J. (2000). *Online communities: Designing usability, supporting sociability.* New York: Wiley.
24. Benford, S., Snowdon, D., Colebourne, A., O'Brien, J. & Rodden, T. (1997). Informing the design of collaborative virtual environments. In *Proceedings ACM GROUP'97* (pp. 71–80).
25. Redfern, S., & Naughton, N. (2002). Collaborative virtual environments to support communication and community in internet-based distance education. *Journal of Information Technology Education, 1*(3), 201–209.
26. Tromp, J., & Snowdon, D. (1997). Virtual body language: Providing appropriate user interfaces in collaborative virtual environments. In *Proceedings ACM VRST '97* (pp. 37–44).
27. Koch, M. (2008). CSCW and Enterprise 2.0—Towards an integrated perspective. In *21st Bled eConference Collaboration:Overcoming Boundaries Through Multi-channel Interaction*, June 15–18, 2008; Bled, Slovenia.
28. Grinter, R. E., Herbsleb, J. D. & Perry, D. E. (1999). The geography of coordination: Dealing with distance in R&D work. *In Proceedings of the International ACM SIGGROUP Conference on Supporting Group Work (GROUP'99)* (pp. 306–315). ACM Press: New York
29. Riemer, K., & Vehring, N. (2008). Should 'virtual' mean 'vague'? A plea for more conceptual clarity in researching virtual organisations. In *21st Bled eConference collaboration: Overcoming boundaries through multi-channel interaction*, 15–18 June, 2008. Bled, Slovenia.
30. Davenport, T., & Prusak, L. (1998). *Working knowledge.* Boston, MA: Harvard Business School Press.
31. Kimiz, D. (2014). *Knowledge management in theory and practice.* Boston, USA: MIT Press.
32. Nonaka, I., & Konno, N. (1998). The concept of "Ba": Building a foundation for knowledge creation. *California Management Review, 40*(3).
33. Jashapara, A. (2004). *Knowledge management: An integrated approach.* Harlow, England: Financial Times Press.
34. Nunamaker, J., Jr., Reinig, B., & Briggs, R. (2009). Principles for effective virtual teamwork. *Communications of the ACM, 52*(4), 113–117.

Author Biography

Blaž Rodič obtained a Ph.D. at the Faculty of Organizational Sciences, University of Maribor. His research interests include the development of new and original methods and tools for simulation and modelling, solutions for reallife optimization problems in manufacturing, logistics and service systems and development of multi-agent simulation models of organisational systems. His current research projects include modelling and simulation of manufacturing processes with the purpose of optimizing the factory layout and manufacturing process (elimination of bottlenecks, minimisation of order production time) and agent based modelling of teams: focus on transfer of knowledge and development of innovative culture.

Model-Driven Design of eMedia: Virtual Technology Transfer Office

Rumen Andreev, Daniela Borissova, Alexander Shikalanov
and Tsvetelina Yorgova

Abstract Establishing a technology transfer office (TTO) is no trivial matter. The goal is to fulfil the gap between research and innovation by involving different kinds of organizational structures aiming to assist public research organizations in managing their intellectual properties that facilitate their transformation into benefits for society. Taking into account the specifics of the transfer of technology as an innovative process described by appropriate business model, the information system is the right choice to help make the appropriate decisions. This article describes an approach to develop of a new e-media based on the proposed business model of TTO. The described model is used for development of an information system. The proposed virtual agents are used as fundamental element of developed e-media to describe some information processing functions which are performed usually by some of media users. The design of described e-media is driven by constructed business model of the office of technology transfer.

R. Andreev · D. Borissova (✉)
Institute of Information and Communication Technologies—Bulgarian
Academy of Sciences, Acad. G. Bonchev St., Block 2, 1113 Sofia, Bulgaria
e-mail: dborissova@iit.bas.bg

R. Andreev
e-mail: rumen@isdip.bas.bg

A. Shikalanov
Faculty of Information Sciences, University of Library Studies
and Information Technologies, Bul. Tzarigradsko Shosse No 119, Sofia, Bulgaria
e-mail: ctmdevelopment@yahoo.com

T. Yorgova
Institute of Mechanics—Bulgarian Academy of Sciences,
Acad. G. Bonchev St., Block 4, 1113 Sofia, Bulgaria
e-mail: yorgova@imbm.bas.bg

© Springer International Publishing AG 2016

A. Lugmayr et al. (eds.), *Information Systems and Management in Media
and Entertainment Industries*, International Series on Computer Entertainment
and Media Technology, DOI 10.1007/978-3-319-49407-4_14

1   Introduction

The innovation from research organization and knowledge transfer to the private sector for commercial application and public benefit requires a formal mechanism of technology transfer office. To better understand the economic impact of academic entrepreneurship needs to explicitly recognizing the academic entrepreneurs and their entrepreneurial behavior across different contexts [28]. Establishing a new technology transfer office (TTO) is no trivial matter and the decision to create one should be made within the context of a long-term plan that takes into consideration the following questions [29]: (1) Does "research commercialization" align with the institution's mission? (2) Do the quality and quantity of research within the institution warrant the establishment of a TTO? (3) Is the institution willing to make a long-term commitment to required institutional changes and to adequately invest in resources and people? The main goal of establishing of TTO is to fulfill the gap between research and innovation. That is why the TTO involve different kinds of organizational structures with basic role to assist public research organizations in managing their intellectual properties in such way to facilitate their transformation into benefits for society. Technology transfer is not a matter of patents rather it is the complex work that takes place at the research and productive organizations activities. The number of TTOs was established over the last 20 years, starting with the US and now spreading over Europe. The scope of their activities is extended from patenting and licensing to collaborative research and company establishing [23]. A technology transfer strategy to perform an effective item-oriented search instead of randomly browsing all patents of the entire database is proposed by Russo et al. [19]. The traditional linear model of technology transfer is constructed as a synthesis of dominant paradigms and the extant literature related to technology transfer within the academic and professional landscape [3]. This model is no longer sufficient, or perhaps even no longer relevant, to account for the nuances and complexities of the technology transfer process that characterizes the ongoing commercialization activities of universities [3]. The TTO should to consider the commercial potential of the invention, as well as prospective interest from the public or private sector [21]. The process of spin-off development is iterative over the different phases of the venture's growth, and policy actions are to be differentiated according to the particular phase of development [27]. The spin-offs often develop early stage of technologies characterized by long development paths and uncertain commercial potential while the private financiers as banks and investors are reluctant to invest in these ventures at an early stage. To bridge this financing gap, governments have set up specialized programs, but few studies have examined the rationale and organization of different types of programs [18].

Improvement of IT infrastructure supports the business activities, information systems and management in eMedia [13, 14]. Factors that have facilitated technology transfer include globalization of business, economic liberalization and encouragement of intellectual properties protection. A generalized model of technology transfer is difficult to find and one that accurately depicts the subtleties of how knowledge and technology are transferred in practice is arguably non-existent [3]. Several authors describe useful frameworks for analyzing businesses, such as profit models [22] and strategy maps [10]. A very first consideration of introducing business information management and systems in the domain of media industries is the particular industry segment. Each segment requires a particular use of information systems especially on operational and knowledge level [13, 14]. The business model can be described as the link between innovation and value creation [4], as the cognitive link between entrepreneurial appraisal of the opportunity and its exploitation [6] or can be represented as the design of organizational structures to enact a commercial opportunity [8].

Considering the specifics of technology transfer as innovation process that is represented by proper business model, the information system is the tool that can realize the required management and decision making. Information systems integrate set of components for collecting, processing, storing data and delivering the information. They are capable to support a specific organizational function with respect to the business outcomes. On the other hand, the information systems involve networks of hardware and software that people and organizations use to collect, filter, process, create and distribute data. Therefore, the information systems and their management is basis of development of new business models of different media products. To develop effective business information systems in particular application areas require new business analytics, information visualization and workflow management. These considerations are taken into account in development of the research prototype of model-driven design of e-media for the goal of TTO considering the organizational function that best fits the system's architecture.

2 eMedia Parameters

Usually communication is considered as a process. It is disregarded the study of the outcome of a communication event. The focus of the scientific research on the communication process should consider its product too. In this context, the media requires the consideration of three viewpoints that reveal key determining features: communication aspects; media content that depends on their role; media realization that concerns their physical properties (media attributes).

Although communication is too complex to be defined in a short definition, there are several characteristics shared by all communications: Communication is a process; Communication is symbolic; Communication is contextual; Communication is purposive; Communication is two-way (bi-directional) [24]. These characteristics are presented to a certain degree by the following definition: Communication is the exchange of meaning between individuals using a common symbol system. Considering communication as a process rather than a product reflects the shift from studying product to studying process that has occurred in a number of communication fields. This characteristic has influence on the construction of the most famous models of communication: Shannon's communication model [20], Garbner's communication model [7], DeFleur's communication model [5] and Westley and MacLean's communication model [26]. The essential elements of the communication process are the followings: Source (sender), Receiver and Massage. The Sender has something to communicate and sends a message to the Receiver. Messages sent used a variety of media or physical bases for carrying messages. If we define communication simply as a process, then we never really get at the important issue of the exchange of meaning. It is necessary to refer to the nature of messages rather than to the process of communicating. As a result we can say that communication is symbolic. What symbols are, how they get their meaning and how we use them to communicate are important communication concepts. Symbols may be objects, written signs, images or sounds. Because of their arbitrary nature they are subject to various interpretations. The use of them in communication implies that the sender and the receiver share a common symbol system that helps them to exchange information. The information exchange is a characteristic of communication that concerns the two-way nature of communication. In interactive communication, a specific message from the sender elicits a predictable response from the receiver. The form of messages is highly constrained by the context of communication. Transactional communication describes a different type of two-way message exchange. In a transactional exchange, the impact of the first message shapes the form of the next messages. It is necessary to realize that communication is contextual, since a context in which communication occur both determines the method of communication and makes it possible. Many miscommunications and misunderstandings arise because the participators in a communication do not share the same context. Generally, communication is done for a purpose, i.e. communication is purposive. Always the communicators have some motivation for communicating that concerns the output of communication.

The determination of the essential characteristics of communication requires study of a communication event taken alone. On other hand, the communication plays different roles in our lives, where we are part of a system and the communication should be considered from system-oriented perspective. In a system the communication is a factor both for maintaining stability and for provoking changes. At the same time it supports the realization of system's functions. Therefore, a functional approach looks at the purposes communication events serve in systems. Looking at functions is a way of categorizing types of communications. It is possible to distinguish three basic functions communication serves—information, persuasion and entertainment. The other communication types realize functions that derive from basic functions. In most cases the communications are informational, since the transfer of information is involved. The term information refers to bare data or facts. The use of information for various purposes and in different context results in realization of different system's functions and determining of various types of communications. A wide variety of communication serves an instructional function, where instruction is considered as information-plus: information plus organizing or interpretative principles. This type of communication is widely use in education systems, where someone give you information and teach you how to use it. Business communications are another type of communication that ensures information plus management principles.

The communication process exists in time as a shared system that is implemented in certain medium. Communicators exist independently, but within this shared system, i.e. they are elements of media environment. Communication occurs in various formats that have an effect on different aspects of an interaction. Our focus is on direct (unmediated) and mediated communications. In direct communications the communicators are the factor that determines all aspects of an interaction like impression formation, relationship formation, communication dynamics and formation of communication types based on information processing. The information processing is first of all communicator's task and concerns cognitive processes of human beings. The definition of cognitive processes is subject of Cognitive Psychology. They include perception, recognition, imagining, interpretation, memorizing, problem solving, thinking, judging and so on. A central metaphor that is adopted by cognitivists is the computer, which serves to provide these researchers important clues and directions in understanding the human brain and how it processes information [15]. Within the information-processing model, humans are routinely compared to computers. This comparison is used as a means of better understanding the way information is processed and stored in the human mind. In mediated communications, the factor of realization of different aspects of an interaction is an agent known as mediator. He does not coincide with the communicators, but is responsible for relationships formation, communication dynamics and realization of various communication functions based on information processing. The mediator is a necessary and characteristic feature of the medium, since he becomes an important element of it. Thus, some basic communication characteristics are guaranteed by the media, not by the media environment.

Usually, the focus of media analysis is on its content and methods of its realization. The word "content" is used to refer to media. However, to be more precise it is necessary to consider content as a specific term in that it means the subject matter of the medium rather than the medium itself. We can define the media content by using the following propositions:

- Content is the essential meaning of media determined by the communication type, communication format, communication context and purposes that a medium realizes;
- Content is something that is to be expressed through some medium and is a result of media production;
- The term content identifies and quantifies the information that is available to media users through various formats;
- The combinations of specific communication types, formats, context and purpose define some type of content referred to as a type of media.

An analysis of media content consist first of determining the communication type, communication format and context that they support. Since media structure depends mainly on these media parameters, the structure of media content is in accordance with the form of a message or series of messages providing of the specific communication. That is why content analysis examines firstly the components of messages and their meaning.

The main media content features are content format and content management. A content format is an encoded format for converting a specific type of data to information that can be easily recorded and transmitted and is suitable for observation, interpretation and processing. The content format depends on the characteristics and qualities of the symbolic system that is shared among media users (communicators). A content management is realized by a set of processes that may support the following features:

- Identification of all key media users and their roles;
- Import and creation of documents and multimedia material;
- The ability to track and manage different versions of a single instance of content;
- Definition of tasks coupled with communications, so that the content manager is alerted to make changes in media content;
- Ability to support access to the content.

Content management systems could take the following forms:

- A document management system and publishing system;
- Service-oriented system;
- Rational data base;
- Information system with decision support functions.

The realization of communication media depends on the ways of data handling. The change from analog information handling to digital information handling is revolutionary. When we think of digital technologies we probably first think of computers. The development of communication technologies is closely connected with the evolution of computer technologies. The using of digital technologies as a basis for realization of media results in construction of e-media. The attributes of e-media are determined by digitalization, computerization and other qualities that are derivation of them. When an attribute of e-media is computer, it is used the term "New Media". The new media can be defined by several propositions [2] (1) New media uses digital computer technology for distribution and exhibition; (2) New media is reduced to digital data that can be manipulated by computer programs (software). The language of New Media can base on objects that rely on digital representations and computer-based delivery shared a number of common qualities; (3) New media guarantee that communication occurring within a computer-mediated format forms and supports all types of relationships—"one to one", "one to many" and many to many". In this way, New Media manifests features that belong to Interpersonal media, Mass media and Individuation media respectively; (4) The properties of New media makes possible of many new forms of media that are determined by the kind of virtual reality implementation; (5) New media as Meta media. Meta media coincides with postmodernism in that they both rework old work rather than create new work. New media plays the role of avantgarde using new methods accessing and manipulating information; (6) New media supports functioning of virtual groups and virtual organization. Computer-mediated communications that help humans form, support and maintain relationships among media users, to regulate information processing and decision making are basis for realization of computer-supported collaboration.

The development of new type of e-media requires changing of some of media parameters like communication function, communication context, communication purposes, common symbolic system, mediated communication or some of new media aspects.

3   Business Model of Technology Transfer Office

The business model concept defining value proposition, configuring value network, choosing partners, looking for ways to reach customers and to implement business strategies, and many other similar decisions. The business model is an abstract representation of business logic of a business entity. Business models exist only as abstract concepts or mental models in the head of people reasoning on them. Since, people have different mental models they will not automatically understand the same thing under a business model. Thus, a generic framework for describing business models is necessary. Such a framework can be understood as a common language shared between model implementers to get the ideas out of their heads in order to formulate them in a way that everybody understands. A state of the art review on business model frameworks can be found in [11]. Business Reference Model is model concerning on the architectural aspects of the core business of an economic entity. It is a generic model of elements, components and relationships. The Component Business Model is result of a conceptual approach to business models proposing a logical representation or map of building blocks. Very often these models represent instances of the Reference Models and concern existing or implemented business models. The Business Model Canvas bases on the "ontological modeling" that carefully defines business model concepts, components and relationships among components. It is obviously that the method of construction of these three types of Business models is component-oriented.

There are two approaches to development of a component-based business model. According to the first business model approach a business model can be divided into seven sub-models. These sub-models can be the value model, the resource model, the production model, the customer relations model, the revenue model, the capital model and the market model [17]. Weill and Vitale [25] have a slightly different approach. They give a systematic and practical analysis of eight so called atomic e-business models: Content Provider, Direct to Customer, Full-Service Provider, Intermediary, Shared Infrastructure, Value net Integrator and Virtual Community. These atomic business models can be combined to form an e-business initiative. Every one of these atomic e-business models is analyzed according to its strategic objectives and value proposition, its sources of revenue, its critical success factors and its core competencies. Linder and Cantrell [12] propose a comprehensive approach to business models. Further, they stress the fact that many people speak of business models when they actually only mean a specific component of a business model. They list the following components: the pricing model, the revenue model, the channel model, the commerce process model, the Internet-enabled commerce relationship, the organizational form and the value proposition.

A business model is simply a business concept that has been put into practice, but for which he develops a number of elements [9]. It identifies four main business model components that range from core strategy, strategic resources over value network to customer interface. Unlike most other authors on business model components Alt and Zimmermann [1] include elements such as mission, processes, legal issues and technology into their framework. The six generic elements are mission, structure, processes, revenues, technology and legal issues.

We use a framework for business model design, which emphasizes on the following four areas that a business model has to address [16]. (1) Product: What business the business entity is in, the products and the value propositions offered to the market. (2) Customer interface: Who the business's target customers are, how it delivers them products and services, and how it builds strong relationships with them. (3) Infrastructure management: How the business entity efficiently performs infrastructural or logistical issues, with whom, and as what kind of network enterprise. (4) Financial aspects: What is the revenue model, the cost structure and the business model's sustainability? These four areas can be categorization by the nine elements as value proposition, target customer, distribution channel, relationship, value configuration, capability, partnership, cost structure and revenue model. The product area is described by *value proposition*—overall view of a company's bundle of products and services that are of value to the customer. The customer interface is described by three building blocks: target customer, distribution channel, relationship. The *Target Customer* is a segment of customers a company wants to offer value to. A *Distribution Channel* is a means of getting in touch with the customer. The *Relationship* describes the kind of link a company establishes between itself and the customer. The infrastructure manager consists of the following elements: value configuration, capability, partnership. The *Value Configuration* describes the arrangement of activities and resources that are necessary to create value for the customer. A *Capability* is the ability to execute a repeatable pattern of actions that is necessary in order to create value for the customer. A *Partnership* is a voluntarily initiated cooperative agreement between two or more business entities in order to create value for the customer. The financial aspect is presented by cost structure and revenue model. The *Cost Structure* is the representation in money of all the means employed in the business model. The *Revenue Model* describes the way a company makes money through a variety of revenue flows.

We construct the business model of Technology Transfer Office in the presented framework for Business Model design. Afterwards, it is developed an implementation of this model that serves as basis for developing of a virtual technology transfer office, which ensure the functioning of a new e-media.

3.1 Business Strategy of Technology Transfer Office "ICT for Energy Efficiency" (TTO "ICTEE")

The mission of TTO "ICTEE" aims to support the successful interaction between researchers and the industry. The main goal is to establish of a pro-innovation infrastructure in Bulgarian Academy of Sciences and implementation of the national innovation strategy in the sectors of Energy Efficiency (EE) and Information and Communication Technologies (ICT). This is a prerequisite to improve the science-to-business relation, promotion of new knowledge and technologies transfer towards Bulgarian enterprises in support of their competitiveness and sustainable development. The innovation in the business activities will increase the number and the level of market of success of innovative products, processes and services developed by research organizations. The *specific objectives* involves: (1) Provision of information access to representatives of various professional groups to the TTO and building a network of offices as a part of the European and national networks for technology transfer; (2) Encouragement of research and development activities aimed at the development of innovative products, providing ICT-based energy efficiency and introduction of novel technologies in enterprises with the purpose of achieving energy efficiency; (3) Protection of intellectual property over the innovative products of RTD organizations, intended for Bulgarian private enterprises, municipal and state organizations.

The *activity of TTO* can be summarized as follows: (1) Assessing the needs and possibilities for improving energy efficiency through the use of ICT in different economic sectors such as energetics, machine-building, transportation, construction, etc.; (2) Providing small and medium enterprises, government institutions and research organizations with services for the evaluation of possible applications of ICT for energy efficiency; (3) Participating as a full member in networks of technology transfer offices as well as in existing or emerging innovation infrastructures; (4) Being a coordinator and an intermediary in the field of energy efficiency innovations through ICT—this activity targets research organizations or individual researchers and inventors; (5) Providing consulting and expert services in the field of technology transfer, intellectual property and financial management of innovation projects by engaging representatives of trade associations, non-governmental and intermediary organizations.

The *services of TTO* are divided in four groups. (1) *Information services:* advancement of novel technological and scientific achievements in the field of energy efficiency and implementation of ICT; support in promoting companies and their products; organization of workshops, seminars, exhibitions, etc.; (2) *Consultancy services:* evaluation and assistance in the protection of intellectual property and patent rights, legal support; development, consultancy and coordination of new project proposals concerning the usage of ICT in the area of energy efficiency; documentation development, certification and registration of new products; market analysis of the market of ICT based energy efficiency innovation products; (3) *Financial services:* facilitation of easier access to external funding and support; access to finance schemes; promotion of energy efficiency related developments towards investment funds. (4) *Technological services*: transfer of technologies, innovations and know-how, scientific solutions to particular problems, related to the usage of ICT for energy efficiency; technology valuation and technology audits; pilot testing of energy efficiency technologies; experts and consultants services, related to technology transfer.

Target customers of TTO are: research organizations, Bulgarian micro-, small and medium-sized enterprises, municipal and state organizations; expert in the field of technology transfer, intellectual property and financial management of innovation projects; SME of the following economic sectors such as energetics, machine-building, transportation, construction, etc.

The purpose of *distribution channel* is to make the right quantities of the right products or services available at the right place, at the right time to the right people. ICT has had an enormous impact on transforming simple distribution channels into value adding components of value propositions. An important element of a channel strategy in a business model is managing channel conflicts. When more than one channel competes for the same customers there is a high chance of channel conflict.

Customer relationship management mechanism defines the different mechanisms they want to use to create and maintain a customer relationship and leverage customer equity. This means using relationship mechanisms to optimize the acquisition, the retention of, and selling of additional products to a firm's customers. A relationship mechanism can contribute to value creation in three distinct ways: either through use, reducing risk or reducing a customer's efforts. *Infrastructure management* describes the value system configuration that is necessary to deliver the value proposition and maintain customer interfaces that is acquired through the firm's *partnership* network. The value *configuration* of a firm describes the arrangement of one or several activities in order to provide a value proposition. *Value network* consists of activities associated with inviting potential customers to join the network, selection of customers that are allowed to join and the initialization, management, and termination of contracts governing service provisioning and charging. Service provisioning consists of activities associated with establishing, maintaining, and terminating links between customers and billing for value received. Network infrastructure operation consists of activities associated with maintaining and running a physical and information infrastructure. The activities keep the network in an alert status, ready to service customer requests. A capability describes the ability to execute a repeatable pattern of actions. A firm has to dispose of a number of capabilities to be able to offer its value proposition. A partnership is a voluntarily initiated cooperative agreement formed between two or more independent companies in order to carry out a project or specific activity jointly by coordinating the necessary capabilities, resources and activities.

A financial aspect is the last block of our framework and is composed of the company's revenue model and its cost structure. The *revenue model* describes the way company makes money. It can be composed of one or several *revenue stream and pricing* elements. The *revenue stream and pricing* element describes an incoming money stream from the value offered by the company. Furthermore it defines what mechanism is used to determine the price of this value offered. Transaction cuts are the main revenue streams of many electronic business platforms that provide the matchmaking facilities for buyers and suppliers. Investment banks are another category of organizations that rely heavily on transaction cuts of the deals they make.

The advertising activity of telling about or praising something publicly, as through a media (e.g. press, TV, web, billboard, etc.) so as to influence the choice, opinion or behavior of those addressed. It can be defined as any paid message communicated by an advertising media. Every product or event enjoying a large attention is interesting to an advertiser.

The *TTO Pricing mechanisms* involve *pay-per-use* when the customer pays in function of the time or quantity he consumes of a specific product or service and *subscription mechanism* when the customer pays a flat fee in order to access the use of a product or to profit from a service. Differential pricing refers to pricing mechanisms that produce prices that are either based on customer or product characteristics, are volume dependant, or are linked to customer preferences, but not based on real-time market conditions. The major mechanisms of this category are *product-feature-dependant, customer-characteristic-dependant, volume-dependant and value-based pricing*. Pricing mechanisms based on product-features are increasingly popular since products and services become more and more configurable. Sellers prefer these variable prices because it makes it harder for customers to compare prices. Bundling of different products and services also fall in this category. Customer-characteristic-dependant pricing mechanisms have existed for a long time but they have known a real boom with the rise of cheap ICTs. Prices can be tailored to the characteristics of every single customer. Volume-dependant pricing is less sophisticated than the former mechanism and simply differentiates prices on the basis of purchased volumes. Value-based pricing puts the customer back into the driving seat and gives him an important role in the price-making process. This means that the final price will strongly depend on the customer's valuation of a value proposition.

3.2 Model of Business Process of TTO

The business process of TTO consists of four groups of business tasks: innovation activities and supporting services, decision making operations, information acquisition and storing, and communications (Fig. 1).

These groups of tasks present four stages of the business process and are result of TTO's mission projection. The mission defines TTO activities, which performance depends on the execution of decision making operations. They need information that is analysis. Information acquisition is a result of using communications. The communications are in the basis of the business process. Their function is determined by the communication context—to deliver information and under information processing to serve for decision making. Therefore, the communication type could be determined as managerial. The model of the TTO's business process

Fig. 1 Model of business process

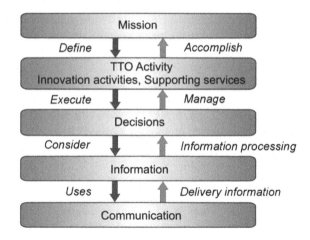

represents the construction of a new e-medium that provides computer-mediated communications and carrying out intelligent functions like decision making.

The TTO activity is determined mainly by the functions of innovation process that could be divided into three levels: (1) Information (2) Connecting and Coordinating (3) Adapt organizational technologies and offer models that lead to effective innovation. The practice requires application of these functions in the innovation process, which guarantee the following achievements:

- Identifying scientific result, ready for transfer;
- Determination of market segment or new technology or market needs;
- Accelerates the process of transfer or commercialization of research results;
- Adding value, including depending on the context of knowledge generation and knowledge absorption;
- Definition of organizational work and strategy for performance of an innovation process

The group of decision making operations is presented on three levels. On each level they perform various tasks in performance of different activities:

Level	Tasks	Activities
Acquisition and dissemination of information	*Support of a database of research results *Use and evaluation of available expertise	*Identification of research results *Offering of IP protection *Assessing market potential
Collaboration	*Support the creation of innovation consortia *Joint tender *Value added creation *Initiating of innovative networks *Join the network	*Finding the right partner for innovative projects *Finding a partner for the contract research *Build innovation capacity of SMEs.

(continued)

(continued)

Level	Tasks	Activities
Adaptation of organizational technology and offering models that lead to effective innovation	*Licensing *Franchise *Joint research and development activities *Co-production *Subcontracting *Delivery *Distribution	*Provide the experts required *Training of staff to work with new technologies *Intermediary provides technology solutions to its customers

An important property of this model of the business process is that it is suitable for the reengineering purposes. It is possible to make changes in anyone stage of the process and their projection on the lower stages ensures their support of the new tasks performing on these stages. Since the communication aspects are fundamental not only for the construction of new e-media, but for the performance of the business process of TTO as well, it is necessary to describe the constitutive role of communication in the TTO.

3.3 Constitutive Role of Communication in TTO

The communications in the TTO serves for supporting of four information flows (Fig. 2).

Since the focus of the TTO business model is the work with individual customers, one of the information flow concerns provision of information for various kinds of customers. They become members of the TTO community and fundamental resource for performance of its activities. For that reason, there are communications that guarantee Membership Negotiation. They realize one to one relationship between the potential members and the TTO kernel. Another information flow relates to Customer Relationship Management in its customer-centric

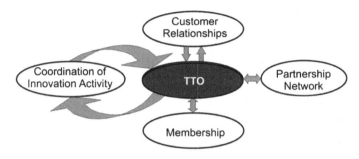

Fig. 2 Communications in TTO

relationship management (CCRM) variant. We neglect the other variants—Business to Business (B2B) and Business to Customers (B2C), since they cannot support The TTO activities. CCRM is a style that focuses on customer profile instead of customer leverage. Customer centric organization helps customers not only to make better decisions, but to drive profitability, as well. CCRM adds value by engaging customers in interpersonal relationships. Customer-centricity differs from client-centricity in that the latter refers almost exclusively to B2B models rather than customer-facing business. CCRM is used for guaranteeing one to one customer service, retaining customers, providing information customers actually want, subscription pricing mechanism. The communications that ensure the information flow supporting a Partnership Network is very important for realization of value configuration element of the TTO business model. They provide *m:m* relationships. The communications that support the coordination of innovation activities implement peer to peer relationships.

4   Implementation of Business Model in TTO

The object model of Virtual office users can be present as shown in Fig. 3. The class *User* is the root of inheritance hierarchy. It has thee attributes *ID*, *UserName* and *Password*. All of this attributes are inherited by subclasses in the hierarchy. This approach ensures latitude to add more attributes in the base class when necessary and all subclasses will have them also. Additionally when it would be decided to add some specific attributes to some of subclasses this will not affect any other classes which do not inherit the changed class.

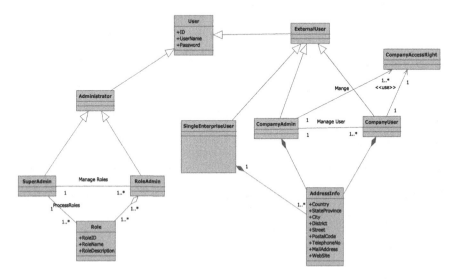

Fig. 3 Object model of virtual office users and their roles

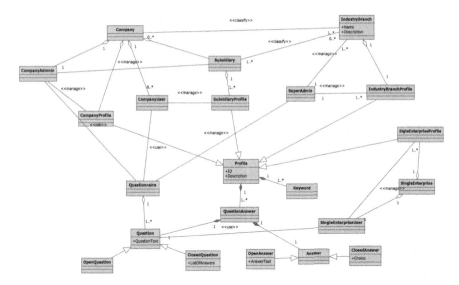

Fig. 4 Object model of profile management

The classes which are direct subclass of *User* are separated in four groups (Fig. 3). These four classes can be separated in two main sets—Administrators and Clients. The reason that a separate direct subclass as Client is not introduced that classes *SingleEnterprisUser*, *CompanyAdmin*, and *CompanyUser* have more differences that similarities in their roles. SingleEnterprisUser models small company even individual users. *CompanyAdmin* class models a user who is appointed to manage other company users—*CompanyUser*. *CompanyUser* class models users who are focused on specific direction of companies' activities or branches. The access rights company users are managed by *CompanyAdmin*. The management is done by applying *CompanyAccessRight* class. The class Administrator is inherited by two subclasses *SuperAdmin* and *RoleAdmin*. *SuperAdmin* has full access to Virtual office data. It is designated to manage all other classes. The *RoleAdmin* class has restricted access to some specific data and functions. This class is designed with a purpose to add some administrators with more specific roles—for example financial administrator, brokerage administrator etc.

The object model of profile management is shown on Fig. 4. Profiles are built on the base of filled questionnaires and Industry branches to which a company belongs. Questionnaires consist of set of open and closed connections. Questionnaires are managed by *SuperAdmin* class. Profiles are used as a source for matching algorithm which is designed to find mutual consiliences between clients searching know how or innovations and clients offering same or similar know how or innovations.

On Fig. 5 is shown a high level architecture of Virtual office software system. It is built according Model View Controller paradigm.

The view part is implemented by *BrowserPages* subsystem. It is based on using *jQuery* framework and uses Ajax approach for data and events exchange between

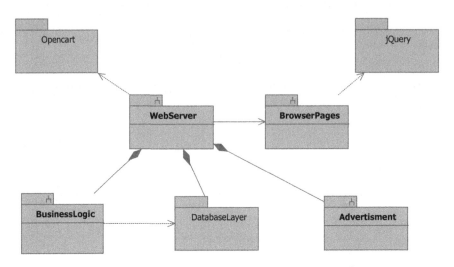

Fig. 5 High level of virtual office software architecture

WebServer subsystem and pages served in users' browsers. The controller part is implemented by subsystems *WebServer* and *BusinessLogic*. *WebServer* subsystem is responsible for serving of web pages. BusinessLogic class implements all business processes related with functioning of Virtual office. The model is contained in database and *DatabaseLayer* package is designed to ensure database independent access to stored models and data.

One of most important business processes implemented is matching clients' interests and communications. The final goal of this business process is to establish a commercial partnerships between companies searching and companies offering know how and innovations (Fig. 6).

The main class modeling this process is *MatchingLogic* class. It information contained in Profile class in order to find coincidences between possible partners and to connect them by establishing a communication between potential partners. The matching logic is applied by filters contained in class Filter. Filters content and matching logic are proprietary of Virtual office development team.

5 Conclusion

The paper presents a new approach to development of a new e-media constructing a business model of Technology Transfer Office which represents a specific communication context. It defines a new communication function, according to which the information is used for decision taking purposes during office management. The media communications use a common symbolic system that is object-oriented. The object-oriented approach to information encoding is used for development of an information system that determines the object-oriented form of media content. Through the usage of computer-mediated communications we design a virtual agent

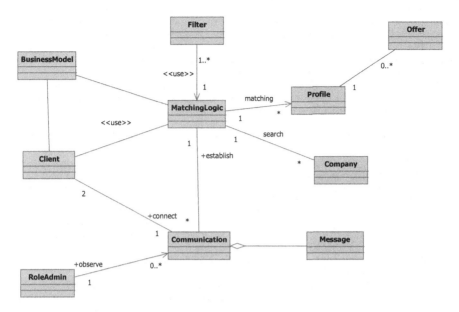

Fig. 6 Design diagram of matching logic

as fundamental element of developing e-media that realizes some information processing functions which are performed usually by some of media users. The design of presented e-media is driven by constructed business model of the office of technology transfer.

References

1. Alt, R., & Zimmermann, H. (2001). Introduction to special section—Business models. *Electronic Markets, 11*(1), 3–9.
2. Black, J., & Bryant, J. (1995). *Introduction to communications* (pp. 364–405). USA: Brown & Benchmark Publishers.
3. Bradley, S. R., C. S. Hayter, & A. N. Link (2013). Models and methods of University technology transfer. *Working Paper* 13–10, June 2013. http://bae.uncg.edu/econ/
4. Chesbrough, H., & Rosenbloom, R. S. (2002). The role of the business model in capturing value from innovation: Evidence from Xerox Corporation's technology spin-off companies. *Industrial and Corporate Change, 11*(3), 529–555.
5. DeFleur, M. L. (1966). *Theories of mass communication.* NY: David McKay.
6. Fiet, J. O., & Patel, P. C. (2008). Forgiving business models for new ventures. *Entrepreneurship Theory and Practice, 32*(4), 749–761.
7. Garbner, G. (1956). Toward a General model of communication. *Audio-Visual Communication Review, 4*(3), 171–199.
8. George, G., & Bock, A. J. (2011). The business model in practice and its implications for entrepreneurship research. *Entrepreneurship Theory and Practice, 35*(1), 83–111.
9. Hamel, G. (2000). *Leading the revolution.* Boston: Harvard Business School Press.
10. Kaplan, R. S., & Norton, D. P. (2004). *Strategy maps: Converting intangible assets into tangible outcomes.* Boston, MA: Harvard Business School Press.

11. Krumeich J., Burkhart T., Werth, D., & Loos, P. (2012). Towards a component-based description of business models: A state-of-the-art analysis. *AMCIS 2012 Proceedings.* Paper 19.
12. Linder, J., & Cantrell, S. (2000). Changing business models: Surveying the landscape, accenture institute for strategic change.
13. Lugmayr, A. (2013). Issues & approach in defining a European research agenda on information systems and management in creative eMedia industries. In E. Stojmenova & A. Lugmayr (Eds.), *Proceedings 1st workshop on defining a European Research agenda on information systems and management in eMedia industries (in conjuction with eBled, Bled, Slovenia)* (pp 17–25). Bled, Slovenia: lugymedia Inc., International Ambient Media Organization (AMEA).
14. Lugmayr, A. (2013). Brief introduction into information systems and management research in media industries. *IEEE International Conference on Multimedia and Expo Workshops (ICMEW).* (pp. 1–6).
15. Marx, M. H., & Cronan-Hillix, W. A. (1987). *Systems and theories in psychology* (4th ed., pp. 403–422). N.Y.: McGraw-Hill.
16. Osterwalder A. (2004). The business model ontology: A proposition in a design science approach, PhD Thesis, University of Lausanne, Ecole des Hautes Etudes Commerciales
17. Peterovic, O., C. Kittl, et al. (2001). Developing business models for eBusiness. In *International Conference on Electronic Commerce,* Vienna.
18. Rasmussen, E., & Sorheim, R. (2012). How governments seek to bridge the financing gap for university spin-offs: Proof-of-concept, pre-seed, and seed funding. *Technology Analysis & Strategic Management, 24*(7), 663–678.
19. Russo, D., Montecchi, T., & Ying, L. (2012). Functional-based search for patent technology transfer. In *Proceedings of the ASME 2012 international design engineering technical conferences & computers and information in engineering conference* IDETC/CIE 2012, August 12–15, 2012, Chicago, IL, USA
20. Shannon, C., & Waver, W. (1949). *The mathematical theory of communication.* Urbana, USA: University of Illinois Press.
21. Siegel, D. S., Waldman, D. A., & Link, A. N. (2003). Assessing the impact of organizational practices on the productivity of university technology transfer offices: An exploratory study. *Research Policy, 32*(1), 27–48.
22. Slywotzky, A. J., & Morrison, D. J. (1997). *The profit zone.* New York, NY: Times books.
23. Tahvanainen, A.-J., & Hermans, R. (2011). Making sense of the TTO production function: University technology transfer offices as process catalysts, knowledge converters and impact amplifiers. Helsinki: ETLA, Elinkeinoelämän Tutkimuslaitos, The Research Institute of the Finnish Economy, 40 p. (Keskusteluaiheita, Discussion Papers, ISSN 0781-6847; No. 1236).
24. Wahlstrom, B. J. (1992). *Perspectives on human communications.* USA: WCB Publishers.
25. Weill, P., & Vitale, M. R. (2001). *Place to space: Migrating to eBusiness models.* Boston: Harvard Business School Press.
26. Westley, B. H., & MacLean, M., Jr. (1957). A Conceptual model for communication research. *Journalism Quarterly, 34,* 31–38.
27. Wright, M., Clarysse, B., Mustar, P., & Lockett, A. (2007). *Academic entrepreneurship in Europe.* London: Edward Elgar.
28. Wright, M., Mosey, S., & Noke, H. (2012). Academic entrepreneurship and economic competitiveness: Rethinking the role of the entrepreneur. *Economics of Innovation and New Technology, 21*(5–6), 429–444.
29. Young, T. A. (2007). Establishing a technology transfer office. In A. Krattiger, R. T. Mahoney, L. Nelsen, et al. (Eds.), *Intellectual property management in health and agricultural innovation: A handbook of best practices.* MIHR: Oxford, U.K., and PIPRA: Davis, U.S.A. Available online at www.ipHandbook.org

Author Biographies

Dr. Rumen Andreev is currently an associate professor at the Institute of Information and Communication Technologies, Bulgarian Academy of Sciences, Sofia. He obtained his Ph.D. in Computer Aided Design from Technical University, Sofia in 1987. He is head of the department "Communication Systems and Services" and director of the Technology Transfer Office. His research interests include computer graphics, human-computer interactions, software engineering, computer aided design, personalized computer-enhanced learning, technology transfer, adaptive and complex systems. He has published in Computers and Graphics, Computer Graphics Forum, Interacting with Computers, Communication and Cognition and others and has presented his research at numerous national and international conferences. He is author of two monographs: "Graphics Systems: Architecture and Realization", North Holland/Elsevier and "Decision Control, Management, and Support in Adaptive and Complex Systems: Quantitative Models", IGI Global. He has professional awards from Marquis' Who is Who in the World, International Biographical Centre, Cambridge and American Biographical Institute.

Dr. Daniela Borissova received M.Sc. degree from Sofia University, followed by Ph.D. from Institute of Information Technologies of Bulgarian Academy of Sciences. Currently, Dr. Borissova is associate professor at the Institute of Information and Communication Technologies of Bulgarian Academy of sciences. She has specializations in Canada, Norway, Albania and Czech Republic. Her main research interests are related to decision support systems, e-learning, modeling and optimization, computer aided design, web design and development of web-based applications.

Dr. Alexander Chikalanov received M.Sc. degree in Mathematics from Sofia University, Faculty of Mathematics and Mechanics, Bulgaria. He obtained PhD degree in Computer Science from Technical University—Sofia, Bulgaria. Currently, Dr. Chikalanov is associate professor at the University of Library Study and Information technology since 2014, where he teaching a course in Computer Science. He has about 35 years sound experience in system analyses assessment of information flows, data acquisition, data processing and documents control, Software quality assurance, data base development and expert system elaboration, Internet based applications, communications, and software. More than 30 successfully concluded projects in the fields of data processing, needs assessment for establishment on information system IT issues.

Ms. Tsvetelina Yorgova is a Ph.D. student—educationally finished protection of Ph.D. thesis in technology transfer and innovation area. She is pursuing work in the field of innovation and technology transfer. Her background is in Industrial Engineering (M.Sc.), while her bachelor's degree is in Electrical Engineering. She is project manager of Enterprise Europe Network for the partner GIS—Transfer Center. Ms. Yorgova worked on Intellectual property management also including exploitation and dissemination of research results, since 2010 in Institute of Mechanics—Bulgarian Academy of Sciences. She also works on building of innovation support in the Bulgarian Technology transfer network from 28 technology transfer offices, through efficient cooperation and collaboration with science, industry, investors, state authorities and other relevant stakeholders. She is an experienced R&D expert with over 5 years of professional experience in providing consultancy services to SMEs in technology transfer, innovation needs assessment, project development and business cooperation. She is national contact point for SME at Horizon 2020.

The Impact of Fluid Publishing on Media Information Management—A Survey of Latest Journalistic Trends as Data-Driven Journalism, Journalism as Process and Metrics-Driven Journalism

Björn Stockleben and Artur Lugmayr

Abstract This chapter introduces "fluid publishing" as a paradigm for journalistic publishing. It identifies and explains the four trends of data-driven journalism, journalism as a process, 24/7 publishing and service personalization as core drivers of fluid publishing. It will give rise to new online publishing formats and require organizational change processes, which in turn create the need for new holistic information systems. Such information systems will have to reconcile the strategic-rational function with a rewarding-emotional aspect, as well as define new journalism-centric metrics embracing high-level concepts of quality in journalism.

1 Introducing the Paradigm of "Fluid Publishing"

Processing information has always been an important aspect of the journalist's business, but it is only recently that business information is becoming an integral part of the journalistic workflow. Until recently, there has been a quite strict distinction between the production of journalistic content and its marketing. Now each author also becomes responsible for the marketing of his content, iterating on the persistent conflict between the economic and public value of journalistic products. Tandoc [1] observed how metrics determined which stories get follow-up coverage and which get taken down to optimize clicks on the homepage. This is a relatively new phenomenon Tandoc coined "de-selection". This kind of metrics-driven

B. Stockleben (✉)
Filmuniversität Babelsberg KONRAD WOLF, Potsdam, Germany
e-mail: b.stockleben@filmuniversitaet.de

A. Lugmayr
Curtin University Perth, Bentley, Australia
e-mail: Artur.lugmayr@curtin.edu.au

© Springer International Publishing AG 2016
A. Lugmayr et al. (eds.), *Information Systems and Management in Media and Entertainment Industries*, International Series on Computer Entertainment and Media Technology, DOI 10.1007/978-3-319-49407-4_15

journalism is on the rise, but the speed of adoption and organizational change varies. Traditional media, mature web-based companies in transition like Slate and Salon and post-web 2.0 startups like BuzzFeed each follow different approaches, as investigated by Robinson [2] and reported in [3]. Even inside the same organization, the pace and quality of adoption of new data-driven strategies can differ immensely between the departments and among the employees, as is evident from Nikki Usher's ethnography at The New York Times [4].

A few years older is the idea of having a conversation with the readers to leverage the wisdom of the crowd in journalistic workflows [5]. Curated social media content has been growing into an integral part of web-based articles. The term "journalism as process" [6] tries to describe this development.

The possibility of publishing without deadlines and maybe even more the continuous social media conversations about news see the classic concept of discrete "issues" on the decline, favoring a 24/7 publishing model with subtle adaptions to the reader's course of the day [4].

While 24/7 publishing adapts to the user behavior in general, the last trend to be considered here is service personalization, which does this for the individual. Online news services gather own user profiles or make use of their audience's profiles on social networking services [7]. In a way, personalization could also be considered as the added value proposition to the customer connected to metrics-driven journalism: The user profiles that are necessarily compiled to support audience analytics are at the same time used to deliver a better service experience to the individual.

This article discusses how the phenomena of vanishing deadlines, journalism as process, metrics-driven journalism and service personalization relate to each other and could lead to a new kind of publishing paradigm which we propose to call "fluid publishing". Fluid publishing describes an idealized, continuous editorial publishing process, driven by qualitative and quantitative real-time feedback of the audience. It serves as a model for designing future business information systems for media businesses, derived from theory and case-studies (Table 1).

2 Method and Approach

The method & approach of this study was exploratory by investigating current trends in journalism. This included a literature review, analyzing the current trends in journalism and identifying key changes. Furthermore, interviews have been conducted with industrial representatives in form of expert groups. Through a thorough analysis we define & coin the term "fluid publishing" and its key parameters & features. We developed a fluid publishing framework and identified its key characteristics.

Table 1 Key references for fluid publishing

Topic	Aspect	Reference
Journalism as a process	Shift from news as a *product* to news as a *transactional object*	[8]
	Conversation with the reader as part of the craft of journalism	[5]
Metrics-driven journalism	Traditional media metrics versus online media metrics in the news business	[23]
	Practical implementation of real-time analytics systems in editorial workflows	[18]
24/7 publishing	Current online publishing practices by example of The New York Times	[4]
	Article on how avant-garde online news websites enable 24 h publishing	[30]
Service personalization	One of the first implementations of a personalized online newspaper	[32]
	Obstacles to commercial uptake of news personalization	[7]
	Microsoft Bot (Chatterbot) alike personalization of generic content	[38, 39, 52, 53]

3   Trend 1: Journalism as Process

Robinson [8:140] describes journalism as a process as follows:

"'process' journalism begins when a reporter (or blogger or commenter) writes an article or blogs a news tip, at which point the news story comprises not only the reporter's work, but also all the comments, blogs and follow-up content sparked as a result of that original tidbit." Dan Gillmor [5] was one of the first to describe this kind of emerging conversation between journalists and their audience. He stated that *"readers (or viewers or listeners) collectively know more than media professionals do. [..] We need to recognize and, in the best sense of the word, use their knowledge."* Later, the concept of "Journalism as process" was formulated in the blogosphere by Jeff Jarvis [6] and Michael Arrington [9] and finally framed academically by Sue Robinson [8]. Jarvis argues that on the web, journalism does not have to be about delivering a perfect, well-researched end product, but an article may be published to spark community comments to evolve the story and support in research. Arrington argues that publishing about rumors helps to find new sources and information to confirm or deny the rumor, often leading to exclusive stories. He adds that transparency about what is known and what not is absolutely necessary to keep the trust of the readership.

Sue Robinson [8] elaborates on the perspective of the changing journalistic workflow, which originally comes from a production background *"constrained by both temporal (press times, work weeks, audience rituals of reading) and spatial (newsrooms, news holes) concerns"*. She describes that the idea of publishing final journalistic products is blurring today, as every social media interaction, change, update or follow-up of an article adds to a story. Instead, she proposes that the former news product *"assumes the characteristics of a transportive and transactional object of professional, social and civic work"*. The idea of news as a transactional object implies that all parties gain some kind of reward from contributing to the transaction. Audience involved in giving information and comments may accumulate social capital, which in some cases might even be used for a professionalization, i.e. in the case of bloggers, as suggested by Robinson.

In this light, journalism as process can be seen as an economization of formerly invisible and informal processes. Whereas research and interviews with sources used to be performed by journalists before publishing and sources and contributors often remained anonymous, the act of contributing to a story may now be very public in form of a comment or a blog post, increasing the social capital of the contributor. This social capital can then be re-invested to accumulate more social or financial capital, according to Franck's theses on the emerging attention economy [10]. The service Klout.com developed an index to quantify this social capital in terms of influence in social networks and an experiment by [11] supports that the Klout score index correlates with credibility for the dimensions of character and competence.

The impact of this kind of economization of the whole news process is a matter to be discussed in a separate case, but it may be worthwhile noting from an information systems point of view that formerly hidden processes now become transparent and measurable. The evolution of the process is similar to the evolution of convergent systems, as discussed in Lugmayr and Zotto [12], Zotto and Lugmayr [13]. Also for the scope of information systems, we see a process that exists as an evolution, where the triple 'convergence, coexistence, and divergence' is king [12, 13].

3.1 Journalism as Process Versus Co-creation

Vehkoo [14] takes a closer look at the phenomenon of crowd sourcing in journalism by a number of case studies of investigative journalism. Aitamurto [15] describes co-creation as an advanced, intense and challenging form of crowd sourcing, where the readers of a magazine are directly participating in editorial processes. Her case study indicates that the adoption of co-creation is laborious and requires larger organizational changes. The difference between these approaches and the phenomenon of journalism as process depicted by Robinson is that the latter seems to build mainly on informal structures and rules, while crowd sourcing and especially co-creation use pre-designed frameworks with explicit collaboration rules and role definitions. Accepting to follow such a framework is a much larger commitment at the start than other informal and less binding forms of collaboration. Bachmayer et al. [16] make a similar differentiation in their classification of collaboration levels in interactive TV formats. It is unlikely that explicit co-creation will be established widely in the daily routines of newsrooms, while the informal and implicit nature of transactions in fluid publishing has the potential to spread widely. Educational issues, and creative methods in media management education have been investigated in [17].

4 Trend 2: Metrics-Driven Journalism

In a nutshell, metrics-driven journalism can be defined as *"the idea of using metrics to inform editorial decision-making"* [18]. The prevailing term for businesses that start employing data analysis to inform operative and strategic decisions is to say that they would become "data-driven" (e.g. [19, 20]). However, the term data-driven journalism is already coined (e.g. [21, 22]) and refers to the usage of data aggregation, analysis and visualization techniques in journalistic research, also often called simply "data journalism". In order to avoid misunderstandings, we do use the term of "metrics-driven journalism" instead, which shall comprise all forms of using quantifiable insights on journalistic workflows as basis for decision making inside media organizations.

4.1 From Web Metrics to Metrics-Driven Journalism

When web metrics were introduced initially, they were mainly used for the purpose of marketing ad space. For a long time, it was possible to determine how successful an article was in terms of clicks, but it was impossible to qualify these clicks any further. The start into metric-driven journalism happened when web analytics tools became integrated better with content management systems, gained the ability to follow user segments down to the level of the individual and, most importantly, began to speak the language of publishers and journalists. Exemplary for these new breed of tools is ChartBeat, which offered real-time monitoring of a publishing site and is able to qualify clicks and identify referrers by platform and user segments. Graves and Kelly [23] cite Kourosh Karimkhany, COO of TPM Media, describing his first experience with ChartBeat as a "real epiphany". Petre [18] highlights that it was one of the first analytics companies to design a visual data dashboard for the needs of journalists. ChartBeat promotes metrics such as "engaged time", i.e. the average time people spend with a site's content and "recirculation", i.e. visitors that stay on the site after they read the article on which they arrived. Other metrics include the number of returning and loyal visitors and all these metrics are meant to promote high quality content, they favour the building of a loyal audience instead of promoting viral one-shots. Table 2 shows ChartBeats and some notable competitors along with their unique sales proposition according to company websites.

Other generic web analytics solutions such as Omniture (now part of the Adobe Marketing Cloud), Google Analytics or Webtrends are as well in use by media companies, yet they do not claim any features tailored to journalistic content.

Table 2 Market overview of leading analytics software for newsroom use

Analytics software	USP
Chartbeat chartbeat.com	Attention-based measures for user engagement and building loyal customerships
Parsely parsely.com	Analyze and predict the users' journey through the content offered— where do they come from, what are they looking for next?
Outbrain engage (formerly: visual revenue) Outbrain.com/engage	Focus on optimization of content-discovery, assisting editorial decisions on article choice and placement, as well as personalized real-time recommendations for readers
Metrics for news metricsfornews.com	Customizable, journalist-centric metrics through integration of web analytics with meta-tagged content

4.2 Web Metrics as News Metrics

While huge advancements have been seen in the use of web metrics in journalism, the "Metrics for News" project by the American Press Institute [54] states that standard web analytics suites are not built with news organizations in mind. Their metrics are not customizable to reflect journalistic values and do not allow journalists to build strategies build on their own criteria. They want to provide information on how to improve the quality of journalistic work itself. This is in line with the findings of Graves and Kelly [23], who state that there is a need for better understanding of measurement data and the measuring of journalistic influence.

The approach taken by metrics for news is allegedly that of meta-tagging articles with properties that shall serve for filtering analyses later. Jeff Sonderman, deputy director of the American Press Institute says *"Compare what you really want to compare. We let publishers compare what works best just within their in-depth enterprise coverage. Or within government coverage. By imposing their own journalism values on their data analysis, publishers can stop chasing page views story-by-story and get smarter about how to excel at whatever kind of journalism they choose to do."*[24]. "Metrics for News" is meant for long term strategic analysis and combines information available in the content management system (CMS) with web metrics, a concept that broadly resembles the idea of the "interactive knowledge stack" [25]. The interactive knowledge stack proposes an open architecture that sees CMS as a tool for knowledge management and seeks to integrate it with other business information sources.

The use of meta-tagging is a surprisingly simple solution to validate editorial assumptions, as it allows to isolate articles that have been crafted following a certain approach and compare them to any other group of articles. Of course, the meta-tagging is based on subjective criteria. A possible next step could be the application of pattern detection to identify strategies across the work of an organisation's journalists, in a very similar way behavioral targeting works for readers currently. The advantage would be that the criteria and categories to be considered would be constructed bottom-up, instead of relying on testing hypotheses that are a priori assumptions derived from the staff's experiences.

4.3　Key Performance Indicators

Graves and Kelly [23] describe the search for a standard measurement ("currency") on the web and the persisting failure to do so, while all other established media succeeded in agreeing upon one primary currency. One reason might be that an ever-evolving web consequently needs evolving indicators. As well it might be that the web as such is still too young as a medium and that it just takes more time till a useful measurement will prevail.

However, there are two current notable trends. The first is the tendency to switch from total reach to relative reach within the potential target group as a measure for journalistic skill. This is applied by the New York Times, as well as at BuzzFeed [26]. A necessary prerequisite is the capability to predict the potential audience for an article. This is not mentioned in case studies, but could e.g. be realized by breaking down customer segments to single categories or watching and evaluating early spreading characteristics of an article. This indicator appears to assess the quality of a journalist to attract audience much better than a mere concentration on absolute numbers, as these may hugely depend on the story as such. It enables new strategies like targeting smaller communities that yet show an intense sharing behavior that Honan [27] reports in his coverage of BuzzFeed. They developed an internal index they call "social lift" that combines the portion of the potential target audience reached with the resonance outside BuzzFeed's core audience.

The second trend is the shift towards measuring attention instead of clicks and visits by taking into account the time a reader spends with an article [55]. As to date, attention is usually operationalized by the total reading time an article accumulates. There are still a lot of shortcomings with this operationalization. As Davenport and Beck [28] explain, attention is a multidimensional concept that primarily addresses the conscious and unconscious mental load an activity causes and does not necessarily correlate with the amount of time spent on that activity.

5　Trend 3: 24/7 Publishing

24/7 publishing can be defined as continuous and immediate publishing of content items, which do not depend on larger publishing units such as daily issues any more. Online media have changed the rhythm of publishing. Online is the first outlet for breaking news and unlike print media knows no deadlines to make it into the next day's issue: "*Journalists who once produced material in a circadian rhythm must now immediately rush any new information to the air (or the web)*" [29]. While the general idea of an issue still has some importance for cross media publications such as newspapers, which combine deadline driven channels with 24/7 channels, web-only media do not provide any references to virtual issues an article may be linked with. Lichtermann [30] reports that the avant-garde of news websites already uses offices in different time zones to deliver content updates around the clock. Still, online media have a rhythm that aligns to the behavior and needs of their audience over the course of the day. Nikki Usher [4] describes this by the case of the New York Times, which starts off into the day with news and concentrates mainly on updates and background stories during the afternoon, with occasional breaking news. While the publication rhythm of the newspaper was defined partly by logistic constraints, as printing presses may rotate the whole night, the flow of content and different forms in online media is increasingly data-driven to address the user context. According to James Robinson, director of news analytics the New York Times uses a combination of quantitative data acquired through state-of-the-art tools and additional research via panels and focus groups to get insights about user motivations and expectations [26]. However, an internal report of The New York Times [31] states that "[...] the vast majority of our content is still published late in the evening, but our digital traffic is busiest early in the morning". In the context of fluid publishing, 24/7 means that journalists are increasingly aware about the rhythm of their audience and different communities relevant to their work and can adapt their processes to this rhythm. The crucial enabling technology are real-time metrics, which increasingly match the actual questions and decisions journalists actually have to take.

6 Trend 4: Service Personalization

Service personalization can be defined as the effort to select or adapt content or interaction model of a service to the individual user based on an implicitly or explicitly developed user profile. Early efforts on service personalization date back to the mid-nineties and notably digital personalized newspapers were among the first prototypes [32, 33]. News were a primary research object in service personalization for TV [34] and radio [35] as well. While having been a research topic for a very long time, only in recent years viable commercial services arose. Krakovsky [7] elaborates some of the reasons for this innovation lag, which lie in the very nature of news, whose relevance to individual does depend on internal and external features, rather than being solely a matter of taste, as with music or movie content. One of the most prominent and successful personalized news service today is Flipboard [36], which relies on social media profiles and explicit choice of individual interest categories to deliver a personalized digital newspaper aggregated from openly accessible web sources. Large social networking services are an enabler to personalization services, as they alleviate the cold start problem of user profiles in personalization, which is described e.g. by [37]. However, there is a certain risk of platform lock-in, as the user profile data usually cannot be exported.

Uhlmann and Lugmayr [38, 39] give a good overview of the research into alternatives for open, interoperable formats for user profiles.

The main role of service personalization in fluid publishing is the increase of granularity of audience measurement and segmentation. Also, it allows to define target groups bottom-up, instead of relying on static customer typologies. Buzzfeed's *social lift* index as described already further above, is only possible if such ad hoc target groups can be inferred from user profiles.

7 Impact of Fluid Publishing on Media Information Systems

If we consider the aforementioned four trends in journalism as aspects of a new publishing paradigm we call "fluid publishing", certain challenges arise for the information management in media organizations who want to implement it. Figure 1 wraps up the key characteristics of the trends and introduces 4 resulting challenges, which are outlined in the subsequent chapters.

8 Challenge 1: Formats

The ideal of fluid publishing would demand a continuous editing process, which flexibly updates articles with input from the community and other sources. The challenge is to find a form to document an ongoing process. The following four formats of fluid publishing are derived from current examples and serve as a basis for developing future formats. They do not pretend to be an exhaustive list.

Fig. 1 Fluid publishing and its constituting trends

8.1 *Updating and Enhancing a Single Article*

Updating a published article is something that is frowned upon in traditional journalism as bad practice. It is seen as a sign of bad initial research and the publication of immature material, as Jarvis explains [6]. However, Arrington [9] argues that in the blogosphere updates are actually good practice and increase transparency and trust of the audience. A major disadvantage of using updates to cover news processes is that readers who already read the article are unlikely to take notice of the changes, unless the article is explicitly marked as a constantly updated evolving story. From a marketing point of view, updates to articles do not give the same opportunity for social media interaction than a new article offers. So updates do rather make sense while an article is still spreading in social media or if the intention is to have the final status of a story in the archive. This may be a reason why updates are rarely heavy edits of the original, but rather small addenda at the top or bottom of the initial article. In any case they ensure that all future readers of the article get the latest version of the story. In a WIRED article, Mat Honan [27] portrays a number of news startups, one of which being the now discontinued service "circanews.com". Circa articles were updated continuously with the latest developments and contextual information. Yet contrary to established journalistic practice, the article was not re-edited to follow a single story arc, but new paragraphs were simply added, with no changes to other parts of the text or any attempt to harmonize the parts. Circa was extremely focused on breaking news first and optimized their workflow according to this end. Obviously, additional editing work would have slowed down the process.

8.2 *Using a Number of Consecutive Articles*

The traditional way of covering a story would be to start with the breaking news, publish a second article once more information comes in and write background stories and comments in the further course of the day. For larger and lasting stories the articles produced may be collected in a dossier. Using consecutive articles in order to tell an evolving story has the advantage that each article may spread independently, but still increases the potential for cross-promotion between the articles. Also, the form of each article may be adapted to the user context in the course of the day, as described earlier. The downside is, that the reader cannot fully catch up on the process by reading just one article, but has to read through all articles. In the click-economy, where the clicks and visits are still the main currency in online media business, this does make sense, yet the transition to attention-centred metrics might favour an approach where users are not forced to click through as many articles as possible, but to get quality information with the least amount of interaction.

8.3   Aggregation of Media Items

The idea of journalism as process materializes most clearly in collections of aggregated media content. More than other social media channels, Twitter makes transparent the interaction between media professionals and the way journalists pick up and validate notions from the crowd and other media. Storify.com was one of the pioneers of aggregating social media items to visualize and document story flows. Scribblelive.com offers a similar aggregation service for CMS integration and is e.g. popular among the public broadcast journalists in Germany for the coverage of live events. This use is related to fluid publishing, however fluid publishing is not bound to events currently happening, but instead emphasizes that the reception process in the audience is tightly intertwined with the journalistic workflow.

8.4   Distributed Editing

The idea of distributed editing is that the editorial work continues on further platforms once an article has been published, especially in the form of social media conversations. Following the idea of news as a transactional object, this would be the natural form of news in the cyberspace. Instead of clearly attributable products, the news object would be like a diffuse cloud with a certain center of gravity wherever a journalist publishes content. Yet as the cloud spans content on both internal and external platforms, it is impossible to keep track of it without the help of tools, indicating an important purpose of information systems in fluid publishing.

9   Challenge 2: Measuring Journalistic Quality

The quest for objective criteria for journalistic quality is as old as journalism itself, as is the discussion on the impact of economic interests on quality. The public function of the journalism remains vital to open and democratic societies, thus the influence of new forms of journalistic workflows such as fluid publishing on the journalistic quality has to be discussed.

The relevance of journalistic core values in new media have been widely debated and the prevailing opinion is that only these values can justify journalism as a profession now that exclusive access to a limited number of channels for both information and publication has ceased to be a formal criterion for distinction. According to Witschge and Nygren [40], this may trigger both a de-professionalization and a re-professionalization along with an orientation at the core values of journalism.

Values may be coded in the form of a company's mission statement, as e.g. outlined by Niven [41] in his approach to the implementation of a balanced scorecard. They ideally are embodied by and passed on among a company's staff. As well they may be coded in shared stories, which is especially the case with established media companies such as The New York Times, The Guardian or the BBC. So company culture can be a corrective to a purely profit-oriented view on publishing. New media startups do not have a culture deeply rooted in traditional journalistic values and thus are—rightfully or not—always suspect of being too much commercially oriented. Yet the main conflict arises from another problem: Journalistic values provide a useful framework to guide journalistic work, but they are hardly quantifiable. Performance metrics are quantified and can be used to formulate clearly assessable goals, becoming the primary indicator for success. So the question to which extend metrics do include journalistic quality or at least are not conflicting with the goal of keeping journalistic quality is an important one.

Petre [18] observed in the newsroom of Gawker, a highly data-driven online news publisher that *"traffic pressures can coexist with a strong perception of editorial autonomy"*. Yet this goes a long with little editorial control of journalistic values, the writers are encouraged to be and market themselves in order to attract traffic to the page. While Gawker staff would have the autonomy to follow high journalistic standards, the decision to actually do so is up to each writer individually.

Held and Ruß-Mohl (2005: 56ff), as reported by Gertler [42: 15], list four ways to measure journalistic quality:

1. Direct measuring of quality criteria, for example through content analysis; dimensions would be topicality, interactivity, transparency, comprehensibility, relevancy right through to objectivity.
2. Audience preferences, because the audience has its own idea of quality; here, market research is deployed.
3. Expert judgments that can be found in sanctioning environments (Press Council) or also in juries; scientifically supported by the multi-stage Delphi method.
4. Indirect indicators that are not measured at the product, but its production conditions; for example the number of editors, educational level and work experience, budget, etc.

Of these four procedures, (2) is already reflected by current metrics. (1) originally addressed manual content analysis, yet can be increasingly automatized and operationalized through new metrics. (3) can as well be assessed automatically, at least to a certain degree, by analyzing the mentioned experts as a dedicated target group, e.g. by analyzing reactions of other media.

Rosenstiel [43:29ff] lists a number of studies that assess journalistic quality based on content analysis and a number of them operationalize different aspects of journalistic quality in a quantifiable, measurable manner. The Project for Excellence in Journalism [43:30] developed the News Coverage Index measuring the breadth of topics covered by a news outlet. As reported by Rosenstiel [43:31f], Lacy and Fico [44] used eight measurements to operationalize journalistic quality:

1. High ratio of staff-written copy to wire service copy
2. Total amount of non-advertising copy
3. High ratio of news interpretations and backgrounders to spot news reports
4. High ratio of illustrations to text
5. Number of wire services carried
6. Length of average front page news story
7. High ratio of non-advertising content to advertising
8. Low amount of square inches of copy per reporter listed with bylines

These characteristics were derived from the findings of a survey of editors by Bogart [45] and combined into a quality index. While some of the measurements are certainly particular to the state of media in the eighties (i.e. the role of news wire services is on the decline, as is the idea of the front page news story), it shows that quality criteria defined by journalists and matching their way of thinking can indeed be operationalized in a way that could be implemented in information systems. However, Rosenstiel [43] argues that systems for automated content analysis are still in their infancy, additionally they pose the question of the selection and implementation of the analysis algorithm. Sentiment analysis arguably is a key technology here [46] to value reactions and interactions of different target groups, allowing to research advanced operationalizations of the complex notion of journalistic quality.

10   Challenge 3: Organizational Change

For a media organization to embrace fluid publishing it needs changes in mindsets, workflows and information management, a complex process of organizational innovation. Nikki Usher's research about the use of web metrics by Al Jazeera English Online [47] concludes:

> [...] we learn that AJE [i.e. Al Jazeera Online] lacked a clear set of organizational norms that dictated how and why journalists should use the powerful metrics available to them [...]. One finding that could be broadly applicable to other newsrooms is that without adequate context, strategy, and guidance, simply having metrics in the newsroom will not impact news production.

Robinson [8] takes a deeper look into the necessary changes in the organizational workflows in order to enable journalism as process. Two observations appear to be of high interest for the design of future information systems for media.

"[...] supervisors within the newsroom struggled with reformulating their relationships with their reporters, who were suddenly no longer physically visible and whose work was often invisible as well" [8: 198]. Due to new roles and jobs in the digital transition the boundaries of the newsroom get blurred in space and time. The 24/7 paradigm knows no clear deadline for user engagement on social media and freelance journalists play a different role now with journalists being encouraged to become their own brand. As access to real-time metrics is essential to fluid

publishing, information systems have to be available to all reporters and editors, including freelancers, at any time and from multiple devices. Moreover, if we go along with Robinson's proposal of news as a transactional object as described earlier, the audience might have to be included in the wider stakeholders of the media business information system.

The second observation is the need for *"[...] physical, public ties to their product [...]"* [8:168] as part of the journalist's emotional reward for her work. In a digital world, journalists have to adapt to new gratifications and Usher [47] indicates that the availability of newsroom metrics can function as a reward in this sense, even if those metrics have no primary relevance in the news cycle. This emotional by-function of the rational evaluation function of metrics should be considered in the design of future information systems. More recently, Petre [18] asserts as a result of her ethnography at Gawker, The New York Times and Chartbeat that "Metrics can be a source of intense stress for writers and editors, but also one of validation and solace". She states that "Chartbeat's dashboard is designed to play a social and emotional role in newsrooms just as much as a rational one".

News startups have a different position when it comes to developing data-driven workflows. Obviously, they can build them up from scratch, often following a key innovation idea. As depicted by Honan [27], being data-driven is the DNA of BuzzFeed and it earns them the trust of both staff and investors. According to Petre [18] Gawker staff are self-selected individuals who value the deal of gaining full editorial freedom against rigid metric-based performance evaluation. Yet one of her finding is as well that "a metrics-driven culture can be just as sticky as a legacy one", meaning that a focusing on criteria that are more difficult to quantify, e.g. as mentioned above in the section on quality, will likely meet resentments.

11   Challenge 4: Designing Information Systems for "Fluid Publishing"

While a lot of tools for real-time audience measurement and analytics that support core aspects of fluid publishing are available, the level of integration into holistic information systems still appears to be low. A first and obvious step would be the deeper semantic integration with content management systems, a direction the aforementioned tool metricsfornews.com is taking. Looking at the organizational levels of IS in media proposed by Lugmayr [48] it appears that the boundaries between the levels are blurring in fluid publishing. As explained in [49] a lot of business information cannot be clearly matched to a certain level or department in the organization. Instead, journalists, marketers and strategists draw largely on the same pool of real-time data and their jobs are overlapping in parts. Every writer also markets her articles and helps developing strategies bottom up. While tasks can still be meaningfully assigned to one of the four levels, job profiles will likely span multiple levels, especially for journalists (Table 3).

Table 3 Organizational level of IS in eMedia [48]

Information system level	Practical scenarios
Operational level	Order processing, transactional services, online subscriptions, audience measurement, simple sales management functions, ...
Knowledge level	Tools for content production, organization of daily tasks, workstation, A/V tools, software tools, work organization tools, ...
Management level	Audience analysis, rating analysis, advertising effect analysis budgeting, production planning, human resource management, inventory, ...
Strategic level	Long term strategic goals, content forms, forecasting, audience forecasting, project planning, portfolio planning, competition analysis, regulation policies, standardization policies, ...

The organizational level model is much tailored to businesses which have a clear separation between development, production and distribution. In fluid publishing, these functions converge essentially in one person and do happen in parallel. To argue that journalism should be considered a service points into the right direction, but the unique characteristic of fluid publishing is that data (metrics) are used in real-time to improve a transactional news object, instead of the usual process of aggregating insights and analyzing them on the management level. I therefore propose to replace the "operational level" with the "transactional level", which comprises all transactions between journalists and audience around evolving news objects. These may include as well sales transactions, although their relation to a news object remains to be explored for transactions other than the purchase of an article.

Table 4 drafts a specific model of information systems for fluid publishing, based on the level model of Information System requirements in eMedia industries as suggested by Lugmayr [48].

Table 4 Levels of information systems for fluid publishing

Information system level	Practical needs
Transactional level	Real-time audience measurement and Analysis to develop a released news object
Knowledge level	Qualitative and quantitative real-time and short-term analysis of audience behavior per writer or resort to develop micro-strategies for future news objects
Management level	Meta-analysis of journalists' performance and micro-strategies to facilitate organizational learning through peer-learning, as well as to optimize human resources planning
Strategic level	Forecasting of changing contextual factors and formats in fluid publishing to inform cost-intensive and/or long-term changes to infrastructure and built-up of new staff competencies

Beyond the introduction of the transactional level also the border between knowledge and management level is blurry in fluid publishing environments. The case studies on The Capital Times [8] and Gawker [18] indicate a tendency to encourage journalists to expose and establish themselves as recognizable personalities on the web. This goes along with a varying, but notable degree of freedom to pursue an individual style and own themes. At Gawker, this freedom seems to go that far so that as long as (very rigid) metric goals are reached, the means are left to the writer. Thus, new media publishers often do more resemble a network than a classic hierarchically structured media organization. Stockleben and Lugmayr [49] argue a shift to more decentralized and cooperative strategy development, as metrics become available to all employees of a media organization. They argue the challenge from an information system perspective is to support organizational learning by analysis of the plethora of micro-strategies continuously developed by the employees. On the knowledge level, each journalist becomes an expert on micro-strategies for his themes and audiences, based on quantitative and qualitative audience feedback, which can be analysed both in real-time and retrospectively. On the level of the management in turn data about an organization's journalists is needed. With the perspective of organizational learning in mind, also a meta-analysis of audience behavior and journalists' micro-strategies would suit the management level well, but as of today this seems to happen mostly in informal exchanges, not systematically.

The strategic level finally calls for mid- and longterm foresight tools. It appears adequate to question the idea of long-term forecast of audience-centred metrics, as the success of any journalistic product depends on many factors, one of being the news environment it gets first released into. Unlike in strategic forecasting in other businesses, any newsworthy event from any domain may shadow any other news, so the eco-system to be considered in a longterm foresight tool for the news business would have to model the world as such. However, capturing longterm changes in audience interaction patterns might be of value. Possibly, a concentration on formats and contextual factors of news productions and consumption should be preferred instead on dwelling on content and themes. In other words, the strategic level should focus on understanding the processes of fluid publishing their evolvement. Journalists can adapt to shifting interest in matters within weeks, but the adaptation of the platform in terms of devices supported and new narrative formats takes months to years, profiting most of long-term strategic foresight.

12 Conclusion

This article has highlighted four current trends in journalism and discusses them in the context of information systems under the new term of *fluid publishing*. It argues how this phenomenon triggers the rise of new domain-specific information system solutions and how these solutions change the structures in news organizations. However, when classifying these solutions along the knowledge levels in organization systems, we find a possible innovation lag between the transactional level and higher levels. Current analytics solution mostly focus on the transactional level, with first mature solutions comprising the knowledge level. Innovation is underway at the management level, with gawker.com as one of the first and most successful implementers, as documented in [18]. Finally, the strategic level is covered, if at all, by classic market research only. The introduced adapted level model for information systems for fluid publishing can give guidance on future research towards holistic information management solutions that integrate business information with both content and content metadata, offering tailored insights for all four levels of organizational information management needs. However, we will see, which impact emerging media technologies, as e.g. Lugmayr [50] or Rakkolainen [51] will have in the world of publishing.

References

1. Tandoc, E. C. (2014). Journalism is twerking? How web analytics is changing the process of gatekeeping. *New Media & Society, 16*(4), 559–575. doi:10.1177/1461444814530541.
2. Christin, A. (2014). *Clicks or Pulitzer?: Web journalists and their work in the United States and France.* Paris: EHESS. Retrieved from http://www.theses.fr/2014EHESS0083
3. Manileve, V. (2014, August 20). *Le journalisme au risque du clic.* Retrieved 24 August 2015, from http://www.inaglobal.fr/presse/article/le-journalisme-au-risque-du-clic-7765
4. Usher, N. (2014). *Making news at the New York Times.* The University of Michigan Press.
5. Gillmor, D. (2006). *We the media: Grassroots journalism by the people, for the people.* O'Reilly Media, Inc.
6. Jarvis, J. (2009, June 7). Product v. process journalism: The myth of perfection v. beta culture. Retrieved 17 August 2015, from http://buzzmachine.com/2009/06/07/processjournalism/
7. Krakovsky, M. (2011). All the news that's fit for you. *Communications of the ACM, 54*(6), 20–21. doi:10.1145/1953122.1953129
8. Robinson, S. (2011). 'Journalism as process': The organizational implications of participatory online news. *Journalism & Communication Monographs, 13*(3), 137–210.
9. Arrington, M. (2009, June 7). *The morality and effectiveness of process journalism.* Retrieved from http://social.techcrunch.com/2009/06/07/the-morality-and-effectiveness-of-process-journalism/
10. Franck, G. (2007). *Ökonomie der Aufmerksamkeit: ein Entwurf.* Dt. Taschenbuch-Verlag
11. Edwards, C., Spence, P. R., Gentile, C. J., Edwards, A., & Edwards, A. (2013). How much Klout do you have … A test of system generated cues on source credibility. *Computers in Human Behavior, 29*(5), A12–A16. doi:10.1016/j.chb.2012.12.034
12. Lugmayr, A., & Zotto, C. D. (2015). Convergence is NOT King—The tripe convergence, coexistence, and divergence IS King. In A. Lugmayr & C. D. Zotto (Eds.), *Media convergence handbook (Vol. 1): Journalism, broadcasting, and social media aspects of convergence and media convergence handbook (Vol. 2): Firm and user perspective.* Germany: Springer Verlag.
13. Zotto, C. D., & Lugmayr, A. (2015). Media convergence as evolutionary process. In A. Lugmayr & C. D. Zotto (Eds.), *Media convergence handbook (Vol. 1): Journalism, broadcasting, and social media aspects of convergence and media convergence handbook (Vol. 2): Firm and user perspective.* Germany: Springer Verlag.

14. Vehkoo, J. (2013). Crowdsourcing in investigative journalism. *Reuters Institute for the Study of Journalism Report*. Retrieved from http://reutersinstitute.politics.ox.ac.uk/sites/default/files/Crowdsourcing%20in%20Investigative%20Journalism.pdf
15. Aitamurto, T. (2013). Balancing between open and closed: Co-creation in magazine journalism. *Digital Journalism, 1*(2), 229–251.
16. Bachmayer, S., Lugmayr, A., & Kotsis, G. (2010). Convergence of collaborative web approaches and interactive TV program formats. *International Journal of Web Information Systems, 6*(1), 74–94.
17. Lugmayr, A., Stockleben, B., Zou, Y., Anzenhofer, S., & Jalonen, M. (2013). Applying design thinking in the context of media management education. *Multimedia Tools and Applications*, 1–39. doi:10.1007/s11042-013-1361-8
18. Petre, C. (2015, May 7). *The traffic factories: Metrics at Chartbeat, Gawker Media, and The New York Times*. Retrieved from http://towcenter.org/research/traffic-factories/
19. McAfee, A., & Brynjolfsson, E. (2012). Big data: The management revolution. *Harvard Business Review, 90*(10), 60–68.
20. Power, D. J. (2008). Understanding data-driven decision support systems. *Information Systems Management, 25*(2), 149–154.
21. Arthur, C. (2010). Analysing data is the future for journalists, says Tim Berners-Lee. *The Guardian, 22*. Retrieved from http://www.septien.edu.mx/septien/maestria/df10/materias/periodismosigloxxi2a/Vista%20previa%20de%20%E2%80%9CAnalysing%20data%20is%20the%20future%20for%20journalists,%20says%20Tim%20Berners-Lee%20_%20Media%20_%20The%20Guardian%E2%80%9D.pdf
22. Parasie, S., & Dagiral, E. (2012). Data-driven journalism and the public good: 'Computer-assisted-reporters' and 'programmer-journalists' in Chicago. *New Media & Society*, 1461444812463345.
23. Graves, L., Kelly, J., & Gluck, M. (2010). Confusion online: Faulty metrics and the future of digital journalism. *Tow Center for Digital Journalism, Columbia University Graduate School of Journalism*. Online at: http://www.Journalism.Columbia.edu/system/documents/345/original/online_Metrics_report.Pdf. Retrieved from http://groupe.dupont.org/system/documents/345/original/online_metrics_report.pdf
24. Stern, R., & Wise, R. (2014b). *RJI Futures Lab update #80: New story metrics from API; and newsroom tracking tool Desk-Net* (Vol. 80). Retrieved from http://www.rjionline.org/futures-lab-update/080-american-press-institute-story-metrics-analytics-desk-net
25. Behrendt, W. (2012). The interactive knowledge stack (IKS): A vision for the future of CMS. In W. Maass & T. Kowatsch (Eds.), *Semantic technologies in content management systems* (pp. 75–90). Heidelberg: Springer. Retrieved from http://link.springer.com/chapter/10.1007/978-3-642-24960-0_7
26. Stern, R., & Wise, R. (2014a). *Futures lab update #85: The future of audience analytics* (Vol. 85). Retrieved from http://www.rjionline.org/futures-lab-update/085-future-audience-analytics-metrics-data
27. Honan, M. (2014, December 17). Inside the Buzz-Fueled Media Startups Battling for Your Attention. Retrieved 6 January 2015, from http://www.wired.com/2014/12/new-media-2/
28. Davenport, T. H., & Beck, J. C. (2013). *The attention economy: Understanding the new currency of business*. Harvard Business Press. Retrieved from https://books.google.de/books?hl=de&lr=&id=FuuKd3on9psC&oi=fnd&pg=PR12&dq=beck+davenport&ots=RK-IFx42Xy&sig=5ltBv5jeAtgqMzMj6SHk9N_uhPQ
29. Harrington, S., & McNair, B. (2012). The 'New' News. *Media International Australia, 144*(1), 49–51. doi:10.1177/1329878X1214400108
30. Lichtermann, J. (2014, July 14). *Report around the clock: How some news orgs use time zones to their advantage to operate 24/7*. Retrieved from http://www.niemanlab.org/2014/07/report-around-the-clock-how-some-news-orgs-use-time-zones-to-their-advantage-to-operate-247/
31. Ellick, A. B., Bryant, A., Sulzberger, A. G., O'Leary, A., Phelps, A., Gianni, E., … Peskoe, B. (2014, March 24). The New York Times Innovation Report 2014. The New York Times.

Retrieved from http://www.presscouncil.org.au/uploads/52321/ufiles/The_New_York_Times_Innovation_Report_-_March_2014.pdf

32. Kamba, T., Bharat, K. A., & Albers, M. C. (1995). The Krakatoa Chronicle-an interactive, personalized newspaper on the Web. Retrieved from https://smartech.gatech.edu/handle/1853/3572

33. Kamba, T., Sakagami, H., & Koseki, Y. (1997). ANATAGONOMY: a personalized newspaper on the World Wide Web. *International Journal of Human-Computer Studies, 46* (6), 789–803.

34. Merialdo, B., Lee, K. T., Luparello, D., & Roudaire, J. (1999). Automatic construction of personalized TV news programs. In *Proceedings of the seventh ACM international conference on multimedia (Part 1)* (pp. 323–331). New York, NY, USA: ACM. http://doi.org/10.1145/319463.319637

35. Stockleben, B., & De Abreu Pereira, N. (2011). Radio frames—Personalization of audio programs. In *2011 IEEE international conference on consumer electronics—Berlin (ICCE-Berlin)* (pp. 306–310). http://doi.org/10.1109/ICCE-Berlin.2011.6031803

36. McCue, M. (2010, July 21). *Flipboard launches world's first social magazine.* Flipboard.com. Retrieved from https://about.flipboard.com/newsroom/flipboard-launches-worlds-first-social-magazine/

37. Lam, X. N., Vu, T., Le, T. D., & Duong, A. D. (2008). Addressing cold-start problem in recommendation systems. In *Proceedings of the 2Nd international conference on Ubiquitous Information Management and Communication* (pp. 208–211). New York, NY, USA: ACM. http://doi.org/10.1145/1352793.1352837

38. Uhlmann, S., & Lugmayr, A. (2011). Portable personality and its personalization algorithms: An overview and directions. In *Media in the Ubiquitous Era: Ambient, Social and Gaming Media: Ambient, Social and Gaming Media, 66.*

39. Uhlmann, S., & Lugmayr, A. (2011). Portable personality and its personalization algorithms: An overview and directions. In A. Lugmayr, H. Franssila, P. Nrnen, P. Näränen, & O. Sotamaa (Eds.), *Media in the Ubiquitous Era: Ambient, Social and Gaming Media* (pp. 66–93). Hershey, USA: IGI Global.\

40. Witschge, T., & Nygren, G. (2009). Journalistic work: A profession under pressure? *Journal of Media Business Studies, 6*(1), 37–59.

41. Niven, P. R. (2010). *Balanced scorecard step-by-step: Maximizing performance and maintaining results.* John Wiley and Sons.

42. Gertler, M. (2013). Meaning-generating propositions of reality by media: Quality attributes and functions of journalism. *Journal of Information, Communication and Ethics in Society, 11* (1), 4–18.

43. Lacy, S., & Rosenstiel, T. (2015). Defining and Measuring Quality Journalism. Retrieved from http://mpii.rutgers.edu/wp-content/uploads/sites/50/2015/04/Defining-and-Measuring-Quality-Journalism.pdf

44. Lacy, S., & Fico, F. (1990). Newspaper quality and ownership: Rating the groups. *Newspaper Research Journal, 11*(2), 42–56.

45. Bogart, L. (1989). *Press and public: Who reads what, when, where, and why in American newspapers.* Psychology Press. Retrieved from https://books.google.de/books?hl=de&lr=&id=DzX-3JA4QZoC&oi=fnd&pg=PA1&dq=bogart+press+and+the+public&ots=YMW0z26S9R&sig=141Io2lJzCYWu2ee0IM6DO4dAPs

46. Lugmayr, A. (2013b). Issues & Approach in Defining a European Research Agenda on Information Systems and Management in Creative eMedia Industries. *The Series,* 17.

47. Usher, N. (2013). AL Jazeera English Online: Understanding web metrics and news production when a quantified audience is not a commodified audience. *Digital Journalism, 1* (3), 335–351.

48. Lugmayr, A. (2013a). Brief introduction into information systems & management research in media industries. In *2013 IEEE international conference on Multimedia and Expo Workshops (ICMEW)* (pp. 1–6). IEEE. Retrieved from http://www.computer.org/csdl/proceedings/icmew/2013/1604/00/06618347-abs.html

49. Stockleben, B., & Lugmayr, A. (2013). Issues and topics to consider for information management research in eMedia industries. In *International series on information systems and creative eMedia, No 2 (2013): Proceedings of the 6th international workshop on semantic ambient media experience (SAME).*

50. Lugmayr, A. (2012). Connecting the real world with the digital overlay with smart ambient media—Applying Peirce's categories in the context of ambient media. *Multimedia Tools and Applications, 58*(2):385–398 (Springer US).

51. Rakkolainen, I. K., Lugmayr, A. (2007). *Immaterial display for interactive advertisements Proceedings of the international conference on Advances in computer entertainment technology* (pp. 95–98). ACM.

52. Uhlmann, S., & Lugmayr, A. (2008). Personalization algorithms for portable personality. In *Proceedings of the 12th international conference on Entertainment and media in the ubiquitous era.* Tampere, Finland: ACM.

53. Lugmayr, A., Reymann, S., Bruns, V., Rachwalski, J., & Kemper, S. (2009). Distributing the personal digital environment throughout your entertainment environment: handling personal metadata across domains. *Multimedia Systems Journal, 15*(3), 187–199.

54. American Press Institute. (n.d.). API's program to create data-driven content strategies. Retrieved August 23, 2015, from http://www.americanpressinstitute.org/training-tools/content-strategy/

55. Edge, A. (n.d.). *Changing the metric: What attention time means for journalists.* Retrieved from https://www.journalism.co.uk/podcast/changing-the-metric-what-attention-time-means-for-journalists/s399/a564942/

Author Biography

Björn Stockleben works as research coordinator of the Master program Cross Media at University of Applied Sciences Magdeburg-Stendal. As well he is working for the innovation group of Rundfunk-Berlin Brandenburg as project manager in EC- and ESA-funded research projects. He is an expert in participative journalism, interactive service design and non-linear AV media, as well as didactics of blended learning and adult education. He holds a master degree in Media Sciences and is a PhD student at TU Tampere, Finland.

Determining the Benefit of Interactive Videos in the Health Sector: Validating a Custom Measurement Instrument

Complete Research

Michael Langbauer, Franz Lehner and Nadine Amende

Abstract Searching for "Windsor knot" on YouTube provides 71.300 alternatives to choose from for those in need of instruction. Learning from a video tutorial in an online portal has become a natural procedure in households. As businesses are starting to realize, video offers a broad spectrum of use cases to foster internal and external knowledge transfer and collaboration. In general, modern media applications are designed to empower the user to choose from a structured compilation of information at will. Harnessing these properties in business settings, interactive video as an example should lead to a beneficiary outcome for its user. To validate this intuition we developed a new software suite to build, manage and view interactive videos and introduced it to a realistic application scenario. In this article we present results of an exploratory factor analysis validating a new measurement instrument designed specifically for the benefit of interactive videos. Data was gathered in a field experiment, in which the interactive videos were used for physiotherapy. We analysed the validity and reliability of the constructs and items. The results show some weaknesses demanding further improvement and adaption of the measurement model, yet also yielding insight into the generation of benefit from such knowledge media on an individual level.

1 Introduction

While traditional forms of media like newspapers and television are still widely spread as information sources, internet-based media types are gaining ground and are changing the rules of the game. Web-based media enable their users to create and share media content (user generated content) using the interactive and collaborative concepts of Web 2.0. Hypermedia, a portmanteau word comprising "hyperlinked" and "media", is a concept to compartmentalize information of various format (i.e. text, audio, pictures, animations, video, etc.) into coherent units

M. Langbauer (✉) · F. Lehner · N. Amende
University of Passau, Passau, Germany
e-mail: michael.langauer@uni-passau.de

© Springer International Publishing AG 2016
A. Lugmayr et al. (eds.), *Information Systems and Management in Media and Entertainment Industries*, International Series on Computer Entertainment and Media Technology, DOI 10.1007/978-3-319-49407-4_16

and integrate them into an ever growing knowledge network by loosely coupling, or linking, them with other information units [31, 44]. As a result, compartmental-ization of information as well as dynamicity in content and collocation create architectures of knowledge sharing, and hypermedia as a concept become knowl-edge media when transformed into interactive products [6, p. 179].

As a result, knowledge media are knowingly or unknowingly already being used by the masses, at first in households [46] and with a slight delay also in companies of all types and sizes [22, 31, 55]. YouTube for instance has experienced unanticipated growth rates in viewership and published content since its launch in 2005 [55]. Taking wikis as a prime example, companies incorporate various types of hyper-media application [47] as instruments for internal and external marketing [49] and customer service purposes [31], for the organisational knowledge management [53] or to support inter and intra corporate collaboration and information exchange [49].

The use of knowledge media applications in businesses is hardly mandatory but voluntary and usually administered as self-services. As such, they aim at self-fulfilment rather than an instrumental value for user productivity. Yet it is possible to improve individual performance indirectly by providing instruction for specific tasks and other work-related purposes [58]. The hedonic aspect of modern forms of business learning applications leads to typical problems for learning systems due to a lack of integration with (core) enterprise systems as well as to a subordinate priority in the workload of employees. For the operator of the platform, web-based media applications hold advantages in comparison to finalized learning and collaboration systems by being cheaper due to central delivery and mainte-nance, and by being in part self-organized [47].

In this study we will look at modern forms of media using the example of interactive videos. In short, "interactive video" is the result of transferring the hypertext concept, to the audio-visual medium video, resulting in dynamic, inter-active and non-linear structures of hyperlinked videos ("hypervideos") enriched with elements of various media formats [65, p. 11]. Therefore, the user experiences advantages as well, namely in the form of self-determined, interactive learning from a medium with high authenticity, vividness and dynamicity [66, p. 359]. With the unique conceptual advantages of interactive videos as a knowledge medium, interactive video instructions and lessons can even be responsive to prior knowl-edge and interests of the individual user without producing and deploying multiple versions for minor changes in content, scope or succession [65, p. 12].

Looking at the market of interactive video software and service, there are several application scenarios for interactive videos to consider, yet they all boil down to the traditional purpose of all forms of media: sharing information. For example by directly linking promotional video footage with products in e-shops, companies might augment the effectiveness of their marketing [65, p. 23]. Shifting perspective to settings with educational [67] rather than commercial purposes, (interactive) video material has a well-documented fit for displaying complex motoric proce-dures [23], e.g. assembling or operating a machine when put into an industrial context. The same idea can be translated back again to households as a private person may be in need of a more seamless visual orientation compared to standard print instructions when assembling furniture. Despite all the suitable applications and laid out advantages for the operating company and especially the user, to the author's best knowledge there is no standard approach of how to measure and explain the benefit of interactive videos.

Yet we have a knowledge base to build upon. Information systems research has always been most interested and also productive in answering this kind of questions. The discipline has brought up various models that offer different perspectives and explanations due to complementary and sometimes contradictory understandings and scopes of the terms "benefit" and "success", nevertheless there is no standardized understanding for them [18]. Deriving a working definition from business economics as a related discipline, Hutzschenreuter [27, p. 179] describes benefit as the subjective fit between the needs of the customer (i.e. user) and the properties of a product (i.e. system), whereas success represents the degree of effectiveness and efficiency in reaching the verbalised goals [27, p. 103]. As we intend to evaluate a hedonic system type that aims at long lasting usage instead of pure performance improvements [58] and intend to measure on an individual level, our research is concerned with the term benefit [27, p. 179].

In addition to the understanding of what is to be measured, the different characteristics and purposes of the specific for information systems (IS) as the research objects have to be considered as well. Consequently, any emergent model describing the benefit/success of a certain IS is always limited to the context of application and type of IS under examination.

Some models have gained enough reputation that they eclipse conceptual alternatives for their respective interpretation of IS benefit/success and are considered as quasi-standard. By continuous validation and refinement, DeLone and McLean's [13, 14, 45] IS Success Model and the Technology Acceptance Model [11, 59] are renowned frameworks used to operationalize benefit in accordance to their concept [29, 45].

Both models can be, and especially the D&M IS Success Model has been applied transcontextual—for different benefit measurement of knowledge media systems. Raeht et al. [46] conceptualized two distinct benefit measurement models for wikis and weblogs that are based on the updated D&M [13] IS Success Model and a literature review to common measures. The resulting instruments elicited both objective and subjective success factors with surveys and interviews. Reisberger and Smolnik [47] analysed the success of a social network with a modified version of the D&M IS Success Model that was extended with specific factors for e-commerce [15]. Hratinski and Monstad [24] developed a measurement instrument to elicit the impact of a video platform on the cultural norms and values within a company in sense of organizational learning process.

Yet with this article we promote building on related studies with some degree of criticism as the common notion of adopting constructs and relationships from long-established models of IS benefit measurement might be systematically problematic. Models like the D&M IS Success Model were designed for radically different system types and initially held as frameworks with verbalized need of adaptation, e.g. for systems that are rather motivated by enjoyment than utility [45]. Therefore, we decided to conceptualize a new measurement model that is explicitly designed for the possibly unique benefit factors of interactive video. To do so, we derived constructs from the use case, operationalized them with known items after a structured literature review and tested their validity in an exploratory factor analysis. This approach of capturing the expected benefits of the application scenario a priori in an expert workshop and contrast the resulting benefit dimensions with the state-of-the-art found in literature is a necessary trade-off between openness and neglecting existing knowledge.

The remainder of this chapter is structured as follows: After providing further information on the characteristics of interactive videos, an existing prototype and the application scenario for a field experiment will be described to provide context for our measurement model. Based on an expert workshop, a subsequent structured literature review will be discussed in its results, i.e. constructs and items. After a brief description of the data collection process in the conducted field experiment, the paper concludes by discussing the outcome of an exploratory factor analysis.

2 Interactive Videos as Media Products and Description of a Prototype

An "interactive video", or "hypervideo", as an organisational concept is a non-linear structure of videos with defined clickable anchors that allows the user to navigate relatively freely within fixed boundaries [41, 65, p. 25]. The authors of the interactive video set navigational and interactional boundaries for example by structuring the primary video content as well as additional information, i.e. annotated texts, pictures, animations, audios, and videos, along paths through a graph of video scenes [41, 54]. As finished media products they combine more or less non-linear structured audiovisual content with interactive control functions [65, p. 18].

Depending on the respective manifestations of the central characteristics, i.e. dynamicity of content, non-linearity and interactivity, interactive videos can take very different shapes. The possible manifestations range from designs for passive content reception with VCR/DVD controls [65, p. 11] to systems with bidirectional content editing at runtime [32]. Existing prototypes confirm the continuity of possibilities offered by the interactive video concept. *Hyper-Hitchcock* allows for the user to call up additional external information and the usage of existing links between scenes. Shipman et al. [51, 52] call this limited utilization of a non-linear structure Detail-on-Demand. Serving the purpose of collaboration in content creation, users of *Advene* can enrich videos by commenting it [1, 10]. Braun and Finke [5] created an interactive video system that tried to mimic a conversation-based learning experience by different forms of annotated information and an avatar.

Chambel et al. [7] developed an environment for individual and collaborative learning where every single user can share his knowledge whenever he chooses.

All these manifestations have in common that they comprise subsystems or components for the creation and the consumption of interactive videos. An "interactive video system" integrates both the "producer" component for authors to generate interactive video applications and the "player" component for users to watch them. With an additional server application, the media data can be stored and streamed to end user devices. For this study we use a prototype integrating all three components to an interactive video system, the *SIVA Suite* (Simple Interactive Video Authoring). Figure 1 provides a comprehensive overview of its architecture and functionality. For more Information see Meixner et al. [40].

In the producer component of the prototype the structure of a new interactive video application is built within the "scene graph". In accordance with the interactive video concept's differentiating property of non-linearity, the scene graph supports branching and looping. Authoring an interactive video with this prototype starts with building the desired navigational structure, including selections for the user as well as conditional and randomized branching. On the basis of the scene graph, annotations of different types (i.e. pictures, rich texts, external links, audio and video) and numbers can then be assigned to and scheduled for any central video scene. The other functions include design setting, tagging of all content elements with key words, editors for scenes, annotations, and the table of content (TOC) editor. The XML-based export function compiles the content designed in the producer into a finished interactive video application including the player in the export file.

The HTML5-based player is composed of several sophisticated functions for macrocontrol and standard web player functionality for microcontrol known from YouTube. Both emphasize the name-giving characteristic of interactive videos in its various levels. Among the macrocontrol elements is a TOC with clickable entries linked to certain content elements. Furthermore, the key word search function

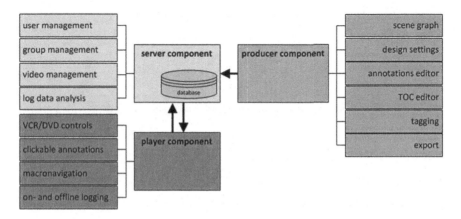

Fig. 1 Architecture of the prototype "SIVA Suite"

results in a hit list of links to the appropriately tagged content elements. The individual usage behavior is recorded and logged by the player for analysis. The gathered information can be transferred to the logging server asynchronously.

The server component provides user, group and video management with possibilities to grant or revoke access rights for certain content or the whole platform. The server also handles bidirectional communication attached to certain content elements.

3 Application Scenario and Field Experiment in the Health Sector

To exploit the features of interactive videos we partnered with a cancer rehabilitation clinic in Germany. The clinic treats approximately 150 patients at a time. The clinic provides medical and physical rehabilitation measures for different kinds of cancer and their respective aftereffects. Along the patient groups, the biggest one is the patients with surgically removed prostates due prostate cancer who are consequently suffering from a loss of bladder control. Bladder control can be regained by strengthening a specific muscle, the pelvic floor, in a rather specific form of gymnastics that is unknown to each participant prior to hospitalization.

As there is a disproportion of the three weeks of stationary rehabilitation and an expectable period of 6–24 months of continuous training before any long term change of conditions can be expected, the clinic had been looking for an instrument to assist their patients in their daily training, especially for the period of time after their initial tuition during stationary rehabilitation. In cooperation with leading

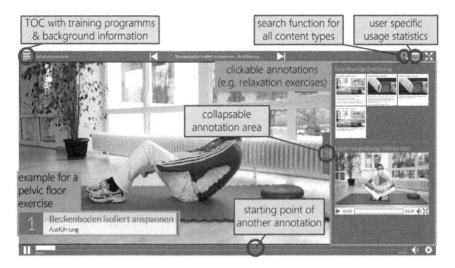

Fig. 2 User interface of an interactive video for therapy

therapists of the clinic, an interactive video application as to be seen in Fig. 2 has been developed to address the identified gap in informational supply.

Within the interactive video we stored two sets of exercises specifically designed to support the patient with instructions for his training without any direct contact to a therapist. The configuration of the application allows for suspending the exercise in favour of respiration or relaxation footage and resuming the set afterwards. Thereby, a virtual trainer that accompanies and counsels the patient for an entire training session has been created. The patient can perform his exercises with audio-visual orientation and chooses the succession of the content in accordance to his needs and wishes.

Additionally, there is a sequence of videos providing detail information concerning important aspects of human anatomy, the rehabilitation process and the utilization of the interactive video application.

4   Theoretical Foundations and Scale Development

The presented application scenario and the underlying need of the clinic was met by our expectation that the key features of interactive videos can indeed noticeably improve a patient's training sessions and thereby contribute to the overall quality of recovery. To validate this expectation we needed a multidimensional benefit measurement instrument on individual level. As it should reflect the clinic's comprehension of possible short and long term benefits on individual level and indirectly also for the clinic, suitable constructs were derived from the clinic's goals for the interactive video application. These goals were elaborated and codified in a workshop with the top management and treatment experts of the clinic.

To evaluate the attainment of the formalized, user-centric goals of interactive video, we needed a suitable instrument to gather data in the field. We conducted a structured literature review [61] in order to base on the state-of-the-art. To generate fitting key words for the following structured literature review, the formulated goals were arranged within the quasi-standard models and theories of IS literature which upholds their prime function of providing a framework for new instruments and also can be treated as a cornerstone of any discussion for the developed instrument [33].

As a first goal, the clinic expects the interactive video application to be comprehended as an additional service and to be appreciated by the patients as such. So the interactive video should increase the level of patient satisfaction both with the therapy in this specific clinic and with the usage of the interactive video. Following Oliver's [43] Expectation-Confirmation Theory (ECT) satisfaction is an "additive function of modified (rather than initial) expectation and conformation" [3]. Models such as the D&M [14] IS Success Model state that user "Satisfaction" plays a pivotal role in the success of information technology as a whole. In IS benefit and success measurement literature user satisfaction is a repeatedly investigated construct that both represents a dimension of benefit in itself and is regarded as a key determinant for acceptance among the targeted group of people.

Acceptance and actual usage has come up as the second goal for interactive video in the experimental context. For going the extra mile in patient care, the clinic expects the patients to show appreciation by utilizing the interactive video with the suggested frequency, intensity and in the desired form of usage. This resonates with behavioural and cognitive psychology and is similar to well-known user-centric constructs in different models of IS acceptance and adoption literature. Fishbein and Aijzen's [17] Theory of Reasoned Action (TRA) posits that human behavior is driven by behavioural intentions which in turn are a function of a person's attitude and "Social Influence" towards the desired behaviour (here: continuous training). Building on TRA in context of information systems, Davis' [11] TAM states the self-reported behavioural intention to "Use" works as a proxy for actual system use. As the main influencing factors on the intention to use as well as the actual use of a system, TAM names "Perceived Ease of Use", "Perceived Usefulness" as the main influencing factors.

As a third and last goal, a more satisfied patient is more likely to have an improved opinion of the clinic that should also lead to patients verbalizing their positive experience and a higher chance of a return in any upcoming stationary rehabilitation cycle. As a causal concept, this expectation corresponds to marketing concepts that by satisfying its patients the clinic can gain in "Reputation" and foster "Loyalty" within his customers, i.e. patients which would return and feel no regret over their decision to use the interactive video. A loyal patient is also expected to show his high regard of the clinic by recommending the clinic and its unique repertoire of treatment measures to others, i.e. positive "Word-of-Mouth".

Based on these goals and our understanding of information systems research literature, we deduced nine search terms: "video AND x" with x = { "perceived ease of use", "perceived usefulness", "intention to use", "satisfaction", "WOM", "reputation", "loyalty", "social influence"}. Starting with 2005 as the year YouTube and thereby awareness for new video delivery techniques and application scenarios took off, we searched academic journal within the EBSCO Host Database Business Source Premier.

From the initial 1291 hits 25 studies provided reasonable measures for our purpose. Double hits and studies with an unfitting orientation were excluded. Reasons to dismiss a study were a (1) focus on different aspects than the benefit (e.g. design, technical, or ethical aspects), (2) the validation of a purely utilitarian rather than a hedonic IS, and (3) not providing sufficient empirical data validating its measures. Table 1 shows the results of each construct including the initial and adjusted number of hits as well as references for the studies that provided measures for it.

The list below shows our understanding of the constructs as well as the chosen alternative for our survey in this e-health field study. In many cases, our search terms, i.e. the names for our constructs, only matched by meaning and not by the identical label. For simplicity's sake we will only name the differing name if needed for their understanding. The construct "Word-of-Mouth" is frequently used in

Table 1 Results of the structured literature review

Construct	Hits		Relevant references
Satisfaction	592	12	[2, 9, 26, 28, 34, 36, 37, 48, 50, 62–64]
Perceived ease of use	35	13	[16, 20, 26, 30, 35–38, 42, 48, 62–64]
Intention to use	64	19	[2, 8, 16, 20, 21, 28, 34–38, 42, 48, 50, 56, 62–64]
Perceived usefulness	47	14	[2, 16, 20, 21, 28, 35, 37, 38, 42, 48, 50, 62–64]
Word-of-mouth	16	8	[19, 25, 28, 30, 34, 39, 62, 63]
Reputation	123	3	[9, 25, 64]
Loyalty	76	5	[20, 25, 30, 48, 50]
Social influence	67	7	[8, 16, 42, 50, 57, 62, 64]

marketing studies (e.g. [39]) and has mostly been found to surface within the "Intention to Use" construct in IS literature (e.g. [16, 63]). Consequently, we disregarded the label within the relevant studies in order to collect relevant items, especially for uncommon constructs such as Word-of-Mouth.

Satisfaction (SAT): SAT is an emotional reaction of a user when using a system as the extent of satisfaction with the system. In many studies SAT is portrayed as Perceived Enjoyment [28, 36, 48, 62–64] as the degree of happiness derived from a system [58] and represents a purely hedonic, intrinsic construct that measures enjoyment without any relation to performance which lead to the original TAM's main influencing factors being PEOU and PU [12]. Lin and Bhattacherjee [34] even went as far as to replace PU and PEOU with Perceived Enjoyment and Social Image, as admiration received for using a system, for the key determinants of intention to use when evaluating hedonic (and not utilitarian) systems. They argue that the use of hedonic systems is entirely intrinsically motivated. As the interactive video application cannot accelerate the healing process but is intended to motivate continuous training, enjoyment and met expectations are intuitive antecedents of continued use. In the light of ECT [43] and interactive video applications not being completely hedonic however, we seek to address the ad hoc statement met or unmet expectation, entailing expectations towards usefulness and ease of use, as well as its consequence on the user's enjoyment. For its focus on emotions we followed the examples of the most frequently used scale for satisfaction [2, 28] and adapted the original items from Bhattacherjee [3]. By also incorporating both positive and reverse coded negative items, we contrast enjoyment with regret and control for inconsiderate answering behavior [48, 50].

Perceived Ease of Use (PEOU): This construct represents an estimate for the mental effort ("Effort Expectancy", e.g. in [38, 42, 48]) or individual capability ("Self-Efficacy Expectancy", e.g. in [26]) as how easy a user can operate a system. Based on evidence from studies testing TAM, PEOU is believed to have a significant impact on the usage decision and the natural subjective evaluation of met expectation towards usefulness [16]. In the presented e-health case, the perceived effort to use the interactive video application is expected to be influenced by voluntary integration into the regular exercise routine as the rather untypical application scenario incorporates navigating through the video while executing the pelvic floor exercises. To address this, we chose items that were specifically designed to test the acceptance of a newly introduced medium into a task that the users are used to executing without [36].

Intention to use (INT): INT as a proxy construct for actual system use goes back to the Theory of Planned Behavior [17] which states that individuals make rational decision based on their beliefs, attitudes and expectancies towards a certain behavior. In the presented application scenario, the desired user behaviour entails parallel usage, in the suggested frequency and length per session. Measures for INT are often combined with a time frame (e.g. [16, 42, 56]) whereas unlimited INT is often referred to as "Continuance" [2, 20, 21, 28, 37, 50]. Other studies also address desired increases of usage in terms of intensity [8] or regularity [36] of use. In the clinical setting, performing pelvic floor exercises is a lifelong necessity for each patient which renders time framed constructs with less meaning than in non-healthcare applications. As it covers the basic willingness as well as the intention to oblige to the suggested intensity, frequency a form of usage, we adapted the items of [42] for INT.

Perceived Usefulness (PU): PU reflects on whether and to which extent a user expects a benefit of interactive videos. In IS benefit measurement literature, usefulness of system is typically determined by its impact on user performance as usually utilitarian systems are targeted. These measures of performance expectancy [42] elicit the subjectively expected impact on efficiency, effectiveness and effort in task fulfilment (e.g. [2, 16, 28, 30, 38, 64]). Applied in educational setting, the performance may also be measured in terms of implicite [21, 36] and explicite [26, 37, 38] learning success. For expressing the perceived usefulness of hedonic systems, enjoyment can also be used as a replacement for PU [34]. In case of the clinical setting users benefit by an enhanced support for their physical recovery. Each patient can perceive and weigh the dimensions of this support differently: The interactive video aims at more effective training sessions by a varying and flexible composition of the training topics and a correct execution of the exercises. According to our understanding for interactive videos, they can lead both performance- and joy-related impacts. To suit the case at hand, we derived our items from scales that focus on general improvement in task execution [35, 38, 63] and learning outcome [26].

Reputation (REP): Following the found literature, "Reputation" is commonly interpreted as Attitude [30, 48], Affect [39] or Trust [9, 25, 26, 64], yet not are commonly used as a substitute or complement for another solution. As the interactive video is a supplement for the rehabilitation at the clinic, we cannot use aforementioned proxies without thorough adoption. Also the previously labled "Loyalty" as the intention to recur is not be found isolated of the system in use, e.g. "Re-Use" [50] of a website. Therefore we created a new simple measure that addresses exactly our need. Connecting the search results for both "Loyalty" and "Reputation" leads to the conclusion that these two terms are too closely related to be separated. Following this train of thought trust in a service provider may be determined by his assumed competence sincerity and benevolence [20, 25, 42, 64] by the customer. In the e-health case at hand, a patient's confidence in the clinic for his personal healthcare is of high importance. In that sense, the reputation as a subjective image and loyalty as the willingness to return [48] for upcoming stationary treatments don't need to be separated which lead to the subsumption under the "Reputation" construct.

Word-of-Mouth (WOM): A user's positive "Word-of-Mouth" about a product in a specific context after a trial phase is believed to reflect the absence of regret towards the initial decision in favour of testing said product [28]. In consequence of the positive experience, and if there is no apparent reason not to share the experience, convinced users are likely to actively or passively recommend the product to others. Transferred to the application scenario at hand, a recommendation of one patient to another or the selfreflecting confirmation of the usage decision can be interpreted as a hint towards benefit expectation [25, 30].

Social Influence (SI): SI states that the use and consequent appreciation for a piece of technology in a given setting can be influenced by important others. Usually, IT is evaluated in business contexts. In those situations using a system is often mandatory or rewarded with a gain of image. In our given context however, the decision whether to initiate or continue use is of increased delicacy: First, use is voluntary which represents an unusual setting for IS benefit measurement. Second, the medicinal application setting makes every decision a patient makes different from casual ones. In order to explore the sentiments that lead to (intention to) use, we follow the majority of studies (e.g. [16, 42] and adapt the correspondent items of the Unified Theory of Acceptance and Use of Technology (UTAUT) by Venkatesh et al. [60]. In contrast to the common notion of keeping the potentially influencing parties unspecific (e.g. in [50], we decided to incorporate our knowledge concerning influencing parties, i.e. doctors, therapists, family and friends, and other patients which go through the identical or at least similar treatment.

Table 2 lists the items and how they were phrased within our questionnaire. In the survey, they were translated into German for using them within the scope of the German project partner. For simplification purposes the illustrated questionnaire contains PVT ("Pelvic Floor Trainer") as an abbreviation for the English translation of the German working title "Beckenbodentrainer" that was used in the German original questionnaire. All items were elicited on a 7-point Lickert-scale. The measures are not included in this paper.

5   Exploratory Factor Analysis

The field experiment was conducted with volunteers among the patients during their hospitalization at the clinic. The experimental setting was planned as follows: At first, all subjects had to fill in a demographic questionnaire. After a short introduction the volunteering subjects were given a task with the interactive video. The task included to find and watch a specific video about theoretical explanations of the pelvic floor and prostate cancer (transfer of factual knowledge) and after that to

Table 2 Scales used in the questionnaire (translated from German)

Phrasing in the questionnaire	Item
The PVT ...	
Is complex to use during exercises	PEOU1
Can only be operated with a high level of physical effort	PEOU2
Forces disturbing interruptions of my training	PEOU3
Demands a high level of mental effort in order to use it correctly during exercises	PEOU4
In the foreseeable future, I plan to use the PVT ...	
In my training routine.	INT1
Parallel to every exercise for orientation	INT2
To improve my knowledge concerning exercise execution	INT3
To improve my knowledge concerning theoretical background for pelvic floor gymnastics	INT4
By using the PVT, I expect ...	
A better muscle development in the course of my exercises	PU1
A more diverse composition of my exercises	PU2
Improvement in my execution of exercises	PU3
Using the PVT for my autonomous training sessions is useful for me	PU4
Incorporating the PVT into my autonomous training routines ...	
Satisfies me overall	SAT1
Fascinates me	SAT2
Disappoints me	SAT3
Frustrates me	SAT4
With the PVT available at this clinic ...	
My impression of the clinic is improved	REP1
I am more likely to consider returning to this clinic in the future	REP2
To use the PVT ...	
Is what I would recommend to other patients	WOM1
Is a decision I would make again	WOM2
I decided to use the PVT because ...	
Doctors think I should use it.	SI1
Therapists think I should use it.	SI2
Other patients think I should use it.	SI3
People who are important to me think I should use it.	SI4

learn (transfer of motoric knowledge) and execute (use of knowledge). Afterwards, the subjects filled in a questionnaire about single benefit constructs.

In total, 32 subjects participated in the field experiment. Because of the target group "patients with prostate cancer", there were solely male subjects. The average age was 63.42 years (min = 45, max = 85, sd = 9.25), which is a typical age for this kind of disease. The patients' physical limitations to conduct the training were in average 0.8 (sd = 1.35), which means that patients are indicating that they have marginal physical restrictions. Thus, they were in a quite good condition to participate in the study and do not distort results. The average usage intensity of computers (PC, Laptop, Smartphone or Tablet) is 2.06 (sd = 2.93). This corresponds to a usage intensity of at least once a month. Internet skills of subjects are 5.2 (sd = 2.02). This corresponds to "rather high" internet skills.

For an evident instrument content validity, reliability, nomological and discriminant validity have to be tested. We can ensure content validity by using a focus group of clinic managers and trainers with which we discussed constructs and measures. The items were adapted to the advice of the focus group. Thus, we identified the constructs "Image" and "Word-of-Mouth" for measuring benefit and selected suitable items. We analysed Cronbach's alpha as a measure of reliability.

Table 3 presents alpha values of each construct. Construct reliability is poor for Perceived Ease of Use, Satisfaction, Image and Word-of-Mouth, because alpha values are smaller than 0.70. If we delete PEOU3 the alpha value will increase to 0.60, which is still not high. Satisfaction has the poorest reliability. Here, each deleted item can increase reliability. The highest improvement in Cronbach's alpha will be achieved, if SAT3 or SAT4 are deleted. Reliability will increase in each case to 0.84. Thus, items are not fitting together. We investigate this aspect further with the results of the exploratory factor analysis. Cronbach's alpha of Image and Word-of-Mouth is lower than 0.70. This can be caused by using only two items. The deletion of any item will not increase reliability for each construct. Intention to use has an acceptable reliability. If INT1 is deleted, alpha will increase to 0.80. Likewise, reliability of the perceived usefulness is quite acceptable. In this case, no possible deletion will increase reliability. Social influence has the highest Cronbach's alpha, which cannot be improved by deleting any item of this construct.

To test the nomological and discriminant validity we conducted an exploratory factor analysis. The factor analysis was a principal components analysis with varimax rotation and with correlated (oblimin) rotation. The varimax solution provided a better grouping of items. Before conducting the exploratory factor analysis, we identified seven factors by using the rule of eigen-values greater than one and the scree test. This confirmed our concept of using seven constructs for benefit measurement. The total variance is explained with 72 %, which is quite high.

The factor loadings of each item are shown in Table 4. For a better readability we deleted item values with poor loadings (<0.30). Some items loaded high and

Table 3 Reliability of measurement instrument

Construct/dimension	Number of items	Reliability coefficient (Cronbach's alpha)
Perceived ease of use (PEOU)	4	0.57
Intention to use (INT)	4	0.75
Perceived usefulness (PU)	4	0.72
Satisfaction (SAT)	4	0.29
Reputation (REP)	2	0.50
Word-of-mouth (WOM)	2	0.45
Social influence (SI)	4	0.82

Table 4 Factor loadings and factor correlation matrix obtained from the exploratory factor analysis

Item/factor	F1	F2	F3	F4	F5	F6	F7
PEOU1	**−0.43**						
PEOU2							**0.83**
PEOU3				−0.31			**0.67**
PEOU4							**0.38**
INT1							
INT2	0.45	0.46				**0.59**	
INT3		**0.88**					
INT4		**0.84**					
PU1			**0.65**				
PU2		**0.64**	0.60				
PU3	0.63	**0.68**					
PU4	**0.85**						
SAT1			**0.64**				
SAT2		0.45	**0.68**			0.46	
SAT3					**0.99**		
SAT4					**0.99**		
REP1		**0.40**					
REP2		0.35		**0.51**		0.45	
WOM1	**0.78**		0.51				
WOM2						**0.81**	
SI1	**0.49**			0.44		0.30	
SI2	**0.58**			0.35		0.42	
SI3				**0.64**			
SI4				**0.83**			

Bold indicates-factor loadings

very high on "parent" factors but also on "foreign" factors. Some items loaded on more than one factor with quite the same loadings. Other items didn't load high or even medium (>0.30) on factors. Therefore, convergent and discriminant validity of constructs is flawed and needs to be interpreted.

6 Interpretation and Conclusion

Each item has at least one factor loading of more than 0.30. Moreover, some items have multiple factor loadings. For these items only their primary loading was taken into account.

The perceived ease of use has to be split in two factors. PEOU1 focuses on general usability, whereas PEOU2-PEOU4 addresses a physical ease of use. In order to investigate further we need to consider that the presented application scenario in fact affords additional physical effort from the patients. Also, the chosen degree of interaction, i.e. manually choose between repeating and exercise or going on to the next in the program, might have been suboptimal. In conclusion, PEOU2-4 loading on one but a different factor than PEOU1, we interpret this as newly found construct resembling a more task-related usability factor present. PEOU4 also has a poor factor loading and might have to be replaced.

Intention to Use shows item loadings to three different factors. INT3 and INT4 address using interactive videos for gaining more knowledge, whereas INT2 elicits the training effect. INT1 focuses on usage intention in general. Consequently, we assume that there is need of dissolving this construct in favour of goal oriented representation of reasons why the individual uses the interactive video application. Depending on the purpose we can distinguish different dimensions of expected benefit. As a knowledge medium, the interactive video can hold epistemic value whereas the usage of each individual interactive video application as a piece of technology is supposed to have a utilitarian and/or hedonic value.

The perceived usefulness shows high loadings across three factors. PU2 and PU3 address the improvement of the training process, whereas PU1 addresses the outcome of the training, e.g. enhanced pelvic floor muscle development. PU2 and PU3 load on the same factor as INT3 and INT4. Thus, varying exercises and improving their execution in combination with improved knowledge about it as expected benefits seem to hint at a combined construct resembling a fit between what the application offers and what the user needs to fulfill his task. PU3-4 load on the same factor as PEOU1 and INT1. Interpreted in conjunction, this factor might stand for a general open-mindedness of patients towards the interactive video application into their training routine as long as it's demand for interaction is adjusted to fit the usage situation, i.e. in the case at-hand performing gymnastics exercises based on video instructions.

SAT1 and SAT2, as representations of positive perceptions of the usage of the interactive video application in the given context, load on the same factor as PU1 referring to a positive impact on the training. SAT3 and SAT4 refer to a negative emotion, when using interactive videos, whereas SAT1 and SAT2 represent a positive emotion. Thus, the satisfaction items should furthermore be harmonized towards either positive or negative phrasing. To improve factor loadings, the negatively scaled items SAT3-4 should be exchanged with their positive counter-parts found in the semantic differential used by Bhattacherjee and Premkumar [4] or replaced as a whole.

The two items of image load on separate factors, rendering the assumed inter-relatedness between reputation and loyalty as inconsistent with the collected data in this case. IMG1 addresses patient's opinion of the clinic, whereas IMG2 addresses the patient's intention to return to the clinic for another therapy. WOM as a construct comprising intention of recommendation and regret of the individual's decision in favour of using can also not be confirmed with the data at hand. These results could be caused by using only two items within each construct. The factor loadings are only medium and might lead to a cancellation of the constructs, replacement of the items or their reassignment to other constructs. For further investigation there is need of assessment of the meaning of the provider of an interactive video for its benefit generation (INT1-2) and the relation between regret and recommendation (WOM1-2) with an individual's benefit.

WOM1 loads on the same factor as PEOU1, INT1 and PU4. WOM2 loads on the same factor as INT2 which can be interpreted as a relation between acknowledging the suggested form of usage and recommending this mode of application to others. WOM1 loading on the same factor as SAT1-2 would suggest that the intention to recommend the interactive video application to other patients seems to be a (potentially) verbalized expression of satisfaction and might be used to determine satisfaction.

Looking at the factor loading of the social influence items, we deduce that the approval of clinical personnel (SI1-2) is anticipated by the patients because the doctor's and therapist's affiliation with the clinic. As a consequence this aspect of influence by others might be negligible. SI3 and SI4 refer to what seem to be more relevant sources of advice, i.e. other patients and relatives.

In conclusion, the factor loading showed interesting relations between different items while there are no exact fits, i.e. all items of one construct loading on the same factor. As the results of our exploratory factor analysis, we interpret the nomological and discriminant validity issues of the literature derived constructs at least partially as positive. It is a result we can build on to improve the measurement model. It shows that the generation of benefit from interactive videos as a non-utilitarian piece of IT is not trivial but demands for further investigation.

The results could also be caused by the small subject size. There has to be further empirical studies with more subjects. Thus, the instrument is actually not applicable. The results induce a modification of the instrument.

We provide this study as a starting point for developing a suitable benefit measurement instrument for interactive videos as an example of modern, media-based learning systems. To the best knowledge of the authors, no specific measurement instrument exists within the IS research discipline.

In future research we plan to correct the measurement instrument with regard to the findings above and add qualitative data as source material for further model and scale development. After testing the revised model in other use cases, a concluding confirmatory factor analysis will determine relationships between the revised constructs.

References

1. Aubert, O., & Prié, Y. (2005). Advene: Active reading through hypervideo. In S. Reich & M. M. Tzagarakis (Eds.), *HT'05: Proceedings of the sixteenth ACM Conference on Hypertext and Hypermedia, Salzburg, Austria, September 06–09, 2005* (pp. 235–244). New York, NY: ACM.
2. Benlian, A., Koufaris, M., & Hess, T. (2011). Service quality in software-as-a-service: Developing the SaaS-Qual measure and examining its role in usage continuance. *Journal of Management Information Systems, 28*(3), 85–126.

3. Bhattacherjee, A. (2001). Understanding information systems continuance: An expectation-confirmation model. *MIS Quarterly, 25*(3), 351–370.
4. Bhattacherjee, A., & Premkumar, G. (2004). Understanding changes in belief and attitude toward information technology usage: A theoretical model and longitudinal test. *MIS Quarterly, 28*(2), 229–254.
5. Braun, N., & Finke, M. (2000). Interaction of video on demand systems with human-like Avatars and hypermedia. In *IDMS '00 Proceedings of the 7th International Workshop on Interactive Distributed Multimedia Systems and Telecommunication Services* (pp. 172–186).
6. Burmester, M. (2006). Usability engineering für interaktive Wissensmedien. In M. Eibl, H. Reiterer, P. F. Stephan, & F. Thissen (Eds.), *Knowledge media design* (pp. 175–200). München: Oldenbourg Wissenschaftsverlag GmbH.
7. Chambel, T., Zahn, C., & Finke, M. (2006). Hypervideo and Cognition. In E. Alkhalifa (Ed.), *Cognitively Informed Systems* (pp. 26–49). IGI Global.
8. Chen, W.-K., Huang, H.-C., & Chou, S.-C. T. (2012). Understanding what determines consumers' expanded use of mobile videophones. *Behaviour & Information Technology, 31* (10), 953–967.
9. Chou, S.-W., & Chiang, C.-H. (2013). Understanding the formation of software-as-a-service (SaaS) satisfaction from the perspective of service quality. *Decision Support Systems, 56*, 148–155.
10. Concolato, C., Schmitz, P., Aubert, O., Prié, Y., & Schmitt, D. (2012). *Advene as a tailorable hypervideo authoring tool*. Paris: France.
11. Davis, F. D. (1989). Perceived usefulness, perceived ease of use, and user acceptance of information technology. *MIS Quarterly, 13*(3), 319.
12. Davis, F. D., Bagozzi, R. P., & Warshaw, P. R. (1992). Extrinsic and intrinsic motivation to use computers in the workplace. *Journal of Applied Social Psychology, 22*(14), 1111–1132.
13. DeLone, W. D., & McLean, E. R. (2003). The DeLone and McLean model of information systems success: A ten-year update. *Journal of Management Information Systems, 19*(4), 9–30.
14. DeLone, W. H., & McLean, E. R. (1992). Information systems success: The quest for the dependent variable. *Information Systems Research, 3*(1), 60–95.
15. DeLone, W. H., & McLean, E. R. (2004). Measuring e-Commerce Success: Applying the DeLone & McLean information systems success model. *International Journal of Electronic Commerce, 9*(1), 31–47.
16. Du, J., Lu, J., Wu, D., Li, H., & Li, J. (2013). User acceptance of software as a service: Evidence from customers of China's leading e-commerce company, Alibaba. *Journal of Systems and Software, 86*(8), 2034–2044.
17. Fishbein, M., & Ajzen, I. (1975). *Belief, attitude, intention, and behavior: An introduction to theory and research, Addison-Wesley series in social psychology*. Reading, Mass: Addison-Wesley Pub. Co.
18. Garrity, E. J., & Sanders, G. L. (1998). *Information systems success measurement, Series in information technology management*. Hershey, PA: Idea Group Pub.
19. Goyette, I., Ricard, L., Bergeron, J., & Marticotte, F. (2010). e-WOM scale: Word-of-mouth measurement scale for e-services context. *Canadian Journal of Administrative Sciences/Revue Canadienne des Sciences de l'Administration, 27*(1), 5–23.
20. Green, D. T., & Pearson, J. M. (2011). Integrating website usability with the electronic commerce acceptance model. *Behaviour & Information Technology, 30*(2), 181–199.
21. He, W., Fang, Y., & Wei, K.-K. (2009). The role of trust in promoting organizational knowledge seeking using knowledge management systems: An empirical investigation. *Journal of the American Society for Information Science and Technology, 60*(3), 526–537.
22. Hippner, H., & Wilde, T. (2005). Social software. *Wirtschaftsinformatik, 47*, 441–444.
23. Höffler, T. N., & Leutner, D. (2007). Instructional animation versus static pictures: A meta-analysis. *Learning and Instruction, 17*(6), 722–738.

24. Hratinski, S., & Monstad, T. (2014). Exploring the relationship between the use of an interactive video website and organizational learning. *New Media & Society, 16*(4), 594–614.
25. Hsu, L.-C., Wang, K.-Y., & Chih, W.-H. (2013). Effects of web site characteristics on customer loyalty in B2B e-commerce: evidence from Taiwan. *The Service Industries Journal, 33*(11), 1026–1050.
26. Hu, P. J.-H., & Hui, W. (2012). Examining the role of learning engagement in technology-mediated learning and its effects on learning effectiveness and satisfaction. *Decision Support Systems, 53*(4), 782–792.
27. Hutzschenreuter, T. (2015). *Allgemeine Betriebswirtschaftslehre.* Wiesbaden: Springer Fachmedien Wiesbaden.
28. Kim, B. (2012). The diffusion of mobile data services and applications: Exploring the role of habit and its antecedents. *Telecommunications Policy, 36*(1), 69–81.
29. King, W. R., & He, J. (2006). A meta-analysis of the technology acceptance model. *Information & Management, 43*(6), 740–755.
30. Kwak, D. H., McDaniel, S., & Kim, K. T. (2012). Revisiting the satisfaction-loyalty relationship in the sport video gaming context: The mediating role of consumer expertise. *Journal of Sport Management, 26*(1), 81–91.
31. Lattemann, C. (2013). Social und Mobile Media in deutschsprachigen Unternehmen 2012. *HMD—Praxis der Wirtschaftsinformatik, 292.*
32. Lehner, F., & Siegel, B. (2009). E-Learning mit interaktiven videos—Prototypisches Autorensystem und Bewertung von Anwendungsszenarien. In A. Schwill (Ed.), *Lernen im digitalen Zeitalter, GI-Edition/Proceedings, P-153* (pp. 43–54). Bonn: Gesellschaft für Informatik.
33. Levy, L., & Ellis, T. J. (2006). A systems approach to conduct an effective literature review in support of information systems research. *Informing Science Journal, 9,* 191–212.
34. Lin, C.-P., & Bhattacherjee, A. (2010). Extending technology usage models to interactive hedonic technologies: a theoretical model and empirical test. *Information Systems Journal, 20* (2), 163–181.
35. Lin, H.-H., Wang, Y.-S., & Chou, C.-H. (2012). Hedonic and utilitarian motivations for physical game systems use behavior. *International Journal of Human-Computer Interaction, 28*(7), 445–455.
36. Lin, J. C.-C., & Liu, E. S. Y. (2009). The adoption behaviour for mobile video call services. *International Journal of Mobile Communications, 7*(6), 646.
37. Lin, K.-M., Chen, N.-S., & Fang, K. (2011). Understanding e-learning continuance intention: A negative critical incidents perspective. *Behaviour & Information Technology, 30*(1), 77–89.
38. Lippert, S. K., & Forman, H. (2005). Utilization of information technology: Examining cognitive and experiential factors of post-adoption behavior. *IEEE Transactions on Engineering Management, 52*(3), 363–381.
39. McKee, D. (2006). Customer self-efficacy and response to service. *Journal of Service Research, 8*(3), 207–220.
40. Meixner, B., Siegel, B., Hölbling, G., Lehner, F., & Kosch, H. (2010). *SIVA suite—Authoring system and player for interactive non-linear videos.* Italy: Firenze.
41. Müller, W., Spierling, U., & Stockhausen, C. (2013). Production and delivery of interactive narratives based on video snippets. In H. Koenitz, T. I. Sezen, G. Ferri, M. Haahr, D. Sezen, & G. Catak (Eds.), *ICIDS'13: Proceedings of the Sixth International Conference on Interactive Digital Storytelling, Istanbul, Turkey, November 6–9, 2013* (pp. 71–82). Berlin Heidelberg: Springer.
42. Oh, J.-C., & Yoon, S.-J. (2013). Predicting the use of online information services based on a modified UTAUT model. *Behaviour & Information Technology, 33*(7), 716–729.
43. Oliver, R. L. (1980). A cognitive model of the antecedents and consequences of satisfaction decisions. *Journal of Marketing Research, 17,* 460–469.

44. O'Reilly, T. (1997). What Is Web 2.0: Design Patterns and Business Models for the Next Generation of Software. *Communications & Strategies, 65,* 17–37.
45. Petter, S., DeLone, W., & McLean, E. (2008). Measuring information systems success: Models, dimensions, measures, and interrelationships. *European Journal of Information Systems, 17*(3), 236–263.
46. Raeth, P., Smolnik, S., Urbach, N., & Zimmer, C. (2009). Towards assessing the success of social software in corporate environments. In: R. C. Nickerson & R. Sharda (Eds.), *AMCIS '09: Fifteenth Americas' Conference on Information Systems 2009, San Francisco, California, USA, 6–9 August 2009,* Curran, Red Hook, NY, 27.11.2014.
47. Reisberger, T., & Smolnik, S. (2008). Modell zur Erfolgsmessung von Social-Software-Systemen. In: M. Bichler, T. Hess, H. Krcmar, U. Lechner, F. Matthes, A. Picot, B. Speitkamp, P. Wolf, & M. Bichler (Eds.), *MKWI '08: Multikonferenz Wirtschaftsinformatik 2008, Munich, Germany, 26–28. February 2008* (pp. 565–577), GITO-Verlag, Berlin.
48. Reynolds, N., & de Maya, S. R. (2013). The impact of complexity and perceived difficulty on consumer revisit intentions. *Journal of Marketing Management, 29*(5–6), 625–645.
49. Richter, A., Heidemann, J., Klier, M., & Behrendt, S. (2013). *Success Measurement of Enterprise Social Networks.* Paper presented at 11th International Conference on Wirtschaftsinformatik, 27 Februar–1 März 2013, Leipzig, Germany. Available at: http://aisel.aisnet.org/wi2013/20. Accessed August 1, 2014.
50. Schaupp, L. C. (2010). Web site success: Antecedents of web site satisfaction and re-use. *Journal of Internet Commerce, 9*(1), 42–64.
51. Shipman, F., Girgensohn, A., & Wilcox, L. (2005). Hypervideo expression. In S. Reich & M. M. Tzagarakis (Eds.), *HT '05: Proceedings of the sixteenth ACM Conference on Hypertext and Hypermedia, Salzburg, Austria, September 06–09, 2005* (p. 217). New York, N.Y.: ACM.
52. Shipman, F., Girgensohn, A., & Wilcox, L. (2008). Authoring, viewing, and generating hypervideo. *ACM Transactions on Multimedia Computing, Communications, and Applications, 5*(2), 1–19.
53. Smolnik, S., & Riempp, G. (2006). Nutzenpotenziale, Erfolgsfaktoren und Leistungsindikatoren von Social Software für das organisationale Wissensmanagement. *HMD—Praxis der Wirtschaftsinformatik, 252.*
54. Stocker, A., Richter, A., Hoefler, P., & Tochtermann, K. (2012). Exploring appropriation of enterprise wikis. *Computer Supported Cooperative Work (CSCW), 21*(2–3), 317–356.
55. Susarla, A., Oh, J.-H., & Tan, Y. (2012). Social networks and the diffusion of user-generated content: Evidence from YouTube. *Information Systems Research, 23*(1), 23–41.
56. Truong, Y. (2009). An evaluation of the theory of planned behaviour in consumer acceptance of online video and television services. *Electronic Journal Information Systems Evaluation, 12*(2), 177–186.
57. Truong, Y. (2009). An evaluation of the theory of planned behaviour in consumer acceptance of online video and television services. *The Electronic Journal of Information Systems Evaluation, 12*(2), 177–186.
58. Van der Heijden, H. (2004). User acceptance of hedonic information systems. *MIS Quarterly, 28*(4), 695–704.
59. Venkatesh, V., & Davis, F. D. (2000). A theoretical extension of the technology acceptance model: Four longitudinal field studies. *Management Science, 46*(2), 186–204.
60. Venkatesh, V., Morris, M. G., Davis, Gordon B., & Davis, F. D. (2003). User acceptance of information technology—Toward a unified view. *MIS Quarterly, 27*(3), 425–478.
61. Webster, J., & Watson, R. T. (2002). Analyzing the Past to Prepare for the Future: Writing a Literature Review. *MIS Quarterly, 26*(2), xiii–xxiii.
62. Yang, H. (2013). Bon appétit for apps: young American consumer's acceptance of mobile applications. *The Journal of Computer Information Systems, 53*(3), 85–96.

63. Yoon, G., Duff, Brittany R. L., & Ryu, S. (2013). Gamers just want to have fun? Toward an understanding of the online game acceptance. *Journal of Applied Social Psychology, 43*(9), 1814–1826.
64. Yu, J., Ha, I., Choi, M., & Rho, J. (2005). Extending the TAM for a t-commerce. *Information & Management, 42*(7), 965–976.
65. Zahn, C. (2003). *Wissenskommunikation mit Hypervideos: Untersuchungen zum Design nichtlinearer Informationsstrukturen für audiovisuelle Medien, Internationale Hochschulschriften* (Vol. 412). Münster, New York, München, Berlin: Waxmann.
66. Zahn, C., Oestermeier, U., & Finke, M. (2006). Designs für audiovisuelle Hypermedien—Kognitive und kollaborative Perspektiven. In M. Eibl, H. Reiterer, P. F. Stephan, & F. Thissen (Eds.), *Knowledge media design* (pp. 357–371). München: Oldenbourg Wissenschaftsverlag GmbH.
67. Zhang, D., Zhou, L., Briggs, R. O., & Nunamaker, J. F. (2006). Instructional video in e-learning: Assessing the impact of interactive video on learning effectiveness. *Information & Management, 43*(1), 15–27.

Author Biographies

Michael Langbauer studied Business Computing (B.Sc.) and Business Administration (M.Sc.) at the University of Passau from 2008 to 2013. Between 2012 and 13 he worked as part time research assistant at the Chair for Information Systems I (Wirtschaftsinformatik I) while finishing his master studies. Since 2013 he started working at the Chair for Information Systems II (Wirtschaftsinformatik II) at the University of Passau for his doctoral studies. His interests in research lie in benefit measurement and interactive videos. He is part of the interdisciplinary research project mirKUL that evaluates the economic viability of interactive videos in practice.

Prof. Dr. Franz Lehner was assistant professor at the Institute for Organizational Research at the University of Linz, Austria, since 1986. Before this he gathered experience in the field EDP as head of the educational centre at a software house and as an independent consultant. From 1992 to 1994 he was professor for business administration and information management (MIS) at the Koblenz School of Corporate Management (WHU, Germany) where he was elected dean of the faculty in 1994. After that a short period followed as president of the new founded Danube-University at Krems which is a centre for postgraduate studies in Austria. In 2004 he accepted a call to the University of Passau where he holds now the Chair for Information Systems II (Wirtschaftsinformatik II) since April 2004. He has published 25 Books (including some as co-author) and more than 100 articles in national and international journals to various topics in the field of information science and information management. His research is focusing on E-Learning as well as Information and Knowledge Management.

Dr. Nadine Amende studied Information Systems at the Martin-Luther-University in Halle-Wittenberg from 2000 to 2007, graduating with a diploma. From 2007 to 2015 she worked as research assistant at the Chair of Information Systems II (Wirtschaftsinformatik II) at the University of Passau before earning her doctoral degree. Her interests in research lie in Information Visualization, models and theories of Success Measurement as well as the Evaluation of Information and Knowledge Management Systems. While being active as a research assistant she took responsibilities in teachings for various lectures at the University of Passau and international partner universities. In 2013 she organized and coordinated the Conference for Professional Knowledge Management (ProWM 2013).

Printed in the United States
By Bookmasters